INCARNATION

Alfred Corn is the author of five books of poetry and a collection of essays. He has taught creative writing at Yale, the City University of New York, U.C.L.A., and Columbia. He is a frequent contributor to *The New York Times Book Review*, *The New Republic,* and *The Yale Review*. He lives in New York City.

INCARNATION

Contemporary Writers on the New Testament

Edited by
ALFRED CORN

PENGUIN BOOKS

PENGUIN BOOKS

Published by the Penguin Group

Viking Penguin, a division of Penguin Books USA Inc.,
375 Hudson Street, New York, New York 10014, U.S.A.

Penguin Books Ltd, 27 Wrights Lane, London W8 5TZ, England

Penguin Books Australia Ltd, Ringwood, Victoria, Australia

Penguin Books Canada Ltd, 2801 John Street,
Markham, Ontario, Canada L3R 1B4

Penguin Books (N.Z.) Ltd, 182–190 Wairau Road,
Auckland 10, New Zealand

Penguin Books Ltd, Registered Offices:
Harmondsworth, Middlesex, England

First published in the United States of America by
Viking Penguin, a division of Penguin Books USA Inc., 1990
Published in Penguin Books 1991

1   3   5   7   9   10   8   6   4   2

LIBRARY OF CONGRESS CATALOGING IN PUBLICATION DATA
Incarnation: contemporary writers on the New Testament/edited by
Alfred Corn.
p.   cm.
Reprint. Originally published: New York: Viking, 1990.
Includes bibliographical references.
ISBN 0 14 01.1583 8
1. Bible. N.T.—Criticism, interpretation, etc.   2. Bible and
literature.   I. Corn, Alfred, 1943–
[BS2361.2.I53   1991]
225.6—dc20   90–21991

Printed in the United States of America

Simone Weil
W. H. Auden
Flannery O'Connor
Robert Fitzgerald

ACKNOWLEDGMENTS

—

I would like to thank David Rosenberg, editor of *Congregation: Jewish Writers Read the Hebrew Bible*, for suggesting this parallel project to me and offering advice as plans became more definite. For many helpful suggestions about the content and scope of the essays, and for friendly encouragement along the way, hearty thanks go to Professor Peter Hawkins of the Yale Divinity School. To the Reverend Wray MacKay I would like to express gratitude for his example and his assistance, offered as the book was being developed. To the authors of each essay, my admiration and thanks for their work, which made the book possible. And to Amanda Vaill at Viking, warm gratitude for shepherding the project to its successful completion.

CONTENTS

—

ix

CONTENTS

INTRODUCTION

—

Alfred Corn

Several times during the development of this collection, when I mentioned it to them, writer friends gave me a wide-eyed stare. Essays on *what?* One didn't need to be a psychic to know what thoughts were racing through their minds: "You're turning into one of those incredible people on television that are always waving the Bible around." Not thus far, at least. I am not a "fundamentalist," in fact, working on this book has made it clearer than ever to me why I am not. One of the disturbing things about fundamentalists to me is that they seem not to read the Bible enough, or not comprehensively. Seizing on one verse or chapter and letting everything follow from that suggests a lack of perspective. It ignores the careful balance established among a series of books composed by different hands over roughly a forty-year period in the second half of the first century of the Common Era. The early church agreed on our present canon of Scripture only after a long, fiery debate that continued into the third century. Comparative reading of the New Testament shows marked differences in the several accounts of the life and teachings of Jesus of Nazareth and of his apostles. To believe that these books are divinely inspired is an inalienable personal prerogative; to say that they were taken down by dictation and immediately accepted as Scripture by all faithful Christians is not consistent with the historical record.

Theologians, expert and inexpert alike, can find scriptural warrants in support of various doctrinal stances, and of course the development of Christianity and its numerous sects and denominations has shown the surprising uses to which the Bible can be put in the process of dogma formation. In fact, the work of founding or challenging doctrine on the basis of scriptural argument is still occurring and is likely to go on. It may be that we are better acquainted now with the hazards involved with scriptural argumentation than we were. The problem of texts, for example: we cannot be entirely certain that the versions that have come down to us are free of copyists' errors or willful tampering by later interests (in fact, there are several instances where it is clear that additions or interpolations have been made). Apart from this problem, most of us must rely on translations, about which there will always be dispute. Still the most widely read and quoted, King James's Authorized Version is beautifully resonant but certainly erroneous in some particulars and composed, moreover, in a seventeenth-century diction hard for the uninstructed reader to decipher with complete accuracy. A careful appraisal of what we really have in our old family Bibles, and of the differences of opinion concerning the meaning of particular words therein, ought to discourage the habit of drawing from them premature, ironclad conclusions about faith and conduct.

Historical record also tells us that an encounter with these texts has over and over again brought on unforeseen, creative events in the lives of those who enter into it with an open mind. Yet those wide-eyed stares of my friends reminded me that a large part of the public accustomed to reading still has only the slightest acquaintance with the Bible and so stands under a disadvantage comparable to the fundamentalists'. Given that biblical texts are the cornerstone of our customs, our laws, our literature and art, our family structure, and our notions of romantic love, this omission is strange and troubling. It can only be explained by the discredit brought to religion since the Victorian era. Too often the church at large forfeited a vital, creative relationship to the Gospel texts in favor of an unbudgeable, flintlike formulation of what they said. And yet we recall that Jesus was more critical of religious smugness and complacency than of any other misdeed or failure he encountered. The content of the gospel proclamation has been more than the exclusive property of a humanly flawed church; its fortunes have not been purely ecclesiastical. If Christian religious practice seems everywhere to be springing into life once again, part of the explanation has to do with an awakening to manifestations of Jesus' teachings outside church walls, and a welcoming of new insights into a present-day understanding of Christian faith.

The original assumption behind the project of gathering these essays was that the New Testament, in whatever translation, is read today and that its readership includes a good many contemporary writers. The Bible and Christian tradition have been the foundation of most of literature in the West since the early medieval period; and that influence continues. It can be seen in the work of all the contributors here and many more besides. Naturally the question arises: Just what is the importance of these ancient scriptures to contemporary imaginative writing? You have here—directly, indirectly, sometimes in a contestatory mode—the varied answers that individual writers were willing to adumbrate. Although none of the authors is a scholar, a good bit of general scholarship is found here as well, and the sum total makes an absorbing and accessible introduction to the New Testament for those readers with only a partial knowledge of it. The simple fact that the contributors are writers themselves gives the twenty-three novelists and poets represented special perspective onto these books, a perspective that their writerly abilities empower them to render in vivid and memorable form. Those among the readership who have some knowledge of the four Gospels but nothing more, or who remember the other books only from a superficial childhood exposure, may find, when they return to the New Testament, a changed sense of what is actually said there.

This book was conceived as a complement to David Rosenberg's *Congregation: Contemporary Writers Read the Jewish Bible*. All of Mr. Rosenberg's essayists were Jews, and of course Gentile writers who read what is traditionally known as the Old Testament might be just as eager to discuss, say, Ruth or Ecclesiastes as Titus or Philippians. This may be a way of saying that there is room for more essays on all of Scripture—and by participants other than those who have ventured to accept the assignment so far. My own methods of finding contributors was a mixture of soliciting recommendations and writing to authors whose work I already knew and admired. Not all of the contributors are practicing Christians, or even theists. Two of them are Jews who had important comment to offer on these texts or on Christianity at large. To treat the New Testament as some sort of club with exclusive membership would have been to ignore what was said in it.

In every case I proposed (for reasons not always easy to state) a subject book to the author. Sometimes the proposal was rejected; sometimes writers suggested alternatives. The assignment was of course not always "the favorite book" of the author undertaking it, and I urged contributors to give themselves free rein in their reactions to the texts confronting them. I was not looking for a definitive summary of scholarly arguments surrounding each book, because such discussions are available already and known to experts in the field of biblical studies. More interesting to me was the personal response of each writer to a given book of the New Testament. I commend my essayists for, among other virtues, their courage. The theology of incarnation argues that spirit and flesh are anything but incompatible and that the practice of sacrifice, at the small scale and the large, is central to any valid "imitation of Christ." I had no difficulty discovering incarnational qualities in this collection, and in the previous work of the authors represented here—which has supported the assumption that Christian Scriptures and tradition are involved in some of the most significant artistic activity of our time. No real surprise there when we consider that these texts are part of a continuing creation inseparable from the written word because it is at one with the divine life in all of us.

INCARNATION

THE GOSPEL
ACCORDING TO
SAINT MATTHEW

—

John Updike

Matthew might be described as the workhorse of the four Gospel writers, the establishment man. His version of the story of Jesus traditionally begins the New Testament and continues to be placed first among the canonical four Gospels, even though Mark has been recognized since the 1830s as most probably the earliest composed, and therefore (presumably) the most authentic and the least overlaid by wishful thinking and concealed doctrinal pleading. Mark has his electric compactness and swiftness of narrative, Luke has those tender human episodes (the annunciation, the birth of John, the nativity in the manger, the twelve-year-old Jesus in the Temple at Jerusalem, the story of Mary and Martha, the parables of the prodigal son and the pearl of great price, the good criminal on the cross, the appearances of the risen Jesus at Emmaus and Jerusalem) absent from the other Gospels, and John has his poetic fire and Platonic thrust. Compared with these writers, Matthew is a drab and not entirely appealing "safe man" who manfully handles Christian belief's awkward lumber—the threats of hellfire and outer darkness and the, to a modern reader, irksome insistence upon Christ's life as a detailed fulfillment of Old Testament prophecies. But one cannot speak of any of the

Gospels as the exclusive product of a writer's personality and inspiration, for all drew upon the same body of oral tradition and contain numerous parallel if not identical passages.

Aside from a few glancing and problematical references in Josephus, Suetonius, and Tacitus, the biography related in the Gospels made no mark in contemporary non-Christian annals. However, Paul's Epistles, which predate even Mark, and the Acts of the Apostles, composed by the author of Luke, verify that there was a historical Jesus, whose life and death exerted a transforming influence upon, first, an inner circle of disciples and followers and, within a generation of his death, groups of worshipers throughout Palestine and, by the next generation, much of the Roman world. The Gospel writers belong, it is likely, to the second generation of Christians after the apostles, though early church tradition claims Mark to have been dictated by Peter, and John to have been the actual work of one of the twelve, John the son of Zebedee, "the disciple whom Jesus loved," recalling these events as a very old man in Ephesus around A.D. 100.

No other texts have suffered such a weight of analysis, yet there is still opportunity for scholars to disagree over such basics as the date, place, and order of their composition, and for significant flaws to be found in every theory. Nevertheless, venerable scholarly consensus dates Mark at about A.D. 65 and places Matthew ten or fifteen years later—certainly after the destruction of the Temple in 70, an event to which Jesus is made to allude in 23:38. Matthew follows, with some deviations and improvements of Greek, Mark's narrative, adding to it a wealth of sayings and teaching present also in Luke: the body of material in common constitutes the well-known hypothetical document Q, named from the German *Quelle*, "source." While Matthew and Luke did not have exactly the same Q in front of them, and small discrepancies abound, it is roughly true that Matthew = Mark + Q and that Luke = Mark + Q + the considerable body of narrative and preachment present only in Luke, called by some scholars S. And if these three "synoptic" Gospels are thought of as thus progressively sedimentary, then the Gospel of John is like a metamorphic rock in which these strata have been violently annealed but in which recognizable veins remain. Nineteenth-century scholars, in working upon the Gospels, naturally thought in terms of men manipulating written texts. Many of the puzzles they formulated, concerning inconsistencies and variations among the texts, disappear if we imagine the Gospel writers as independently drawing upon a lively body of oral history—a body that threatened, as the Christian community became more scattered and diverse, to become ever more distorted and open to inauthentic, notably Gnostic, incursions. By the last quarter of the first Christian century, a written testament was necessary if the movement was to remain coherent. Luke's dedication of his Gospel to Theophilus evokes a scene of growing confusion wherein "many have undertaken to arrange in narrative form such accounts of the momentous happenings in our midst as have been handed down to us by the original eye-witnesses and ministers of the Word."*

Those of us who call ourselves Christians, then, look *through* the Gospels that did emerge from the first century as through a cloudy glass toward a brilliant light. But the Gospel writers, whether rememberers or editors of others' memories, themselves were looking through accretions of written and oral history toward events as distant from them as World War II is from us. Their thumbprints, as it were, cannot be rubbed off the glass; at the outset of this century Albert Schweitzer demonstrated in his book *The Quest of the Historical Jesus* that no pleasingly liberal Jesus—no purely political revolutionary stripped of superstitious accretions, no sweet Jesus who is all beatitude—can be extracted from the Gospel record, which is supernatural to its core. Yet Mark, by itself, is a rather cryptic storm of parable and miracle, which begins when Jesus appears, fully grown, "coming from Nazareth in Galilee," to be baptized, and which ends at the point where three of his female followers come to the tomb in search of his crucified body and are greeted by "a young man in a white robe" who tells them that Jesus "has risen: he is not here." Though he also tells the women, "Do not be afraid," the text of Mark judged to be authentic ends with the sentence "They said not a word to anyone, because they feared." The triumphant and redeeming end of the story, Christ's miraculous resurrection, is mysteriously muted in this ending, and a writer of the second century,

---

* This and all subsequent translations are taken from E. V. Rieu's 1952 translation *The Four Gospels*, for the Penguin Classics series.

in a style of Greek plainly not Mark's, appended twelve verses out-lining some of Jesus' postresurrection appearances to the apostles and containing his charge to them to "go into every part of the world and preach the Gospel to the whole creation." These added verses, included in all Bibles, are canonical but not Marcan; in what survives of *echt* Mark Jesus disappears from the tomb as casually as he appears at the Jordan to be baptized by John. There is no nativity story, and no follow-up of the empty tomb. Nor is there much explanation of Jesus' announcement "The time has come, and the Kingdom of God is at hand. Repent and put your trust in the Good News." The news we are given concerns a young man, a paragon of vitality and poetic assertion, who after an indeterminate period of itinerant preaching and miraculous healing in Palestine is taken prisoner in Jerusalem by the Roman authorities at the request of the Jewish priesthood and ignominiously put to death, crying out on the cross, in his lan-guage of Aramaic, *"Eloi, Eloi, lama sabachthani*—My God, my God, why hast thou forsaken me?"

Matthew takes up the task of giving these events a cosmic context, by knitting them tight to the sacred texts of the Jewish people col-lected in what is now called the Old Testament. Matthew is viewed by tradition as the most specifically Jewish of the Gospel writers: Eusebius in his fourth-century *Historica ecclesiastica* quotes Papias, the bishop of Hierapolis around 130, as saying that "Matthew com-piled the oracles (or sayings) in the Hebrew language, but everyone translated them as he was able," and Eusebius cites Irenaeus as claim-ing that "Matthew published a gospel in writing also, among the Hebrews in their own language." The contemporary biblical scholars who edited the Anchor Bible edition of Matthew, W. F. Albright and C. S. Mann, propose that the disciple Matthew, a former tax collector identified elsewhere as Levi, in fact was Matthew the Levite, who as a Levite would have been "a Pharisee, educated, and from an orthodox . . . background." The author of the Gospel of Matthew, whatever his actual name, was, they believe, "a conservative-minded Jew" especially interested in the Law and aware of "Messianic titles (the Prophet, the Righteous One) already archaic in the time of Jesus." Without wishing to present Jesus as the new Moses, Matthew shows a "consuming interest in the spiritual history of Israel as a chosen people" and "in carefully preserving sayings of Jesus which re-establish the true principles of the Mosaic Law."

Certainly Matthew can be wearisomely legalistic, beginning with the badly stretched genealogy from David to Jesus that opens his Gospel. Eleven times—and each time dampening credibility rather than, as in the original cultural context, creating it—he claims that something occurred in order to fulfill what the Lord had spoken through the prophets: the virgin birth, Bethlehem as the birth site, Herod's massacre of children under the age of two, the flight of Joseph and Mary with their infant son to Egypt, their eventual settling in Nazareth, Galilee as the site of Jesus' ministry, his healing of the sick, his modesty, his speaking in parables, his curious choice of both a donkey and a colt to enter Jerusalem upon, and Judas' acceptance of thirty pieces of silver all take their significance from having been foreshadowed by texts in Isaiah or Jeremiah. For the sake of a verse of the Psalms, "They gave me gall for food, and for thirst they gave me vinegar to drink" (Psalm 69:21), Matthew altered Mark's "They offered him wine mingled with myrrh" to ". . . mingled with gall." It would appear that Jesus himself came to see his life in terms of Israel's hopes of a Messiah. In Mark 14:27, he quotes Zechariah, "I shall strike the shepherd and his sheep shall be scattered," to give the dignity of foreordainment to his disciples' coming abandonment of him. But it is hard not to feel that words are being put in Christ's mouth when Matthew has him, in 26:53–54, say to a disciple who has drawn a sword, "Do you suppose that I could not call upon my Father and that he would not in a moment have a greater force than fifty thousand Angels at my side? But then, how could the Scriptures be fulfilled which say, it shall be thus?" And a few verses farther on, Matthew's Jesus rebukes the crowd that has gathered at his arrest, "I see that you have come out with swords and sticks to capture me as though I were a brigand. Day after day I sat in the Temple, teaching, and you did not arrest me. But all this has happened so that what the Prophets wrote may be fulfilled." This appeal to the Prophets has a parallel in Mark (14:49) and in Luke, but in Luke assumes a quite different quality: "When I was with you in the Temple day after day, you did not raise a hand against me. But this is your hour. Night takes command" (22:53). In John, which names Peter as the disciple who took the sword and cut off the right ear of the high priest's servant, there is no parallel.

A legal passion peculiar to Matthew insists that "while heaven and earth remain, the Law shall not be docked of one letter or one comma* till its purpose is achieved" (5:18). Jesus assures his auditors, "Do not imagine that I came to abolish the Law and the Prophets. I came, not to annul them, but to bring them to perfection" (5:17). The parallel passage in Luke has no such assurance, nor does it contain Matthew's strictures on oath taking or his stress upon inwardness and secrecy in performing acts of prayer, fasting, and almsgiving: "But when you practise charity, do not let your left hand know what your right hand is doing, so that your charity may be in secret; and your Father who sees in secret will render you your due" (6:3–4). And only Matthew's list of Beatitudes ends with "Happy those that have been persecuted for righteousness; for theirs is the Kingdom of Heaven"; the young church was already suffering persecution, and hence Matthew speaks through Jesus to the imperiled faithful of A.D. 80. The threat of hell seems especially vivid in Matthew, and ready to hand, to brandish as a menace: in two separate places (5:29–30; 18:8–9) he repeats the ferocious admonishment found in Mark 9:43–48:

If your hand leads you into evil, cut it off: it is better for you to come into Life maimed than, with both hands, to depart into hell, into the fire that cannot be put out. And if your foot leads you into evil, cut it off: it is better for you to come into Life crippled than, with both feet, to be cast into hell. And if your eye leads you into evil, pluck it out: it is better for you to come into the Kingdom of God with one eye than, with two, to be cast into hell, where their worm does not die and the fire is never quenched.

These are among the hardest of the not unnumerous hard sayings of Jesus, and Matthew brings them to the fore; his presentation

---

* In Greek the words are *iota* and *keraia*, the latter being small horns attached to some letters of Hebrew; the King James translation has it "one jot or one tittle," and the Standard Revised "not a letter, not a stroke."

delights in a moral perfectionism. "You then must be perfect, as your Father in Heaven is perfect" (5:48). The Kingdom of Heaven is very precarious of entrance, a matter of jots and tittles of the ancient Law: "The man who abolishes one of these little rules and teaches people to forget it shall count for little in the Kingdom of Heaven" (5:19).

What is this Kingdom of Heaven? At times it seems to be a revolutionized earth, an earth brought under the rule of God; at others, a realm of an otherworldly afterlife, the opposite of hell and outer darkness. And yet again it seems a new state of inner being, a state of moral perfection that is not so much the ticket to the Kingdom but the Kingdom itself. In Luke, Jesus tells his disciples, "Watch as you may, you will not see it come. People will not be saying 'Here it is!' or 'There!' And the reason why is this—this Kingdom of God is within you" (17:20–21). The most extended statement concerning the Kingdom, and the longest compilation of Christ's instruction, comes in Matthew, chapters 5 through 7, and it is this so-called Sermon on the Mount, or Great Instruction, that would be the sorest loss if Matthew's Gospel, in that precarious welter of first-century Christian testimony, had vanished along with Q and Matthew's supposed version in Hebrew. Luke's shorter version of the sermon, delivered not on a mountain but on a plain, in 6:17–49, is less than half as long, and strikes a merry note peculiar to itself: "Happy, you that weep now; for you shall laugh." Matthew does not mention laughing, but his extended collection of the sayings of Jesus holds many touches of that sublime gallantry, that cosmic carefreeness which emanates from the Son of Man:

Count yourselves happy when the time comes for people to revile you and maltreat you and utter every kind of calumny against you on account of me.

Let your light so shine upon the world that it may see the beauty of your life and give glory to your Father in Heaven.

If anyone strikes you on the right cheek, turn the left towards him also. If anyone sees fit to sue you for your tunic, let him have your cloak as well. If anyone impresses you to go a mile, go along with him for two.

Love your enemies and pray to those that persecute you, so that you may become children of your Father in Heaven, who causes his sun to rise on the wicked and the good, and rains on the just and the unjust alike.

Do not amass for yourselves treasure on earth, where moth and rust destroy, and thieves break in and steal.

Learn from the lilies of the fields and how they grow. They do not work, they do not spin. But I tell you that not even Solomon in all his glory was robed like one of these.

Do not judge, lest you be judged.

Do not give holy things to dogs, nor scatter your pearls in front of swine, or they may trample them underfoot, and turn and tear you to pieces.

Ask and you shall receive. Seek and you shall find. Knock and the door shall be opened to you. For everyone that asks receives; every seeker finds; and to everyone that knocks the door is opened.

These commands do not form a prescription for life in this world. The auditors are described as "filled with amazement at his teaching; for he taught them like one with authority and not like the Doctors who usually taught them." The concept of amazement recurs in this part of Matthew. In the next chapter, the disciples are, in Rieu's translation, "amazed" at Jesus' stilling the wind and sea, and Jesus is "amazed" at the faith of the centurion who comes to Jesus to heal his paralyzed son.

Two worlds are colliding; amazement prevails. Jesus' healing and preaching go together in the Gospel accounts, and his preaching is healing of a sort, for it banishes worldly anxiety; it overthrows the commonsense and materially verifiable rules that, like the money changers in the temple, dominate the world with their practicality. Jesus declares an inversion of the world's order, whereby the first shall be last and the last first, the meek shall inherit the earth, the hungry and thirsty shall be satisfied, and the poor in spirit shall possess the Kingdom of Heaven. This Kingdom is the hope and pain of Christianity; it is attained against the grain, through the denial of instinctive and social wisdom and through faith in the unseen. Using natural metaphors as effortlessly as an author quoting his own works, Jesus disclaims Nature and its rules of survival. Nature's way, obvious and broad, leads to death; this other way is narrow and difficult: "Come in by the narrow gate, for the way to destruction is a broad and open road which is trodden by many; whereas the way to life is by a narrow gate and a difficult road, and few are those that find it" (1:13–14).

Life is not what we think and feel it is. True life (sometimes capitalized "Life" in the Rieu translation, as in the quotation from Mark above) is something different from the life of the body: "He that wins his life will lose it, and he that loses his life for my sake shall win it" (10:39). Christ's preaching threatens men, the virtuous even more than the wicked, with a radical transformation of value whereby the rich and pious are damned and harlots and tax collectors are rather more acceptable. The poor, ignorant, and childish are more acceptable yet: Jesus thanks God "for hiding these things from wise and clever men and revealing them to simple folk" (11:25). Even ordinary altruism is challenged, and decent frugality, in the incident of the woman who poured precious ointment over Jesus, to the amazement and indignation of the apostles. They object, "That might have fetched a good price, and so been given to the poor." The blithe, immortal answer is given: "You have the poor among you always; but me you have not always" (26:11). Over against human perspective stands God's perspective, from which even sparrows sold two for a farthing have value. Just so, each human soul, including those of women and slaves and Gentiles, has value. From our perspective, the path of righteousness is narrow; but the strait gate leads to infinite consolation: "Put on my yoke and learn from me, who am gentle and humble in heart—and you will find rest for your souls. For my yoke is easy and my burden light" (11:28–30). Fulfillment of the old Law turns out to be close to lawlessness: circumcision, dietary restrictions, strict observance of the Sabbath, familial piety, pharisaical scruples are all swept away by the new dispensation. Said John the Baptist: "He will baptize you in the Holy Spirit and fire. His winnowing-fan is in his hand. He will clear his threshing-floor and gather the grain into his barn" (3:11–12). Said Jesus: "The blind see once more; the lame walk; lepers are cleansed; the deaf hear; dead men are brought back to life, and beggars are proclaiming the Good News. Happy the man who finds no fault in me" (11:5–6).

Christ's easy yoke drew dozens and then thousands and millions into Christianity, which for the first three centuries of its existence was professed in the Roman Empire under penalty of death. Neither in terms of Judaic Scripture and religious practice nor in the context of other world religions was the transformation of value Jesus introduced totally new; but it felt new to those who embraced it, in the aftermath of his brief ministry and alleged resurrection. He is the new wine, and of all the Gospel writers Matthew takes the most trouble to decant him from the old skin. The Judaic God had walked in the Garden with Adam, joked with the devil, bullied Job, and wrestled with Jacob: still, it was a scandalous act to send his Son to earth to suffer a humiliating and agonizing death. The concept profoundly offended the Greeks with their playful, beautiful, invulnerable pantheon and the Jews with their traditional expectations of a regal Messiah. Yet it answered, as it were, to the facts, to something deep within men. God crucified formed a bridge between our human perception of a cruelly imperfect and indifferent world and our human need for God, our human sense that God is present. For nearly twenty centuries now, generations have found comfort and guidance in the paradoxical hero of the Gospels, the man of peace who brings a sword, the Messiah who fails and shouts his despair aloud, the perfect man who seems to drift, who seems in most of his actions merely reacting to others, as they beg him to heal them, or challenge him to declare himself the King of the Jews ("The words are yours," he replies), or ask him, as does his Father in Heaven, to undergo crucifixion.

In the Lutheran Sunday school I attended as a child, a large reproduction of a popular painting in a milky Germanic Victorian style showed a robed Jesus praying in Gethsemane, his hands folded on a conveniently tablelike rock, his lightly bearded face turned upward with a melancholy radiance as he asked, presumably, for this cup to pass from him, and listened to the heavenly refusal. I was a mediocre Sunday-school student, who generally failed to win the little perfect-attendance pin in May. But I was impressed by the saying that to lust after a woman in your heart is as bad as actual adultery and deserving of self-mutilation, because it posited a world, coexistent with that of trees and automobiles and living people around me, in which a motion of the mind, of the soul, was an actual deed, as important as a physical act. And I took in the concept that God watches the sparrow's fall—that our world is everywhere, at all times, in every detail, watched by God, like a fourth dimension. Some of the parables—the one in which the prodigal son received favorable treatment, or those in which foolish virgins or ill-paid vineyard workers are left to wail in outer darkness—puzzled and repelled me, in their sketches of the dreadful freedom that reigns behind God's dispensations. But the parable of the talents bore a clear lesson for me: Live your life. Live it as if there is a blessing on it. Dare to take chances, lest you leave your talent buried in the ground. I could picture so clearly the hole that the timorous servant would dig in the dirt, and even imagine how cozily cool and damp it would feel to his hand as he placed his talent in it.

Like millions of other little citizens of Christendom I was infected with the dangerous idea that there is a double standard, the world's and another, and that the other is higher, and all true life flows from it. Vitality, perhaps, is the overriding virtue in the Bible, and the New Testament, for all its legalisms, obscurities, repetitions, and dark patches, renews the vitality of the Old. From certain verbal prominences, burnished by ages of quotation like kissed toes on bronze statues of saints, and certain refracting facets of the tumbled testamental matter an iridescence shudders forth which corresponded, in my consciousness as a child, to the vibrant, uncaused moments of sheer grateful happiness that I occasionally experienced. I still have them, these visitations of joy, and still associate them with the Good News. "Know too," Matthew's Gospel ends, "that I am with you every day to the end of time."

THE GOSPEL
ACCORDING TO
SAINT MARK

—

PARTS OF A JOURNAL

Mary Gordon

To write of this subject in this way is to acknowledge my place among the noninnocent.

It was not something you wrote about, or even anything you read: it was what you heard. To come to it this way is strange, even false-seeming. The Bible as Literature. The Gospel as Narrative. Christ the character. Exposition. Denouement. These are words from a later time, a time in which experience is less sensually apprehended, less natural. The first encounter with it was before memory; it was a story that had nothing to do with history or print. We did not read the Bible; we were Catholics. In our house there was, of course, a Bible— the translation: Douay-Rheims. We did not record in it the memorable events: birthdays, marriages, deaths. We rarely looked at it. We didn't need to; we were encouraged not to. We heard the truth and the truth would set us free. The truth was not for reading.

Inevitable, like the seasons, were certain narrative events. The Passion, of course, and Christmas, the Ascension, Pentecost; but the stories took on the flavor of certain weathers. The narrative imprinted itself on household objects: toys. I had a puzzle of Jesus and the children; for my Bible stamp book, I licked the multiplication of the loaves and fishes, Lazarus in his tomb. Above the examining table in my doctor's office Jesus gave the blind sight. The narrative was part of bodily life, like food or shelter. You were never apart from it.

Did I draw distinctions among the four evangelists? At the beginning of the Gospel, the priest always said whom the story was according to. I never listened. Did I have any sense that certain stories were retold in different ways, that one writer included events that another left out, that some embellished on a simple incident and some condensed? Of course not. I stood, and heard. There was no notion of a text. We were not the people of the book; we were the people of the priestly utterance, the restricted information, interpreted, rendered safe only when spoken through the consecrated lips.

I cannot write about the Gospels in a form that suggests a coherent experience of it as a written whole; this would be untrue to what it was for me. The Gospels appeared to me as scenes. Not moving: static. Unconnected to each other, with a separateness that seemed sacred in itself, each scene with me like the color of my eyes.

And yet, it would be retreating into a kind of false innocence to pretend that my contact with the Gospels ended when I heard them as a child—or as an orthodox believer. In college, fearing I had touched the profane, I studied the New Testament. Hearing people talk about translations from the Greek, versions from different manuscripts, shocked and titillated me. They were talking about it as they would talk about an ordinary work: the epic of *Gilgamesh*, which we also read that term. I have read the Gospels as an adult, read them silently, alone, not leaving aside the literary sophistication that is part of me as well. But it is reading like no other reading: never disengaged, hooked to memory, belief, loss of belief, the knowledge that it has been a source of pain (in the impossibility of its standards) and growth (perhaps for the same reason). How, then, do I write about it? Perhaps without the illusion of cohesion. But not innocently. No.

I
She Is Not Dead, but Sleeping

The daughter of Jairus. The daughter of somebody important, someone with the confidence (would my father have had it?—yes; the other fathers in the neighborhood would not) to push through the crowd and get Jesus' attention.

The daughter of privilege. The apple of her father's eye. Servants tend her, but they are helpless. How beautiful she is: eyes closed, immobile. On her pallet. The word is exotic; it means the climate is temperate enough not to need a bed. The lightest covers. In the warm evenings, the breeze is caressive to the skin.

When Jesus gets to the house, He is told she is already dead. He doesn't listen. "She is not dead, but sleeping."

If He can say it to her, He can say it to anyone. Perhaps death is always only a perceptual error.

Talitha cumi: in the middle of the English two foreign words. Immediately we are told what it means: Little girl, I say to thee: arise.

She gets up and walks. She is twelve years old.

For years, I measure my age against hers. I am younger than she at first. Then one year we are the same age: it could be I rescued from death. By the time I realize that I am older than she, I no longer believe in the possibility of my own resurrection.

He tells them not to speak of it and to give her something to eat. I imagine Him leaving the house, leaving the others to what is always for me the food in the Gospels: bread and fish.

Reading it now, I discover that Jesus is interrupted on His way to Jairus's house. He is interrupted by a hemorrhaging woman. She doesn't even try to get His attention; she only wants to touch His cloak. Now I realize that this in itself was a daring act; perpetually menstruating, she was in a state of perpetual defilement. And Jesus, having cured her almost against His will (it is her contact with His clothing that dries up her hemorrhages), recoils for a moment, in the grips of a taboo: "aware that the power had gone out of him." The King James renders it "immediately knowing in himself that virtue had gone out of him": the old confusion in words, virtue—

virtù—and power. In any case, strength and/or virtue are destroyed by contact with the defiled woman.

Jesus is not frozen in a state of primitive recoil. He does not call the woman unclean; He doesn't even refer to her former uncleanness. Jesus changes: something we were never taught to think of, something we were thought to think of as unimaginable. Impressed with the woman's faith, her self-forgetfulness, He overcomes his own initial primitive response. There is room in the Kingdom even for the menstruating woman. She need not be set apart.

I have never heard anyone speak of this.

Only after this contact with the hemorrhaging woman does He go to Jairus's house, to be told that He is too late, the girl is dead. She is not dead, but sleeping. She is twelve years old. Is it that she is dead to childhood? Jesus escorts her into womanhood; He permits her maturity. He allows her to move from the recumbent position of the privileged girl child to the ambulatory state of adulthood. He urges the others to bring her food. And then He leaves her.

I am reading the New English Bible. It doesn't say: "She is not dead, but sleeping." It says: "The child is not dead, she is asleep." I feel that something has been stolen from me. I require the exact words. I look in the King James: "The damsel is not dead, but sleepeth." Worse. Pure literature. No good to me at all.

I don't have a copy of the Douay-Rheims. I ask my mother. She says she thinks she lost it when she moved.

II
The Fig Tree

Jesus curses the fig tree for conforming to natural law. Why is this incident exciting? It induces a kind of masochistic thrill: to observe sympathetically someone whose demands are, literally, supernatural, requiring not just heroism but betrayal of causality. Simone Weil took the parable terribly to heart: she identified with the fig tree. We are all less fruitful than we might be; we are all in the grips of nature. We would like to blossom, out of season, at a word.

The petulant, irritable Jesus. He appears often in Mark. Mark's tone is harsh. It wasn't something we were listening for in church:

tone. But the idea of gentle Jesus meek and mild is certainly extra-textual. Just after He curses the fig tree, He drives the money changer from the Temple, another thrilling episode. No one could possibly identify with the money changers. Their shock, their venal faces registering mercantile outrage, the upraised arm of Jesus, brandishing the rope He uses as a whip, the doves, loosed from their cages, disoriented in the Temple courtyard. It is violent: male.

He is often impatient with the pressing demands of the crowd; He is caught between the demands of the eternally growing multitude and His mystical nature that requires solitude. There are always more blind, deaf, possessed. He keeps wanting to escape from them. We never noticed it. But, even as He broke out of the frozen attitude of recoil from the menstrual taboo, He breaks out of the attitude of wearied impatience with the needs and the stupidity of the crowd. He says to the father with a possessed child: "What an unbelieving and perverse generation! How long shall I be with you? How long must I endure you?" This because the father insists upon Jesus actually laying on hands; he doesn't believe in the power of his own faith. Finally, though, Jesus responds to the father's less than fully mature needs and says: "Bring him to me."

III
Bread to the Dogs

A Gentile woman comes to beg Jesus to drive the evil spirit out of her daughter. He says to her: "Let the children be satisfied first, it is not fair to take the children's bread and throw it to the dogs." The interpretation of this cruelty from the altar was that Jesus was testing her to show the greatness of her faith. But it also could be simple xenophobia: He thought originally that He was preaching to Jews. She beats Him on His own linguistic grounds. "Sir, even the dogs under the table eat the children's scraps." She bests Him using the technique He uses against the Pharisees: turning His own words against Him. But what a time for word play: who would say this to a mother, distraught over her child's possession?

She seems, however, to be one of the importunate women from whom Jesus learns. He sends her home; her daughter is cured. He has taken His first step in allowing the world outside the Law of Moses into the Kingdom.

We were never allowed to think of Jesus as someone who learned, or grew or developed. Particularly in relation to a woman.

IV
The Devils

"He would not let the devils speak because they knew who he was."

The possessed man, whose voice is the voice of his possessing spirit, also recognizes Jesus. "What do you want with me, Jesus, son of the Most High God? In God's name do not torment me." For Jesus was already saying to him, "Out, unclean spirit, come out of this man."

To personify evil as something existing outside the self, therefore capable of being removed from the self without impairing the self's integrity. As if evil were detachable, a growth, but one that moved and spoke. And yet the devils seem willing to cooperate with Jesus in His healing. It is their idea to enter into the pigs. *Their* idea or *His* idea: the identity of the devil in relation to the identity of the possessed man is confused: this is evident from the confusion of number: "*My* name is Legion, *he* said, there are so many of *us*." The notion that the spirit seeks embodiment in the created world. Better to be embodied in a pig than to be bodiless.

The ability of evil to recognize God. To name Jesus, even against His will to be named. To conspire in breaking the messianic secret.

To frame evil in these terms is consoling. It implies the possibility of exorcism. Fifteen years ago, when the film *The Exorcist* came out, it was fashionable to consider hiring those priests who were qualified exorcists to try to cure the mentally ill. How long did the fashion last? What stopped it?

It would be helpful to someone who loved a mad person or a criminal to be able to conceptualize evil this way, as something apart from the person, randomly visited upon him, and perhaps as randomly removable. It lessens the crushing pressure of self-blame: a kind of healing in itself.

The stark visual drama of pigs hurtling over a mountaintop. The animal world responds to the authority of God, so it takes on a kind of animal force. Mark mentions the number of pigs: two thousand. We believe anyone who knows numbers. Any good storyteller, or liar, knows this.

V
The Blind Man and the Trees

"The people brought a blind man to Jesus and begged him to touch him. He took the blind man by the hand and led him away out of the village. Then he spat on his eyes, laid his hands upon him, and asked whether he could see anything. The man's sight began to come back and he said, I see men, they look like trees, but they are walking about. Jesus laid his hands on his eyes again; he looked hard and now he was cured so he saw everything clearly."

The pleasure of partial vision. Did Jesus allow the man only as much vision as he could tolerate? Was the fullness of the visible world too much of a shock all at once? I keep thinking how pleasant it would have been, that partial state: no sharp differentiations, yet an awareness of a life, moving: proof that there are others outside the self.

What does it say, really, about Jesus as healer? There's something almost comic about the situation: I see men as trees walking. Back to the drawing board. But there is something wonderfully noncoercive about Jesus' role, a sort of patience as healer, and an eagerness to hear the man's version of his own experience. Jesus takes him out of the town. Respectful or reclusive? Or was it cruelty to take the man out of his pleasant distortion? Would it have been merciful to leave the man in the vagueness of perceptual half-truth? Was Jesus tempted to do that first, and then, respecting the man's right to painful sight, did He reject the temptation? Why does it seem like a loss of innocence? As if Mr. Micawber were given a compulsory course on economics. Illusion is not enough; more is demanded. Vision. Testimony. Distinctions made.

VI
Jesus and the Children

How we have fixed on this scene! Or did we fix on it before the Victorians fell in love with childhood? It's not, after all, a staple of Renaissance iconography, where the only interesting children were angelic or divine.

He was interested in children in a way that was really original. I look in the Biblical Concordance for references to children in the Old Testament: "In sorrow bring forth children" . . . "Give me children or I die" . . . "The father's children shall bow down" . . . "Seled died without children" . . . "The children rebelled against me" . . . "As arrows in the hand, so are children" . . . "Do not have mercy on her children" . . . "The children's teeth are set on edge." Job pleads for the sake of the children, but Elisha sends a bear after the boys who made fun of him. Nowhere, though, is there concern for the education, the upbringing of children, the inner lives of children, the idea that they exist not as possessions, as markers, as earthly immortality, but in themselves. Jesus' concern for them is practical: how do we treat children to help them grow? How do we help children achieve salvation? He seriously thinks of their souls.

Jesus seems genuinely to want the physical presence of children, their company. We often hear Him trying to keep people away, or see Him trying to get away from them, but He rebukes the disciples for shooing the children away. He is described in a state of affectionateness. Surely, He is the only affectionate hero in literature. Who can imagine an affectionate Odysseus, Aeneas? Even a novel would be queasy dwelling too long on a scene like this. Affection— a step, many steps below passion, usually connected to women. He is both maternal and paternal with the children. "He put his arms round them, laid his hands upon them, and blessed them."

And yet it is exactly this scene, this event, that generates His most harsh dualism. It is in relation to protecting children that He urges His followers to mutilate themselves in the face of temptation that might prove too strong. He puts His hands on the children and then urges His followers to cut off their own hands. He embraces the children and in the next breath tells the rich man that if he will not give up everything he cannot enter the Kingdom of God. He blesses the children and then says, "There is no one who has given up home, brothers or sisters, mother, father or children . . . who will not receive in this age a hundred times as much—houses, brothers and sisters, mothers and children, and land—and persecutions besides; and in the age to come eternal life."

But of course it is exactly this extremism that makes Jesus not Victorian and therefore not sentimental. Is it possible to have a vision that is at once sentimental and eschatological? This may be the one new contribution of the TV evangelists: the angel with the flaming sword is guarding home and hearth. And, of course, the TV. Usually, though, it is the eschatological that prevents the sentimental; and for that reason, if for no other, it is desirable.

He is a complicated character. "Character" in both senses of the word: literary and colloquial (as in "He's a real character," implying the capacity for surprising behavior). Without our knowing it, without our being permitted to articulate it, was the very complexity of Jesus' character, the self-contradictions, the progressions forward and backwards, what made Him so compelling, so that even after belief had ceased, we brooded on the figure?

In Jesus, the rejection, always, of the middle ground.

VII

The Abomination of Desolation

The end of the world. This Gospel occurred at the beginning of autumn, the last Sunday in Pentecost. But the words "the abomination of desolation" seared and still cause reverberations. The days were beginning to be short, night would fall suddenly, without transition: darkness took over the face of the earth. You went inside the house, feeling vaguely guilty, anxious. There wouldn't be enough time. For what? Homework? Salvation? Simply, time was the devourer, seeking what it might devour.

In the fifties, it was mixed up with fear of the bomb, mixed up with the mornings of air-raid drills spent hunched under desks or in the basement by the furnace, where the focus of my fear was not my own burning flesh but how would I find my mother. I knew it would be chaotic. My mother worked. Suppose she was on her way home, caught, ordered somewhere else while I roamed looking for her.

And then there were the false Messiahs. Sermons concentrated upon those. The false Messiahs of modern life, offering pleasure, prosperity. I knew myself susceptible to their lure. "If anyone says to you, 'Look, here is the Messiah,' or 'Look, there he is,' do not believe it." But whom would you believe? How would you tell the false Messiah from the true? I had no faith in my powers of discernment; I knew myself persuadable. To go off with the false Messiah, without my mother and without Jesus—the possibility terrified me and seemed, of all the possibilities, the most likely, knowing as I did my weaknesses and faults.

"Alas for women with child in those days, and for those who have children at the breast!" I knew I wanted children; I felt those words were for me. Now I think: how many men would take into consideration the hardships of pregnancy and nursing?

"Learn a lesson from the fig tree. When its tender shoots appear and are breaking into leaf, you know that summer is near." He uses for His own narrative purpose the natural behavior of the fig tree, which He formerly cursed. Is He making amends?

The abomination of desolation. I have never heard a phrase that so fully captures the horror of annihilation. Desolation. We think of it as a species or adjunct of loneliness. But older meanings are more concerned with physical devastation. In the midst of devastation, there must be a terrible sense of loneliness, in the confusion and destruction, the quiet horror: I am alone.

"But in those days, after that distress, the sun will be darkened, the moon will not give her light; the stars will come falling from the sky, the celestial powers will be shaken. Then they will see the Son of Man coming in the clouds with great power and glory. Heaven and earth will pass away; my words will not pass away."

The end of anxiety, and chaos: glory. Light-filled but silent, or perhaps only the sound of wind, rushing. When I thought of the word that would not pass away, did I think of the Logos? Of course not, but there must have been something comforting about the *word*, removed as it was from all the assaultiveness of apocalyptic imagery, that gave solace.

So by the time I left church, I was calmed down.

VIII
The Anointing by Mary

The figure of Mary was confused and conflated in my imagination. She was Mary, the sister of Lazarus, who chose the better part (my ally, my hope in my rejection of the domestic for the intellectual); she was also the sinful woman, the prostitute. In my archetypal imagination, then, it was possible to be a contemplative and a prostitute, but not a contemplative and domestic, and not a prostitute and domestic. It was this Mary whom I saw anointing Jesus.

It is Luke, not Mark, who suggests that the woman who anoints is a prostitute, and also that she wipes His feet with her hair. The story in Mark is much less erotically charged, but, as Elizabeth Schussler-Fiorenza points out, it is politically more important. Schussler-Fiorenza thinks that Mark's version—an anointing of the head rather than the feet—is more likely, since a foot washing would have been more commonplace and less worthy of note. "Since the prophet in the Old Testament anointed the head of the Jewish king, the anointing of Jesus' head must have been understood immediately as the prophetic recognition of Jesus, the Anointed, the Messiah, the Christ. According to the tradition it was a woman who named Jesus by and through her prophetic sign-action. It was politically a dangerous story."

It's the only story I've ever referred to in fiction. I describe it as justifying the sins of fat Renaissance bankers. In fact, it is the triumph of the aesthetic over the moral. According to John's Gospel, it is Judas, the betrayer, who urges attention to the poor and his decision to hand Jesus over to the authorities comes just afterward. Yet what is the Gospel all about if not attention to the poor?

IX
The Man in the Sheet

An inexplicable passage. We are with Jesus in the Garden. Judas has just betrayed Him; one of the disciples has cut off the high priest's servant's ear. (In Mark, Jesus does not replace the ear.) Jesus says, "Do you take me for a bandit, that I was within your reach as I taught in the temple, and you did not lay hands on me. But let the scriptures be fulfilled." Then the disciples all deserted Him and ran away.

Among those following was a young man with nothing on but a linen cloth. They tried to seize him, but he slipped out of the linen cloth and ran away naked.

This is an image not susceptible to language. Silently, the identityless young man slips out of his linen cloth. They can't catch him. Where does he go, naked? We imagine him, running silently—but where? We have seen him to the side in early paintings. He is Mystery. Is he an angel? Lazarus? The embodied erotic other? He is entirely without context. He has nothing to do with context. At a point of almost unbearable tension, when Jesus has shown himself most truly vulnerable in human terms: the distraction of the running body. Unseizable. Without history or future. Faceless. Unknowable: the blank screen, the object of desire.

X
The Men He Wanted

"He then went up to the hill country and called the men he wanted."

When I listened to the names they meant nothing to me; it was a signal for me to think my own thoughts. Now I understand that included in Jesus' group were a tax collector and a zealot—that is to say, an employee of the hated Roman Empire and a member of the party politically committed to overthrowing it. "And Judas Iscariot, the man who betrayed him." There was a place made even for the betrayer, only he unplaced himself.

This is perhaps the most important model that the Gospel offers us: the model of inclusiveness—of nonexclusiveness. The church that later specialized in excommunication didn't learn it from Jesus' example of choosing a group of followers. The modern world, with its explosion of information, gives us more information, perhaps more than we can use, about people's differentness from ourselves. We have to know that most of the world is unlike us, whoever we are. The crucial need, then, for the accommodation of difference. Can this be done without the genius leader, followed to the point of death? The history of the twentieth century has taught us the dangers of that kind of enterprise. What we have never had is the glimpse of a genius leader committed to embracing differences. It is not possible to imagine any longer: we have to posit a different kind of human being, to whom differentness meant something we can no longer recognize.

XI
The Empty Tomb

After the black shock of the Passion, the lightness of Easter. Lighter in tone—a different palette, but also insubstantial, incorporeal after the relentless physicality of Good Friday. But Mark, the harshest, the sparest of the Gospel writers, gives us an unhopeful Easter. Many scholars believe that the manuscript actually ended with a failure of nerve. The women, seeing the angel at the empty tomb, are terrified. The angel tells them to bring the message of Christ's resurrection to the disciples, but they don't. It is believed that the original manuscript ended with this verse: "Then they went out and ran away from the tomb, beside themselves with terror. They said nothing to anybody but they were afraid."

How extraordinary, to end a heroic narrative with the words "they were afraid." Frank Kermode points out that Mark's ending really should read, "They were scared, you see"—an abnormality more striking even than ending a book in English with the word "yes," as Joyce did *Ulysses*.

To a modern, of course, the inconclusiveness, the pessimism, are satisfying, and more in keeping with the dour Mark, who found the disciples wanting, blind and uncourageous at every turn. The Gospel as we have it ends with Jesus' exhortation of the apostles to evangelize; it moves to His Ascension and ends, with an unsatisfactorily dense, abstracted condensation, "Afterwards Jesus himself sent out by them from east to west the sacred and imperishable message of eternal salvation."

What would the history of the church have been had the one of the Gospels ended, not with the promise of victory, but with the proof of defeat?

THE GOSPEL
ACCORDING TO
SAINT LUKE

—

Annie Dillard

It is a fault of infinity to be too small to find. It is a fault of eternity to be crowded out by time. Before our eyes we see an unbroken sheath of colors. We live over a bulk of things. We walk amid a congeries of colored things which part before our steps to reveal more colored things. Above us hurtle more things, which fill the universe. There is no crack. Unbreakable seas lie flush on their beds. Under the Greenland icecap lies not so much as a bubble. Mountains and hills, lakes, deserts, forests, and plains fully occupy their continents. Where, then, is the gap through which eternity streams? In holes at the roots of forest cedars I find spiders and chips. I have rolled plenty of stones away, to no avail. Under the lily pads on the lake are flatworms and lake water. Materials wrap us seamlessly; time propels us ceaselessly. Muffled and bound we pitch forward from one filled hour to the next, from one filled landscape or house to the next. No rift between one note of the chorus and the next opens on infinity. No spear of eternity interposes itself between work and lunch.

And this is what we love: this human-scented skull, the sheen on the skin of a face, this exhilarating game, this crowded feast, these shifting mountains, the dense water and its piercing lights. It is our lives we love, our times, our generation, our pursuits. And are we called to forsake these vivid and palpable goods for an idea of which we experience not one trace? Am I to believe eternity outranks my child's finger?

The idea of infinity is that it is bigger, infinitely bigger, than our universe which floats, held, upon it, as a leaf might float on a shoreless sea. The idea of eternity is that it bears time in its side like a hole. You believe it. Surely it is an idea suited for minds deranged by solitude, people who run gibbering from caves, who rave on mountaintops, who forgot to sleep and starved.

Let us rest the material view and consider, just consider, that the weft of materials admits of a very few, faint, unlikely gaps. People are, after all, still disappearing, still roping robes on themselves, still braving the work of prayer, insisting they hear something, even fighting and still dying for it. The impulse to a spiritual view persists, and the evidence of that view's power among historical forces and among contemporary ideas persists, and the claim of reasoning men and women that they know God from experience persists.

"A young atheist cannot be too careful of his reading," C. S. Lewis observed with amusement. Any book on any subject—a book by a writer the young atheist least suspects of apostasy—may abruptly and unabashedly reveal its author's theist conviction. It may quote the Bible—that fetish of Grandma's—as if it possessed real authority. The young atheist reels—is he crazy, or is everyone else?

This Bible, this ubiquitous, persistent black chunk of a best-seller, is a chink—often the only chink—through which winds howl. It is a singularity, a black hole into which our rich and multiple world strays and vanishes. We crack open its pages at our peril. Many educated, urbane, and flourishing experts in every aspect of business, culture, and science have felt pulled by this anachronistic, semibarbaric mass of antique laws and fabulous tales from far away; they entered its queer, strait gates and were lost. Eyes open, heads high, in full possession of their critical minds, they obeyed the high, inaudible whistle, and let the gates close behind them.

Respectable parents who love their children leave this absolutely respectable book lying about, as a possible safeguard against, say, drugs; alas, it is the book that kidnaps the children, and hooks them.

But he . . . said unto Jesus, And who is my neighbor?

And Jesus answering said, A certain man went down from Jerusalem to Jericho, and fell among thieves. . . .

And he said unto him, Who is my neighbor?

But a certain Samaritan . . . came where he was. . . .

And went to him, and bound up his wounds . . . and brought him to an inn, and took care of him.

And he said unto him, Which now, thinkest thou, was neighbor unto him that fell among the thieves?

And he said unto him, Who IS my neighbor?

And Jesus answering said, A certain man went down from Jerusalem to Jericho, and fell among thieves.

Who IS my neighbor?

Then said Jesus unto him, Go, and do thou likewise.

This and similar fragments of biblical language played in my mind like a record on which the needle has stuck, moved at the root of my tongue, and sounded deep in my ears without surcease. Who IS my neighbor?

Every July for four years, my sister and I trotted off to Presbyterian church camp. It was cheap, wholesome, and nearby. There we were happy, loose with other children under pines. If our parents had known how pious and low-church this camp was, they would have yanked us. We memorized Bible chapters, sang rollicking hymns around the clock, held nightly devotions with extemporaneous prayers, and filed out of the woods to chapel twice on Sunday dressed in white shorts. The faith-filled theology there was only half a step out of a tent; you could still smell the sawdust.

I had a head for religious ideas. They were the first ideas I ever encountered. They made other ideas seem mean.

For what shall it profit a man, if he shall gain the whole world and lose his own soul? And lose his own soul? Know ye that the Lord he is God: it is he that hath made us, and not we ourselves; we are his people, and the sheep of his pasture. Arise, take up thy bed, and walk.

Who shall ascend into the hill of the Lord? or who shall stand in his holy place? He that hath clean hands, and a pure heart; who hath not lifted up his soul unto vanity, nor sworn deceitfully.

The earth is the Lord's, and the fulness thereof; the world, and they that dwell therein. The heavens declare the glory of God; and the firmament sheweth his handiwork. Verily I say unto you, that one of you shall betray me.

Every summer we memorized these things at camp. Every Sunday, at home in Pittsburgh, we heard these things in Sunday school. Every Thursday we studied these things, and memorized them, too (strictly as literature, they said), at our private school. I had miles of Bible in memory: some perforce, but most by hap, like the words to songs. There was no corner of my brain where you could not find, among the files of clothing labels and heaps of rocks and minerals, among the swarms of protozoans and shelves of novels, whole tapes and snarls and reels of Bible. I wrote poems in deliberate imitation of its sounds, those repeated feminine endings followed by thumps, or those long hard beats followed by softness. Selah.

The Bible's was an unlikely, movie-set world alongside our world. Light-shot and translucent in the pallid Sunday-school watercolors on the walls, stormy and opaque in the dense and staggering texts they read us placidly, sweet-mouthed and earnest, week after week, this world interleaved our waking world like dream.

I saw Jesus in watercolor, framed, on the walls. We Sunday-school children sat in a circle and said dimly with Samuel, "Here am I." Jesus was thin as a veil of tinted water; he was awash. Bearded men lay indolent about him in pastel robes, and shepherd boys, and hooded women with clear, round faces. Lake Gennesaret, the Sea of Galilee—it was all watercolor; I could see the paper through it. The southern sun, the Asian sun, bleached the color from thick village walls, from people's limbs and eyes. These pastel illustrations were as exotic, and as peculiar to children's sentimental educations, as watercolor depictions of lions and giraffes.

We studied the Gospel of Luke. In that world, people had time on their hands. Simon Peter, James, and John dropped their nets and quit their two boats full of fresh fish: "And when they had brought their ships to land, they forsook all, and followed him." They had time to gather at the side of the lake and hear harsh words. They had time to stand for the Sermon on the Mount and the sermon on the plain. A multitude followed Jesus and the twelve into a desert place belonging to the city of Bethsaida. The day wore away while Jesus spoke to them of the Kingdom of God; then he had his disciples feed them—"about five thousand men"—on five loaves of bread and two fishes, which Jesus blessed and broke, looking up to heaven.

Luke's is the most reasoned, calm, plausible, and orderly Gospel. It does not claim divinity for Christ, but a glorious messiahship; Jesus is the holy teacher who shows the way; he leads Israel and all the world back to a prayerful acknowledgment of the fatherhood of the one God. The coming of Jesus, attended by signs from heaven, does not interrupt the sacred history of Israel; it fulfills it. But Luke's Gospel is calm and plausible only compared to the swirling bewilderments of Mark and the intergalactic leapings of John. All of the Gospels are unprecedented, unequaled, singular texts. Coming at Luke from our world, we stagger and balk. Luke is a piece torn from wildness. It is a blur of power, violent in its theological and narrative heat, abrupt and inexplicable. It shatters and jolts. Its grand-scale, vivid, and shifting tableaux call all in doubt.

In a hurried passage, Jesus walks by Levi the tax collector and says, "Follow me." That is all there is to that. He calms the storm on the lake from his skiff. He heals the centurion's servant at a distance from his house; he raises a widow's young son from his funeral bier. He drives demons into the Gadarene swine and over the cliff. He performs all with his marble calm, by his fiery power which seems to derive from his very otherness, his emptiness as a channel to God. He moves among men who, being fishermen, could not have been panicky, but who nevertheless seem so in contrast to him: "Master, master, we perish!" Jesus is tranquil in his dealings with maniacs, rich young men, synagogue leaders, Roman soldiers, weeping women, Pilate, Herod, and Satan himself in the desert. Resurrected (apparently as a matter of course), he is distant, enlarged, and calm, even subdued; he explicates Scripture, walks from town to town, and puts up with the marveling disciples. These things are in Luke, which of all the Gospels most stresses and vivifies Christ's common humanity.

Long before any rumor of resurrection, the narrative is wild. Jesus dines with a Pharisee. A woman—a sinner—from the town walks in; she has heard that Jesus is in that house for dinner. In she walks with no comment at all, just as later a man with dropsy appears before Jesus at another house where he is eating. The woman stands behind him in tears; the men apparently ignore her. Her tears, which must have been copious, wet Jesus' feet. She bends over and wipes the wetness away with her hair. She kisses his feet and anoints them with perfume from an alabaster flask.

After some time and conversation with the Pharisee, Jesus says, "Seest thou this woman? . . . Thou gavest me no kiss: but this woman since the time I came in hath not ceased to kiss my feet. . . . Her sins, which are many, are forgiven; for she loved much." To the woman he says, "Thy faith hath saved thee; go in peace." (This is in Luke alone.)

The light is raking; the action is relentless. Once in a crushing crowd, Jesus is trying to make his way to Jairus's twelve-year-old daughter, who is dying. In the crowd, a woman with an unstoppable issue of blood touches the border of his robe. Jesus says, "Who touched me?" Peter and the other disciples point out, with exasperated sarcasm, that "the multitude throng thee and press thee, and sayest thou, Who touched me?" Jesus persists, "Somebody hath touched me: for I perceive that virtue is gone out of me." The woman confesses, and declares she was healed immediately; Jesus blesses her; a message comes from Jairus's house that the daughter has already died—"Trouble not the Master."

"Fear not," says Jesus; he enters the child's chamber with her parents and Peter, James, and John; says, "Maid, arise." She arises straightway, and he commands her parents to give her meat. Then he calls the twelve together, gives them authority over devils and power to heal, and sends them out to teach and heal. When they come back he preaches to multitudes whom he feeds. He prays, teaches the disciples, heals, preaches to throngs, and holds forth in synagogues. And so on without surcease, event crowded on event. Even as he progresses to his own crucifixion, his saving work continues: in the garden where soldiers seize him, he heals with a touch the high priest's servant's ear, which a disciple impetuously lopped off; hanging on his cross, he blesses the penitent thief, promising him a place in paradise "this very day."

Historians of every school agree—with varying enthusiasm—that this certain Jewish man lived, wandered in Galilee and Judaea, and preached a radically spiritual doctrine of prayer, poverty, forgiveness, and mercy for all under the fathership of God; he attracted a following and was crucified by soldiers of the occupying Roman army. There is no reason to hate him, unless the idea of a God who knows, hears, and acts—which idea he proclaimed—is itself offensive.

In Luke, Jesus makes no claims to be the only Son of God. Luke is a monotheist: Jesus is the Son of Man, and the Messiah, but Jesus is not God's only-begotten Son, of one substance with the Father, who came down from heaven. Luke never suggests that Christ was begotten before all worlds, that he was very God of very God, that eternity interrupted time with his coming, or that faith in his divinity is the sole path to salvation. The substance of his teaching is his way; he taught God, not Christ. The people in Luke are a rogues' gallery of tax collectors, innkeepers, fallen women, shrewd bourgeois owners, thieves, Pharisees, and assorted unclean Gentiles. He saves them willy-nilly; they need not, and do not, utter creeds first.

Salvation in Luke, for the followers of Christ, consists in a life of prayer, repentance, and mercy; it is a life in the world with God. Faith in Christ's divinity has nothing to do with it. The cross as God's own sacrifice has nothing to do with it; the cross is Jesus' own sacrifice, freely and reluctantly chosen, and of supreme moment on that head. That Jesus was resurrected in flesh and blood means in Luke, I think, that he was indeed the Messiah whom God had promised to lead the people—now all people—by his teaching and example, back to prayerful and spiritual obedience to God their father and creator.

Still, his teachings are as surprising as his life. Their requirements are harsh. Do not ask your goods back from anyone who has taken them from you. Sell all that thou hast, and give it to the poor. Do not stop to perform a son's great duty, to bury a father. Divorce and remarriage is adultery. Forgive an enemy seven times in one day, without limit. Faith is not a gift but a plain duty. Take no thought for your life. Pray without ceasing. Unto everyone which hath shall be given; and from him that hath not, even that he hath shall be taken away.

The teachings that are not harsh are even more radical, and harder to swallow.

Consider the lilies how they grow: they toil not, they spin not; and yet I say unto you, that Solomon in all his glory was not arrayed like one of these.

If then God so clothe the grass, which is to day in the field, and to morrow is cast into the oven; how much more will he clothe you, O ye of little faith? . . .

Your Father knoweth that you have need of these things.

But rather seek ye the kingdom of God; and all these things shall be added unto you.

Fear not, little flock. . . .

Ask, and it shall be given you; seek, and ye shall find; knock, and it shall be opened unto you.

For every one that asketh receiveth; and he that seeketh findeth; and to him that knocketh it shall be opened.

"Fear not, little flock": this seems apt for those pious watercolor people so long ago, those blameless and endearing shepherds and fishermen, in colorful native garb, whose lives seem pure, because they are not our lives. They were rustics, silent and sunlit, outdoors, whom we sentimentalize and ignore. They are not in our world. They had some nascent sort of money, but not the kind to take seriously. They got their miracles, perhaps, but they died anyway, long ago, and so did their children. Salvation is obviously for them, and so is God, for they are, like the very young and the very old in our world, peripheral. Religion is for outcasts and victims; Jesus made that clear. Religion suits primitives. They have time to work up their touching faith in unverifiable promises, and they might as well, having bugger-all else.

Our lives are complex. There are many things we must consider before we go considering any lilies. There are many things we must fear. We are in charge; we are running things in a world we made; we are nobody's little flock.

––––––

In Luke, Christ's ministry enlarges in awfulness—from the sunny Galilean days of eating and drinking, preaching on lakesides, saying lovely things, choosing disciples, healing the sick, making the blind see, casting out demons, and raising the dead—enlarges in awfulness from this exuberant world, where all is possible and God displays his power and love, to the dark messianic journey which begins when Peter acknowledges him ("Who do you think I am?") as the Christ, and culminates in the eerie night-long waiting at the lip of the vortex as Pilate and Herod pass Jesus back and forth and he defends himself not.

Jesus creates his role and succumbs to it. He understands his destiny only gradually, through much prayer; he decides on it, foretells it, and sets his face to meet it. On the long journey to Jerusalem, which occupies many chapters of Luke, he understands more and more. The narrative builds a long sober sense of crushing demand on Jesus the man, and the long sober sense of his gradually strengthening himself to see it, to cause it, and to endure it. (The account of his ministry's closure parallels the account of its beginning three years previously; Jesus very gradually, and through prayer, chooses, creates, and assumes his tremendous and transcendent role. He chooses his life, and he chooses his death.)

In that final long journey to Jerusalem, the austerity of Jesus deepens; his mystery and separateness magnify. The party is over. Pressure rises from crowds, pressure rises from the Jewish authorities.

His utterances become vatic and Greekish. Behold, we go up to Jerusalem, he tells his disciples. If anyone wishes to follow me, let him deny himself, take up his cross day after day, and so follow me. For the Son of Man is coming into his glory. What awaits him is uncertain, unspecified, even unto the cross and upon it; but in the speeches of his last days, in this village and that, his awareness becomes stonily clearer. Privately, often, and urgently, he addresses his disciples in dire terms: When they call you before the magistrates, do not trouble yourself about what you are to say. I have a baptism to undergo. The days will come when ye shall desire to see one of the days of the Son of Man, and ye shall not see it. "And they understood none of these things."

On the way to Jerusalem he addresses the Pharisees, who bring him a message from Herod ("that fox"): "I must walk to day, and to morrow, and the day following: for it cannot be that a prophet perish out of Jerusalem." He adds an apostrophe: "O Jerusalem, Jerusalem, which killest the prophets, and stonest them that are sent unto thee; how often would I have gathered thy children together, as a hen doth gather her brood under her wings, and ye would not!"

And he does walk, that day, and the next day, and the day following, soberly, wittingly, and freely, going up to Jerusalem for the Passover in which he will not be passed over. There is little mingling with crowds, and only four healings, two of them provokingly on the Sabbath. His words are often harsh and angry. "Thou fool," he has God saying to a rich man. "Ye hypocrites," he calls his disciples. In one of his stories an outraged master says, "Depart from me, all ye workers of iniquity." I am come to send fire on the earth. But those mine enemies . . . bring hither, and slay them before me.

He enters the city on a "colt" and is at once discovered driving the money changers out of the Temple. "Whosoever shall fall upon that stone shall be broken; but on whomsoever it shall fall, it will grind him to powder." As for the temple in which they stand, "there shall not be left one stone upon another. . . . These be the days of vengeance."

The crowds around Jesus are so great in Jerusalem that the Roman authorities must take him at night, as he quits the garden. There he has prayed in an agony, "Father, if thou be willing, remove this cup from me: nevertheless not my will, but thine, be done." Then he has prayed *more* earnestly, and his sweat fell down to the ground. Betrayed to the soldiers, he shuttles back and forth between Pilate and Herod all night; the cock crows; Peter denies him; and in the morning Pilate takes him—him supremely silent, magnificent, and vulnerable—before the chief priests and Jewish rulers, and before an unspecified crowd. They cry, "Release unto us Barabbas." And their voices and those of the chief priests prevail. As Roman soldiers lead Jesus away, "there followed him a great company of people." Where were they a minute ago, that they could not outshout the claque for Barabbas?

In Luke alone, after Jesus on the cross commends his spirit to the hands of God and dies, a Roman soldier is moved to say, "Certainly this was a righteous man." Luke alone recounts the incident on the road to Emmaus. Two disciples walking to Emmaus are talking about Jesus' crucifixion, which has occurred three days previously, when a stranger joins them and asks what they are talking about; the disciples, surprised, explain. The stranger interprets messianic prophecies in Scripture for them, beginning with Moses, which seems to surprise them not at all. In the village, they invite the stranger in. When at table he takes the loaf, gives thanks, and breaks it, then their eyes are opened, they recognize him, and he vanishes.

Amazed, they walk that night all the way back to Jerusalem—another seven miles—and tell the others. And while they are speaking, Jesus appears yet again. They are "terrified," but Jesus says, "Why are ye troubled? and why do thoughts arise in your hearts?" He shows them his wounded hands and feet, and they are full of joy and wondering, and very far from recognizing that, among other things, ordinary hospitality is called for—so Jesus has to ask, "Have ye here any meat?" (They give him broiled fish and a piece of honeycomb.) Then the resurrected Jesus explains scriptural prophecies concerning the Messiah's death and his resurrection on the third day; charges them to preach to all nations; leads them out as far as Bethany (two miles east); blesses them; and is carried up to heaven.

When I was a child, the adult members of Pittsburgh society adverted to the Bible unreasonably often. What arcana! Why did they spread this scandalous document before our eyes? If they had read it, I thought, they would have hid it. They did not recognize the lively danger that we would, through repeated exposure, catch a dose of its virulent opposition to their world. Instead they bade us study great chunks of it, and think about those chunks, and commit them to memory, and ignore them. By dipping us children in the Bible so often, they hoped, I think, to give our lives a serious tint, and to provide us with quaintly magnificent snatches of prayer to produce as charms while, say, being mugged for our cash or jewels.

In Sunday school at the Shadyside Presbyterian Church, the handsome father of rascal Jack from dancing school, himself a vice-president of Jones & Laughlin Steel, whose wife was famous at the country club for her tan, held a birch pointer in his long fingers and shyly tapped the hanging paper map—shyly because he could see we were not listening. Who would listen to this? Why on earth were we here? There in blue and yellow and green were Galilee, Samaria itself, and Judaea, he said (and I pretended to pay attention as a courtesy), the Sea of Galilee, the River Jordan, and the Dead Sea. I saw on the hanging map the coasts of Judaea by the far side of Jordan, on whose unimaginable shores the pastel Christ had maybe uttered such cruel, stiff, thrilling words: "Sell all that thou hast. . . ."

The Gospel of Luke ends immediately and abruptly after the Ascension outside Bethany, on that Easter Sunday when the disciples had walked so much and kept receiving visitations from the risen Christ. The skies have scarcely closed around Christ's heels when the story concludes on the disciples: "And [they] were continually in the temple, praising and blessing God. Amen."

What a pity, that so hard on the heels of Christ come the Christians. There is no breather. The disciples turn into the early Christians between one rushed verse and another. What a dismaying pity, that here come the Christians already, flawed to the core, full of wild ideas and hurried self-importance. They are already blocking, with linked arms, the howling gap in the weft of things that their man's coming and going tore.

For who can believe in the Christians? They are, we know by hindsight, suddenly not at all peripheral. They set out immediately to take over the world, and they pretty much did it. They converted emperors, raised armies, lined their pockets with real money, and did evil things large and small, in century after century, including this one. They are smug and busy, just like us, and who could believe in them? They are not innocent, they are not shepherds and fishermen in rustic period costume, they are men and women just like us, in polyester. Who could believe salvation is for these rogues? That God is for these rogues? For they are just like us, and salvation's time is past.

Unless, of course—

Unless Christ's washing the disciples' feet, their dirty toes, means what it could, possibly, mean: that it is all right to be human. That God knows we are human, and full of evil, all of us, and we are his people anyway, and the sheep of his pasture.

Unless those colorful scamps and scalawags who populate Jesus' parables were just as evil as we are, and evil in the same lazy, cowardly, and scheming ways. Unless those pure disciples themselves and those watercolor women—who so disconcertingly turned into The Christians overnight—were complex and selfish humans also, who lived in the material world, and whose errors and evils were not pretty but ugly, and had real consequences. If they were just like us, then Christ's words to them are addressed to us, in full and merciful knowledge—and we are lost. There is no place to hide.

THE GOSPEL
ACCORDING TO
SAINT JOHN

—

THE STRANGEST STORY

Reynolds Price

The Gospel of John is the most mysterious book in the New Testament; and that larger book is as filled with mysteries of date, authorship and intent as any in history. But say for the moment that the oldest surviving tradition about John is correct—it was written by John bar Zebedee, the Beloved Disciple of Jesus; and it appeared in the city of Ephesus around A.D. 90. Though it makes no detectable pretense to the formal order and beauty of a work of art, think of its predecessors in Western narrative.

They include early Middle Eastern epics, from *Gilgamesh* through the Old Testament; all of Greek poetry and prose, with its cult of the great man, its tragic gaze and worship of eros, its bracing obscenity; then the prime Latin classics—shocks like the scurrilous lyrics of Catullus, the urbane sideline comment of Horace, the mockery of Juvenal, and Petronius' salacious *Satyricon*. That much at least lies behind John, and some of it might well have been known to his audience.

Given the traditional author and date for his book, and despite such flamboyant predecessors, a powerful case can still be made that this last Gospel—no more than a pamphlet and written in a Greek of no special distinction—is the most original and outrageous work, in any type of prose or verse, that had yet appeared in the West.

And if two thousand years of pious handling had not dimmed both John's story and its demand, his Gospel would still be seen as the burning outrage it continues to be, a work of madness or blinding light. Its homely but supremely daring verbal strategies, the human acts it portrays and the claim it advances—from the first paragraph—demand that we make a hard choice. If we give it the serious witness it wants, we must finally ask the question it thrusts so flagrantly toward us. Does it bring us a life-transforming truth, or is it one gifted lunatic's tale of another lunatic, wilder than he?

Again, who wrote it—when, where and why? Any discussion of such matters must simplify ruthlessly; but an increasing number of students now agree that the Gospel of John originated and was shaped to its present form in the vicinity of the city of Ephesus, then in Asia Minor, now in Turkey. The current wide-ranging tendency is to date it in the years between the death of Jesus, near A.D. 32, and the end of the first century, sixty-odd years later—no long wait, in narrative cultures. Any veteran of a society devoted to the spoken transfer of urgent memory—a culture like that of the American South till the 1970s or immigrant American Judaism or most Indian tribes—will know how easily vivid tales and speeches can pass intact through generations, even centuries.

My nieces, for instance, never knew their grandfather Price. He was born in 1900 and died in 1954, well before their births. Yet since infancy, they have heard my brother and me tell stories of our father's acts and traits. They can now repeat many of the stories precisely. And they have retained them apparently because the words give them an obvious but complex pleasure, a pleasure they are likely to pass to their children, who may well be born a century after my father. Admittedly, my nieces have heard no claims that Grandfather Price was the only Son of God; so the stories they know are clean of worship, though not of strong hope to win allegiance.

Raymond Brown, John's most judicious recent student, concludes that the Gospel appeared between A.D. 90 and 100. Whenever and by whomever it was written, edited and published, our first external evidence comes from Bishop Irenaeus, writing as a missionary from

Gaul in about 180, some eight or nine decades later than the Gospel's appearance. He tells us that as a boy in Asia Minor, he had listened avidly to the memories of old Polycarp, a pupil and friend of Jesus' own pupil, the Beloved Disciple John. Irenaeus adds that—after Mark, Matthew and Luke had published their Gospels—the Gospel of John was published in Ephesus by John, that same disciple who had leaned on Jesus' chest at the supper before his arrest. Irenaeus says also that John lived in Ephesus, down into the reign of the emperor Trajan (who came to power in 98 and died in 117).

Such testimony might seem unexceptionably credible to a student of memory and its modes of conversion to story; but New Testament scholars are often comically nervous at the prospect of simple solutions. And early in the twentieth century, a majority of scholars doubted Irenaeus. Even more scornfully, they dismissed the possibility that "a simple Galilean fisherman" could have written such a complex and elevated work. But in recent decades, with a broadening knowledge of unorthodox theology in first-century Palestine, more and more students are returning to a saner view—one that sees no human or literary problem in accepting the testimony of men who had met and heard pupils of John bar Zebedee, the Beloved of Jesus.

Again I hack a path through hundreds of theories; but my own studies convince me that no skeptic has shown sufficient cause to doubt the tradition, as relayed by Irenaeus. In the face of the Gospel's unrelenting display of accurate geographical and cultural knowledge and despite its pervasive atmosphere of eyewitness, quite independent of other Gospels, then the suggestion that a fisherman who studied with Jesus might not have been as competent a theologian as his modern doubters is amusingly small-minded.

Whatever the answers to the mysteries of John, they are all concealed in the space of a single lifetime, one that might easily have spanned the six or seven decades after Jesus' death and resurrection. And if we assume that John bar Zebedee was a man in his early twenties when he followed Jesus in about A.D. 30, then we may reasonably guess that at least the first edition of the Gospel is the product of the mind of a man in his eighties, or a little older. (In all the mountain ranges of commentary—the all but endless attempts to explain John's dislocations, his stops and jolting starts, his glaring clarities and sudden fogs—I have never met with an intelligent attempt to see it as an old man's book. Yet an arresting case can be made for its being the product of a large but aging mind, a mind at hurried final work on the scenes and words of its distant youth—now precise and lucid, now vague and elliptical, all its procedures screened through the thought of intervening years.)

The first indisputable fact is that, not long after the end of the first century, the Gospel was acknowledged throughout the scattered and threatened world of Christianity as one of the four unparalleled stories of the acts and the meaning of Jesus. None of the other first-century Gospels mentioned in Luke 1:1 has yet come to light. So John with all its bafflements has, from near the first, been seen as the unmatched pearl of the four. And it stands unchallenged still as the crown of firsthand witnesses to a life as outrageous, and as crucial in the history of the world, as any life known.

Yet again, the heart of that outrage is seldom noticed. And a poll of modern readers would likely show that John stands with Luke as the most beloved of Gospels, primarily because of its many consolations. A further poll might show that Christian readers at least prize John for two reasons—his steady picture of a Jesus who boldly announces his godhead yet knows our human weakness so well that he promises the love and hope that most hearts crave. Few readers versed in Anglo-Saxon culture fail to know some of the words by heart, and in the King James Version—"For God so loved the world, that he gave his only begotten Son, that whosoever believeth in him should not perish, but have everlasting life." . . . "Let not your heart be troubled: ye believe in God, believe also in me. In my Father's house are many mansions: if it were not so, I would have told you. I go to prepare a place for you . . . that where I am, there ye may be also."

But centuries of familiarity with such assurance—and with John's near-omission of an awful Judge who spreads his terror through the other Gospels—has muffled the rank outrage of John. Seen head-on, John demands that his readers choose—is he a truthful reporter, as he vows, or a fantast? Is he fraudulent or raving? And if we rule that John's report rings true, then all the questions must be judged once more in the matter of his hero. Is this man Jesus a whole-cloth fictional creation, a village lunatic, a deluded visionary, a skillful charlatan, the "only begotten Son of God"; or as he announces, is he somehow God himself? If Christian readers can make the effort to approach John fresh, in a new and relatively literal translation, they may begin to see what atheists and agnostics will sight at once—the hair-raising newness of one slender tract. Anyone coming to the book afresh will see it with ease.

Forget that you ever read a Gospel; forget you ever heard of Jesus. Read John watchfully and what do you see? For me, first and last, he offers two things. The things are a few human acts, which John calls "signs," and some speeches. The story concerns the final years of one man's life. The important speeches come from that man. Alone among Gospel writers, John claims that he himself witnessed the signs and heard the speeches. He claims to report a few of them—and those truly—and he adds in clarification, at 21:25, "There are many other things Jesus did which, if written one by one, I think the world itself couldn't hold the books."* Also near the end, and again in his own voice, John says that he makes his record for an urgent reason—to convince each reader "that Jesus is the Messiah, the Son of God, and that, believing, you get life in his name."

Compared with the world's other urgent stories, however—among them, the early books of the Hebrew Bible, the Koran and the founding texts of most Eastern religions—John delivers his strike in a few thousand words and ends. He can be read through in under an hour; and he stands, after Mark, as the second-shortest of the Gospels (the others of which, I repeat, he may well not have known). What is the story he can tell so quickly? Does he mean us to read it as "realistic," even by his time's different standards of veracity? If he writes symbolically, allegorically, anagogically, does he give us sufficient signals when he goes into a nonrepresentational gear, into rigged descriptions of acts that never happened or improvisations on the gestures and voice of a distantly remembered Jesus? Again, is John's passion to change human life a folly, a delusion or a sanely built plan?

———

* Hereafter all quotations from John are translated by me, as near to the Greek as I can manage. And since the Greek is unpunctuated, I have let the English reflect the fact, this side of obscurity.

With unprecedented daring, he packs the whole story into his first three paragraphs (1:1–18). A further shock lies in our eventual discovery that we knew the whole story from the first page but were unaware of our knowledge. "In the beginning the Word was. The Word was with God, and God was the Word." The Word, then, or the Idea, is one of God's infinite natures—a nature that was present before the creation of things and that caused all things. After a glance at another John, who will forerun the Messiah, John the evangelist races with a speed and aim as sure as the start of Genesis toward his first outrage. Though he would be refused by the world, "the Word became flesh and tented among us, and we saw his glory." In the early years of our era then, God's active power embodied itself in a visible man called Jesus.

Having calmly hung the assertion before us, John begins his human story. The Word has now been among us through the years of his childhood and has grown to manhood in ways undescribed. Now at a moment of historical time that ends in the known Palestinian governorship of Pontius Pilate, the Word in its tent of flesh—Jesus from the village of Nazareth in Galilee—comes south to the teacher called John (the evangelist never calls him the Baptist). This John is performing a ritual washing of sinners near Jerusalem. Though the evangelist omits the scene, Jesus apparently accepts this rite that he cannot need. At once John both recognizes Jesus as the Messiah and predicts his unsuspected nature, the shock and scandal he will bring to his people.

Jesus Messiah will not be the longed-for chieftain to lead his people in victory over Rome. He will be more nearly the Suffering Servant whom Isaiah foresaw—"He was despised and rejected by men . . . by his wounds we are healed." In another flare of insight at 1:29, this baptizer finds yet another name for the man Jesus who walks before him—"Look, the Lamb of God, who takes away the sin of the world." Lambs are common objects of affection. They are also slaughtered by the thousand, in sacrifice to God's just wrath in his Temple, a few miles west of the baptism site. But while the baptizer sees so far at the start, even he fails to glimpse the horror to come in the life of this lamb and the glory to follow.

Among those around the baptizer are five particular men. At least three of them are from Galilee—Andrew, his brother Simon (whom Jesus soon calls Peter or "Rock") and Nathanael. The fourth is Philip. Is the unnamed fifth that man whom John later calls "the pupil [or "disciple"] whom Jesus loved"? Since John bar Zebedee is always named by other Gospels as one of the first four pupils called by Jesus, the guess seems likely. All five men seem young, impressionable and game to roam; and they are so impressed by the baptizer's witness, by the undescribed magnetism of Jesus, by Jesus' assent to Nathanael's belief that here indeed is the Messiah, they promptly leave John and follow Jesus home.

In chapter 2, back in Galilee, he soon astounds the new disciples, his mother and numerous others with a first display of power, the first unearthly sign. He changes water to delicious wine at a wedding in Cana, a town near Nazareth. (Despite the symbolic meanings deduced by two millennia of commentators, it seems unlikely that John would describe such a homely kitchen-wonder unless he had been present and convinced of its actual and inexplicable occurrence.)

Then, with his pupils, his mother, and now his brothers, he visits the fishing town of Capernaum on the Lake of Galilee. The other Gospels tell us that, hereabouts, Jesus found and enlisted more disciples, to a final number of twelve. John will later mention others—Judas, Thomas Didymus and "the pupil whom Jesus loved"—but he passes over their calling in silence. And he omits the numerous early Galilean signs and wonders described by Mark and repeated in Matthew and Luke.

Next Jesus and the pupils go to Jerusalem for Passover, the solemn spring feast in memory of the night when God spared those with lamb's blood on their doors. It is the first of four such visits described by John (the other Gospels describe only one). And here at Jesus' first appearance on the main stage of his country, he at once scores his fame on the public air by committing a serious breach of the peace. With an impromptu whip, he drives the licensed livestock dealers and money changers from the Temple. Unaccountably, such a blasphemous outburst goes unpunished; and on the same visit he is free to perform other signs, unspecified.

Then he moves in bold opposition to the Jesus of Mark, who demands that his pupils keep silent about his nature. In chapter 3, this Jesus, now on the edge of fame, tells Nicodemus, a member of the Jewish ruling council who visits him by night, that he Jesus is the only son of God. He is sent, here and now, from the depths of God's love to save whoever believes in him. Here and constantly hereafter, Jesus affirms that eternal life is available to those who believe in him, and to them alone. (In the teeth of such a blasphemous claim, strangely Nicodemus makes no reply; but when Jesus is dead, John alone tells us that Nicodemus shares the burial costs.)

In the remaining three-fourths of the Gospel, Jesus will give more signs; he will suffer death and rise from the dead. By the end of John's third chapter, however, the story has set its pattern and made its sole demand, *Believe in this man or die forever.* But who is the man and what do we mean if we say we believe in him? How would that belief change our daily lives, our thoughts and acts? What would be the long-range outcome of such a vague faith? The balance of the story, and the speeches, tell us grandly and with no trace of doubt in the voice of the teller.

At this point in my own reading, I begin to notice John's strangest departure from the memories of Jesus recorded in other Gospels. John takes almost no notice of the man's ethical teaching. The parables, with their lessons on daily life and their guideposts to eternity; the eloquent moral teachings in Matthew and Luke, with their awful threats for failure and their sometimes tedious suspension of narrative thrust—John has no room for a syllable of these.

He surely remembers or knows of the teaching. In so many cases, he knows of places, times, customs, acts and speeches that ring entirely true but are absent from the other Gospels. Yet the fact is that John omits Jesus' teaching with the same ease as many other things we may eventually want from him—some account of Jesus' early life and education, say, a physical description of the man and much more.

The fact that we read John in the context of its three companion Gospels obscures the astonishing fact that, if John's were our only report, not even Christians could claim that Jesus was a moral teacher, a probing witness of human life who declared God's will that we love our neighbors as we love ourselves (and the converse, so often ignored by Christians—that we love ourselves as we do our neighbors). Admittedly John reports that as Jesus bids farewell to his disciples at the Last Supper, he says "This is my command, that you love one another as I have loved you. No one has greater love than this, to lay down his life for his friends." But though the command is taken by Christians to apply to all human beings, Jesus gives it to his pupils only, alone in a dark room fouled with the threat of his death. Did he mean it for the world?

From that flagrant first visit, Jesus leads the pupils into the Judaean countryside, where, with the authority of their master, they proceed to baptize. And we hear that the baptizer again acknowledges that Jesus is Messiah: "He must grow greater. I must shrink." Word also reaches Jesus of the beginning of hostility from the liberal political-religious party, the Pharisees; and he and the pupils return to Galilee. Hereafter John's story is revealingly strung on the twin poles of Western realistic narrative—country and city: Galilee and the capital, a three- or four-day walk apart. Among numerous differences, the country Jesus is far more human and humane than the coruscating mage he becomes in Jerusalem.

In chapter 4, on the return trip north when the disciples leave him briefly alone, Jesus meets a woman by a well near Shechem in Samaria. That a male Jew should associate freely with a hated Samaritan, much less a woman, is scandal enough. But in the midst of an initially lighthearted conversation, in which Jesus tells the woman that he knows she has had five husbands and is now living with yet another man, he launches an image that—if we credit John—comes from the core of Jesus' sense of mission and that states his literal offer to mankind. He tells this restless pariah that, in his person, he is somehow food for humanity. He is all forms of nourishment for hungry man, *Partake of me and live forever*. But how do I partake of you? No one in all John's gospel asks him.

Through the remainder of the story, Jesus will ramify the terms of his offer in increasingly daring ways. But here at the start in 4:14, he offers this likably feisty outcast "a spring of water welling up to eternal life." At first she scarcely hears him. What wins her sudden, unwarranted belief that he is the Messiah is his uncanny knowledge of her past. But when she calls her townsmen, and they prevail upon Jesus to stay for two days and explain himself further (an explanation we do not hear), they also accept his words; and with no further sign, these Samaritans, so long shunned by orthodox Jews, come to believe his one demand—"We know that this man is really the savior of the world."

Back in Galilee, on another visit to Cana, Jesus gives his second sign on home ground. He heals the son of an official in the employ of the king, one of the lesser Herods. The man has come from Capernaum to beg his help, "Sir, come down before my boy dies." For the first time, this sovereign Jesus in 4:48 sounds a complaint often heard in other Gospels, "With no signs and wonders, could you ever believe?" But then in words alone, at twenty miles' distance and with no mention of pity or compassion, he heals the boy by telling the father, "Go home. Your son's alive." The man believes, heads downhill to Capernaum and is met by servants who tell him that the boy was cured at one o'clock the previous afternoon, at the moment Jesus spoke.

The other Gospels begin Jesus' career with pictures of his first long rush of compassionate healing. John has waited this late, a fourth of the way through his story. And he has all but concealed the common thread of such reports by the other evangelists—their insistence that belief in the power of Jesus is somehow a condition of his love, his unearthly power. In John we almost never hear the other Gospels' awesome pre-echo of King Lear's threat to an apparently ungrateful daughter, "Nothing will come of nothing." This Jesus *can* act and *will*, whether we trust him or not. And in John, he is far more sparing of his power.

As if to prove his mastery of fate, in chapter 5 he returns to Jerusalem for an unspecified feast; and there on the Sabbath, he goes to the curative pool called Bethesda (whose detailed description by John has only lately been confirmed by archaeologists). Here he cures a man lame for thirty-eight years. Because Jesus heals in the Sabbath rest, and because the sign is followed by his defense of such work, many readers see the sign chiefly as a demonstration that Jesus is Lord of the Sabbath. They are partly right, but surely at the expense of sufficient notice that, in this his first face-to-face cure, Jesus heals instantly and without request. Nor does John say, like the other evangelists, that Jesus heals from a loving heart. This man can and *does*, when and where he wills, for his own inscrutable reasons. His power exists for himself, as *evidence*. If he heals us, the motive may only be reflexive—the light of our wonder revealing his face, not warming our hearts.

When those powers in the city, whom John calls simply "the Jews," learn of this breach of the Sabbath, they challenge his right. Jesus tells them in 5:17, "My father works now and I work." The flat assertion is his first public announcement in Jerusalem of quasi-divine authority, but it is barely a warning of the full claim yet to come. Understandably, we hear of a mounting hatred, "Then all the more the Jews hoped to kill him." Heedless, Jesus expands on the powers of his sonship in 5:25, "An hour is coming when all those in tombs will hear [the Son's] voice—the doers of good will come out to a resurrection of life; the evildoers to a resurrection of judgment." So in words that more than compound his deeds, Jesus casts his fatal die in the game that will kill him and work his triumph. John never says why the enemies fail to kill him on the spot. They have more than ample provocation, though they cannot know how much more they have yet to bear.

In chapter 6 we hear only that Jesus is back in Galilee by the lake, "doing signs on the sick" and drawing crowds. For the first time, we are told that, though Jesus and the pupils withdraw to a mountain for Passover, a crowd of five thousand gathers. Again at this point John avoids the chance to let his Jesus teach (so, oddly, do the other gospels—perhaps a memory of the real occasion: with so many round him, teaching was impractical). In 6:5, Jesus' one expressed concern is for their nourishment, "Where can we buy bread so they may eat?" This far into our knowledge of Jesus, it strikes an odd note—how can this man lower his gaze and plan a mass picnic? Yet he does. On their human hunger, Jesus builds a new sign, another practical kitchen-wonder that works his deeper purpose. For only when he transforms a boy's lunch of bread and fish into an overabundance for the crowd are they convinced that Jesus is "really the prophet coming into the world," an understandably false identification.

Knowing that these men are about to seize him and make him king, in 6:15 Jesus slips off alone. This is the one moment in any Gospel when we are plainly told that numbers of men have begun to see Jesus as not only a spiritual but a political leader (and a far graver threat to both the Jerusalem authorities and the Roman overlords than a mere rural thaumaturge with blasphemous delusions).

Evening comes and the pupils leave also, by boat for Capernaum. When they have gone three or four miles (the lake there is seven miles wide), night overtakes them; and a storm blows up. Suddenly they see Jesus walking toward them on the water and are rightly afraid. But as he nears them in 6:20, he says—for the first time in their hearing—a phrase that means literally "I am. No fear." And they welcome him in, with no sign of hearing a wonder.

In Mark's account of the same incident (6:48–50), Jesus says nearly the same, employing the identical pronoun and verb—*egō eimi*. Most English versions translate the clause as "It is I." As far as it goes, they are right. But *egō eimi*—"I am"—is also the name that God reveals to Moses in Exodus 3:14, "Tell the Israelites 'I Am has sent me to you.'" John has used the clause one previous time, in 4:26. When the Samaritan woman says that she knows the Messiah is coming, Jesus says "I am [he], speaking to you." There also, translations blur the possibility that, even so early, John's Jesus confides to an outcast, not merely his exclusive Sonship but his very identity with God the Father. If the storm-tossed disciples hear even a trace of the claim, it seems a wonder that they stay in the boat and do not leap to swim for dry ground.

Next day, missing Jesus, the crowd finds him at Capernaum. And at last he speaks to them in the first of the startling "I am [something]" metaphors. He told the Samaritan woman that he had living water to give, but he did not say that he was the water. Now in 6:35 he is ripe for a bolder leap, "I am the bread of life. . . . Who comes to me will never hunger." This man speaks not in the short-story parables of other Gospels but in self-made metaphors that show John's Jesus as a lyric visionary poet, not a prose storyteller. We cannot know how such self-regarding claims sounded to John's first readers, much less to Jesus' own audiences (assuming that the speech is a memory of John's, not a creation or extrapolation). But we can share their amazement, if not revulsion, when in a matter of moments Jesus thrusts his metaphor of nourishment a further horrific step in 6:53, "Amen amen I tell you, unless you eat the flesh of the Son of God and drink his blood, you have no life in you."

To say that one can give "living water" may be no more than the poetic claim of a spiritual teacher. To call oneself the "bread of life" approaches the megalomanic. But for one man to thrust through the Hebrew dread of eating blood and of human sacrifice and apparently to demand the actual consumption of his physical body is a deed that cries for drastic response—exile, confinement for lunacy, immediate stoning. Or obedience.

For by now, a third of the way through his pamphlet, John has boldly shown us (who know Mark, which John may not) that even the raw-boned first evangelist evades how entirely Jesus *means* what he says. The man is no fraud, no country magician with God on the brain. He has shown his power over inhuman nature (water to wine, the storm on the lake). He has healed the sick no doctor could heal. Crowds of the desperate follow his tracks. He wields language as though he were making it, word by word, from the empty air (by implication of course, he has—he made the air and he willed human language). And though again the Jews balk at immediate stoning, John admits in 6:66 that "after this, many of his pupils went back and walked with him no more." By the end of this taut chapter, John's revelation of his man's meaning is all but complete. The greater part of Jesus' remaining acts and words will only cut old impressions deeper and compound the outrage.

With the start of chapter 7, we learn that because Jesus is not ready to die in Jerusalem, he continues to "walk" in Galilee, presumably giving more signs. John specifies no one act from the time; but if we are to take his chronology literally, Jesus "walks" at home from the early-spring Passover to the autumn Feast of Tabernacles. Some of the signs are almost surely described in other Gospels; but John has only three more deeds to tell in his shapely story—Jesus' penultimate affront to "the Jews" (raising a putrid corpse from the tomb), then his own acceptance of judicial death and his resurrection.

Though his disbelieving brothers urge him to visit Jerusalem for the feast (are they eager for his death?)—and though Tabernacles had by now become the feast most associated with the messianic hope of the Jewish people—Jesus refuses to go. But once the brothers leave, he slips into the city secretly. Knowing of the deadly hostility against him, and having told his brothers "My time is not yet come," why does he take the risk? John makes no guess but we may suspect that his all-knowing Jesus foreknows that his doom is some way off.

Only midway through the observance, at 7:14, does he show himself and begin to teach in the Temple. As always, John withholds the precepts given. Instead he launches an extended report of one more wrestle between this man and his enemies. And another of John's boldest strokes is visible in all the stages of this match as it spreads through the center of his story, chapters 7–10. John permits us to see—and in scalding light, as no other evangelist sees or dares—that the enemies of Jesus are, by their standard of reason, more than justified in their fierce revulsion, if not their brute vengeance. If nothing else exculpates them for a modern reader—even the injunction *Eat me, flesh and blood*—then let him suspend any bias he may feel for or against John and his Jesus and look again at the end of chapter 8, verses 48–59. I am aware of no more audacious scene in literature nor of one more carefully built toward its climax, a blinding, unforeseeable bloom of vast megatonnage.

    The Jews said to him "Aren't we right to say you're Samaritan and have a demon?"

    Jesus said "I have no demon but I honor my Father. You dishonor me. I am not seeking glory for me. There is One who seeks though and is judging. Amen amen if a man keeps my word he shall never in any way see death."

    The Jews said to him "Now we know you have a demon. Abraham died and the prophets and you say 'If a man keeps my word he shall never in any way taste death.' Are you greater than Abraham our father who died? Or the prophets who died? Who are you?"

    Jesus said "If I glorify myself my glory would be nothing. My Father glorifies me. You say 'He is our God.' You do not know Him. I know Him. If I said I did not know Him I'd be lying like you. I know Him and I keep His word. Abraham your father was glad to see my day. He saw it and laughed."

    So the Jews said to him "You're not even fifty and you've seen Abraham?"

    Jesus said to them "Amen amen I tell you before Abraham was I am."

    They took up rocks to throw at him but he hid himself and left the Temple.

We heard Jesus in private, in the storm, say "I am" to the pupils, with the chance of a simpler meaning. Unmistakably though, his assertions of "I am [something]" have continued—*bread, drink, the light of the world*. But here in the Temple, God's literal home, and in the hearing of his mortal foes, at last he stamps out any remaining doubt of his meaning with an outright definition. He does not say "I am food" or "I am light for your path," not "I am the only Son of God" but "I am God himself, here and now; I have always been, will always be." In Leviticus 24:16, Moses commanded that "anyone who blasphemes the name of Yahweh must be put to death. The whole assembly must stone him." And only by hiding himself at this moment, does Jesus—a man who claims to be God Yahweh—escape a justified lynch mob, with an ample stock of stones at their feet: shards from the Temple construction around them, the Temple that only forty years hence will be again a hill of rubble, destroyed by Rome.

Any reader who by now has begun to feel that John is the master artificer among evangelists—that, working with similar but highly individual memories, he cuts and splices with a freer and more imaginative hand—must face, at the end of 8, the odd fact that John does not sustain this vast surge of force and climb to the next and tallest of his towering waves of theophany. Maybe, however, his art has not failed him. May he not be hewing to his irresistible memory of the visit? In any case, from his first great climax, he swoops to earth and describes a further Sabbath cure in Jerusalem. In 9:6 through the medium of clay which he makes from spit, Jesus heals a man born blind. Though the sign precipitates a touching response from the man and comic confusion among the Pharisees, it does little more in the ongoing story than deflate the pressure of chapter 8 in a new but familiar round with the Pharisees, who by now are predictable straight-men.

Then with no description of Jesus' actions and whereabouts from early October till mid-December, John hurries in chapter 10 to the next Jerusalem visit, at the feast of Hanukkah. The Jews approach him with a question that at first seems to predate his recent claim to divinity, "How long will you hold our souls in suspense? If you are the Messiah, tell us plainly." But then we recall that nothing in our present understanding of the messianic hope suggests that the Jews expected a *divine* Messiah, only a strong wise man. This time Jesus, as he so often does in other gospels, sidesteps. He says in 10:25–26, 30 that his acts declare his identity and mission, "The acts I do in the name of my Father, these witness to me but you do not believe. . . . I and the Father are one."

Here an alert reader may begin to reflect that the Jews have an advantage denied to us. They can watch Jesus' acts in progress; yet they are still doubtful, having already told us that they believe in demons and black magic. What of us, this late, who see the alleged acts only through ancient words? Do we accuse John of lying, delusion or insufficient evidence? Considering that the techniques of full-blooded narrative realism will not be developed till the nineteenth century, what more could John give us than this film of words? Whatever we, as vicarious witnesses, may wish to do at this crux of the story, Jesus' live audience seize their familiar stones. But again he escapes and withdraws a few miles across the Jordan to John's old baptismal site. There he is visited by many, and many believe.

We are now in the exact midst of John's campaign to win or hold us, chapter 11 of twenty-one. Only two more signs remain to unfold. After the vertiginous heights of 8, where else can he take us? In the relative calm of Jesus' Transjordanian retreat, he learns of the sickness of his friend Lazarus, the brother of Martha and Mary of Bethany, a village near Jerusalem. Till now John has told us nothing of this family, but here he specifies that Jesus loved them (the only ones beyond the circle of pupils for whom John claims such an honor). Despite his love, Jesus refuses to hurry. He lingers a further two days. And then against the fearful advice of his pupils, he goes up to Bethany to find that Lazarus is already dead and has been in the tomb four days.

Meeting Jesus in the road, Martha rebukes his delay; but with words as prized by Christians as any in the New Testament, in 11:23, 25–26 he makes her the promise that anyone bereaved of a loved one wants, "Your brother will rise again. . . . I am the resurrection and the life. Whoever believes in me, though he dies, shall live." Still, at a second rebuke, from Mary, at the sight of Mary's tears and those of "the Jews" around her, Jesus "groans in his soul" and also weeps—the nearest approach to a human passion shown by this man who is also God (in the only other entirely human moment, John told us in 4:6 that Jesus was tired from a journey). He asks that the door-stone be taken off the tomb. Martha, the forthright sister, says "Lord, by now he stinks." But the stone is removed. Jesus looks up and—for the stated purpose of informing his audience—he thanks God for hearing his prayer, a peculiarly unlikable moment (as if our *liking* had any weight now). Then he shouts "Lazarus, come out."

Any reader with a willing imagination can watch the great moment; anyone who saw the filmed *Last Temptation of Christ*, with its brilliantly imagined raising of Lazarus, knows the visual and emotional force, the terror and joy, that lurk in those words. In the two other raisings, in Mark 5 and Luke 7, both of virtual children—Jairus's daughter and the son of the widow of Nain—we see no detail of the corpses' reaction to the rousing word and touch. But in John 11, we have the hard facts—this stinking body was once a live man with two quite different sisters, a man of sufficient wealth to own a tomb cut into live rock. And without an actual touch by Jesus, in prompt response to words alone, at 11:44 the Greek says literally, "Came out the one having died, having been bound his feet and hands with bandages and his face bound round with a napkin. Jesus says to them 'Free him and let him go.' "

However much more we want from the story—Lazarus's first words, the response of his sisters and the mourners (what do you do with a friend and brother who was four days dead?)—John ruthlessly turns our eyes elsewhere. And the rest of the chapter gives us only the reaction of those men who gather in the Sanhedrin, the ruling council presided over by Caiaphas the high priest.

These powers-that-be explicitly grant the fact of the miracle—it is odd that none of the Gospels, even Mark, the least artful, takes the chance to point out that the mortal enemies of Jesus never question his inhuman power or attempt to expose its fraudulence. But for the first time now, in 11:48–50, they privately sound a calculating note, far grimmer than the old impulsive anger, "If we leave him like this, everyone will believe in him and the Romans will come and take from us both our place and the nation." Caiaphas deepens the tone by sounding a blindly ironic note, "It is better that one man die for the people than that all the nation die." And serious plans begin for a human sacrifice.

Somehow Jesus learns of the plan (is his source the nameless disciple who in 18:16 is said to know the high priest?). Again he retreats with the pupils, this time to Ephraim in the desert. Apparently he stays there till, in chapter 12, six days before the spring Passover he comes back to Bethany—less than a mile from Jerusalem—for a supper at the home of Lazarus and his sisters. John says nothing of Jesus' purpose in the dangerous visit. But when sister Mary unexpectedly bathes Jesus' feet with an exorbitant amount of expensive perfume, and Judas protests the waste, in 12:7 Jesus foreshadows his purpose, "Let her be. She has kept it for my burial day." He knows that his fateful hour has come and that Mary's open heart has unknowingly prophesied his end. Six nights from now, he will lie torn, dead and cold.

The remainder of the book, nearly half its length, will unroll John's version of that last week—the man who is God agrees to die, as the high priest has dimly foreseen, and to "be glorified," whatever that may mean. The external lines of the story are scored as deeply in Western minds as any other, in high and low art; and I will not follow it as closely as before. What seems more useful is a chart of John's differences from other Gospels—differences of act, focus and meaning.

First and basic to the entire account is his claim that Jesus both enacted and confirmed his divinity in Galilee a few years ago. Here in Jerusalem in sight of the Temple for more than a year, in acts and metaphors, he has bruited the claim at center stage. And within the Temple courts and in a suburb yards away, in the months from the winter solstice till now, Jesus has thrown down his wildest "I am" gauntlet and publicly raised the rotting corpse of a man of evident wealth and standing.

So in 12:14, when he courts messianic identity and makes his assback re-entry to the city, John (in contrast to the welcoming crowd) sees him, not as the teacher-Messiah-king of the other gospels, but as something utterly new on earth, a chance once-given and not to be repeated.

In other Gospels, the four days that lie between this hollow triumph and Jesus' final supper with the pupils are packed with incident and speeches. But John vaults through them in thirty-seven verses of chapter 12. Jesus makes repetitive and oddly unremarkable statements of his mission. The thermonuclear flare of 8 is never revived, not before his death; and he works no further wonder in the city. Likewise "the Jews" seek no more debate. Their course—and Jesus' intent—are firmly set for lethal collision, as we have known since Lazarus rose (and since chapter 1). John cannot lack memory or hearsay of the time. The thin story line then is likely explained by two things—the fact that he has already established "the Jews' " grounds for violence, and John's own rush toward Jesus' farewell and "glory."

John's third large innovation in the Passion story appears in his memory of Jesus' last supper with the pupils on Thursday evening. Knowingly or not, John contradicts the chronology of the other Gospels. Mark, Matthew and Luke state that the supper is the Passover feast. John calmly states that the supper is "[the night] before the feast of Passover" and leaves us a quandary—is his memory accurate, and the other Gospels wrong, or has he jogged the calendar by a day to provide a synchrony he will soon reveal?

Then John alone gives us the moment after supper when Jesus strips, girds himself with a towel, pours water into a basin and washes the feet of each disciple, including presumably Judas. Each time the act begins before me, I pull back and think, "The withering or frozen I Am of John would not do this." And it is I Am's most human act since his early chat with the Samaritan woman, since spitting on dirt to heal the blind man or weeping at the thought of Lazarus dead.

Christian commentators propose dozens of implicit theological meanings for the foot washing. I've read many of them in the hope of understanding. But at last they seem foolish excess baggage for a moment so charged with the credible shock of human meeting. For as the scene moves to its end—at 13:6 when Jesus reaches Peter and Peter objects—John wins me with a last exchange, the unforeseeable depth of which even Mark, with his notes of Peter's memories, cannot match. "Peter said 'You'll never wash my feet, not in this eon.' Jesus said 'If I don't wash you, you have no share of me.' Peter said 'Lord, not only my feet but my hands and head too.' "

Then while the other Gospels report a few of Jesus' words at the supper—the establishment of a bread-and-wine memorial to himself, the news of his coming betrayal—John is alone in reporting long speeches from Jesus. In fact, a glance at one of those useful New Testaments with the words of Jesus printed in red will indicate that where Matthew is reddest near the start, and Mark and Luke red fairly evenly throughout, John's long red stretch is held for now, chapters 13 through 17.

It is this long arc of speech in so little time that gives John an air of weight and ponderosity equal to Matthew's and Luke's, where speech so often impedes story. In John the pupils ask a few questions and occasionally whisper among themselves, but the valedictory voice of Jesus fills the air. A great part of the favorite texts of Christians come from these chapters, yet few believers notice or mind that most of chapter 16 is a virtual repetition of 13:31–14:31. At least some of the more static repetitions may result from a later editor's anxiety to tack on to John's first edition yet another surviving report of Jesus' words. But for me—and for many non-Christian readers—the lengthy wait does not simply leave us impatient for the coming doom. It leaves us wondering what, if anything, is new and indispensable (to either John's purpose or our own stake while we read) in the slow and uncharacteristic farewell.

If we trust that John is reporting verbatim Jesus' actual leavetaking, then we face a document at least as fascinating as, say, the last words of Cleopatra or Francis of Assisi would be. If we cannot make that trusting leap, but do assume that John is attempting a faithful memory—a scrupulous *impression* of what Jesus said at the real event— we may conclude that first-century Middle Eastern eloquence was as circling and numbing as it is today. Then we can search for the new.

First, we see that the words are spoken to the disciples in a private gathering, to a small group and one that has been with Jesus almost from the start. To what extent are we to assume that whatever Jesus says is valid also for other and later believers? The question is seldom noticed—modern Christians gladly sweep past it—and since it goes unanswered by John, I will not risk a public guess, however strongly the words have braced the lives of millions of readers. For the remainder of the speech, the following points seem new, both to the pupils and to us as readers.

Jesus is going away to the Father. And he goes specifically to prepare a place where the pupils may follow him. Only then will he return to them. In his absence meanwhile, he will ask the Father to send a substitute, a spirit whom Jesus calls the Counselor. (At 16:8–9, his first clear reference to a punishment of sin, he adds that the

Counselor will convict the world for failing to believe in him.) He goes on in 13:34 and again in 15:12 to urge that, with the help of that Spirit, the pupils obey his second command (the first command is "Believe that I am"), "Love each other as I loved you." And in 15:13 for the first time in the Gospel, Jesus makes an ethical observation which he seems to claim as valid for all mankind (it is not a precept, notice), "No one has greater love than this, that he lay down his life for his friends." Newly tender at 15:15, he knows the pupils by calling them servants no longer but friends. He promises that the pupils will suffer for his sake but that, on his return, their joy will abound. Then they will know the answers to all questions, 16:25, "I have said these things in metaphors to you. The time is coming when I shall speak no longer in metaphors but will plainly explain the Father to you."

At last in 16:30 the pupils—who have hardly understood more than the tragicomic bunglers who are their counterparts in other Gospels—show a redeeming insight: "Now we know that you know everything and have no need that anyone should question you. By this we believe that you came from God." Here I always recall that, of the four evangelists, John is much the least harsh on the pupils. Can the fact be weighed with the many other pieces of evidence that he was one of the Twelve?

At the start of chapter 17, as if the disciples' final warmth has completed some long-delayed circuit of power, Jesus prays. Now that "those you gave me" have believed, "Father, glorify me beside you with the glory I had before the world was." With a further prayer for those who will come to believe through the pupils' teaching— but strangely with no request for a bread-and-wine memorial—Jesus rises and leads his friends downhill, out of the city and across a small stream to an olive grove, a familiar haunt. Except for the final sign he will give, his communication with the pupils is ended. From first till last, from the time with John the Baptist till now, John tells no more of Jesus' will than can be contained in one sentence, *Believe that I am and love one another.* And at no point has Jesus explained his reason for the death he has all but begged from the Jews and now strides to embrace.

It is generally assumed that John's sense of Jesus as all-knowing and divinely serene makes him omit from chapter 18 the next scene reported by the other Gospels, that appalling hour when the pupils sleep oblivious while Jesus prays that the crisis pass and he not die. In the oldest account of this nadir, Mark 14:32–42, the muffled horror of Jesus' dread is conveyed with a power matched only by John's account of the crest, "Before Abraham was, I am." And it may well be that John chose to suppress the moment as a private human lapse, undeserving of public scrutiny.

But given the gritty eyewitness nature of so many narrative details in John, another possibility suggests itself. If, as Mark reports, John bar Zebedee was one of the sleeping pupils, then the same man—the aged John the Evangelist—may have had no memory of the moment. (Though Mark's details have the ring of hard fact, and though the eloquence of his Jesus' words far surpasses anything written elsewhere by Mark, he never tells us who witnessed Jesus' solitude and conveyed its memory. Anyone who knows the topography of those few square yards at the base of the Mount of Olives may easily assume that one of the sleepers roused briefly and overheard Jesus' agonized prayer.) Certainly John's unique details of the ensuing arrest in the garden suggest eyewitness—the torches and lanterns of the posse, their stumbling panic when Jesus again says "I am," the name of the man whose ear Peter lops off in the fracas.

Each of the gospels has a varied account of the remaining events of that Thursday night and Friday morning. In chapters 18 and 19, John's unique details include the news that one of the pupils (John?) is known to the former high priest Annas and so gains admission for himself and Peter to the courtyard near where Jesus is first questioned. John gives us Jesus' unremarkable reply to Annas—he has always spoken the truth publicly, never in secret. There is nothing in the disappointingly undramatic scene to suggest imaginative heightening where it might well be expected.

And though John says that Annas sent Jesus on to the high priest Caiaphas for further questioning, he tells us nothing of that meeting, though the other Gospels call it a meeting of the Sanhedrin. Thus he misses the chance to reiterate the only explanation he offers for Jesus' death—the earlier ironic foresight by Caiaphas that "it is better that one man die for the people than that all the nation perish." Again, was John simply absent from the meeting and lacking in direct memory? (Compare Mark's charged account in 14:53–65. When

Caiaphas asks Jesus if he is the Messiah, Jesus replies *Egō eimi*—"I am." And Caiaphas tears his robe, the ritual response to high blasphemy.) By now it is early morning; and "the Jews" lead Jesus on to the residence of Pilate, the Roman governor.

All the Gospels insist on the blood hatred for Jesus felt by the Jewish priests and the Pharisees and by the Passover crowds who, five days ago, greeted him as king. Each evangelist implies that the hatred of Jesus' own people is finally the cause of his execution. Some readers find a hotter anti-Jewish hostility in John than elsewhere, but I see no such bias. Right or wrong, in 18:31 John is the one evangelist who says why "the Jews," having made their decision to execute Jesus for blasphemy, bring him to the Roman governor for confirmation—they do not have the judicial right of capital punishment (as opposed to their early near-lynchings). Though John joins other Gospels in mitigating the responsibility of Pilate, he does not give Matthew's account of Pilate's washing his hands of guilt. And nowhere does John echo the historically disastrous moment in Matthew 27:25 when the Jews are reported as crying "Let his blood be on us and our children."

From whatever distance John's Jesus endures his mental and physical trials, at no point does he yield an inch to his accusers. His final words to Pilate in 19:11 are, from Pilate's point of view, so absurd as to guarantee harmless lunacy.

> "You could have no power against me unless it were given to you from above. . . ."
> After this Pilate wanted to free him. But the Jews shouted "If you free this man you are not a friend of Caesar."
> So hearing these words Pilate brought Jesus out and [condemned him].

As John warned us then in 1:11, "his own did not accept him." And though their refusal gets slim sympathy from John, he is again the one evangelist who grants how understandable is the rage of Jesus' enemies for his elimination.

The account in chapter 19 of the crucifixion and burial is also strikingly idiosyncratic. One of the most important differences is John's implication, never directly stated, that Jesus is crucified at the hour when, a few hundred yards away in the Temple courts, priests are slaughtering Passover lambs—ritual substitutes to bear God's wrath and spare the people. John proceeds to omit some of the credible details of the other gospels (that Simon of Cyrene helps carry the cross, for instance); but he adds minor details that are now known to be historically plausible (that four Roman soldiers are in the execution party, that the soldiers come to break Jesus' legs and hasten death but, finding him apparently dead, pierce his chest with a lance as insurance). And there are two striking innovations.

The first is to be expected. None of the four Gospels pays special attention to the brutal agonies of mind and body implicit in crucifixion; they can assume that each of their contemporary readers has witnessed the common ghastly sight, one that appalled even so hardened a lawyer as Cicero. But Mark, Matthew and Luke provide incidents that dramatize the private pain of Jesus and the sympathy of nature itself—the mockery of witnesses, Jesus' words with the two thieves who hang beside him, lowering skies, an earthquake that opens tombs and raises "many bodies of the sleeping saints."

Though John's Jesus gives almost no signs of suffering, he does uniquely say that he is thirsty and then sucks a drink of sour wine from a sponge held toward him. But he spares us the desolate cry in Mark and Matthew, "My God, my God, why have you abandoned me?" And his last words are a richly ironic claim of relief, acceptance and triumph—"It is finished" [or "accomplished"]—his death is one of the least finished acts in human history.

From the point of view of narrative texture, the second important innovation is John's report in 19:26–27 of something not mentioned in other Gospels. Though John has not referred to Jesus' mother since the wedding in Cana, Jesus on the cross provides for her care, bequeathing her to the pupil "whom he loved." In contrast to other Gospels, which imply that no pupil was brave enough to stand by the cross, John affirms that the Beloved Disciple was not only present but "from that hour took her to his own." (Her actual name, given elsewhere as Mary, and the Beloved's name are never recorded in John. Of the other disciples mentioned, none other's name is suppressed except that of James, the brother of John bar Zebedee.)

Despite a century of captious debates on the identity of the Beloved and on the symbolic significance of "mother" and "woman," it seems inescapable for any student of Western narrative strategy that, whatever "Beloved" connotes, the pupil in question is John bar Zebedee. And the otherwise pointless interjection at 19:35 is nothing less than an underlining of the fact, "The one that saw it bore witness and his witness is true. He knows that he speaks true, that you may believe"—the first of two such statements of purpose in the gospel.

That intense air of recall, the one relief in such painful matter, is suspended for a quick account of the surprisingly lavish embalming and burial of the corpse in a new garden tomb near Golgotha. John reports that the burial is handled by two secret adherents of Jesus, the till-now-unmentioned Joseph of Arimathea and Nicodemus, whom we encountered on the first Passover trip to Jerusalem.

Like other Gospels, John tells us nothing of the thirty-odd hours of Friday night and Saturday when Jesus lies dead. Where are the pupils and what are they doing? After all, it is Jesus' story, not theirs. And with Sunday morning, and throughout the resurrection appearances, John comes to life most startlingly as a grainy and credible eyewitness. Again his version is independent and has the feel of authority. All the gospels admit a fact detrimental to their case in first-century Palestine—the empty tomb was discovered by women (women being thought unreliable witnesses). But where the other Gospels mention small groups of women, in 20:1–2 John tells us only that Mary Magdalene comes to the tomb early, while it is still dark; and finding the stone removed from the door, she runs to tell Peter and the Beloved.

The two men of course run toward the tomb, the Beloved outstripping Peter, stopping at the open door and bending to look inside. He sees the grave clothes lying there empty; but for unexplained reasons, he does not enter. Some readers think that John praises the Beloved (that is, himself) tacitly—the Beloved does not need to make a thorough inspection; he understands at once. When Peter arrives, with characteristic boldness, he steps in and sees not only the grave clothes but the headcloth, folded separately. If those details are provided for us by the Beloved, it is significant that he scrupulously preserves Peter's apparent greater courage.

Likewise in the four remaining scenes that John reports. The Beloved is absent for the tomb-side meeting between Jesus and Mary Magdalene (another example of John's emotional generosity and the only Gospel record of a major risen appearance to a woman). The Beloved also pays no special part in Jesus' first appearance to the disciples, minus Judas and Thomas, or in the next, when doubting Thomas is the center of attention. Even in the final muted but deeply resonant appearance by the Lake of Galilee, though the Beloved is the first of the pupils to recognize Jesus when he calls from shore, the Beloved receives no special notice in the scene that follows.

The resurrected Jesus who returns in visible form to his pupils and friends in Matthew, Luke and John has been studied more obsessively than any other figure in Western narrative; by comparison, Hamlet and Don Quixote are slighted. Paul's flat-footed account in 1 Corinthians 15:3–8 is our earliest record, written about twenty years after the events. Mark as well has no scenes that show the risen Jesus (the appearances mentioned in Mark 16:9–20 are a later addition to the original, which ends at 16:8). In Matthew, the risen Jesus meets his pupils only once, on a nameless mountain in Galilee. There is no report of physical contact nor any physical detail, only a visible presence and words. Luke in chapter 24 gives detailed accounts of two meetings, one between the risen Jesus and two followers on the road from Jerusalem to Emmaus and a second in which Jesus surprises the pupils at a meal, asks them for food, eats "part of a broiled fish," then leads them out to Bethany and departs to heaven.

Of John's four appearances, only one seems to coincide with another Gospel's—John 20:19–23 may harmonize with Luke 24:36–49. The early-morning appearance to Magdalene is unique, like the second Jerusalem appearance to the Eleven in 20:26–29—the occasion on which Thomas is given a chance to probe the actual hand-and-side wounds of the risen Jesus, to acknowledge this palpable being as his "Lord and God" and then, like the others, to receive the unthinkable power to forgive sin (a power unmentioned elsewhere).

What is most extraordinary—and for me, most compelling and convincing as story—is the complex event recorded in chapter 21. Students now widely acknowledge that the earliest edition of John ends at 20:30–31 with a retrospective definition of the Gospel's scope and purpose—"So Jesus did many other signs before the pupils which are not written in this scroll but these have been written so you may believe that Jesus is the Messiah the Son of God and that, believing, you may have life in his name." The whole of the ensuing 21 is an appendix then but one with such intimate connections of manner, tone and vocabulary to the original text as to seem unquestionably a piece of the same firsthand tradition, saved here by a later editor, if not by the evangelist himself in a later edition. I will look at it closely later.

It is a natural inference that 21 reports Jesus' final meeting with the pupils. We can at least know that John has told all he wanted to tell—*The man returned from the tomb and forgave us, feeding us one last time, near home*. So with two brisk but emphatic repetitions, the appendix ends; and the book ends again—the Beloved is the source of this story too, and Jesus did so much more among us that the world itself could not hold the books if all were described.

That seems a fair outline of the story. Yet it can be pressed further down, to a sentence—the force that conceived and bore all things, came here among us, proved his identity in visible acts, was killed by men no worse than we, rose from death and walked again with his early believers, vowing eternal life beside him to those who also come to believe that he is God and loves us as much as his story shows. None of the other active world religions says anything remotely similar or comparable. John's story, in fact, which became the orthodox Christian faith, is repugnant to Judaism, Islam, Buddhism and all the beliefs of India and Japan. There is no parallel in the theologies of John's contemporaries—the dead myths of Greece or Rome, with their demigods and deified bureaucrats. Again, John hands us a brand-new thing.

Then what do we think? Were we meant to read it at all? As he wrote, did the Beloved or whoever wrote on his behalf imagine an audience of almost utterly alien people, Christian or otherwise, two thousand years later? If he could have glimpsed our existence, in a century of profound doubt, would he repeat for us his hope to win our belief in the divine nature of Jesus? Would he think his Gospel still a useful, if not sufficient, brief in the case? Or was he chiefly thinking, there in his old age and near the end of his century, of the small community of his own already convinced pupils in Asia Minor? They were anyhow friends whom he would soon leave; and he may well have worked at their urging in the prospect of their no longer having his speaking memories and meditations, the unsurpassed power of his comprehending voice.

If he meant to write for such a private audience, then he was essentially providing them with a prompt book—this careful, though occasionally clumsy, set of a few sketchily rendered acts and a few thousand important words (from a horde of both) to coach the memories of pupils already learned in the lore and meaning of the Beloved Disciple's Jesus. But what if we could have asked him a further question—did he so much as guess that his brief document, as it left his hands, could be expected to win and hold the belief of generations who would lack a direct eyewitness teacher and perhaps have no other account than his own pamphlet with its stupendous claim and promise?

Whatever his hopes, surely no other ancient firsthand document continues to press its force on so many lives. The only recoverable fact is that we have it. With all its mysteries of authorship, editing and the nature of its editors (probably no more than two or three people are involved), it has stood in the midst—sometimes near the head—of our culture this long. How can an interested reader use it, here and now?

This late in the twentieth century, it seems more than unlikely that a sane non-Christian, first-time reader can spring to believe that Jesus of Nazareth, crucified in about A.D. 32, was an earthly condensation of the God who made everything, known and unknown. Without a powerful nudge from that same invisible God (further obscured by the disasters of our own history), how can a rational life yield to an old and preposterous pamphlet which asks no less than a seismic change of mind and heart? (The ignorant and mad yield daily to less.)

What would yielding mean? The question brings us again to the one broad command of John and his Jesus, *Believe that Jesus is the Messiah, the Son of God, and God incarnate*. Suppose that I assent, *I do believe*. What next? Despite the fact that, in 15:10, Jesus urges the disciples to keep his commands, it is important to recall that only one other command is reported by John, the last-minute injunction that the disciples "love one another." Nowhere does this Jesus commend the Mosaic Law, as he does in other Gospels. His miraculous signs are benign in effect—healings, feedings and two resurrections—but are far past all human hope of emulation. And the least attempt to copy Jesus' acts, his gestures and words, will promptly land us in blasphemy, if not jail or the mental ward.

So far as we can learn from John, then, individual assent to the divinity of Jesus is the one vital act of response that a reader must make—eternal life will follow, whatever that is (and in 14:2–3, it appears to be a continuing existence with Jesus in some extraterrestrial good place, though again Jesus himself makes the promise solely to the disciples, not to a subsequent world of believers).

Say that John is the one surviving Gospel. Given the disappearance of a great mass of early Christian writing, it might easily be. Say that we have no other believing *narrative* testimony to the man and his meaning. Would Christianity have survived the death of the last disciples and apostles? Would the memory of Jesus have lingered any more powerfully in the world's imagination than the memory of Socrates, Alexander, Joan of Arc or a made-up figure like King Lear?

Unless the Holy Spirit had inspired belief in many more hearts, the answer is surely no. Original and powerful as he is, John would not be enough. Neither would Matthew nor Luke, though their reports of the teachings would lodge Jesus firmly in the history of ethics. Paul and all the other writers of the New Testament would have gathered dust as eccentric exhibits in the history of mystery religions. Only Mark—with his blunt air of no-nonsense reportage, his bat-out-of-hell commitment to vivid action over slowed-down speech and his brick-wall collision at 16:8—might have gone the long way toward keeping Jesus strong among us: a young man coming to John for baptism, learning in that instant of God's will for him, choosing disciples, working compassionate miracles, incurring the wrath of officialdom, revealing his mystic status as Son in a nighttime mountaintop transfiguration, then choosing death as a substitute for man and apparently—*apparently*—rising from the tomb. It's at least a story worth hearing and weighing.

What of John, though, with his patent design on human lives (lives in his own time, if not ours) and his wild demand? It turns out, to his good, that three more Gospels also survive and that each provides a good deal that we miss in John—three more distinct angles on the presence, acts and words of Jesus. I have noted numerous ways in which John, with a tranquil mastery worthy of his teacher, stakes down the tent of his own story with the hard pegs of contemporary Palestinian detail, then floats it on the literal air of a voice unlike any other on human record.

But a glance back at 8:48–59 will strengthen the point—the man's rising voice, insane if not true, and the all but murderous counter-voices, mounting as unstoppably as the peroration of an organ fugue. In chapter 4, the delicate comedy of the well-side meeting in Samaria is another scene in which acts and words seem to mock the likelihood of invention (though no one is present but Jesus and the woman; will Jesus tell the pupils later?). And nothing reported from Jesus' earthly life is more convincing as *story* than the homely but ghoulish prelude to the raising of Lazarus. Our worst fear has happened; our best hope may follow—and suddenly does. Yet the scene that mostly defeats my doubts, that bears the homeliest signs of straight report-age, is the most uncanny of all.

Look back at the whole of chapter 21, the dawn appearance of Jesus by the lake to his fisher friends. Even a sanely conservative student like Raymond Brown suspects that the scene is an amalgam of two memories of the resurrection, one involving Peter and a miraculous haul of fish and another involving a meal and the commissioning of Peter as shepherd of the flock. To indicate the tortures that even the most sensible biblical commentators inflict upon themselves, I should add that Brown's suspicion rises mainly from the lack of any mention of a meal in other early references to a resurrection ap-pearance to Peter. I might point out that there is likewise no early mention of swimming or nudity; but that does not perturb Brown—nude swimming being, it would seem, more natural to nocturnal fisherman than breakfast.

As a reader who has known the story for forty-six years, who has read it dozens of times and translated it, I continue to respond to what I see as a patently seamless web of story—the large amount that is said so quickly, the huge amount that goes unsaid. An ex-periment in extrapolation, however risky, will sketch my point.

After the appearances of a risen Jesus in Jerusalem, seven of the disciples—for whatever reasons—have returned to their home and their old work (though we know their old work from other gospels, not John's). Peter is already their leader. He decides to fish at night, a propitious time on the Lake of Galilee; and six others agree to come with him. They work all night and catch nothing. Dawn commences and they see a strange man standing on shore. In their village world, a stranger is rare. He calls to them, "Boys, anything to eat?" (The Greek noun is the plural of *paidion*, a diminutive of *pais*, boy— thus an easy greeting.) When they shout back their failure, the man says to cast to the right. Impressed by his strangeness, they gamble on a throw; and at once they haul an enormous catch.

"Therefore," John says, "the disciple that Jesus loved said to Peter 'It's the Lord.' " Does the Beloved know Jesus first because of their special intimacy (as he may have trusted in the resurrection without close study) or because of the fish?—never in the Gospels do the disciples catch a single fish without help from Jesus. Yet so certain is the Beloved that he stays aboard to draw the heavy net to shore. The fiery Peter, overjoyed, tucks up his shirt for speed (under it, he is naked) and throws himself in, to swim toward Jesus. The five others also stay with the catch. Even a further appearance of the Lord does not force them to sacrifice their welfare, only a hundred yards from shore. John's focus continues on them through verses 8–9—their landing, their seeing a charcoal fire with fish and bread.

Despite his apparent readiness for breakfast, Jesus invites them to bring their own fish. And only here, at verse 11, does the focus return to Peter. "So Peter got up and hauled in the net of big fish— a hundred and fifty-three and with all the number still the net was not torn." So Peter gets up—from *where?* I may be crossing legitimate bounds, but here again I suspect the skipping movement of an old man's memory. Peter has dropped from John's gaze for the time of the rash independent swim; what John most remembers is what the Beloved was doing, conserving a haul. But now Peter returns to mind; he "gets up" from where he is panting on shore, or kneeling near Jesus, and resumes his earthly duty. He helps his friends draw in the fish that will feed their dependents (we know from Mark that Peter at least has a family).

Jesus calls them to eat. Still awed, they hang back, knowing but speechless—even the Beloved, who in any case almost never speaks in the Gospel. So Jesus "comes over, takes the bread and gives it to them. Also the fish." John tells us nothing about the meal. Did Jesus partake; were there any exchanges? As with Peter's swim, John again jerks forward to 21:15, "So when they had eaten. . . ." And the threefold questioning of Peter follows, rising in Jesus' laconic intensity, Peter's shamed answers, and Jesus' repeated "Feed my sheep." *I was the shepherd. Now I am leaving. Serve for me.*

From here to the end, John's eye is fixed on Peter and the Beloved; we hear nothing more of the other five pupils. And no words to them or to the Beloved are reported. If the Beloved is identical with John the Evangelist, then whatever his part in this last meeting, he effaces its memory with silence. The Beloved is mysteriously glanced at a final time. After Jesus' prediction of Peter's death by crucifixion in verse 18, Peter turns, sees the Beloved and says to Jesus "Lord, this man—what?" Jesus speaks his haunting peremptory last words, "If I want him to stay till I come, what's that to you? You follow me." And again with the confirmation in verse 24 that the same Beloved is the author of this book, John rests his case.

As ever, the risen Jesus makes no ethical demands and, after the meal, no practical request to anyone but Peter—no exhortation to spread the word of his glory worldwide. Given the godly Jesus of John, we might have expected signs with an extra degree of wonder after his rising, acts of the glorified Son of God. But his risen acts are all of a piece with his former life—if anything, more homely. He speaks with a woman, satisfies a doubter and assists a failed boatload of fishermen. As ever, again he enacts his name—*I am. Grasp that.*

Nothing in all this unprecedented book, nothing in any other Gospel, consistently comes so near to convincing me of John's reliable witness as this last scene. By "reliable," I mean its tenor of honest report—*I saw this happen; now I tell it to you.* There are hundreds of invented scenes in Western fiction and drama that win our momentary belief. To mention only two, look at Mistress Quickly's description of Falstaff's death in the second act of Shakespeare's *Henry V* or Anna Karenina's final moment before she flings herself under the train. But nothing that I have encountered elsewhere, in a lifetime's reading, surpasses the simple conviction, the pure-water flow of John 21.

As literate a scholar as C. S. Lewis has said much the same of John's whole story.

I have been reading poems, romances, vision literature, legends, myths all my life. I know what they are like. I know that none of them is like this. Of this text there are only two possible views. Either this is reportage—though it may no doubt contain errors—pretty close to the facts; nearly as close as Boswell. Or else, some unknown writer in the second century, without known predecessors or successors, suddenly anticipated the whole technique of modern, novelistic, realistic narrative. If it is untrue, it must be narrative of that kind. The reader who doesn't see this has simply not learned how to read.

And to Lewis's salutary desk thumping, I can add one unquestionable fact. The whole of chapter 21 can be converted into first-person narrative by a simple change of pronouns. Note the effect in a few examples:

Simon Peter said to us "I'm going fishing." We said "We're coming with you." So we went out and got in the boat but all night we caught nothing. . . . We others came on in the little boat towing the net of fish . . . and when we landed we saw a charcoal fire laid with fish laid on it and bread. . . . Jesus came over, took the bread and gave it to us. Also the fish. This was the third time Jesus showed himself to us after being raised from the dead.

Admittedly, such a recasting is not sufficient proof that a firsthand narrative memory lies behind John 21; but all fiction writers and most careful readers know that third-person narratives—with their detachment, their stance well back from the action—can seldom be altered by a mere switch of pronouns. The phenomenon applies, though less directly, to all John's narratives of miracles—the water-to-wine, the healings, the raising of Lazarus—the trial and crucifixion, the race to the empty tomb and the other two resurrection accounts that involve the disciples. Hovering just at the edge of each event, or caught in its center, is the powerful sense of a pair of human eyes, so fixed in a lover's rapt attention as to vanish nearly from our reading minds and leave us face to face with the act and the moving bodies.

Is it all "true," then—a prosaic report, screened no doubt through long decades of thought and teaching but an earnest try at the visible, audible facts of a life lived in an actual place and time? Was John the Beloved a young man possessed of photographic memory, with an added genius for verbal recall? Even in a life of following Jesus on his restless swings through Palestine, was the young John making the kind of careful notes that recent findings of scrolls and papyri have proved were possible, not only in settled communities but among endangered fugitives? On the face of the book before us, neither chance is unlikely. If John's raw notes—his travel diary, say— were to be discovered tomorrow in a desert cave and we knew thereby that he appeared to document his life at the heels of Jesus, then what would be changed?

To look at only one change of many—at once the inadequacies of other Gospels would glare in a new light. None of them makes specific claims to be an eyewitness, and their subsequent repute precludes that possibility. But if our John is really the Beloved Disciple, then we would not only need to adjust the chronology of Mark, Matthew and Luke (Papias, after all, recorded in about A.D. 130 that Mark set down Peter's memories, "though not in order"). To the other evangelists' accounts of Jesus' ethical teaching, we would have to add John's theophanic shockers—the man's equations of himself to God, the elaborate metaphors of himself as food. And John's account of the resurrection would, more than ever, complicate our response to an unimaginable action that John insists we take as *event*, not symbol—hard, palpable, edible event that aims at every human heart, "whoever believes."

Beyond such practical adjustments in our view of the remainder of the New Testament, each reader would then make whatever private changes seemed apt, urgent or neither. At the least, those responses would range from an unquestioning conversion to belief in Jesus' claims all the way to a repelled dismissal of the mad outrage or massive fraud. As I have noted, a number of sober students have lately moved in the older direction, hearing and seeing the steady presence of John bar Zebedee, the Beloved, behind the full length of the charged few pages—a voice at least that means to stay, as Jesus granted, till he comes again. Once you have moved that far of course, your questions and choices have only begun.

Still, with every relevant manuscript discovery of the past century, we come closer to understanding that, once we concede the nearly intolerable premise of John's theology, nothing in his book is past the scope of a watchful, sensible man of his time—certainly nothing past the mental or narrative reach of a man who stood, to the end of his long life, as the single pupil in a group of twelve who could be called Beloved. With the availability of uncluttered new translations, attentive to the rapt storytelling of the Greek, we can meet John's knowledge face to face. Bizarre as it is in so many parts, he says in the clearest voice we have the sentence that mankind craves from stories—*The Maker of all things loves and wants me*. In no other book our culture owns can we see a clearer graph of that need, that tall enormous radiant arc—fragile creatures made by God's hand, hurled into space, then caught at last by a man in some ways like ourselves, though the ark of God.

THE ACTS OF
THE APOSTLES

—

THE CHURCH SET FREE

Larry Woiwode

The Acts of the Apostles is the most narrative book of the New Testament, and one of two books composed by Luke, the only Gentile included in the canon of Scripture. Acts appears between the Gospels and the Epistles—those letters directed to specific congregations within the early Christian church, as it came to be known (one of the many historical pieces of information we gather from Acts 11:26)—and Acts is, as it were, the Genesis of those epistles. Luke was a physician and a scholar, and this is the second of his books of instruction—"so you will understand the subject in which you're being catechized"—to an auditor known only as Theophilus, or "lover of God," a name that might be symbolic, though it as likely refers to an actual person, since it was common enough in Luke's time.

The title of the book is its best description. In succinct, dramatic episodes, or series of unfolding acts, Luke lays down not only the history of the beginnings of the Christian church, but every major theme and conflict that will come to affect that church through the centuries. Acts is the most wide-ranging and diverse book of the New Testament (and second in length perhaps only to Luke's Gospel;

I won't count verses); and in order to gather its main themes in an orderly way, I'm dividing it into three sections. This division is actually suggested by Christ in the first chapter, when he says to his apostles, "But you shall receive power when the Holy Spirit has come upon you; and you shall be my witnesses both in Jerusalem [division I], and in all Judea and Samaria [II], and even to the remotest part of the earth [III]." I should also mention that I quote from the New American Standard Bible, which is the most literally accurate version available in English—although on occasion, where the reader might hear and miss the King James, I refer to it. Actually the New King James, based on recent scholarship, often duplicates the NASB, which, besides its word-for-word translation—shunning the pitfalls of paraphrase—has a rough poetic growl akin to the Koine, or street-language Greek (in contrast to literary Attic Greek) of the original. When I quote from within the chapter the narrative has reached, I don't include a reference, but if I refer forward or backward in the book, or to another book of the Bible, I do.

I
The Holy Spirit and the Apostles' Ministry in Jerusalem

Luke opens Acts by reminding Theophilus of his "first account" (The Gospel According to Saint Luke) but hardly has the words out of his mouth before he mentions Jesus being "taken up, after He had by the Holy Spirit given orders to the apostles," and then he shifts into the forty-day period surrounding the postresurrection appearances of Christ, and by the third sentence of the book Jesus is speaking, and the apostles responding, in dramatic fashion. And then in the breathtaking backstep that is characteristic of Luke, he takes us to the moment of the actual ascension, a recapitulation of the close of his Gospel, when Jesus "was lifted up while they looked on, and a cloud received him out of their sight."

Luke's point in this, to employ the earlier quote, is that the Holy Spirit, who has been promised through the centuries by the prophets, and also by Christ, will soon be given to the apostles. They hurry from Mount Olivet back to Jerusalem, "a Sabbath day's journey"—less than a regular day's journey, since the apostles, devout Jews all, wouldn't travel after sunset—and in Jerusalem they gather, minus one, in an "upper room" with about a hundred others, including women.

Just as we begin to wonder about the twelfth apostle, Judas, Peter rises and says, "Brothers, the Scripture had to be fulfilled, which the Holy Spirit foretold by the mouth of David concerning Judas, who became a guide to those who arrested Jesus. For he was counted among us, and received his portion in this ministry." (Now this man acquired a field with the price of his wickedness; and falling headlong, he burst open in the middle and all his bowels gushed out. And it became known to all who were living in Jerusalem; so that in their own language that field was called Hakeldama, or Field of Blood.) "For it is written in the book of Psalms, *Let his homestead be made desolate, and let no man dwell in it,* and *His office let another man take.* It is therefore necessary that of the men who have accompanied us all the time that the Lord Jesus went in and out among us—beginning with the baptism of John until the day that He was taken up from us—one of these should become a witness with us of His resurrection."

Here, from Peter's mouth, is the authoritative definition of an apostle, and I have quoted at length to render a sense of Luke's taut, dovetailed technique. He was a Greek, but his packed concision often out-Greeks the Greeks of Greek drama, and is a forerunner of writing of the kind we won't witness in its full-blown application until our own stark, purged fiction of the twentieth century. It is necessary to note, too, that with the possible exception of Matthew's Gospel, Acts, more than any other book of the New Testament, pointedly interweaves the correspondences between the Law and the Prophets and the New Testament, and so is commonly turned to by the church for its teaching of the doctrine that has come to be known, in its broadest terms, as the Covenant—to be defined soon.

After Peter's speech, Joseph called Barsabbas and Matthias are put forward. The apostles pray, and then, perhaps surprisingly to some, draw lots ("The lot is cast into the lap but the whole disposing thereof is of the Lord"—Proverbs 16:33), and the lot falls to Matthias. That completes chapter 1. The loose threads of the gospels have been gathered, in order to prepare us, now that Christ has ascended, for the most significant single event of the New Testament church.

Unless you have read your Bible carefully from Genesis, the opening sentence of Luke's next chapter might seem inauspicious: "And when the day of Pentecost had come . . ." But the careful reader will note the introduction of a new word into the canon: Pentecost. John Calvin, the much-maligned reformer who is one of the humblest and most self-effacing of commentators, says in his *Commentaries* that "as the Law was given to the people of old fifty days after Passover (*Pascha*), written by the hand of God on tables of stone, so the Spirit, whose work is to write that Law in our hearts, the same number of days after the resurrection of Christ, who is the true Passover, fulfilled what had been prefigured in the giving of the Law." He says that "it was upon a feast-day, when a great multitude always gathered at Jerusalem, that the miracle was performed, that the fame of it might be the greater," and concludes: "It was called the fiftieth day, the reckoning being made from the feast of the firstfruits."

On the fiftieth day, or Pentecost, then, "suddenly there came from heaven a noise like a mighty, rushing wind, and it filled the whole house where they were sitting. And there appeared to them tongues as of fire distributing themselves, and they rested on each of them." This is one of the two times in Scripture when the Spirit is rendered visible. Before, as Jesus stepped from the Jordan where John had baptized him, "he saw the Spirit of God descending as a dove, and coming upon him," and now, in this electrifying instance, so that all the senses of those present are confirmed in the promise that Christ's followers will be baptized with water and then fire, the fiery minister becomes visible for the final time.

They *see* the Spirit, and then are filled with it, "and began to speak in tongues, as the Spirit was giving them utterance"—a matter of concern to the church still: the "gifts of the Spirit" and the concept of "a second baptism," to be discussed in conjunction with Cornelius and his household. The immediate effect, we see as a crowd gathers, is that although the speakers, who are Galilean, are at first suspected of being drunk, yet "Parthians and Medes and Elamites, and residents of Mesopotamia, Judea and Cappadocia, Pontus and Asia, Phrygia and Pamphylia, Egypt and the districts of Libya around Cyrene, and visitors from Rome, both Jews and proselytes, Cretans and Arabs— we hear them in our own tongues speaking of the mighty deeds of God." So presently the gift is the hearing in many languages of speech that makes sense.

Then Peter, "taking his stand with the eleven," in an alteration from the man who, less than two months before, denied even knowing Jesus, gives one of the great sermons of the New Testament. He quotes from the prophet Joel, who foretold this pouring out of God's Spirit, in order to explain the present phenomenon, and then with growing authority, quoting now from Psalms, he places Jesus before them as their "Lord and Christ"—the anointed one, the Messiah. There is the charged vivacity of conviction in every turn of his message, yet its thought is complex; he sets in proper balance the issue of the will of God in relationship to personal responsibility—"This Man, delivered up by the predetermined plan and foreknowledge of God, you nailed to a cross by the hands of godless men and put to death."

Peter adds that when David wrote in Psalms that the Lord would not permit "His Holy One to undergo decay" David wasn't speaking of himself: "I may confidently say to you regarding the patriarch David that he both died and was buried, and his tomb is with us to this day. And so, because he was a prophet, and knew that God had sworn to him with an oath to seat one of his descendants on the throne, he looked ahead and spoke of the resurrection of Christ." Peter mentions, in reference to that psalm, 16, that Christ "was neither abandoned to Hades nor underwent decay," giving some credence to those who have rewritten the Apostle's Creed by deleting "He descended into Hell." Peter's exegesis indeed suggests that the "harrowing of hell," which has received considerable treatment by poets and writers, wonderful as the idea might be, is most likely myth.

It would be remiss not to mention, too, that there are present-day Jewish spokesmen who interpret Peter's crucifixion statement, and other New Testament passages (particularly when read in the Christian church), as anti-Semitic. Peter was of course himself a Jew, as were the apostles, as was Jesus, and implicit in Peter's sermon is the proclamation of the fulfillment, in Christ, of the Law and Prophets, the basis of the Jewish faith. He himself now stands as a prophet, newly anointed by the Holy Spirit, and his words fall in the vein of those spoken by all the prophets since Moses to God's Israel (Deuteronomy 32:5; 2 Kings 17:20; 2 Chronicles 25:7; Ezekiel 3:7–9; Amos 9:7; etc.); it is out of that context (or text) and tradition that

Peter now speaks, as his hearers—"Jews living in Jerusalem, devout men, from every nation under heaven"—would recognize. And it is under this aegis, when they are "cut to the heart" and ask what they can do, that Peter tells them to repent and be baptized: "For the promise is to you and to your children"—a call to the Covenant.

Three thousand are baptized that day.

The Covenant can scarcely be spoken of separate from baptism, so to conclude this discussion I'll confine myself to the mode of baptism, and now speak of baptism's place in the Covenant. Whether we view the Covenant as a five-point structure with similarities to ancient suzerain codes, or as a movement from that which is waxing old to that which is new (Hebrews 8), in relation to the two Testaments, it begins in the Garden, with God's implied promise of eternal life to Adam and Eve, and thus Adam's and Eve's offspring, if they do tend the Garden (the first picture of Paradise) and do eat all but one fruit—that of the tree of the knowledge of good and evil. That one they do eat, breaking the Covenant, and the repercussions of their fall precipitate the Flood, when a further Covenant, sealed by the rainbow, is established with Noah and his descendants: the cycle of life will continue in its seasonal pattern, and humankind never again be removed from the earth by a flood.

The Covenant then attaches, as an "everlasting Covenant" with broadening promise, to Abram and his seed after him (see Genesis, chapters 15–17). Abraham, whose name changes when he is called into the Covenant (as Saul's name shall change in Acts), will be the "father of many nations" and will inherit, with his seed after him, "all the land of Canaan, for an everlasting possession" (a further picture of Paradise), and now a sign of this Covenant is instituted: "Every man child among you shall be circumcised." Not just Abraham's offspring, we learn (Genesis 17:13–14), but every child born within his house, whether his or a servant's, and every servant bought—all of his household (Genesis 17:23).

So those of the Covenant are not all of the same familial or racial or ethnic identity, and not all remain within it or faithful to it, though they all bear the sign and seal of it, circumcision, as the Covenant moves on, excluding Ishmael and Esau, to Isaac, then Jacob, the father of the twelve tribes of Israel—each of whom keeps genealogies so that the duties and inheritances of each tribe remain clear (such

as the priesthood limited to the descendants of Levi) and all of whom
continue to circumcise everyone in their households, whether they
travel into Egypt or Babylon, up to and including Christ, of the tribe
of Judah, on the eighth day, as prescribed (Genesis 17:12), so that
when Peter says in his sermon on Pentecost that "the promise is
to you and to your children," his hearers would understand: the
Covenant; my household.

Proselyte baptism began to be practiced by those within the Covenant, to symbolize the cleansing of an outsider before he was circumcised; and when Christ submitted to the baptism of his cousin,
John the Baptist, he initiated the sign and seal of the New Covenant:
baptism. But the familial or "household" nature of that Covenant
remained, as we see over and over in Acts: in the baptism of Cornelius
and his household, Lydia and her household, Crispus and his household, the Philippian jailer and his, and so forward to the present.
This pattern of the Covenant, made explicit in Acts, is why so many
otherwise diverse branches of the church baptize infants, who may
or may not remain faithful members of the Covenant—just as adults
who receive a "believer's baptism" may or may not.

As for the mode of baptism, any mode would seem acceptable,
since it is unlikely that there was enough available water in semiarid,
mountainous Jerusalem, with aqueducts supplying even the drinking
supply, for three thousand to be immersed by about fifty in one day.
Or sufficient water for immersion in a jail and several other locations
mentioned in Acts. I would permit myself or my children to be
baptized by sprinkling, pouring, cupping and patting, and even immersion, perhaps, unless the claim was made that immersion alone
was acceptable, since that tends to suggest the mode itself is effectual.

We learn that those baptized "were continually devoting themselves to the apostles' doctrine and fellowship," and also this: "Now
all who believed were together, and had things in common, and sold
their possessions and goods, and divided them among all, as anyone
had need"—a kind of communal living soon to be probed.

In the next chapter, Peter and John go to the Temple in Jerusalem,
confront a lame man ("Gold and silver have I none," Peter's speech
to him begins), and tell him to walk. The man leaps up, praising
God, and creates such a stir a crowd gathers. To this crowd Peter
preaches his second recorded sermon, similar in content to the first

but with the mention that God raised up Jesus, first of all, for the Jews, and the effect of this is two-pronged: the number of believers grows to five thousand, but the Sadducees, a sect that did not believe in the afterlife, and the priests and Temple guards appear, "greatly disturbed," and place Peter and John in jail overnight.

The next day the rulers and elders of Jerusalem gather, with Annas the high priest present, and ask Peter and John, "By what power, or what name, have you done this?"

"Then Peter, filled with the Holy Spirit, said to them, 'Rulers and elders of the people, if we are on trial today for a good deed to a helpless man . . . let it be known to all of you, and to all the people of Israel, that by the name of Jesus Christ the Nazarene, whom you crucified, whom God raised from the dead—by this name this man stands here before you in good health.' " The council, not quite sure what to do, with the healed man there, commands Peter and John not to speak or teach anymore in Jesus' name, and they answer, "Whether it is right in the sight of God to give heed to you rather than to God, you be the judge; for we cannot stop speaking what we have seen and heard."

The council threatens them further but finally lets them go.

Almost immediately there is this: "And the congregation of those who believed were of one heart and soul; and not one of them claimed that anything belonging to him was his own; but all things were common property to them. . . . For there was not a needy person among them, for all who were owners of land or houses would sell them and bring the proceeds and lay them at the apostles' feet, and they would be distributed to each, as any had need."

If anybody wondered whether the Holy Spirit was of the same Lord God Jehovah who had opened the earth under Korah, Dathan, and Abiram, after their rebellion against Moses, and had consumed 14,700 then with a plague (Numbers 16), or had sought out Achan when he concealed spoils from Jericho under his tent, and had had Achan and his family burned by fire (Joshua 7), then they were to witness the case of Ananias and Sapphira, husband and wife, who sell a piece of property for the common cause. Ananias comes and lays "a certain part" of it at the apostles' feet—and now watch the power that these feet assume:

"Ananias [Peter says], why has Satan filled your heart to lie to the Holy Spirit and keep back part of the price of the land for yourself. While it remained, was it not your own? After it was sold, was it not in your control? Why have you conceived this thing in your heart? You have lied not to men but to God." Then Ananias, hearing these words, fell down and breathed his last. So great fear fell upon all those who heard these things. And the young men arose, and wrapped him up, carried him out, and buried him. Now it was about three hours later when his wife came in, not knowing what had happened. And Peter answered her, "Tell me whether you sold the land for so much?" And she said "Yes, for so much." Then Peter said to her, "How is it that you have agreed together to test the Spirit of the Lord? Look, the feet of those who have buried your husband are at the door, and they will carry you out."

And they do.

Whether this is further proof for the teaching of a trinitarian God, or whether it is "just," in the sense that some argue against the "justice" of Jehovah, it does suggest the continuity of His character, and confirms that the apostles' power wasn't their own. The proceeds held back were for the common coffer, the establishment of which we might assume to be an element of "the apostles' doctrine." Or is it? In Leviticus (chapter 25, etc.) and Deuteronomy (15, etc.) and Proverbs (14 and 29, etc.) and elsewhere (Matthew 25:34ff), there are commands to provide for one's own and not to turn away the needy in their hour of need, and since the apostles' followers had grown from two hundred to over five thousand in a matter of days, perhaps this means was their only way of meeting, in all sincerity, the needs of their followers.

When history was attended to with a scrupulousness that our present age lacks, and there wasn't a craze of "end times" eschatology, as now, commentators took to heart Jesus' prophecy that the Temple and city would be razed within the lifetime of those he was speaking to (Mark 13:1–23; Luke 21:5–24), and they recognized in the history of Josephus, who recorded the terrible and entire destruction of Jerusalem in the year 70, the fulfillment of Jesus' prophecy. Such commentators view the apostles' consolidation of resources as a liquidation of what would have been otherwise lost (besides a preparation for the coming famine, 11:28–29), and so a form of stewardship applicable to the situation they were in, and not the perdurable model for the church. How tithe without property or income? How remain independent of the sometimes tyrannical Roman Empire, which then governed Israel, without funds to meet every contingency of the growing group?

Surely it's at least partly the failure of the contemporary church to provide for its own that has caused its members to turn to the government as benefactor. I am sensitive to the concern for foreign missions and missionaries, considering "the Great Commission" (Matthew 28:19–20; Mark 16:15) and the unfolding of Acts itself; but it seems inadvisable for a church to expend its monies in a foreign field as long as local members are in need. It is exactly this need that has allowed the social gospel and liberation theology to gain ascendence, as it were, in impoverished lands. Indeed, unless the local church is taking care of its own, a mandate made explicit by this portion of Acts, it seems presumptuous of it to suspect that its concerns lie far afield. Could it be that the daily, sometimes disorderly demands of needy members is too trying to deal with, and the call of foreign cultures too exotic to resist?

Certain portions of the church have also ignored the middle portion of that Great Commission, which states, after the command to make disciples of all nations (again, the Covenant), that these disciples must be taught "to observe all things whatsoever I have commanded you." "Whatsoever" would include all of the Law and Prophets and the New Testament, and represents quite a task; and I would say, again, that unless the local church is engaged in such teaching, so that members are being cared for and fed ("Feed my sheep," Jesus says to Peter) in this most important spiritual realm, then the local church should probably not presume upon its ability to carry its teaching into a foreign culture.

Finally, however we wish to interpret the action taken against Ananias and Sapphira, it is necessary to note that the property isn't quite communal, as Peter defines it to Ananias himself: "After it was sold, did it not remain under your control?" This isn't the socialism that certain theologies propose but a kind of corporate investment, and Peter is pinpointing the canny greed beneath Ananias and Sapphira's untruthfulness: though the property was under their control, they wanted a bit more on the side for themselves, just to be safe.

A contemporary commentator, Mark Rushdoony, suggests that the action taken against Ananias and Sapphira—by the Holy Spirit, note, who is God: "the same in substance, equal in power and glory," as the Westminster Catechism puts it—was a necessary form of discipline for the small but burgeoning (five thousand members added in a matter of days) new church. This is a further realm in which the present-day church has proved remiss: discipline. In many denominations, actual discipline, such as censure or excommunication, is so seldom practiced it can be termed nonexistent, to the church's detriment; discipline is the only means of maintaining a healthy church (1 Corinthians 5), yet nowadays delinquent pastors, even, escape censure, and the world outside cries, properly, "Hypocrites!"

Note the effect of the disciplining of Ananias and Sapphira from above, the real source of church discipline (Matthew 18:18): within two verses we learn that the number of believers keeps growing daily—so fast, in fact, that the high priest and the Sadducees of the established church, "filled with jealousy," clap the apostles in a public jail. An angel of the Lord releases them, instructing them to teach in the Temple, and when the supreme council, or Sanhedrin, sends for the apostles and they turn up not in prison but in the Temple, and are called in to explain this, their response is more to the point than before: "We must obey God rather than men."

The council wants to kill them. Gamaliel, a Pharisee (a proponent of the resurrection from the dead), intervenes, however, in the first tie in Acts to Saul—a nearly hidden thread in this book so closely woven it yields increasing details with each reading. Gamaliel sends the apostles out of earshot and cites the instances of men who have risen up, claiming to be somebody, yet have come to nothing: "And so in the present case, I say to you, stay away from these men and let them alone, for if this plan or action should be of men, it will be overthrown; but if it is of God, you will not be able to overthrow them; or else you may even be found fighting against God."

The apostles are flogged, and warned never again to teach in Jesus' name, yet the chapter ends: "And every day, in the temple and from house to house, they kept right on teaching and preaching Jesus as the Christ."

They have not moved beyond Jerusalem, and chapter 6 is notable for the choosing of "the Seven," an action that branches of the church interpret as the institution of the office of deacon, although "deacon" is never used to identify any of the seven, while "evangelist" is (21:8). Whatever the office, it rises out of a squabble. Hellenistic Jews complain that their widows ("The stranger, the fatherless, and the widow among you shall be fed"—Deuteronomy 14:29) are being neglected by native Judaeans in the serving of daily meals, so the apostles call up their disciples. "It is not desirable for us to neglect the word of God in order to serve tables," they say. They ask the disciples to select "seven men of good reputation, full of the Holy Spirit and wisdom," to take charge of this task. Psychology might suggest that since the problem concerns women, it would be wiser to appoint women; but the "statement found approval with the whole congregation."

The seven are brought forward, and the apostles pray, then lay hands on them, as the Levitical priesthood laid hands on sacrificial animals—an act that in the New Testament will come to picture the giving of the Spirit, or ordination to a specific office, or sacrificial giving over to God. Stephen, "full of faith and the Holy Spirit," is one of the seven, and we learn right away that he isn't merely going to wait tables; he performs "great wonders and miracles among the people." If the seven are deacons, then we see acts of nearly apostolic dimension from this deacon, and his ministry moves forward with such power that false witnesses from the freedmen's synagogue (composed of those slaves, circumcised into the Covenant, who have since been freed) are suborned to say he has been speaking blasphemies against Moses and God. So Stephen, too, is called before the Sanhedrin.

In the mixture of misunderstanding and untruths stated by the witnesses, this appears: "We have heard him say that this Nazarene, Jesus, will destroy this place"—Jerusalem, of course, which would be another reference to the prophecy of Christ that past commentators viewed as being fulfilled in the year 70.

The high priest asks if this is true, and Stephen gives the council a lengthy recapitulation of Jewish history, beginning with Abraham, then moving to Moses, some of whose acts he explicates in a new light, adding luster and dimension to Moses' calling as Israel's prophet; and then in a brush past David and Solomon, Stephen concludes in the language of Moses: "You stiffnecked and uncircumcised in hearts and ears, you are always resisting the Holy Spirit, just as your fathers did. Which of the prophets did your fathers not persecute? And they killed those who previously announced the coming of the Righteous One, whose betrayers and murderers you have become."

Then Stephen looks up and says, "Behold, I see the heavens opened up and the Son of Man standing at the right hand of God." The council drives him out of the city and starts stoning him, the Old Testament punishment for blasphemy; and as the stones strike home, Stephen calls out, in signification of the New Testament, in a variant of Christ's cry from the Cross, "Lord Jesus, receive my spirit!" And then, as he sinks to his knees, another variation: "Lord, do not hold this sin against them!"

Luke concludes, "And having said this"—and it can hardly be said less vindictively—"he fell asleep." The first martyr since the giving of the Holy Spirit. Only after this action subsides, it registers with us that the robes of the witnesses, who by Old Testament law were compelled to cast the first stones, have been laid at a young man's feet. This is Saul.

II
All Judaea and Samaria, and the Conversion of Saul

Before we return to Saul, I want to insert a note about Luke's use of feet in the book of Acts. The focus, first, renders incarnate the prophecy of Isaiah (52:7), "How lovely on the mountains are the feet of him who brings good news." It is a theme recapitulated by Saul himself, as Paul, in Romans 10:15, and Luke is pointing to both the power and the peace of those who convey the gospel by the most common mode of transportation then available, foot power, out into the widening world. Whether Luke purposely intended the connection to Isaiah, or is employing a literary symbol, pales beside the content of his focus; it is clear that Luke's considerable literary talents are being employed to the utmost as the Holy Spirit speaks what the Spirit wishes to communicate through him, because no human mind could channel and arrange the structure and patterns that at certain moments in Acts step off through whole tracts of the Old and New Testaments while applying to a situation the reader noted only this morning.

For me, a writer, aware of how much more complex each story or book grows with each sentence added, it was the power of these patterns and structure in Scripture, and their ability to interlock with one another through as many levels as I could hold in my mind, that convinced me that the Bible couldn't possibly be the creation of a man, or any number of men, and certainly not the product of separate men divided by centuries. It was of another world: supernatural. I was forced to admit, under no pressure but the pressure of Scripture itself, that it could be only what it claimed to be, the word of God. Do I believe that? I do. Do I believe in it? I do indeed, since it was its clarity and complexity itself that drew me in so deep I was left resting in belief.

What I have found surprising since is the vague interest in Scripture, when it is present, of contemporaries who say they are Christian, as if Christianity or Christ himself derives from any other source. Are linguists or historians, or even eminent theologians, as wise as Scripture? Some seem to assume so. No doubt I am "word" oriented, but I am also a fairly common representative modern, as much at home in New York City as in the country or the academy; and what I find even more surprising is that those who look to Scripture to formulate their beliefs, if not their theology, will exclude verses that disagree with their personal views or with contemporary cultural trends, rather than wrestling with the passages as further revelations of the source of their beliefs, as Jacob wrestled with the preincarnate Word, present in his arms in the form of an angel.

Scripture itself doesn't claim it will be easy; and once you dismiss portions of it, for whatever reason, you're saying that other auditors may dismiss what they wish, or that the whole of it is dismissible, which leaves you without Christ—or, anyway, without the Christ of Scripture, who himself kept quoting Genesis, Deuteronomy, and Isaiah.

Either it is the word of God or it isn't, I tend to think, and sense the red flags of fear of the Falwellian go up. My view is actually more Augustinian, in that I believe one must study the whole counsel of God, precept by precept, in order to begin to understand the heavenly city He has built—and is building here on earth, through the acts of the apostles, first, and then through the Holy Spirit that has set His church free. This Holy Spirit inspired and is present in every verse of Scripture (1 Timothy 3:16), and Scripture is the blueprint for the church in its ensuing actions. I am aware of those who wish to follow the "leading of the Spirit," but I don't believe we need to look to that leading to decide which suit jacket to wear, for instance, when the Spirit has already spoken, through the prophets and the apostles, directly to every essential any believer needs to possess to live a faithful life (1 Timothy 3:17); and so, à la Augustine, it seems more fruitful to me to study what stands rather than to attempt to draw on the airiness of leading. The pitfalls of this attitude were addressed years ago by T. S. Eliot, in a sentence that also seems to cover certain temptations in the neo-orthodoxy proposed by Barth, wherein if the Spirit doesn't illuminate the reading, say, of the sixth commandment, then one may apparently conveniently ignore it, or any other troublesome text of Scripture; in his essay "Thoughts After Lambeth," Eliot writes, "Certainly, any one who is wholly sincere and pure in heart may seek for guidance from the Holy Spirit; but who of us is always wholly sincere, especially where the most imperative of instincts may be strong enough to simulate to perfection the voice of the Holy Spirit?"

So to pass over whatever might seem, from a human point of view, unhappy or "culturally irrelevant"—a dispensationalism of convenience, to my mind—is nearly as blind a view as the one that will formulate an entire theology and world view on the basis of a favorite verse or two.

"And Saul was heartily in agreement with putting him to death," chapter 8 opens, referring to Stephen, precisely because of Stephen's teaching from Scripture; and in an application like a burst of light in its brilliance, the adversary, the one who would curtail or restrict that Word, now stands before us. Saul, who has studied "at Gamaliel's feet" (22:3), now joins the growing opposition against the apostles' followers in Jerusalem. "Beyond measure I persecuted the church of God, and wasted it," he declares in Galatians 1:13, "and I profited in Judaism above many of my equals in my own nation, being more exceedingly jealous for my ancestral traditions."

The church in Jerusalem is "scattered abroad," largely through Saul's zeal, it seems, and with the sometimes omniscient eye of Acts we now follow Philip, one of the seven ordained with Stephen, into Samaria, the next area of ministry mentioned by Christ. The Samaritans, not actually Gentiles, were Jews of mixed heritage who wouldn't worship in Jerusalem and rejected portions of the Old Testament, and so were abhorrent to orthodox Jews. This is why Christ's parable about the Good Samaritan arrived with such impact—that an outcast Samaritan, and not a priest or Levite, would aid that injured man!

In Samaria Philip performs a series of healings and begins to gather adherents, including Simon, a former sorcerer and magician. When Peter and John arrive, as they do, Simon sees them administer the Holy Spirit by the laying on of hands, and offers them money for this power. "May your silver perish with you," Peter says, always forthright, "because you thought you could obtain the gift of God with money!," reminding us of Peter's confrontation with Ananias and Sapphira, and perhaps also more recent history that brought about the Reformation, and thus Protestantism: Luther's objections to the sale of indulgences.

The apostles start back for Jerusalem, but an angel of the Lord directs Philip to take a desert road toward Gaza, and he sees an Ethiopian eunuch, the court treasurer of Candace, queen of Ethiopia, rolling along in a chariot, reading from Isaiah. Philip runs and catches up, and the eunuch, wonderfully imperturbable, asks him to explain a passage from Isaiah 53. "And Philip opened his mouth and beginning from this Scripture he preached Jesus to him." Again, we see Christ incarnate in Scripture, as propounded by Augustine's maxim: "The New is in the Old concealed; the Old in the New revealed."

The eunuch says, "Look! Water! What is to prevent me from being baptized?" Nothing, apparently, once the eunuch confesses that "Jesus Christ is the Son of God," because Philip baptizes him. Was there water of sufficient depth in the desert to immerse? One wonders. Then, however, in the strangest turn of this strange encounter, Philip is "snatched" by the Spirit to Azotes, some twenty miles off—literally "spirited away," in the idiom our language has adopted to accommodate the event.

Saul now receives letters from the high priest to the synagogues in Damascus, commissioning him to arrest any of "the Way" that he finds there; apparently some of the disciples have fled north. Saul travels with a troop toward Damascus in an account that becomes so novelistic I might as well present it that way. Saul and his cohort are nearly to Damascus when a flash of light envelops Saul and stuns him. He falls to the ground and hears, "Saul, Saul, why do you persecute me?"

"Who art Thou, Lord?" he asks, aware of who he's dealing with.

"I am Jesus whom you persecute; but rise, enter the city, and it shall be told you what you must do."

The troops with Saul haven't seen what he has, but have heard the voice, and as Saul rises there is a further discovery: he's been blinded. The men have to take him by the hands and lead him into Damascus. He lies in bed there for three days, blind, refusing to eat or drink.

And now another Ananias, a "disciple at Damascus," enters the action, or is entered; the Lord tells him in a vision to go to a "street which is called Straight" (compare Matthew 7:14) and ask for Saul, who is praying and, in a vision of his own, has seen Ananias arrive and lay on hands to restore his sight. But "Lord," Ananias says, "I have heard from many about this man, how much harm he did to your saints at Jerusalem."

"Go, for he is an instrument of mine, to bear my name before the Gentiles and kings and the sons of Israel; for I will show him how much he must suffer for my name's sake."

Ananias obeys, lays hands on Saul, and says, "Brother Saul, the Lord Jesus, who appeared to you on the road by which you were coming"—outside confirmation of the incident—"has sent me so that you may regain your sight, and be filled with the Holy Spirit."

Immediately, we learn, "there fell from [Saul's] eyes something like scales"—another phenomenon covered by an English idiom—"and he arose and was baptized." Note that nobody seems to leave the room, where there must have been water, and that "immediately he took food and was strengthened." Daily sustenance is never neglected by our physician-writer of Acts; nor is the larger implication of it as the "bread which came down from heaven," as Christ has literally done in this instance both to arrest and alter Saul.

Saul begins to "proclaim Jesus in the synagogues" with such eloquence his life is threatened, and the disciples have to lower him over the city wall in a basket—a subtle reminder of Moses' escape from Pharaoh. And now the seamless weaving of time in Acts becomes apparent; we learn in Galatians 1:17–18 that Saul at this point spends three years in Arabia, while Luke communicates a sense of events taking place one after the other, for now Saul travels to Jerusalem and attempts to associate with the disciples. They're afraid of him. They've surely heard of his persecuting zeal, and perhaps have received word of his conversion secondhand; then he was in Arabia. It is somewhat of a comfort, actually, for those who have been brought to Christ late in life, to see that even the apostles mistrusted a convert (and not just a convert but one called to be an apostle), since the church often holds itself at a distance from a convert with a past, as if to say, "How can this person expect to be a part of us?"

Barnabas, a Cypriot and perhaps somewhat of an outsider (singled out for his generous giving in 4:36–37), befriends Saul and becomes, in a sense, Saul's advocate to the apostles. Saul moves "freely in Jerusalem," opening up a further phase of missionary work to the city, until his preaching again imperils his life, at which point he is sent by the apostles to Tarsus, his hometown in Cilicia.

The omniscient eye of Acts now turns on Peter, at this moment in Lydda, where he is informed of the death, in nearby Joppa, of Dorcas, a woman "abounding with deeds of kindness and charity." Peter goes to the room where she is laid out, "and all the widows stood beside him weeping, and showing all the tunics and garments that Dorcas used to make while she was with them." Peter sends everyone from the room, as Christ did in similar situations, and for the first time since Christ's ascension, the momentous miracle we might have expected on Stephen's behalf is touchingly extended to this lowly but diligent seamstress: Peter raises her from the dead.

It soon becomes apparent why we're with Peter, for another pair of visions is about to merge, signifying a calling from death that will set the disciples off into the entire world. We move for a moment to Caesarea, to Cornelius, a Gentile Roman soldier, "a devout man, and one who feared God with all his household, and gave many alms to the Jewish people, and prayed to God continually." That afternoon an angel appears to Cornelius in a vision and tells him to send for Peter, who will tell him what he is to do. Cornelius dispatches a soldier and a pair of household servants, after explaining matters to them—in a more credulous world, clearly. The next morning, as they approach Joppa, Peter goes up to a rooftop to pray; he gets hungry, and as a meal is being prepared he falls into a trance and sees heaven open and something like a sheet, held at four corners, descend, and in it sees "all kinds of four-footed creatures, and crawling things of the earth and birds of the sky," and then a voice says, "Arise, Peter, kill and eat!"

Peter, obviously appalled at the implied contradiction of the dietary laws of Leviticus and Deuteronomy, says, "By no means, Lord; for I have never eaten anything unholy or unclean."

"What God has cleansed," he hears, "no longer consider unholy."

This happens three times. As Peter tries to puzzle it out, the men from Cornelius appear at the gate, asking for him. "Behold," the Spirit says, in a further conjunction, "three men seek you." Peter is told to join the trio "without misgivings; for I have sent them Myself." The men from Caesarea repeat Cornelius's story, and the next day Peter and six others (now three trios) travel back to Caesarea. Cornelius has gathered relatives and friends at his house, and at the sight of Peter he falls at his "feet" to worship him. Peter is at first corrective—"Stand up; I myself am only a man"—and again forthright: "You yourselves know how unlawful it is for a man who is a Jew to associate with a foreigner or to visit him; and yet God has shown me that I should not call any man unholy or unclean." The first part of Peter's forthright statement must refer to a Jewish tradition, since no specific prohibition of its sort appears in Scripture (or anywhere that I can find), and it is this propensity for tradition in Peter that will eventually get him into trouble (Galatians 2:11–14) with another apostle.

Cornelius relates his vision with slight variations ("a man stood before me in shining garments") for the third time we've heard it in this chapter of triads—a pattern whose purpose will take on more than mere literary trinitarianism when we see it applied to Saul's stories of his conversion. At the conclusion of Cornelius's report,

Peter opens his mouth and out comes the interpretation of his vision and the entire event: "Of a truth I now understand that God is no respecter of persons"—a moment of particular applicability to our author, Luke. Peter then preaches on this theme: "Of Him all the prophets bear witness, that through His name whoever believes in Him shall receive remission of sins," and as he says this, the Holy Spirit falls on the entire assembly, "and all the circumcised believers who had come with Peter were amazed. . . . For they were hearing them speaking with tongues and exalting God."

"Surely no one can refuse the water for these to be baptized who have received the Holy Spirit just as we did, can he?" Peter asks, then orders the assembly "to be baptized in the name of Jesus Christ."

The appearance of the Holy Spirit, and the visible effects of its appearance, as we observe them in the second chapter of Acts and here, has beleaguered the church during different eras. Traditionalists, as we might call them, maintain that the gift of tongues was for a given time and purpose: so that the gospel of Christ (still oral, not yet written) could be spread with alacrity in the early phases of the church, through this area of the Roman Empire with its polyglot of languages. A later view was that the phenomenon of tongues was merely a facility for languages or dialects given to foreign missionaries; Acts itself supplies support for this tradition, if we note the specific purpose in each instance of the use of tongues—they aren't generally employed for personal, pietistic ends, but seem either the significator of the Spirit received, as here, or, when the crowd gathers after Peter's sermon on Pentecost, a means of enabling immediate understanding.

In the present-day church, in both Roman Catholic and Protestant branches, there is a charismatic movement that has gained in force and adherents, for whatever reasons, since Vatican II. Charismatics hold that the "gifts," such as speaking in tongues, interpreting tongues, prophesying, and so forth, continue to this day, and in most cases recognize the appearance of these gifts as "baptism by the Holy Spirit" or a "second baptism." Paul speaks definitively on tongues in 1 Corinthians, chapters 12 and 14; although he tells the church at Corinth not to forbid speaking in tongues, he says that "though I speak more in tongues than any of you, I would rather speak five words of understanding than ten thousand in tongues" and mentions that "tongues" must take place in a proper, orderly way, and always be interpreted, if used in the church. In his notable chapter on love (1 Corinthians 13) he mentions that if he speaks in the tongues of angels but doesn't have love, he is nothing, and further says (13:8) that "tongues shall cease."

Unfortunately, ardent charismatics sometimes view believers who haven't experienced a second baptism as second-rate Christians, or ones who need to "graduate," and they might argue that since God is eternal and unchangeable He wouldn't cease something He Himself began. I would agree with this, but would add that He uses different means, at different times, of expressing His unchangeability, such as the Flood, which He Himself has said He won't use again. In Ephesians 4:5, we find that there is "one Lord, one faith, *one baptism*," which is illustrated over and over in Acts; baptism, as the sign and seal of the Covenant, performed by men, takes place before or after actual conversion, which is by the Spirit of God. So we see Peter order the household of Cornelius to be baptized after people there, already speaking in tongues, are obviously converted. Yet the Philippian jailer's whole household—children included, we assume— is baptized without any such outward manifestation of the Spirit, but on the basis of the jailer's confession of faith.

The work of the Holy Spirit in conversion is the "one baptism," and the many gifts that believers might manifest after this baptism (enumerated in 1 Corinthians 12, Galatians 5, etc.) don't necessarily have to be those that charismatics cherish; and nobody, or nobody that I've heard from, has yet claimed the Spirit's special gift to Philip: bodily transport (not just in one's mind) to another location.

In Jerusalem, where word of what has happened at Cornelius's has arrived, Peter recounts the events in "orderly sequence," and as we observe his adherence to details (including Cornelius's side of the vision), we understand the meaning of "faithful witness," and the necessity for such witness before Scripture was recorded. "When they heard this, they quieted down, and glorified God, saying, 'Well then, God has granted to the Gentiles also the repentance that leads to life.'" A wonderful moment of resigned reconciliation, perhaps in acknowledgment that the great prophecies of Isaiah (chapters 42,

49, 54, 55, 60, etc.) have been fulfilled, and the blasted bunch of mixed beasts in that sheet—the Gentiles of every nation on the earth—have been added by this action to God's Israel.

But there is still a division in the disciples, as some go off to preach to both Jews and Gentiles, and some "to Jews alone." Herod Agrippa I, as if to take advantage of this division, puts James, the brother of John, one of the "sons of thunder," to death. This meets with such general public approval that Herod has Peter arrested, intending to execute him after the feast of the Passover. Soldiers are placed on guard over Peter, and he has to sleep between two of them, bound with chains, "but prayer for him was being made fervently by the church to God." On the night that Herod plans to send for Peter, an angel again appears in the prison, strikes Peter to awaken him, and tells him to follow, and we receive a sense of how close the apostles must have been, day by day, to the otherworld, because Peter, though participating in the moment, "did not know that what was being done by the angel was real, but thought he was seeing a vision."

Out in the street, he comes to himself and makes it to the house of John Mark, where people are praying, most likely for him. A servant, Rhoda, hears him at the gate and runs to tell the others. They say, "You're out of your mind" and "It's his angel," as if they, too, are caught up in a night vision. Peter is at last let in, but goes "to another place"; and in the continuing nightmare, Herod executes the guards, and then, during a public address, when a crowd exclaims that Herod has the voice of a god and not a man, an angel of the Lord strikes *him* "because he did not give God the glory, and he was eaten by worms and died."

All of these angels. Considering their ubiquitousness, it might be helpful to examine one in particular: the Angel of the Lord. This is the angel who appears to Abraham at the moment he intends to sacrifice Isaac (Genesis 22), to Joshua after he crosses into Canaan (Joshua 5) and orders Joshua to remove his sandals, because he is on holy ground, as Moses was instructed to do in the presence of the burning bush; and in these and many other instances, as in the wrestling match with Jacob, this angel is considered to be God, or the preincarnate appearance of Christ. In many instances in Acts, then, and particularly when the angel is the "Angel of the Lord," I take it to be a postresurrection manifestation of Christ, who most dramatically appears to Paul on the Damascus road, and whose "spirit" appears at other times. Jesus is, in fact, in a very real sense, though a distinct person of the Trinity, the Holy Spirit—"the same in substance, equal in power and glory."

Why is it that we moderns, wrapped in our scientific veneer, believe in Carlos Castaneda's Don Juan and UFOs and reincarnated spirits who consort with movie actresses, but have trouble with angels?

III
All the World, and the Prosecution of Paul

The remainder of Acts, or more than half, is dedicated to the broader missionary work of the church, and the prosecution brought against Saul, soon to be Paul, as a result. He and Barnabas return to Antioch, to the church first called Christian, from Jerusalem, where they have been distributing aid to a city already affected by famine, and are "set apart" by order of the Spirit, and then the laying on of hands, for the expansion of the kingdom, now that the barrier between peoples has been broken down. There is no special missionary board originating in a higher church at Jerusalem: it is the local Antioch church that sends them out; there will be no visits to missionary societies when they return, and no tours to churches while on "furlough" with pleas for support. They are commissioned and sent out by a fledgling local church.

And now the great sea voyages of Acts begin. Paul and Barnabas sail from Seleucia to Cyprus, Barnabas's homeland, preaching the gospel in synagogues across that island, and it is here that Saul becomes Paul. The proconsul at Paphos asks to hear the word of God, and as Paul and Barnabas speak to him, a magician, Elymas, keeps contradicting them, until finally Paul, through the power of the Spirit, accuses him of being a son of the devil, and calls down on him the state Paul himself suffered: blindness. Elymas goes about "seeking those who would lead him by the hand," though we never learn if he reaches his Damascus. The proconsul, Sergius Paulus, is converted.

Some believe Paul took the name of this notable convert, but I suspect there's more to the matter: when God calls a prophet out of a previous state of unbelief or idolatry, as he called Abram, he often demands a change of name; in this case, all that Saul hated, all that Saul once persecuted, Paul now is.

He and Barnabas sail from Cyprus to Pamphylia and travel overland to Pisidian Antioch, where, in the synagogue on the Sabbath, they are asked by synagogue officials to give "a word of exhortation." Paul's sermon, like Stephen's, begins with a recapitulation of Israel's history, though his main thrust is that Christ's resurrection means, for Jews specifically, eternal life—of especial import to this former Pharisee.

He and Barnabas are asked to speak on the next Sabbath, and the whole city turns out, but now the Jews oppose them, and Paul says that since they "judge themselves unworthy of eternal life, behold, we are turning to the Gentiles." He and Barnabas are chased out of town.

At their next stop, Iconium, after again speaking in the synagogue—"I am not ashamed of the Gospel of Christ, for it is the power of God for salvation to every one who believes, to the Jew first and also to the Greek," Paul says in Romans 1:17—and calling both Jews and Gentiles to the faith, dividing the city along lines of belief and unbelief, Paul and Barnabas catch wind of a plot to stone them. They flee to Lystra, where they run into problems of another kind. Paul heals a lame man, and a crowd claims that the gods have come to earth. The crowd wants to offer sacrifices to Paul, whom they call Hermes, since he is the chief speaker, and Barnabas, renamed Zeus. So the world of unbelief will do its own renaming, too, to suit the purposes of the church to its ends, and it takes a great deal of effort on Paul's part to restrain the crowd. He tells them he has come to preach the God who created heaven and earth, so they can turn from their empty idols, and at that moment Jews from Antioch and Iconium appear, stone Paul, and drag him from the city, leaving him for dead.

This is the pattern of the latter portion of Acts: the proclamation of the gospel, a wholehearted response on the part of some, and then the restraining response of civil or church authorities, generally directed against Paul, whose missionary zeal equals his earlier zeal for persecution—though at this point all that seems ended. As the disciples stand around, however, Paul rises, enters the city, and then goes with Barnabas to Derbe and Lystra, then on to Iconium and Antioch, encouraging those churches in a new note for Paul: "Through many tribulations we must enter the kingdom of God."

Elders are appointed in the new churches, setting up the authority of local church government, and then Paul and Barnabas sail off again to Antioch, where they communicate what they've done, and spend "a long time." We don't know exactly how long, or the length of time Paul has been away, but from the chronology supplied in Galatians 2:1 we understand that it has been fourteen years between Paul's last visit to Jerusalem and the one he is about to undertake, for the apostolic event called the Jerusalem Council.

As with many matters of the church, then and now, the Jerusalem Council rises out of dissension; men from Judaea are saying to the church in Antioch, "Unless you are circumcised according to the custom of Moses, you cannot be saved." Paul and Barnabas dispute this claim, and it is decided that they should go, along with others, to the apostles and elders in Jerusalem and consult with them on the issue, an act that has led, through the centuries, to the formation and calling of councils and assemblies and synods (over and above the local church government) through most of the church.

At this first council, Peter rises and explains how God has called in the Gentiles, making "no distinction between us and them." Paul and Barnabas relate the "signs and wonders" God has performed among the Gentiles, and then James, the brother of Christ, rises and, like Christ, quotes from Amos, who is recapitulating Jeremiah—both of whom foresaw this widening of the kingdom.

Then James suggests this: "that we write to them that they abstain from things contaminated by idols and from fornication and from what is strangled and from blood." This finds approval with the assembly, and Barsabbas and Silas are chosen to accompany Paul and Barnabas, to deliver the first written communication, or epistle, of the Christian church (the entire text of which is reproduced by Luke), to the church at Antioch. The assembled congregation receives it with joy, "because of its encouragement," and Silas and Barsabbas further encourage them with "a lengthy message." The number of modern churches that would be encouraged by this method would be easy to count. I know of pastors who have been approached by church members if their sermons last thirty minutes, with the admonition that if this keeps up the Sunday roast will be ruined. For many moderns God seems merely another amulet of convenience.

Immediately after this, in the intimate, dramatic mode in which Luke has cast his entire book, Paul says to Barnabas—and we can imagine Paul turning to Barnabas, smiling, perhaps putting a hand on his shoulder—"Let us return and visit the brethren in every city in which we proclaimed the word of the Lord, and see how they are." It would be pleasant to be able to say that their camaraderie continues, but this is the occasion for one of the most shocking disagreements in Acts, and it is included, surely, to edify the present-day church. Barnabas wants to take John Mark along, but Paul points out that though John Mark began the first journey with them (12:25), he "deserted them" in Pamphylia (13:13), and such "sharp disagreement" arises between the two that faithful Barnabas separates himself from Paul and sails off for Cyprus with John Mark.

"All happy families are alike, but an unhappy family is unhappy after its own fashion." So Tolstoy opens *Anna Karenina*, with a maxim that applies equally to this family, the intimate body of believers, which is really more than a family: they are members of one another. Paul is saying that from his point of view, John Mark (to whom some ascribe The Gospel According to Mark) has not been as thoroughgoing as he might be in his service to Christ, although Barnabas obviously disagrees, and it is in exactly this fashion that the church, even when it is faithful, has disagreed over the ages: when one person's sense of the extent of faithful service, or a varying interpretation of proper faithfulness, is set against another's.

So Paul chooses Silas, and they begin traveling through Cilicia and Syria, "strengthening the churches." There is a curious moment in Derbe, when Paul meets Timothy, "the son of a Jewish woman who was a believer," but whose father is Greek. Paul wants Timothy to travel with him, and circumcises him, in spite of the Jerusalem document Paul has been reading in the churches, because the Jews in the area know that Timothy's father was a Gentile. We presume Paul makes this concession to keep from unnecessarily offending fellow Jews, but it is a compromise of magnitude, considering the document he is carrying, and some missionaries, far afield, sometimes wonder if they can't engage in similar compromise, or even subterfuge. I don't believe it's a question that can be answered easily (and don't intend to try), but one side of the answer would have to include the acknowledgment that Paul was an apostle who was spoken to directly by the Holy Spirit.

This Spirit now forbids Paul "to speak in Asia," and the "Spirit of Jesus," in one of those postincarnate manifestations, forbids him and his group to enter Bithynia, so they go from Mysia to Troas, on the coast, where Paul has his "Macedonian vision"—in the night a "man of Macedonia was standing and appealing to him, and saying, 'Come over to Macedonia and help us.' "

At this moment, just when we feel there can be no more surprises in this well-woven book, and certainly no technical ones, the next sentence goes: "And when he had seen the vision, immediately we sought to go into Macedonia, concluding that God had called us to preach the gospel to them." Nearly unobtrusively, in a shift of personal pronoun, Luke is present. This is analogous to only one other moment in Scripture, as far as I know, in Ezra, near the middle of chapter 8, when an orderly genealogy breaks into the first person. Now there is a sense of fresh air in the sails, with a person clearly familiar with the sea among the group, and they run "a straight course to Samothrace, and on the day following to Neapolis," and finally reach Philippi.

Nobody is there to meet them, certainly not the man who beckoned, and on the Sabbath they go outside the city to a river, where they suppose (or perhaps they've heard), Jewish believers gather to pray. There was probably no synagogue in Philippi, a Roman colony, for, as Calvin notes, "it was a capital offense for Greeks and Romans to celebrate the Sabbath, or practice Jewish rites."

At the river they encounter Lydia, a seller of purple fabrics, "a worshiper of God," and the Spirit opens her heart to Paul's message. She and her household are baptized, and she immediately says, "If you have judged me to be faithful to the Lord, come into my house and stay." There are few instances of such moving hospitality (perhaps Abigail's to David), and Lydia has since embodied for many Christians the attitude (see *Open Heart, Open Home*, by Karen Mains) they are to have. Certainly hospitality is a lost art; and I believe one can even say, considering this and other passages in Scripture (Romans 12:13; 1 Timothy 3:1; 1 Peter 4:9; etc.), a spiritual failing in the modern church. We entertain out of social exigency, or because we have to, or it's our turn, but seldom out of gratitude, or the stirring of the Spirit in us, understanding that hospitality is a gift of God and a necessary attribute of Christian virtue.

If more of our churches taught this, we might see the effects we do in Lydia's case. A group of believers gathers at her house, or anyway a locus of worship is established, for we next learn that as the disciples are going to "the place of prayer," another woman, a servant girl with a "spirit of divination," follows them, crying, "These men are bond-servants of the Most High God, who are proclaiming to you the way of salvation!" She does this for days, until Paul commands the spirit to leave her. The girl's owners, who hold her in spiritual bondage (to be discussed in connection with Sceva's sons), realize they've lost their source of income, and drag Paul and Silas before the authorities. "These men," they say, "are throwing our city into confusion, being Jews, and are proclaiming customs which it is not lawful for us to accept or observe, being Romans."

Paul and Silas are beaten with rods, thrown into jail, and locked up in stocks by a man memorialized since as the Philippian jailer. At midnight, as Paul and Silas pray and sing hymns of praise, there is an earthquake (no angel this time), and the prison doors spring open. The jailer wakes, and we can imagine his incredulity, his shock and shaggy disarray, though perhaps not his next action: he draws out his sword, impetuous as Peter, intending to kill himself, since death seemed a jailer's end if there were escapees. So we see a man with the moral temerity to judge himself and carry out his own execution, even though the broken-open jail isn't his fault. Paul prevents him, pointing out that nobody has escaped, and the jailer, who must by now feel tossed in every direction, and surely has been observing and listening to Silas and Paul, "came trembling," fell at their feet, and said, "Sirs, what must I do to be saved?"

"Believe in the Lord Jesus Christ, and you shall be saved, you and your household," they say, emphasizing again the Covenant. They speak to him in his quarters, where he bathes their wounds, and then they in a sense do the same: they baptize him and his household. The jailer then feeds them, as Paul was fed after his recovery from the Damascus encounter, causing one to wonder if the sacrament of Communion or the Lord's Supper was celebrated after these incidents and others (20:11, for example). The passages aren't clear enough to speak to this with certainty, but it's clear that the jailer, who is rejoicing "greatly," has cause to rejoice even more the next day: the city magistrates send policemen to say he is to release Paul and Silas. And now Paul lodges a protest; he says, "They have beaten us in public without trial, men who are Romans, and have thrown us into prison, and now they are sending us away in secret?"

Paul's appeal to his Roman citizenship, which will be insisted on by him for the rest of the book, draws him under the purview of civil authorities (not that he hasn't faced them before) and ultimately carries him to Rome, where tradition, not Scripture, has it that he was executed. For now, however, having thrown a scare at the authorities, he goes to Lydia's house, and then he and Silas, minus Luke (did the civil disruptions dismay our gentle physician?), travel to Thessalonica, where they speak in the synagogue and again stir up the established church so much that a mob assaults the house where they're staying. They have to steal away by night to Berea. There the more noble-minded Bereans examine "the Scriptures daily, to see whether these things [said by Paul] were so," but a mob from Thessalonica arrives, and Paul is hurried away into Athens, where he is to wait for Silas and Timothy.

Paul wait? The only one Paul waits on, to paraphase him, is God. His spirit is so provoked by this "city full of idols" that he speaks in the synagogue "with the Jews and the God-fearing Gentiles," and then moves to the marketplace, where Stoic and Epicurean philosophers engage him in debate—a picture of the prevailing sources of wisdom of that historical period. Paul, who is one of the great rhetoricians and logicians of the age (see Romans) is apparently able to hold his own, and eventually he is brought to the Areopagus, on Mars Hill, to face not the authorities, for a change, but a larger audience: "for all the Athenians and the strangers visiting there used to spend their time in nothing other than telling or hearing something new."

To this audience of philosophical intellectuals Paul mentions that he has seen a local altar inscribed TO AN UNKNOWN GOD, and says that the God they are worshiping in ignorance he is here to proclaim. He says that this God is the creator of all things, the Lord of heaven, a sovereign Spirit, the uniter of nations, the determiner of time and events, and not far from anyone; "for in Him we live and move and exist, as even some of your own poets have said, 'For we also are His offspring.'" The crowd scoffs when Paul mentions the Resurrection, but there are converts, two of whom are named: Dionysus and Damaris.

From here Paul travels to Corinth, where he meets Priscilla and Aquila ("because Claudius had commanded all the Jews to leave Rome"), with whom he works at the trade they have in common, tent making, the means by which Paul—a self-supporting missionary not beholden to that mission board or series of churches—pays his own way (20:34; 2 Thessalonians 3:7–10). At Corinth, through Paul's teaching, Crispus, the chief ruler of the synagogue, "believed on the Lord with all his house" (the Covenant again), and there are further converts. In a vision Paul is instructed to remain in the city, because it is safe, and Luke, more calendarlike now, tells us he remains eighteen months. When Gallio is named deputy of Achaia, however, Jewish leaders bring Paul before his judgment seat, accusing him of persuading the people to worship God contrary to their law. Gallio won't hear the case, since it isn't a matter "of wrong or a vicious crime," and Paul goes free.

He sails with Priscilla and Aquila to Syria, speaks briefly at Ephesus, parts from his tent-maker friends here, and goes on to Caesarea, then Jerusalem, and home to the church in Antioch. There's a slight elision then of Paul, who dominates two-thirds of Acts, as we see his disciples Priscilla and Aquila taking aside and correcting a disciple in Ephesus named Apollos, who is preaching the baptism of John but seems unaware of the Holy Spirit. Does Priscilla, or Prisca (Romans 16:3), execute in this instance church authority? She certainly joins her husband in straightening out Apollos' doctrine, but there is no record of her teaching on her own. Paul arrives in Ephesus from yet another journey, and discovers disciples who indeed haven't heard of the Holy Spirit; he teaches them, baptizes them, and lays on hands, and they begin to speak in tongues. Is his teaching, then, to be seen as authoritative?

What I'm edging toward, of course, is the issue of women in church office. To many this is an issue of the past, decided decades ago, when women began to be ordained as pastors in some denominations, or when Mary Baker Eddy set up her own church; indeed, a black woman was recently ordained a bishop in the Episcopal church, although she remains unrecognized by the Archbishop of Canterbury. The oldest Christian institution, however, and the largest, the Roman Catholic church, has so far resisted feminist claims; and the small denomination of which I am a member, the Orthodox Presbyterian church, recently completed a three-year study on the role of women in church office—a sixty-page document packed with citations from Scripture—and came to the conclusion that the offices of elder and deacon are not open to women, if our reference is Scripture alone. *Sola Scriptura*, the rallying call of civilizations during the period of the great reformers—Hus, Luther, Calvin, Knox, and Zwingli—is no longer popular; the decision was not popularly received, nor did it find "approval with the whole congregation" (6:5). It was a decision reached by a committee of men, of course, and the lone dissenter to the majority opinion, the president of a seminary on the West Coast, agreed with the others on the office of elder but felt that the diaconate, considering references to Phoebe, was open to women. Our denomination has asked local congregations to respond to the decision, and this is one of the tasks I've been working at when I'm not busy with Acts. I haven't yet reached any definitive answers, if I ever will, so if anyone is waiting breathlessly for yet another male's opinion on the subject I can only say, as for Acts and the rest of Scripture, "To be continued after further study."

Paul remains in Corinth for two years, teaching in the house of Tyrannus, a schoolmaster most children suspect they've met, and a practice begins that has been used by a series of charlatans ever since: handkerchiefs and aprons are carried from Paul and used to heal and to drive out spirits. Not that I believe Paul was a charlatan, or that evil spirits are nonexistent. In Shirley Nelson's recent *Fair Clear and Terrible*, a careful examination of the Frank Sandford Shiloh cult, there is a firsthand account of having to wrestle down a man possessed that will set your hair on end. The society that will accept Castaneda's Don Juan, an image of the malevolent shape-shifter, or an actress's New Age "Deep Throat" who speaks in the same retrograde platitudes as Edgar Cayce's familiar (see *Unholy Spirits*, by Gary North), can't countenance the idea of evil.

There have been enough recent books (the above, *The Ultimate Evil, Children of the Lie*, etc.) informing us of something amiss, and enough recent news reports to assure us that the worship of Satan does take place, and often demands human sacrifice, as the worship of Moloch did; and enough random violence, such as the shooting of children on a school playground, to suggest that man is indeed not getting better and better, as another banal platitude goes. The teaching of Christ is that one cannot serve two masters: it's one or the other, you're either for me or against me, he says; and Paul, in Romans and elsewhere, emphasizes that one is in *bondage* to one or the other. Which is why Christians are referred to as servants or slaves, and call upon the Holy Spirit to displace the Spirit or spirits they once served.

A kind of exorcism trade sets up in Corinth, and the seven sons of a chief priest, Sceva, begin to command evil spirits to leave by "Jesus whom Paul preaches," until one spirit says, "I recognize Jesus, and I know about Paul, but who are you?" The man possessed then attacks a pair of the sons and tears their clothes so badly they run off naked. The scene does not depict a neutral middle ground, no more than the rest of Scripture does, but a spiritual warfare in which good is set against evil.

When news of the attack gets around, fear falls on the city, and a period of confession and repentance begins, including the first recorded book burning: magicians and sorcerers gather together their incunabula and begin "burning them in sight of all; and they counted up the price of them and found it to be fifty thousand pieces of silver." This is done of their free will, we see, in a repentant mode, as if to say, "This black magic I here abjure." It is not imposed upon them by a censor, and so is an admission that the "arts" they practice are the reverse of, or in opposition to, the gospel of Paul.

There is a different reaction from another, as it were, special-interest group. Demetrius, a silversmith who fashions shrines to Diana, assembles the artisans and workmen of the city and says, "Men, you know that our prosperity depends on our business. And you see and hear that not only in Ephesus, but in almost all of Asia, this Paul has persuaded and turned away a considerable number of people, saying that gods made with hands are no gods at all." The danger, he tells them, is not only that their trade will fall into disrepute but that the temple of Diana will be treated as null. They begin shouting with rage, "Great is Diana of the Ephesians!," and the whole city is caught up in the confusion. The crowd grabs two disciples, but the town clerk finally persuades them to disperse and pursue legal means if they have a complaint, or they'll be culpable for their uproar, in this, one of the earliest labor riots, here in opposition to the gospel.

Paul wants to be in Jerusalem for Pentecost, and on the way there he calls the Ephesian elders to him in Miletus and tells them that in spite of trials and humiliations he has never shrunk from teaching and preaching in every circumstance; that the Spirit has informed him that further bonds and afflictions await him, but he doesn't consider his life of any account, or as dear to him as the gospel. He says they will never see his face again, and warns them to be on guard for themselves and their church, because wolves will soon enter, "speaking perverse things," and ravage the flock; he reminds them how for three years he admonished them with tears, coveted nothing of what they had, and worked with his hands to earn his own way, after the example of Christ, who "Himself said, 'It is more blessed to give than to receive.'"

He kneels with them and prays, and they begin to weep and embrace and kiss him, particularly grieved because he has said they won't see him again. They won't, and to follow Paul's course we move to Jerusalem. James and the elders there suggest what can be seen as another form of subterfuge: that Paul take part in a ritual purification along with others, so that the Jewish hierarchy can't accuse him of disdaining Mosaic Law. But when Paul appears in the Temple, Jews from Asia seize him, claiming that he has not only preached against the Law but brought a Gentile into the Temple; he hasn't, but was seen in the company of an Ephesian. Now an uproar rises in Jerusalem as Paul is dragged from the Temple and its doors slammed behind him, a clangorous detail: the established Jerusalem church has shut Paul out, and the only direction he can travel now is away from it.

There is such widespread disturbance in Jerusalem that a Roman commander arrives with centurions. He stops the crowd from beating Paul but has him bound with chains and brought to the barracks, and there occurs what I view as one example of the "gift of tongues." Paul speaks Greek to the commander, Claudius Lysias, who realizes that Paul isn't the Egyptian who led four thousand in a revolt (again, shades of Moses), and then honors Paul's request to address the rioting crowd. In a shift to "the Hebrew dialect," Paul tells the Jerusalemites how he persecuted Christians to death, and then recounts his experience on the road to Damascus. The crowd appears to listen with interest—and it is a wonderful story in itself—but when Paul mentions how, during a later visit to Jerusalem, the Lord appeared to him and told him to preach among the Gentiles, people in the crowd pull off their cloaks and throw dust in the air, crying, "Away with such a fellow from the earth, for he should not be allowed to live!"

Lysias orders Paul scourged, thinking this will prompt him to confess why he has so upset the crowd; but as Paul is tied in place with thongs, he says to a centurion, "Is it lawful for you to scourge a man who is a Roman and uncondemned?" The soldier runs to Lysias to ask what to do, permitting us to examine the question of civil disobedience, which has since affected the church, is affecting it now, and threatens to affect it in ways it never has if the protests against abortion, for instance, continue to escalate.

If the Jerusalem Sanhedrin, the government and hierarchy of the Old Testament church, can also be viewed as a civil authority, as it seems it partly was, then the apostles went contrary to that authority *when they preached the gospel*, as they were forbidden to do (chapters 4 and 5); but their command to preach arrived from Christ, who, to those who accept him as Messiah, is the Lord of the Church. The apostles certainly get into plenty of trouble, and do cause civil strife, but only through the preaching of the gospel, and the trouble always originates within the established religion—whether it's the idol makers in Ephesus, the Sanhedrin, or local synagogue authorities. As before, Paul has here appealed for relief from that religious authority to a higher civil rule, the Roman government under which Judea was a protectorate, and for his civil rights under that rule; and now Claudius Lysias arrives and says, "Tell me, are you a Roman?"

"Yes," Paul answers.

"I acquired this citizenship with a large sum of money," Lysias, most likely once a slave, says to Paul.

Paul says, "I was born free," and in the considerable dimension of meaning Paul is claiming that he is a natural-born Roman citizen, an inheritor of the rights of that citizenship, and also that he was born into the Covenant established with Abraham and Moses, and that as an inheritor of that Covenant, which is fulfilled in Christ (whose atoning sacrifice releases every member from the bondage of the Law, which none were anyway able to keep, and from the bondage of sin and evil), he has been absolutely freed.

Lysias then sets Paul before the Sanhedrin, and when Paul testifies that he has lived a life of good conscience before God until this day, the high priest has his mouth slapped. "God is going to strike you, you whitewashed wall!" Paul cries. Bystanders rebuke him for reviling the high priest, and Paul says, either in irony or in respect, "I was not aware, brothers, that he was high priest; for it is written, 'You shall not speak evil of a ruler of your people.'" Noticing then that the council is divided between Sadducees and Pharisees, he cries out, "Brothers, I am a Pharisee, a son of Pharisees; I am on trial for the hope and resurrection of the dead!"

A new uproar begins, this one religious, as Pharisees rise in Paul's defense, and such dissension develops that the commander is afraid Paul will "be torn to pieces." He takes Paul back to the barracks, then learns of a conspiracy to kill Paul, and under cover of night has him escorted by soldiers to Caesarea, the court of Felix, the governor. He says he will hear Paul's case before his accusers, and they arrive with an attorney, who claims that Paul has caused dissension among Jews and desecrated the Temple; Felix, after hearing both sides, keeps Paul in custody but allows his friends to minister to him. Felix has a "more exact knowledge of The Way," we read, and soon learn why; in a few days he returns with Drusilla, "his wife who was a Jewess," and summons Paul before them to "speak about faith in Jesus Christ." At Paul's mention of self-control and the judgment to come, Felix gets so frightened he locks him up again. For two years Felix keeps this up, until he is succeeded by Porcius Festus.

The chief priests approach Festus with their complaints against Paul, begging him to try Paul in Jerusalem (after setting an ambush), and Festus tells them to come first to Caesarea. Paul again maintains his innocence, then appeals to the emperor, Caesar, and Festus says, "To Caesar you shall go."

Herod Agrippa II and his sister, though, stop for a visit, and when Festus mentions Paul to them, Agrippa asks to hear him. So the next day Paul, who is getting good at courtroom procedures, appears in the midst of the pomp set out for the king, and we're reminded of the trial of Christ, who in the working of Providence, was tried by a civil authority, Pontius Pilate, and declared innocent ("I find no wrong in this man"), so that His innocence and atoning death, fulfilling God's sense of perfect justice, could be applied to those who believed in Him.

Agrippa tells Paul he may speak in his own defense, and Paul mentions his strict upbringing and his zeal in persecuting Christians, "not only locking them up in prisons" and casting his vote for the death penalty, but trying "to force them to blaspheme." Paul then recounts again his experience on the road to Damascus; and as we hear a second variation from his own mouth of the actual experience, we remember the three recountings of the conjoining vision of Cornelius and Peter and follow Paul's words even more closely, noting new emphases, or the deletion or expansion of certain details (such as the more complete commission from Christ in verses 16 through 18) for this new audience, although the central story remains unshakable, and realize that through this pair of examples Luke is instructing Theophilus about the relationship of the three Gospels (minus John's, which has a specific intent) known as the synoptics. There have been, through the centuries, discussions of the "harmony" of these Gospels, and here Luke structurally illustrates their conjunction: each was written by a different man, with a specific audience in mind, on a different occasion, so there will be variants, or varying details, or different emphases, but in each the central unshakable message is the same, as Paul's recountings of this single event in his own life are. And now, as if to drive this home, Paul says in summation that in everything he has ever said he has stated "nothing but what the Prophets and Moses said was going to take place," that Christ would be a light to both Jews and Gentiles.

"Paul!" Festus cries out. "You're out of your mind! Your great learning is driving you mad!"

One appreciates Luke even more for not suppressing this remark out of fear that it's exactly what many might think. Paul turns to Agrippa and says, "King Agrippa, do you believe the Prophets? I know that you do."

Agrippa answers, "In a short time you will persuade me to be a Christian!"

Paul replies, in a note of humility and pragmatism, "I would to God, that whether in a short or long time, not only you, but also all who hear me this day, might become such as I am, except for these chains."

Paul is sent away, and Agrippa says to Festus, "This man might have been set free if he had not appealed to Caesar."

But Paul has testified that he was born free, and now as he begins the months-long sea journey toward Rome, still in chains, and under the guard of a Roman soldier, his testimony surfaces with further strength. Luke, who is with him, notes that he is allowed to greet friends at Sidon.

After considerable rough sailing, Paul warns the captain not to leave a port in Crete, because it's October and winter storms are beginning, but is overruled. For more than two weeks the ship is driven by a storm that blots out stars and sun, in a passage resonant of Homer, and it is Paul who, in spite of his earlier warnings, encourages the crew—an angel of the Lord has assured him that none will perish, he says—and persuades them to eat. When the worst happens, and the ship runs aground off Malta, breaking up in the waves, and Paul's assurance proves true, we're reminded of Jonah on his way to Nineveh, and of Christ stating that his sign will be only the sign of Jonah, and of Paul's own words "a night and a day I have spent in the deep" (2 Corinthians 11:25)—the length of time Christ spent in the tomb.

And when a viper appears from the kindling used for a fire on Malta and fastens itself to Paul's wrist, and the natives wait for him to die, Paul rises free even of this, unaffected. He is to reach Rome, he's been told again by the angel who brought word that none on the ship would perish; and when he nears the city, and crowds travel out to greet him, Paul thanks God and takes courage, though he stands in chains. The desire of his heart has been granted: he has arrived in Rome, freed into the eternal life his mentor Gamaliel taught through their Messiah, whose reign was not to be over a mighty political kingdom similar to David's or Solomon's but over a spiritual one in which He is the firstfruits: eternal life. Whatever any church or civil authority has done to Paul, or tried to do, he has attained the authoritative peace of resting within that life by faith.

He is permitted to rent his own room in Rome, and although the local Jewish authorities visit him, and some believe and some do not, there isn't the slightest suggestion of any disturbance; and although a soldier still stands guard over Paul, and Paul for the next two years resides under the shadow of Caesar, we read at the close of Acts that Paul is "welcoming all who came to him, preaching the kingdom of God, and teaching concerning the Lord with all openness, un-hindered."

Those teachings have by now reached the remotest parts of the earth, even North Dakota, where I now live. Last year in our local church there was a study of Acts, and these are some of the residual questions from it that I consider as I sit in church on Sunday with approximately fifty others, many of them farmers, in this southwestern corner of the state distinguished by its mesas and buttes; and when the door to the left of the pulpit, leading to a small meeting room, is inad-vertently left open, I can see out a rear window to the ascending plain in its conjunction with the sky, blue against green or gold or white, depending upon the season, and my considerations suddenly become less important than this picture of heaven over earth—a demarcation of the interim in which we carry out our present-day acts.

THE EPISTLE OF
PAUL THE APOSTLE
TO THE ROMANS

—

David Plante

I recall the winter light coming through the windows of the class-room, and the nun, Mère Sainte-Epiphane, standing in that hard light, her long black skirt hiding her shoes so she appeared to float a little above the unpolished wooden floor, telling the class in Canadian French that we shouldn't try to read the Bible because we wouldn't understand it. Only those who had devoted their lives to the study of the Bible understood God's word properly. We should rely on them for explanations and not try to interpret the word of God according to what we might want that to be, because not what we wanted God to be was true, but God in himself was true, and the truth of his word required knowledge we did not have.

About Saint Paul, we were taught that he was the man, the military man, who most understood Christ's teachings, and therefore the church's. Paul was the authority on all interpretations of the Bible, and what the laws of the Bible he interpreted most had to do with was what everyone in the class of pubescent adolescents most thought about: the body of flesh.

Mère Sainte-Epiphane, who heard this from we had no idea what higher power because we didn't think she herself read the Bible, relayed to us that according to Saint Paul we had a body and a soul, and the body was always trying to destroy the soul by drawing our attention to it rather than allowing us the full attention to the soul it needed for our salvation. To save our soul, we must strictly control our body, as Saint Paul did.

We were not, however, responsible for what we dreamed.

A colored holy picture of the saint was passed from student to student, all at our desks, for us to study. He was a Roman soldier wearing armor that reproduced the chest muscles, the nipples, the curves of the groin of his body, and he had a halo over his head. His picture made us entirely aware of our body, but his teaching was that we, as soldiers of Christ, must subject our body to a will above our body, a will that said the soul, not the body, mattered. We were put in armor by Saint Paul that exactly reproduced our naked body, that reminded us all the time we wore it of our naked body, and that didn't allow us to expose our body to be touched, even by ourselves.

One afternoon, in the attic where I liked to go after school to look through the cardboard and wooden boxes that'd been packed away there before I was born, I lifted old sheets of newspaper that covered a box filled with books and, taking these out to examine them, found a large book that interested me for being so big and heavy, with a thick green binding and a silver top stain. I looked through books for pictures, not text, and I opened this one onto a picture of Christ walking along a dirt road and as if followed by the devil, both figures rather different from the Catholic Christ and devil—smoother, softer, vaguer about the edges, and in pastel colors—and I was so struck by the difference I became suspicious and examined the book more closely. I held in my hands a Protestant Bible. Quickly, I went down the ladder with it, and in the kitchen, where my mother and brother were having tea at the table, I held the book up and shouted, "I found a Protestant Bible in our house." My mother and brother didn't seem interested. I went to the door that led to the cellar and threw the Bible down the stairs.

"Go get that," my brother said.

"No," I answered. "It's a Protestant Bible."

My mother asked, "How did it get into the attic?"

"I don't know," I said. "But we've got to get rid of it."

"Go get it," my brother said again, and I insisted, "No." He went down the cellar stairs, picked it up, and came back, smoothing out the crumpled pages.

I went up into the attic again and, looking through more books, forgot the Bible.

Some days later, drying the dishes my mother washed, I remembered the Bible and asked where it was. She looked out the window over the sink, then said, as if about an act that had been horrible but necessary, "It's gone."

What had most frightened me about the Protestant Bible was that I knew it was read in an entirely different way from the Catholic. A Protestant interpreted the truth of God's laws in whatever way he wanted.

But the Protestant Bible was gone.

Then one of my brothers, the one who had rescued the Bible I'd thrown down the cellar stairs, married a Protestant. My mother and I thought she was wonderful: so free, so bright, so outgoing. Not like us. But my father disapproved of her for being Protestant, my father who was in no way free, bright, outgoing.

Protestants were freer than I. Protestants could be as aware of their bodies as they wanted, and in the locker rooms and on the beaches where my older brother and my new sister-in-law took me sometimes on a summer Sunday, they enjoyed this awareness. In our family, the body, especially that of my father, was a secret. If I was obsessed by my body in private, I was embarrassed by it in public. The Catholic meaning of the body was private, and the Protestant was public, and these meanings were very different from one another. Even Saint Paul would not be an absolute authority to a Protestant, but someone whose words about the body and soul could be read in the way he wanted to read them.

When I became a freshman in a Jesuit college, I had to take courses in theology, and I learned, to some extent, the authoritative readings of the Bible. But the more I learned the official interpretations, the more I was drawn to the unofficial, or what I imagined the unofficial, ways, for the freedom of being able to read as I wanted, and I turned from Knox's Roman Catholic translation of the Bible to the King James as a deliberate act of rebellion, and also with the excited sense that I was reading a work that was, according to strict church law, forbidden, as was *Leaves of Grass*, by Walt Whitman. I bought the

Protestant Bible in a bookshop in Boston and kept it hidden in my room. As I studied the Catholic Bible, I read, for inspiration, the Protestant, which, for everything that I as a boy had been told made the Protestant Bible an occasion of sin, freed me from the rules of the Catholic. I read the King James Version of the Bible as I imagined a Protestant would read it—not necessarily for understanding of God's intent, but for inspiration; not to learn the impersonal laws governing all men, but for an entirely personal movement in my soul.

I wanted the Bible to inspire me with a movement in my soul equal to the movement I felt, in body and soul, when my roommate opened the door and came in at the end of an afternoon from a class and threw his books on the floor and threw himself on his bed, his worn buckskin shoes on, and asked me how my day had been. I wanted to find in the Bible a Protestant Saint Paul who, superseding the Catholic one, would justify me in my freedom to love my roommate, physically and spiritually. The only justification needed from the Protestant Bible, I imagined, was to feel the truth of a certain passage, even if I did not understand it. Justification in the Catholic Bible was intellectual, was Scholastic. I wanted to read the Bible for inspiration in the same way I was inspired by my roommate to love him, and I also wanted my reading of the Bible to inspire my love for him.

And so I read the Protestant Saint Paul. (I never did read the Catholic, because my courses at college didn't require me to.) I read:

> Professing themselves to be wise, they became fools,
> And changed the glory of the uncorruptible God into an image made like to corruptible man, and to birds, and fourfooted beasts, and creeping things.
> Wherefore God also gave them up to uncleanness through the lusts of their own hearts, to dishonour their own bodies between themselves:
> Who changed the truth of God into a lie, and worshipped and served the creature more than the Creator, who is blessed for ever. Amen.
> For this cause God gave them up into vile affections: for even

their women did change the natural use into that which is against nature:

And likewise also the men, leaving the natural use of the women, burned in their lust one toward another; men with men working that which is unseemly, and receiving in themselves that recompense of their error which was meet.

And even as they did not like to retain God in their knowledge, God gave them over to a reprobate mind, to do those things which are not convenient;

Being filled with all unrighteousness, fornication, wickedness, covetousness, maliciousness; full of envy, murder, debate, deceit, malignity; whisperers,

Backbiters, haters of God, despiteful, proud, boasters, inventors of evil things, disobedient to parents,

Without understanding, covenant breakers, without natural affection, implacable, unmerciful:

Who knowing the judgment of God, that they which commit such things are worthy of death, not only do the same, but have pleasure in them that do them. [Romans 1:20–32]

How could I, in my superseding Protestant freedom, interpret this passage in Saint Paul's Epistle to the Romans, the passage appearing in the very first chapter, in terms of which I, alas, found myself reading the entire epistle?

Panicked, I had to defend myself against the Protestant Saint Paul, who horrified me. I had to find something wrong with him. I told myself, what this passage implies, among other terrible things, is that God "gave over men" to burn in their lust for one another as a punishment for worshiping the creature more than the Creator; that God "filled" people who didn't retain him in their knowledge with "unrighteousness, fornication, uncleanness," and the rest of it. So, for one man to make love with another was not a sin in itself, but a punishment for worshiping the creature rather than the Creator, a punishment for which these people are to be further punished, receiving in themselves that recompense of their error which was meet, which was to become backbiters, haters of God, despiteful, proud, boasters, inventors of evil things, and on and on, including disobeying their parents and being made unmerciful.

The truth about myself as a practicing Catholic was that I loved God, in himself, and never thought of him as a corruptible man or, much less, as a four-footed or creeping thing, though I must confess I did think of him as a bird, a dove, in his manifestation as the Holy Spirit, for which not I but the entire church should be condemned. I loved God, but, for some reason, God nevertheless punished me by making me fall in love with my roommate. This was very clear: he didn't punish me by making me a backbiter, etc., because I loved my roommate. He punished me, for no reason that I could imagine myself guilty of, by making me fall in love with my roommate.

Mère Sainte-Epiphane was right. I shouldn't have read the Bible without proper guidance. I didn't understand.

The very awareness Saint Paul had of the lustful body indicated his attachment to it. "O wretched man that I am! Who shall deliver me from the body of this death?" There was a strong point to seeing Saint Paul's thorn in the flesh, even if it were not sexual, as a constant, painful awareness of the body, an awareness he thought was the ruination of his soul. But to a person, as I was as an adolescent, for whom laws against the flesh were also laws against the spirit, Saint Paul's condemning the body condemned the soul. His struggle to free the soul was nullified by his condemnation of the body.

I knew it was unjust to him that he, the great radical who proclaimed the end of the Law, should, in the end, be known above all as the man who stood for the law; unjust that his strictures against the flesh should override his amazing proclamations of the freedom of the spirit. And yet he did see the two, body and spirit, as incompatible, and in that he was a danger to me.

In that first year of college, I didn't doubt that I loved my roommate any more than I doubted I loved God. Saint Paul said that was impossible.

I'll call myself Daniel and I'll call my roommate Charlie.

Daniel and Charlie were sitting in a bar in the old North End of Boston. They were in a booth with tall sides that had dates and names carved in the dark wood. The table was wooden, too, and carved with dates and names. Daniel was apprehensive because he and Charlie were under age, and every time Charlie asked the waitress for another two beers, Daniel got worried that she would ask for their IDs. Charlie didn't seem to worry, but said to the waitress, joking, "I like this place. It's where the real he-men hang out." She said, "You bet."

Charlie and Daniel were discussing circumcision, the pros and cons. It was a way for two young men to talk about male sex.

Charlie said, "I can't understand why removing a baby's foreskin should have become a law of religion. Why?"

"Is it, do you think, a sin for a Jew not to be circumcised?" Daniel asked.

"I think that a Jew who isn't circumcised isn't a Jew, according to Judaic Law, so, not being a Jew, an uncircumcised Jew wouldn't be sinning because he wasn't circumcised. He wouldn't be anything."

"Can you imagine circumcision being such an issue it defines by religious law what you are?" Daniel said.

"As I said, I don't understand," Charlie said.

"Saint Paul talks about the circumcision of the spirit taking the place of the circumcision of the flesh."

"Does he?"

"Christians are supposed to have circumcised souls. That's what makes them Christian."

"I don't know what that means."

"It means, I think, not abiding by the letter of the law, but the spirit."

Charlie smiled. "Do you feel you have a circumcised soul, Dan?"

Daniel smiled back. He said, "I do, and my soul so abides by the spirit rather than the letter, I don't believe in sin anymore."

"That seems radical," Charlie said. "What made you decide that?"

"It just occurred to me that what I thought was sinful I did only because of a Church law that condemned it. In fact, there's no reason at all for it to be condemned, because in itself it's—" He stopped for a moment to drink beer and try to cool down, for what he had to say he must say dispassionately to convince Charlie of it. "—it's completely natural," he said, "as natural as having a foreskin."

Charlie didn't ask what it was, but he asked, "How do you know it's natural?"

"My spirit tells me," Daniel said.

"I don't know if that'd pass in an examination on syllogisms, Dàn."

"Well, take it this way," Daniel said, leaning across the table toward his friend, "take it the way Saint Paul would take it, if Saint Paul were myself or if I were Saint Paul. He says over and over, in Romans, that people can't live fulfilled lives according to the law, but only according to the spirit, and the spirit is above the law. He even says that it's only because of laws that there are sins, and without laws there wouldn't be sins. He says that he knows that there is nothing unclean of itself, but a thing is unclean to someone only if he thinks it is unclean. He also says that a man is happy who doesn't condemn himself for what he allows himself. I can quote you chapter and verse for these—the first, chapter 5, verse 13; the second, chapter 15, verse 14; the third, chapter 15, verse 22—"

"You mean," Charlie said, "you've read the Bible?"

"The Protestant," Daniel said.

"And?"

"And it made me want to talk with Saint Paul. I want to tell him that he contradicted himself so badly in his letters, especially in Romans, that everything he says is canceled out, or would be canceled out if he himself had been responsible for the contradictions. But I believe something else, something greater than himself, something above the laws of logic, made him contradict himself, and instead of this condemning his writing, it—this something greater than himself—saved it, at least for me."

Charlie, leaning with his elbows on the table edge and his shoulders hunched forward, looked at Daniel.

Daniel said, "I'd say to Saint Paul, 'You may not be aware of it, but something in your writing knows that the body and soul are not opposed to one another, but as much one as our great American poet Walt Whitman said they are.'"

"I thought you'd have to get Walt Whitman in there," Charlie said.

Daniel said, "I'm talking to Saint Paul, I'm saying to him, 'You wrote, "To be carnally minded is death," and you also wrote, "My brethren, ye also are become dead to the law of the body of Christ; that ye be married to another, even to him who is raised from the dead, that we should bring forth fruit unto God," which is an image based on carnal love for the body of Christ, it seems to me, however mystical the marriage is. No, you can't use the imagery of sexual love on one level, on what you consider a high and justified level, and condemn sex on another, what you consider a low level. And you do that all the time. You could say that it's impossible to act out on the low level what is possible on the higher level, so the lower level must be condemned. Well, if you think that, you should use an entirely different set of references for the higher level. Don't you see that you can't use an image of what you damn, which is the body, for what you praise, which is the soul? You say over and over that the body and the soul are separate and opposed, and the true believer must put off the carnal body to take on Jesus, but in the end you go back on yourself and, as though giving in to a passion greater than your strong intelligence you use the image of the body to identify what you repeatedly insist has nothing to do with our mortal bodies: the body of the church itself, the mystical body of Christ? "For as we have many members in one body, and all members have not the same office: So we, being many, are one body in Christ, and every one members one of another"—Romans, chapter 12, verses 4 and 5. Don't you see that it's when you allow yourself to be inspired— as, in chapter 15, verse 22, you say a happy man does without condemning himself—you, despite your personal struggle to separate the body from the soul, unite the body and the soul and make them one in images that transcend the personal? Don't you see that in your use of images of the body to make sense of the soul you are inspired as if by grace beyond your thinking, and beyond contradiction too? Don't you realize that your very awareness of the body, instead of condemning you, gives substance to the very faith that will save you and us all?' "

Charlie said, "I think you should tell that to the Jebbies."

Daniel laughed.

Daniel and Charlie left the bar because Charlie had a date. Daniel walked to the MTA station with him so Charlie could get a trolley, and then he continued to walk. He went along streets lit by street-lights toward Faneuil Hall, and up Cornhill to the courthouse, and up onto Beacon Hill behind the statehouse; then at Louisburg Square, where the dim, old-fashioned lamps seemed to hiss, he turned down to the dark Boston Common.

As Daniel passed the hill on the Common, he saw Saint Paul at the top, looking up into the nighttime sky, in which the stars defined a great body, Christ's, risen with arms outstretched, which Saint Paul contemplated with greater love than Daniel would ever have for anyone in his life.

THE FIRST EPISTLE OF
PAUL THE APOSTLE
TO THE CORINTHIANS

—

Frederick Buechner

The Greek rhetorician Alciphron wrote in his memoirs, "Never yet have I been to Corinth, for I know pretty well the beastly kind of life the rich enjoy there and the wretchedness of the poor," and from the time of Aristophanes on, the city could even claim the distinction of having its name made into a verb. To "corinthianize" meant to go to the dogs. Situated on the narrow isthmus that connects Greece proper with the Peloponnesus, it was a major center for trade and shipping. Its population was largely immigrant, and sailors from everywhere under the sun prowled its streets, bringing their gods with them—Isis and Serapis from Egypt, Astarte from Syria, Artemis from Ephesus, to name just a few. The most striking geographical feature of the place was a steeply rising peak known as Acrocorinth, and on its summit—to symbolize her ascendancy both over all rivals and in the hearts of the citizenry—there stood a temple to the goddess Aphrodite, which according to the Greek historian Strabo employed the services of some one thousand sacred prostitutes. "Not every man should go to Corinth" was an ancient byword whose reasonableness seems beyond challenge.

Saint Paul should have taken it to heart. Around A.D. 50 he arrived there for the first time, and the book of Acts gives a brief but vivid account of the consequences. He went to live with a Jewish couple named Priscilla and Aquila—tent makers like him—who had left Rome when the emperor Claudius ordered all Jews out. They introduced him to the local synagogue, and as a distinguished guest he was invited to address the congregation. His zealous promotion of the claim that a Nazarene named Jesus, only some twenty years earlier crucified in Jerusalem, was the Messiah and Lord of life of ancient Jewish expectation so horrified some of the synagogue leaders that they told him as a blasphemer and heretic to leave and never show his face again. This he did, but not before taking with him a number of Jews he had converted to the new faith, including a man named Crispus, the synagogue's ruler. In the house of one Titus Justus, who to add insult to injury was the synagogue's next-door neighbor, he set up a Christian church, where for a year and a half he preached the Gospel, until he decided to continue his missionary activities elsewhere. This journey eventually landed him across the Aegean in the city of Ephesus, and it was there, a few years later, that he received from the converts he had left behind in Corinth a letter which First Corinthians is in part an answer to.

Paul's responses to the specific questions that they posed and to the local problems they asked him to advise them on by no means constitute the most important or interesting part of the Epistle, but they give a rich sense of the kind of document it was written to be. Paul was not primarily concerned with setting forth religious doctrine, as he did in Romans and Galatians. He made no attempt to present an orderly résumé of the Christian faith. He was simply trying to set his Corinthian friends straight on the concrete matters that immediately concerned them, and only in the process of doing that did he get sidetracked into some of the most eloquent, moving, and self-revelatory passages that he ever wrote.

You can't help wishing you knew more about those concrete matters. There is just enough here to tantalize. Was the Sosthenes he mentions in his opening salutation the same Sosthenes that the Corinthian Jews beat up after their unsuccessful attempt to get Paul into trouble with the Roman proconsul Gallio, who threw the whole pack of them out of court, saying in so many words that the internecine squabbles of the Jews bored him to death? And how about

Chloe, whose "people"—slaves? household members?—brought Paul news in Ephesus of certain goings-on that the Corinthians themselves had apparently chosen not to mention in their letter? She seems to have been one of the few well-heeled members of a congregation that otherwise, Paul tells us, consisted mainly of the lower orders, the more or less down and out. It would be especially interesting to know more about Apollos, an Alexandrian Jew who preached in Corinth after Paul's departure. Is it possible that Paul's disparagement of philosophical eloquence and, in Second Corinthians, his acerbic references to "super apostles" (11:5 and 12:11) are allusions to him? Is it conceivable that Luther was right in identifying him, not Paul, as the one who wrote the eloquent Epistle to the Hebrews? Or, as others have believed, was it Priscilla, Paul's hostess, who wrote it? Her name is mentioned ahead of her husband's in the passage in Acts that describes them as the ones who took Apollos aside and "expounded to him the way of God more accurately," suggesting perhaps that, theologically speaking anyway, she was the one who called the shots in the family. In any case they were both of them with Paul in Ephesus when he wrote his letter, and he sends their greetings back home along with his own.

But if Paul gives us only a fragmentary picture of the dramatis personae, he leaves us in no doubt as to the general situation they were involved in. It is clear that one way or another all hell had broken loose. Foreshadowing the fate of Christendom from then on, the small church had already split up into a number of factions. One of them followed Paul himself; another, his successor Apollos; another, the apostle Peter; and a fourth, Christ. (This last faction may have been a group of Christian Gnostics who denied the humanity of Jesus.) There had also sprung up a group of charismatics, or *pneumatikoi*, who claimed to have such spiritual gifts as prophecy and speaking with tongues and who seem to have been given not only to playing at spiritual one-upmanship with each other but to looking down their noses at pretty much everybody else. One member of the congregation and his stepmother were living together as man and wife despite the fact that Roman as well as Jewish law condemned such a relationship. Others were gorging themselves and getting drunk at the Lord's Supper, which at this early point was not the ritual wafer and sip of wine that it later became but still a full meal that the whole church ate together, presumably in the house of one of its members. And so on. Things couldn't have been much worse. Paul wrote that he could not "address [them] as spiritual men, but as men of the flesh, as babes in Christ, for while there is jealousy and strife among you, are you not of the flesh and behaving like ordinary men?"

Jealousy and strife were probably the least of it. The church in Corinth, and everywhere else for that matter, was indeed ordinary men and women who, spiritually speaking, hadn't cut their first teeth yet. It was slaves, dockhands, shopkeepers, potters, housewives, bronze workers, leather workers, and what have you. They were no better than anybody else, and at least in one sense worse, because, "sanctified in Christ Jesus" as Paul believed them to be, so much more was expected of them and should have been forthcoming. They were in fact Christ's body, as Paul wrote to them here in one of his most enduring metaphors—Christ's eyes, ears, hands—but the way they were carrying on, that could only leave Christ bloodshot, ass-eared, all thumbs, to carry on God's work in a fallen world. What came forth from them was just the kind of wretched tangle they were in at the moment and, harder still for Paul to deal with, the wretchedness it gave rise to within himself. This is what First Corinthians is essentially about—Paul's sense of futility and despair at war with his exultant hope, the terrible tension between the *in spite of* and the *because of* of his restless and often anguished faith.

He fielded their questions as best he could—questions about sex and marriage, about the role of women in church, about whether or not it was proper to eat meat, which in a Gentile city like Corinth had probably all been dedicated to some godling or other, down to the last lamb chop. His answers tend to be pedagogic, avuncular, appealing more to tradition than to theology. It was better to marry than to burn, he told them, in a phrase that has echoed down the centuries. Women should be veiled in church and not speak. It couldn't matter less that the meat they ate had already been offered up to Serapis or Astarte—that was just the sort of religious pedantry that Christ had set them free from—but if by eating it they shook the faith of some Christian friend to whom it did matter, then of course they should abstain for the friend's sake. But there is no mistaking that for Paul the real question lay deeper down than any of these. "The word of the cross is folly to those who are perishing," he wrote. Was it possible that it was folly, period? It seems clear enough that in his heart of hearts that was the question that haunted him above all others.

The message that a convicted felon was the bearer of God's forgiving and transforming love was hard enough for anybody to swallow, and for some especially so. For Hellenized sophisticates—the Greeks, as Paul puts it—it could only seem absurd. What uglier, more supremely inappropriate symbol of, say, Plato's Beautiful and Good could there be than a crucified Jew? And for the devout Jew, what more scandalous image of the Davidic King-Messiah, before whose majesty all the nations were at last to come to heel? Paul understood both reactions well. "The folly of what we preach," he called it, and he knew it was folly not just to the intellectually and religiously inclined but to the garden-variety Corinthians who had no particular pretensions in either direction but simply wanted some reasonably plausible god who would stand by them when the going got rough. Paul's God didn't look much like what they were after, and Paul was the first to admit it. Who stood by Jesus when the going got rough, after all? He even goes so far as to speak of "the foolishness of God." What other way could you describe a deity who chose as his followers not the movers and shakers who could build him a temple to make Aphrodite's look like two cents but the weak, the despised, the ones who were foolish even as their God was, and poor as church mice?

To pray for your enemies, to worry about the poor when you have worries enough of your own, to start becoming yourself fully by giving of yourself prodigally to whoever needs you, to love your neighbors when an intelligent fourth-grader could tell you that the way to get ahead in the world is to beat your neighbors to the draw every chance you get—that was what this God asked, Paul wrote. That was who this God was. That was who Jesus was. Paul is passionate in his assertion, of course, that in the long run it is such worldly wisdom as the intelligent fourth-grader's that is foolish and the sublime foolishness of God that is ultimately wise, and nobody heard him better than William Shakespeare did when he wove the rich fabric of *King Lear* around precisely this paradox. It is the Fool, Edgar, Kent, Cordelia, Gloucester—the foolish, weak, despised ones—who in their fatal loyalty to the ruined king triumph, humanly speaking, over the powerful cunning of Regan, Goneril, Edmund, and the rest of them. "Upon such sacrifices, my Cordelia, the gods themselves throw incense," Lear says to Cordelia—that is their triumph—just as, before him, Paul quoted Isaiah's "What no eye has seen, nor ear heard, nor the heart of man conceived, [that is] what God has prepared for those who love him."

But Paul was as aware as Shakespeare was that when the final curtain rings down, the ones who loved this God of love end up just as dead as the ones who never gave him the time of day, and he was aware that any Corinthians shopping around for a new religion were aware of it too. So it was a matter not only of what could look more foolish than the Gospel he preached but perhaps even of what could actually *be* more foolish. Terrible as that possibility was, he did not flinch from putting it down in black and white. "If for this life only we have hoped in Christ," he wrote, "we are of all men most to be pitied."

He must have considered the possibility that, as Edmund believed, the only god worth a hoot is the god of raw Nature; that it is the fittest, not the fairest, who survive longest; and that in the long run the only law that matters is the law of the jungle. "If Christ has not been raised," he flatly said, "then our preaching is in vain and your faith is in vain. . . . If the dead are not raised, 'Let us eat and drink, for tomorrow we die.' " It is impossible to read these words without having the sense that he is speaking here not just theologically, apodictically, but personally, out of his own darkest misgivings. "We are fools for Christ's sake," he wrote, meaning fools as holy as Christ himself was holy. But if Christ ended up as dead as everybody else, then Paul knew they were also damned fools, and Christ himself had been fooled most tragically. "To the present hour we hunger and thirst, we are ill-clad and buffeted and homeless. . . . We have become, and are now, as the refuse of the world, the off-scouring of all things." That is how he described his life as apostle to the Gentiles, but it was the inner buffeting and homelessness that were the worst of it.

Paul was no beauty if the description of him in the apocryphal Acts of Paul and Thecla is to be believed. "Bald-headed, bowlegged, strongly built, a man small in size, with meeting eyebrows, with a rather large nose. His letters are strong, but his bodily presence is weak." You see those meeting eyebrows knotted, see the way he holds his bald head in his hands, his big nose lost in shadow, as he writes out of his grimness. But something extraordinary keeps him going on those bowlegs of his anyway, in spite of everything. He has himself seen Christ after the crucifixion. That is what keeps him going through thick and thin, that is what keeps him firing off his letters like rockets.

In this letter he does not describe what it was like to see him, simply states it as a fact; but it is described elsewhere, and doubtless he told them about it in Corinth when he was there . . . the light that blinded him for days afterward, the voice calling him by name. He never forgot the sheer and giddy grace of it, of Christ appearing to him of all people, professional persecutor of Christians as he was at the time; of Christ not only forgiving him but enlisting him, signing him up. Everything Paul ever did or wrote from that moment on flamed up out of that extraordinary encounter on the Damascus road. And there was something else, if anything, even more extraordinary. If death was not the end of Christ, then it was not to be the end of any of them. "For as in Adam all die, so also in Christ shall all be made alive." They were all of them *in Christ*—one of his favorite phrases—as Christ was also in all of them, and thus life, not death, was to be the last thing for them too. Nor was it to be some disembodied life, either, as the Greek dualists argued with their dim view of bodies generally, but life as themselves, wearing some marvelous new version of corporeality, not of flesh and blood any longer but of "spirit . . . imperishable . . . raised in Glory."

"Lo! I tell you a mystery." His tone becomes lyric, exultant. "We shall all be changed, in a moment, in the twinkling of an eye, at the last trumpet. . . . Thanks be to God, who gives us the victory. . . . Therefore, my beloved brethren, be steadfast, immovable, always abounding in the work of the Lord, knowing that in the Lord your labor is not in vain." The great nostrils swell.

That is the farthest and deepest his eyes have seen, farther even than the depths of the dark, the brightest thing he has to tell. Then in the next breath he is down to brass tacks again, explaining to them how the money for the Jerusalem church is to be collected, how it is to be sent there, where he plans to travel next and when. Who knows when the last trumpet will sound? In the meanwhile, for all

of them, there is much work to be done. Yet in the meanwhile too—
he has already written them of this—there is much to rejoice in this
side of the great Joy.

There is among other things the Lord's Supper, which some of the
Corinthians have been turning into a three-ring circus. He berates
them at first. The sentences are short and sharp. They have behaved
outrageously. He is outraged. "What shall I say to you?" Then abruptly the language changes and his tone with it. The words start to
come with a kind of twilight hush to them. They have an almost
dazed quality, as if he is so caught up in the scene he is describing
that he is more there than here. He hadn't actually been there, of
course; but he knew some who had been—Peter, for instance, his
old colleague and sometime adversary. Peter must have spoken of
what he remembered about the last time they had all of them eaten
together, and it is such memories as his that Paul is presumably
drawing on here, though that is not what he says. He "received [it]
of the Lord" is what he says. Who knows what he means—perhaps
that it was the significance of that last meal, the full truth of those
last words, that he received. In any case, he remembers details,
remembers that the night of his betrayal was when it happened,
remembers how the bread was taken, broken, with thanks given for
it, remembers the wine. For the first time you realize fully how few
years had gone by since it all happened. There were men and women
around still who had eaten and drunk with Jesus, if not that final
meal, who knew the sound of his voice, could have picked him out
in a crowd. Paul remembers what he said: that the bread was his
body, the wine was his blood. It was he himself they were eating
and drinking, taking his life into their lives, into them. This meal
was their proclamation of what his death had done and meant, and
for anybody to make a drunken shambles of it was to risk sickness
and death. It was their consolation and the Lord's great gift to them
till he came back again in his glory. And there were other gifts.

Not even in the Gospels is there a more familiar passage than in
the thirteenth chapter of First Corinthians. "Though I speak with
the tongues of men and of angels . . ." "When I was a child, I spake
as a child," "through a glass, darkly": words as familiar as these are
like coins worn smooth with long handling—after a while it is hard
to tell where they came from or what they are worth. Paul has been

speaking about spiritual gifts—prophecy, tongues, healing, miracles, and so on—and making the point that they should not be the cause of still further divisiveness, people gifted one way disparaging people gifted another. He sees all Christians as parts of Christ's body and each part in its own way as necessary as every other. "The eye cannot say to the hand, 'I have no need of you.' " Each gift is to be cherished. "But," he says then, "earnestly desire the higher gifts," and at that point he sets off into what turned out to be perhaps the most memorable words he ever wrote.

The highest gift of all is *agape*, he says. Without it even faith, almsgiving, martyrdom are mere busyness, and even great wisdom doesn't amount to a hill of beans. The translators of the King James Version render the Greek word as "charity," which in seventeenth-century usage was a happy choice—charity as the beneficence of the rich to the poor, the lucky to the unlucky, the powerful to the weak, the lovely to the unlovely. But since to our age the word all too often suggests a cheerless and demeaning handout, modern translators have usually rendered it as "love." But agape love is not to be confused with eros love. That is what Paul is at such pains to make clear here.

Eros love is love that reaches upward. It is love for what we need to fill our emptiness, love for what is lovely and lovable. It is Dante's love for Beatrice as well as Cleopatra's for Antony, the child's love for the parent, humankind's love for God. William Blake engraved the picture of a tiny human figure with a ladder pitched toward the moon and underneath, in block capitals, the words I WANT! I WANT! Those are the words that eros always speaks. Not so with agape. Agape does not want. It gives. It is not empty. It is full to overflowing. Paul strains to get the distinction right. Agape is patient; eros champs at the bit. Agape puts up with anything; eros insists on having things its own way. Agape is kind—never jealous, boastful, rude. It does not love *because* but simply loves—the way the rain falls or the sun shines. It "bears all things," up to and including even its own crucifixion. And it has extraordinary power.

The power of agape—otherwise quite powerless—is perhaps nowhere better seen than in the tale of Beauty and the Beast, where Beauty does not love the Beast because he is beautiful but makes him beautiful by loving him. Ultimately, in other words, agape is

God's love for humankind, and only as God's gift are humans enabled at rare moments to love that way themselves—transformingly, unconditionally, no matter what. Thus when Paul says "Love never ends," he is not being sentimental or merely rhetorical. There is no doubt that eros ends. Even in its noblest forms it ends when the desired becomes undesirable or when desire ends, or when, as between old lovers, it ripens into something milder, if cooler and calmer, with more of compassion in it and less of passion. Agape, on the other hand, is as without end as God is without end because it is of the essence of God. That is what Paul experienced on the Damascus road where he found that the One who had every cause to deplore him loved him. For as long as the moment lasted, anyway, the beetle-browed, bowlegged Christian baiter put away his own childish things and in an unutterable instant saw Truth itself not through a glass darkly for once but face to face; understood, as he put it, even as he was understood.

He himself was the first to admit that he remained in many ways as much of a mess as the rest of us—full of anguished doubts and depressions, hostilities, exaltations, hang-ups, whatever he meant by "the thorn in the flesh," which he interpreted in his second letter to Corinth as God's way of keeping him "from being too elated." The bitter and the better of him, it is all there in the words with which he closes his letter, the words that he tells us he is writing with his own hand: "If any one has no love for the Lord, let him be accursed. Our Lord, come. The grace of the Lord be with you." A malediction, a prayer, a benediction, in that order. They are all mixed up together, as God knows they were all mixed up in Paul himself. But then: "My love be with you all in Christ Jesus. Amen," so that the very last thing of all that he does is send them his love—*agape* is again the word he uses—the most precious thing he ever received, the most precious thing he ever had to give.

THE SECOND EPISTLE OF
PAUL THE APOSTLE
TO THE CORINTHIANS

—

"YE ARE OUR EPISTLE"

Alfred Corn

Bible reading was one of the themes of my childhood. Certainly we had it at church and Sunday school, but my family also had a morning Scripture reading at breakfast every day, along with a short homily from a monthly devotional publication called *The Upper Room*. In my early teens I decided to go all this one better and read *all* of Scripture. This I did, day by day, chapter by chapter, in order, in the King James Authorized Version, from Genesis through Leviticus and Numbers, Chronicles, Proverbs, Micah, the Gospels, the Epistles, and Revelation, with a doggedness and dutifulness that takes me aback now. I was very good at "sword practice" in Sunday school: contestants lined up with their black calfskin-bound Bibles in hand were all given a verse to locate. *I beseech you therefore, brethren, by the mercies of God, that ye present your bodies a living sacrifice, holy, acceptable unto God, which is your reasonable service.* "Twelfth chapter of Romans, verse one!" The first to identify and find it read out the verse and was declared the winner.

Thinking back now and trying to estimate the results for me as a writer from exposure to this subversive book and its peculiar diction, I can immediately see two. First, I became aware that there are several kinds of language and that unaccustomed ways of putting things are often the most memorable and powerful. *Consider the lilies of the field, how they grow; they toil not, neither do they spin: And yet I say unto you, That even Solomon in all his glory was not arrayed like one of these* (Matthew 6:28–29). The second lesson was that reading, engagement with texts, directed and shaped human life. The Bible's importance prepared me to see other texts as important also. The act of reading itself makes for a certain kind of mind, as we can begin to see in a time where reading is being crowded out by other media.

Jews describe themselves as "the people of the book," and so would I. The Gospel of John calls the Christ a "Word" (a *logos*, a speech, or reasoning), and in that generic sense he is also a book, "the Word of God." It is a multiple identity. That bipartite name Jesus Christ points to the truth that Jesus (or Joshua or Yeshua, a name meaning "God saves"), was an actual human being who was anointed (*Christos* in Greek means "the anointed") with another spiritual identity. I see also that there is never an incident in the gospel narratives of a formal anointing, in the old way of, say, Saul and David: "My kingdom is not of this earth." Instead, there was the baptism administered by John, presumably unnecessary for one who had nothing to repent of. But then death was also unnecessary for the Son of God; another meaning of baptism is as a prefiguration of death—and resurrection. The fleshly Jesus departed from this life; the Christ, the Logos, the divine identity comes to us through texts. And this is the Resurrection renewed. When the Nicene Creed says, "And rose again, according to the Scriptures," surely more is meant than "And rose again—at least the Bible says he would and says he did." It must also mean, "He rose, and still does by means of the Scriptures."

But not by Scriptures alone. We can encounter the flesh-and-blood actuality of the risen Christ in persons as well, exactly to the extent that they have become "words" themselves, become embodiments of text, readable, instructive, and filled with compassion—"living sacrifices." The spread of the gospel, the conversions of the early church are described in the twelfth chapter of Acts this way: "But the word of God grew and multiplied." It is in this spirit that Saint Paul can say, in 2 Corinthians 3:2–3 (Authorized Version), "Ye are our epistle written in our hearts, known and read of all men: Forasmuch as ye are manifestly declared to be the epistle of Christ ministered by us, written not with ink, but with the spirit of the living God; not in tables of stone, but in fleshy tables of the heart." This baroque metaphor, much like some of George Herbert's, is Saint Paul's strong revisionary transformation of the verses in Jeremiah 31 concerning a new covenant, where we read, "I will put my law in their inward parts, and write it in their hearts." In both Jeremiah and Paul, spiritual change is figured as a kind of writing, with the faithful as a new, incarnate text.

It follows that the circumcision that Paul urges is one of the spirit, which makes the actual fleshly operation superfluous. Paul is the noted Puritan of the New Testament, not merely in his insistence on freedom from "defilement" but also in the antisacramental direction of his arguments. If the right spiritual connections have been made, fleshly enactments of them, apart from baptism, strike him as unnecessary. And so they are, once the major premises of his theology have been accepted. Reading his letters one after another, though, can be wearying, at times offensive, so intent is he on hammering home his convictions. His devaluation of Judaism sounds anti-Semitic to modern ears. And then, far from encouraging the weakening of patriarchal structures in society, he has specific regulations for conduct directed at women only (even though he did say in Galatians, "For as many of you as have been baptized into Christ have put on Christ. There is neither Jew nor Greek, there is neither bond nor free, there is neither male nor female: for ye are all in Christ Jesus"). Nor is there any getting around the persistent bias against "the flesh" in Saint Paul. He expected the end of the world to come at any moment and thought it unwise for people to marry and beget children on the eve of destruction. As a well-trained Jew, he had no patience with sexual libertinage or Greek customs concerning physical relations between people of the same sex. Judaic sexual restraint seems to have combined in Paul with a strand of Platonic antimaterialism acquired in the Hellenized ambience of the Diaspora to produce a thoroughgoing asceticism in his temperament. Again, because he expected the approaching end of the world, he was little concerned with reforming the social order. Slaves were not to revolt against their masters, and freemen were to obey their governments, even when these were unjust. Everything would be set to rights in the next age.

For these and other reasons it has become commonplace to denigrate Saint Paul and his writings, so that, for example, George Bernard Shaw could reverberate against Paul's "monstrous imposition upon Jesus." To prefer the sayings of Jesus as recorded in the Gospels need not, however, prevent us from discovering passion, intellectual power, and literary skill in Paul. Certainly he is the most vividly realized human *character* in all the New Testament. His adult life is amply described (some details mistaken) in Acts, but, more important, we have his own account of himself in the epistles. And what a portrait emerges: of a man now supremely confident of his gifts and mission, now excruciatingly vulnerable to criticism; at a loss for words, provided with an abundance of them, even to excess; now thundering like Jove, now pleading like a lover; reproving, stroking, "building up," applying brimstone, balm, or honey as needed; and always, always serving his Lord with devotion absolute, at a personal cost frightening to consider and for very few others in human history possible to duplicate. One often hears dismissals of Jesus as being too much the Lamb, too convinced about the importance of turning the other cheek—in short, a Milquetoast (notwithstanding what he said about the smug and hypocritical of his day). Well, Paul gives us another picture of active life "in Christ." The fact that he is one of the chief saints of Christian tradition gives hope to some of us with short fuses and a propensity to judge.

Historically the church has moved in a more sacramental direction than Paulinism would seem to have urged, no doubt under the weight of considering what incarnation must actually mean. But the Protestant insistence on spirit rather than rote and unfelt ritual is indisputably valuable. Could we consider the Protestant-Catholic debate as analogous to the dialogue between soul and body—or perhaps between the rational and the irrational?

The religious solution for me has been to be confirmed in a denomination (American Episcopal) where the inherited strands of Catholicism and Protestantism both are active and in fruitful dialogue. It's sobering to reflect just how syncretistic and evolutionary Christianity is, the product of ages of religious practice in many different circumstances. It was built on the foundation of a religion that combined Middle Eastern, Egyptian, and Canaanite elements, and added to that strains from Hellenistic and Roman traditions. When it moved into northern Europe, an influence from Celtic and Druidic sources changed its flavor; and when it came to America, more emphasis came to be placed on individual conscience and on social justice. Christianity has been formed on the assumption that God speaks through history, human devotion, and the response of the church to changed conditions, to form a new body of opinion and practice concerning worship and human conduct. Contemporary Christianity is open to insights from non-Western cultures it encounters in Asia and Africa, from Native American religious practice, and from its parent religion, Judaism, most particularly as both traditions struggle to understand and discover meanings in the Holocaust.

Not all of Saint Paul's strictures concerning conduct or the invalidity of Judaism, which reflected tensions and customs of his time, need to be followed in our day. His recommendations concerning the subservience of women, the obedience of slaves, and acceptance of unjust governments have been put aside in favor of something better. It is impossible not to be impressed by the Lutheran pastor Dietrich Bonhoeffer's death in the concentration camps as a result of his struggles to overthrow Hitler's social order. The work of Roman Catholic liberation theologians has had far-reaching political consequences in Latin America. As I write this, Archbishop Desmond Tutu of Capetown is actively involved in the struggle against apartheid in South Africa. The Reverend Barbara Harris has just been consecrated a bishop of the Episcopal church. And several denominations are coming to realize their mistake concerning love between members of the same sex as more about church history becomes known (see John Boswell's *Christianity, Social Tolerance, and Homosexuality*) and the example of devotion among gay members of congregations becomes manifest. Here, no doubt, Protestantism is at work, reminding that the spirit is the point, not specific fleshly enactments.

The fact is that Christians today have not only the Bible for a guide but also church tradition, still evolving under the direction of the Holy Spirit—which often sends the church back to Scripture, or to a chapter of it different from the one up to now held in highest esteem. Does Saint Paul contradict himself? Yes, he does. He was a human being, subject to error; and he was not aware at the time he wrote Romans or Galatians or 2 Corinthians that his words would one day be part of a new canon of Scripture. Even if he had thought so, would the pressures of his circumstances—as a man who supported himself as an artisan (a tent maker) and much of whose time was spent as an active missionary often persecuted and several times imprisoned—have allowed him to produce works perfect in argument, expression, and charity?

————

Saint Paul's model for his writings was the community letter of the Jewish Diaspora, sent out from Jerusalem in order to inform the synagogues of the religious calendar for the year and keep them up to date about any changes in religious practice. Two such examples are found in 2 Maccabees 1:1–9 and 1:10–2:18, where the Jerusalem authorities urge the adoption of the new feast of the Dedication, which came as a result of the Maccabean War. Such letters typically began with a salutation, a thanksgiving, a prayer, the body of the message, and a concluding benediction. Saint Paul would have heard such letters read to the congregation in his native Tarsus, and, according to Acts 9, he was himself carrying such a letter to Damascus when he underwent his blinding vision. Some time after Paul's conversion, the Christian apostolic council in Jerusalem sent a letter (see Acts 15) to the churches in Asia Minor with instructions concerning religious faith and practice. It must have seemed natural to Saint Paul, then, after the founding of his churches in Greece, to continue to guide them by epistles when he was not present.

Coming from Macedonia, Paul made his first visit to Corinth late in 50 C.E., gathering a few converts around him and instituting the little "assembly" (*ekklesia*) active in the homes of its members when he left in the summer of 51. One of the most moving chapters in church history is this earliest form of communal worship, the faithful crowded into the houses of one of their members, the flickering light from an oil lamp set in a wall niche playing over the sun-browned Jewish, Greek, and Mediterranean faces intent on the prayers being pronounced; and then the setting out of the love feast that became the prototype of the Mass.

It was in Corinth that Paul wrote his first surviving epistle, now called 1 Thessalonians, the earliest text of the New Testament. These early epistles and most of his other attested writings were spiritual but also personal, and subject to personal vicissitudes. The composition is not consistently methodical. Organization is more spontaneous than constructed, rhetorical rather than logical, metaphoric rather than expository. Hebrew Scripture was a frequent resource, but of course no other writings of what we now call the New Testament were available to him. (One of the motives for recording the Gospel narratives must have been as a corrective to the authority of the Pauline letters that began to be circulated among the churches.)

Saint Paul had no body of doctrine to build on; he is the first Christian theologian, and it is clear that he is often at sea in trying to formulate coherent interpretations of Jesus' proclamation. The great Pauline contradiction is between Law and Freedom, which he could not resolve because, within Christian thought, it cannot be resolved in final terms: the debate concerning what we must do, what we may do, and what we may be forgiven for has never been settled and probably never will be. As suggested before, the Christian spirit is evolutionary, revisionist. All questions are examined first in the framework of law inherited from Judaism and then held up to the light of Jesus' teachings to form new guides for action. Evolutionary Christianity sees it not as religion but only idolatry that would require animal sacrifice or maim human lives by insisting on present conformity to metaphors and rigidities appropriate to earlier historical periods. Yet Saint Paul knew that it was equally meaningless to prate of grace and forgiveness where there is no discoverable intention to abandon malice, cynicism, greed, oppression, and violence. If not now, when? as Rabbi Hillel said. (Evolution in Judaism has been less dramatic, but definite, especially after the destruction of the Temple and the introduction of Talmudic practice. It's common to hear Reform Judaism depreciated, but its precedents and principles are sound. On the opposite side, when one hears of ultraorthodox proposals in Israel to tear down the mosques on the Temple Mount, rebuild the Temple, and reinstitute the old cult practice, the sense of impending tragedy is enormous. I share the consternation of those Israelis who see such a plan as a great wrong. The destruction of one temple does not justify the destruction of another, particularly given that the surviving foundation wall of the old Temple has become a place of universal spiritual meaning. To discard post-Yavneh Judaism tends to dishonor nearly two thousand years of Jewish ancestors, by suggesting that their worship was defective, a view that, considering the record of faithfulness and achievement, cannot be valid.)

———

A letter to the Corinthians obviously has to be written from somewhere else. After Paul left Corinth in the autumn of 51, he wrote a letter to the Corinthian church (as he says in 1 Corinthians 5:9), but this has been lost. The letter now called 1 Corinthians (written from Ephesus, probably in the autumn of 54) is his second to the Corinthian congregation. Paul made another journey to Corinth, most likely in the spring of 55. After that visit, he wrote a third letter, now lost, referred to in 2 Corinthians 2:3–4 as "the tearful letter," apparently a very personal and anguished response to news of strife and faithlessness in the Corinthian church. 2 Corinthians, written from Macedonia, probably in the late summer of 55, after a period of extreme hardship in Asia, is then actually his fourth letter to the church at Corinth of which any trace survives.

Attestation for this letter is not as strong as for 1 Corinthians. We have no record that it was circulated in the first century C.E.; in fact, its first mention comes up not before circa 145, as part of Marcion's canon of Pauline writings, and only as that canon is represented in Tertullian's *Against Marcion*. Beginning in the eighteenth century there has been a lively tradition of debate about the integrity of the letter itself. Many scholars propose that chapters 1 through 9 are part of one letter, and chapters 10 through 13 part of another, the two fragments joined together by a later editor and presented as a single, unitary epistle. If so, these later chapters would be drawn from yet a fifth letter to the Corinthians. According to this theory, the fifth letter would have been written from Thessalonica or Berea in the summer of 56, shortly before Paul's third projected visit to Corinth, referred to in chapter 13 of 2 Corinthians as it now stands. On the other hand, other scholars have argued that 2 Corinthians is a single letter, perhaps composed in two parts, after an interval of a day, a week, or longer. Both views are defensible and have been defended. The nonscholarly reader, without deciding the issue, can still note that there is a difference in tone and content between the two parts—and also accept the scholars' assertion that the passage running from 6:14 to 7:1 is almost certainly a later interpolation, since it interrupts Paul's argument and is written in a style different from his.

Both parts of 2 Corinthians are concerned with the spiritual well-being of the community and with the upcoming collection to be made for the church in Jerusalem. The intensity Paul brings to the issue of this collection might seem surprising, given that he himself asks no support from the church. In his letters he more than once reminds readers that he is a self-supporting artisan, a tent maker (which gives special poignance to his metaphors concerning the "earthly tent" where we dwell, in the opening passage of 2 Corinthians 5). We can theorize that the collection for the Jerusalem church was important to him not only because he saw the elders there as being in need of support but also because he wanted to bring quantifiable proof to them of the success of his ministry. The Jerusalem church was the conservative wing, worshiping in the Temple, upholding the Law, skeptical of Gentile converts, and dubious about Paul, who after all had never seen or known Jesus during Jesus' earthly ministry. Throughout all the early letters there is a strenuous effort at self-authentication. By force of argument, by force of personal history, almost by sheer will, he intends to convince his hearers that he is a true apostle, called of the Lord, and possessed of right doctrine. It sometimes makes for painful reading, so that one plausible theory for the "thorn in the side" Paul mentions without identifying is precisely this question of the doubt cast on his right to be counted as an apostle.

Any speaker trying to establish personal legitimacy has to face the problem of listeners' will to contradiction. Numbering one's achievements invites disparagement. Paul knows this, and from the eleventh chapter of 2 Corinthians forward, he dances around the problem with the help of a rhetorical strategy: "I speak as a fool," he says. Foolishness here (Greek, *aphrosyne*) has to do with the "boasting" Paul is forced to do in order to establish apostolic credentials. The contrasting term would be *sophrosyne*, "moderation" or "modesty," a cast of mind much more appropriate for one who understands all his merit to be a gift of grace. I don't think it is merely the wish to convince his hearers that makes Paul reluctant to boast. He sees the sin of pride in boasting and would prefer to avoid it. But the welfare of the fledgling Corinthian church is at stake, and "boast" Paul must in order to convince his hearers that he is the equal of the "chief apostles," almost certainly meaning Peter, James, and John, whose knowledge of Jesus was firsthand. So we have the famous speech about the tribulations Paul has suffered, demonstrably harsher than others':

> Are they ministers of Christ? In my madness I say it: I am, more than they. With more labors, more imprisonments, many more beatings, often near the point of death; five times I took the thirty-nine lashes from the Jews, three times I was beaten with rods, once stoned, three times shipwrecked, and spent a day and night in the water; often on the road, with danger from rivers, danger from brigands, danger from my own people, danger from foreigners, danger in the city, danger in the wilds, danger at sea, danger among false brothers; with toil and hardship, often sleepless, in hunger and thirst, often famished, cold, and naked. Aside from externals, there was the day-by-day pressure on me, my anxious concern for all the churches.

> [2 Corinthians 11:23–28, *translated by Richmond Lattimore*]

Boasting or not, this passage rings true, and to most of us the truth will excuse the immodesty. Moderation is a virtue, but a pale one next to the kind of dedication, passion, and endurance outlined here, which shames me and probably shamed the Corinthians. Of course Paul has already made the point, in the first chapter of 2 Corinthians, that sufferings do more than simply establish credentials—they increase our ability to comfort others who suffer:

> Praised be the God and Father of our Lord Jesus Christ, the father of all mercies and the God of all consolation, who comforts us in every affliction of ours, so that we are able to comfort those who are in every affliction through the consolation we ourselves have received from God. For as the sufferings of Christ abound for us, so through the Christ our consolation abounds. If we are afflicted, it is for your comfort and salvation; if we are

comforted, it is for your comfort, which works in endurance of those same sufferings which we also undergo; and our hope in you is firm, since we know that as you are sharers in our sufferings, so also are you sharers in our consolation.

[2 Corinthians 1:3–7, *translated by Richmond Lattimore*]

The Greek words translated here as "comfort" or "consolation" are *paraklesis* (noun) and *parakalein* (verb), from which comes the name Paraclete—the Comforter, or Holy Spirit. The sense, however, is stronger than the softly quilted connotations the word "comfort" has taken on in modern English; it actually meant "to call for support," "to strengthen," "to encourage." Paul's assertion is that his personal sufferings always act to summon the Holy Spirit, who strengthens and encourages him, first for his own trials, and then, having become a permanent resource, is available through him as a resource for others who suffer and whom he will strengthen.

————

Apart from face-to-face encounter or the intermediary of texts, there is another, rarer way that life in the spirit may come to people: a personal experience of revelation, the tearing away of the veil separating the human from the divine. This is what happened to Saint Paul on the road to Damascus, and his private apocalypse became his chief credential for apostleship. The problem with private visions is of course that they are private; the visionary's word is the only warrant of authenticity, and we know that anyone discussing visions is usually considered a liar or a fool. When Saint Paul comes to the question of his vision, he again resorts to the rhetorical strategy of claiming to be doing some foolish boasting and, what's more, refers to himself in the third person:

I must go on boasting and speak of visions and revelations of the Lord. I know a man in Christ who, fourteen years ago, whether he was in or outside his body I cannot say, only God can say—a man who was snatched up to the third heaven. I know that this man—whether in or outside his body I do not know,

God knows—was snatched up to Paradise to hear words which cannot be uttered, words which no man may speak. About this man I will boast; but I will do no boasting about myself unless it be about my weakness. And even if I were to boast it would not be folly in me because I would only be telling the truth.

[2 Corinthians 12:1–6, *New American Bible*]

Early cosmologies are numerous and conflicting, but in one of them the third heaven was the highest, the realm where Paradise was located, as Paul's next parallel sentence suggests. The tradition of a heavenly journey was a common feature of Jewish apocalyptic literature before Paul and after. A well-known later instance was the story of Rabbi Akiba's otherworldly voyage to Paradise. In Islam there is Muhammad's legendary night journey, which left the earth from the Temple Mount in Jerusalem. The question of being outside the body (Greek, *ekstasis*) or in it is left undecided by Saint Paul. In Hebrew tradition, these journeys were taken physically; in analogous Greek accounts, bodiless rapture was the mode of transcendence, as in the myth of Er in book 10 of Plato's *Republic*.

Paul's experience on the road to Damascus, then, belongs to a widespread visionary tradition, at least as presented in 2 Corinthians. In conveying the content of that experience he must reckon with the same problems that have faced other visionaries who attempt to leave some sort of record as to what happened to them. The problem of being thought of as a fool he counters by conceding that he is speaking foolishly. The problem of veracity he handles by referring to himself in the third person, in an effort to assume an objective stance. The problem of the ineffability of mystic experience he cancels simply by saying that the "words" he heard in the third heaven are secret, not permissible to repeat.

Readers could wish that Saint Paul had been less circumspect here. Granted that mystical and visionary writing can never expect as much assent as worldly, factual reportage, still it has been a fairly constant theme in the West as well as the East throughout recorded history. Apart from glimpses in the life of Saint Paul, the New Testament has the startling example of the book of Revelation; and I have already mentioned Akiba's story as an instance in rabbinic literature.

Among medieval Christian mystics one of the most striking is Hildegard of Bingen, whose writings Dante may have known. His *Commedia* is no doubt the single greatest visionary work in Western literature, but the writings of Dame Julian of Norwich, Saint John of the Cross, and Saint Teresa of Avila are also landmarks in the mystic tradition, followed in later centuries by Jakob Boehme, Sor Juana, Thomas Traherne, Emanuel Swedenborg, and William Blake. With the advent of Romanticism, visionary writing takes on a less legendary and more introspective character, but it has continued from Wordsworth, Shelley, and Victor Hugo even up to the present, in both poetry and prose. It's fair to say that visions are a permanent human potential, and I recently read of a survey in which a surprisingly high percentage of interviewees acknowledged that they had undergone experiences that might be termed "visionary." Some of these may have been drug-induced, a commonplace in modern society since the late 1950s, but not all.

The "Vision of Dame Kind" that W. H. Auden reports as having experienced one evening in the early 1930s was not drug-induced but altogether "natural" and apparently beneficent. I've often wondered if it was at all like the one that I myself was subject to about eight years ago. I had just emerged safe from a situation that I rightly felt to be a close brush with death. It was a sunny midday in early spring. I was taking a walk in the Grove Street cemetery in New Haven, a self-described atheist out enjoying the first pink-and-white blossoms on the cherry trees. I sat down on one of the flat tombstones, squinting in the sunlight as I placed a tape cassette of Bach keyboard music into a portable player. A four-voiced fugue began playing, brilliant strands of harpsichord counterpoint interweaving into a golden sonic tapestry superimposed over the grass and trees and sunlight I was seeing. And suddenly I knew with complete certainty that the world and everything in it was a Creation, so complex as by contrast to simplify the Bach fugue into a child's bare, unaccompanied nursery song; but that Bach, too, had had a similar intuition and did the best he could, by heaping harmonic complexity on melodic intricacy and formal *rightness* to convey, however incompletely, some notion of the universal order and its greatness. I felt the sun and earth revolve around each other, the irresistible tug of grass, tree, and creature toward light and heat, the interweaving of earth, breezes, sky, and *something else* in perfected counterpoint, and myself at the heart of things simply allowing these sensations and intimations to play through me. The ground beneath, holding the bones of those who died in earlier centuries, the invisible action of earthworms, roots, and moles, was like a flowing river, as flexible as the breezes, as permeable as the sky, the bass notes of the immense opus that God—yes, I was forced to see—had made. The sun sent brilliant iridescent shards of light through my eyelashes as I squinted and squinted, trying both to normalize and to accept the moment as it happened. This was an "in the body" experience, but it was also a period of *ekstasis*, or ecstasy, which I cannot—I speak as a fool—convey completely. Nor was it the last of its kind. The others have been less abstract, steadily more human; but I think I will resist including those here, as I tend to resist them in my life; they interfere with getting the task done.

———

To return to the question of whether 2 Corinthians is two letters or one, it occurs to me that if it is two letter fragments joined by a later editor, that editor, with enormous Hellenistic subtlety, saw a potential unity in the two parts and composed them into one. A much-discussed passage in the third chapter concerning veiling and revelation will help explain what I mean: "Whenever anyone turns to the Lord the veil is removed. Now the Lord is the Spirit, and where the Spirit of the Lord is, is freedom. And we all, with unveiled face, beholding as in a mirror the splendor of the Lord, are being transformed into the same image, from splendor to splendor, as from the Lord, the Spirit" (2 Corinthians 3:16–18, translated by Victor Paul Furnish, in *The Anchor Bible*). This last phrase has the force of "by the Lord who is the Spirit," *apo Kyriou Pneumatos*, in Greek. Here, as in the conclusion of chapter 13 in 1 Corinthians (the "through a glass, darkly" passage), we have Paul's sense of a deepening and clarifying vision of divinity. In the verses here, increased understanding also takes the form of personal transformation: the faithful, by steady contemplation of "the splendor of the Lord," come to share in that splendor.

A rich complex of themes revolves around Paul's concept here.

First, there is the Genesis assertion that God created human beings in God's own image; we are "image and dust," as the Jewish sage Abraham Joshua Heschel puts it. Second, there is the idea that Jesus, as the Son of God and very God, was God's clearest icon on earth. Paul was probably aware also that a number of Hellenistic mystery cults had their initiates gaze at an icon of the god whose power was sought in order to effect a personal transformation. As a well-instructed Jew, he had no dealings with idols or graven images, however; nor had he ever seen the Jesus that the chief apostles knew. The gazing he recommends is a spiritual one, "beholding as in a mirror" not an icon but "the Lord, the Spirit." This beholding is progressive, leading "from splendor to splendor," the final goal a complete congruence between the beholders and their Lord.

He does not state it in so many words (in order to avoid boasting), but it is clear from the context, and from other writings of Paul (particularly in Philippians 3:17, where he recommends to his adherents, "Be imitators of me"), that the immediate image of the Lord being offered to the Corinthians is Paul's very own. No, not his own, but the image of the Lord *in* him, acquired first from his Damascene vision, then from association with the other faithful, then from his personal sufferings, not excluding the "thorn in the side," and from a steady communion with the Lord who is the Spirit, who has come to him to "comfort" and strengthen him in his trials. Many Christians can attest to the fact that one of the earliest and strongest intimations of the identity of the Christ came to them by seeing it in the face of someone else. In fact, I have often thought that the importance of the apostolic succession in Catholic churches has much less to do with the laying on of hands than with the unbroken linkage of a certain gaze, a sort of visual Eucharist that has been handed down from senior to junior communicants for nearly two thousand years. Qualities of soul and love, for those who have eyesight, enter into us at the gates of the eyes.

There is also Paul's moving discovery, suggested by the use of the phrase "beholding as in a mirror," that the process of patterning is reciprocal. As the divine "image" becomes more and more perceptible in the gaze of his followers, Paul becomes more and more assured that it has been present in him to begin with and is now being passed on to his flock. Throughout 2 Corinthians Paul seeks for proofs of grace, the evidence for a living Christ. Hence the emphasis on a deepening and clarifying divine image, with the quantifiable evidence of the collection for the Jerusalem church, with the catalogue of hardships he has endured, and with the "comfort" (*paraklesis*, or strengthening) that arrives to help the faithful not be overwhelmed with suffering. We can be reminded of Rudolf Karl Bultmann's assertion that the cross and the Resurrection are inseparable: belief in the redemptive efficacy of the cross amounts to belief in the Resurrection, whether or not the Resurrection occurred as an event in history. "Resurrection" for the Christian means resurrection to bear a new cross; and *paraklesis* comes to Christians often as not through the gaze, the *text* of another believer, which is resurrection also.

The first nine chapters of 2 Corinthians are written mostly in the first person plural. Suddenly chapter 10 begins with "I Paul," a series of passages noted for being the most intimate writings of Paul to have survived, and including brief accounts of his vision and his tribulations. Don't we see in the first nine chapters a more general, more Christlike identity, indicated not only by the first person plural but by the scarcity of autobiographical reference, and a more general kind of exhortation? With chapter 10, however, the book suddenly becomes palpably personal, *incarnate*, and it is "I Paul" speaking. This new tone and content might have continued to the end; certainly the two-letter hypothesis would be stronger if it had. And yet by the beginning of the thirteenth chapter a transformation has been worked. When Paul talks of his upcoming visit, he becomes an abstract judge again; indeed, the projected visit takes on the aura of a sort of rehearsal for the Last Judgment, with Paul as the representative of Christ:

> This is the third time I shall be coming to you. "A judicial fact shall be established only on the testimony of two or three witnesses." I said before when I was there the second time—and I repeat it now in my absence—to those who sinned before and to all the rest, that if I come again I shall not spare you. You are, after all, looking for a proof of the Christ who speaks in me. He is not weak in dealing with you, but is powerful in you. It is true he was crucified out of weakness, but he lives by the

power of God. We too are weak in him, but we live with him by God's power in us. Test yourselves to see whether you are living in faith; examine yourselves. Perhaps you yourselves do not realize that Christ Jesus is in you—unless, of course, you have failed the challenge. I hope you will understand that we have not failed. We pray God that you may do no evil—not in order that we may be approved but simply that you may do what is good, even though we may seem to have failed. We cannot do anything against the truth, but only for the sake of the truth. We even rejoice when we are weak and you are strong. Our prayer is that you may be built up to completion.

[2 Corinthians 13:1–9, *New American Bible*]

The mixture of third person and first person singular and plural tells us that Saint Paul is speaking in more than *propria persona* alone. As an emblem or icon of Christ he will come to Corinth and remind the congregation of the Christ who is already in them, a Christ who will judge whatever part of them that is not Christ. This is inseparable from the process that will have them "built up to completion," from splendor to splendor, as they clarify their reflection of the divine image. Paul has just demonstrated by the text of his letter how this gradual transpersonalization is to take place. If a text can become incarnate, it can also record a process of transformation into spirit once again, "a living sacrifice." In fact, the medium of the letter is a wonderfully apt metaphor for the way the Christ communicates with his followers of these latter days. Like Paul, he is physically absent from them. He comes to them in spirit, by written texts, through the Eucharist, through persons who embody his Word. One reason why Paul is valuable for us is that his situation is closer to ours than Peter's, James's, or John's was. No more than Paul did we see the historical Jesus. We have to rely on the methods Paul outlines in order to be in communication with the divine image. And we have to communicate it to each other, for comfort and strength. "For I long to see you, that I may impart unto you some spiritual gift, to the end that ye may be established; That is, that I may be comforted together with you by the mutual faith both of you and me" (Romans 1:11–12, *Authorized Version*).

When Paul arrives for the third time, he will embody that Word, bestirring the congregation to feel it weakly or strongly incarnate within themselves and so discover whether they are divided or whole. As Paul looks at them, both he and they, in this lull after so many sufferings, will see the Word reflected. He will himself be their strengthening epistle; and they will be his.

THE EPISTLE OF
PAUL THE APOSTLE
TO THE GALATIANS

—

Anthony Hecht

I

In the first chapter of *The Structure of Complex Words*, William Empson sets out some of the ground rules he means to observe and some of the problems he intends to face. Among these problems is one he calls "Range," which concerns the breadth of meaning a word may afford, and the overlaps from vaguely synonymous words.

> One can . . . drag the idea of Range into the puzzle about "thrifty" and "miserly"; it is clear that the behavior thought proper for a farm labourer might be given a different name when adopted by the squire. But it would only be useful to put this into the definition if you were dealing with a simple and clear-cut society. And then again, there might be much odder uses of the Range idea about misers. Some people think they can recognise misers by their manner or their smell or something, so that any sign of thriftiness in one of these men will be called Miserly.

Empson was an unusually liberal as well as liberated man, without, so far as I know, the least taint of racial prejudice or bigotry about him. But this passage of his contains an enthymeme, or a suppressed premise, of which he may himself have been unaware, so much is it a part of received, or folk, tradition of, alas, great antiquity. No mention is made in this passage (or in the surrounding context) of Jews; but Jews were commonly associated with miserliness (most critics mistakenly call Shylock a miser, though there is no evidence for this in the play), and from the Jew to the medieval *foetor Judaicus* (Jewish stench) is the corollary association putatively explaining why misers might be recognized by their "smell or something." Luther makes casual mention of this even in the period around 1523, when he was best disposed towards the Jews and acknowledged that Jesus Christ was born as one. He remarks:

I would advise and beg everybody to deal kindly with the Jews and to instruct them in the Scriptures; in such a case we could expect them to come over to us. If, however, we use brute force and slander them, saying that they need the blood of Christians to get rid of their stench* and I know not what other nonsense of that kind, and treat them like dogs, what good can we expect from them?

Brutality, be it noted, is rejected on purely pragmatic grounds; and by 1543 Luther had grown far less charitable as regards the Jews, urging that their homes and synagogues be set on fire, that they be deprived of their prayer books and the Talmud, that rabbis be prohibited under threat of death from teaching, that passports and traveling privileges of all Jews be abrogated, their rights to lend money rescinded, and concluding, "Let us apply the same cleverness as other nations," namely expulsion.

All this bears upon St. Paul's Epistle to the Galatians first because Luther, starting at the age of thirty, delivered a great trilogy of lectures on the Psalms, Romans, and Galatians between 1513 and 1516. More important, shortly after the birth in 1526 of his son Hans, "Luther again developed severe anxiety, this time protracted and bordering on deep melancholia," as Erik Erikson reports. In this

*The topic is also dealt with by Sir Thomas Browne in *Pseudodoxia epidemica.*

condition his "conscience" expressed itself as an inner voice that mocked him.

> "You alone know everything? But what if you were wrong, and if you should lead all these people into error and into eternal damnation?" [jeered the voice]. . . . He was able to overcome this voice sometimes [Erikson says] only by a kind of cosmic grandiosity putting his teaching above the judgment of even the angels on the ground that, since he so deeply knew it was right, it must be God's teaching and not his own. In his own support he quoted Galatians 1:8—"But though we, or an angel from heaven, preach any other gospel unto you, let him be accursed."

One of the problems of Paul's Epistles, especially of Romans and Galatians, is the curious authority they seem to furnish for the Reformation—curious because while the Christian church had dealt with many varieties of heresy in the course of its history, a very long time had to elapse before this seemingly irreconcilable split began to show itself. Galatians, a text not easily accessible, is, if anything, made more obscure in the King James Version. For example, as regards 2:6–10, Raymond Stamm says of Paul's original formulation:

> This sentence of ninety-five Greek words, strung together with relative pronouns and tumbling participles, is typical of Paul's headlong style. What he started to say was that James and Peter and John had found nothing lacking in his conception of the gospel and recognized the equality of his apostleship by shaking hands with him. But having dictated the first six words, he interrupted with a reminder that God plays no favorites; then after a fresh start he broke the sentence again to give the reason why these pillar apostles recognized him; and finally he wrote an appendix to it to give the details of the agreement to divide the mission field [James, Peter, and John to be apostles to the Jews, "the circumcised," and Paul to the Gentiles, "the uncircumcised"] and remember the poor.

This "stylistic" observation could be extended to other parts of the epistle, which presents many puzzles as regards its tone, which, according to one commentator, is by turns "haughty, aggressive, defensive, abusive, sarcastic and self-justifying." But leaving aside such personal and idiosyncratic matters for the moment, the account above offers no comment on the possibility that the meeting between Paul and the pillar apostles may be the one mentioned in Acts 15, or that Acts 15 presents a large assortment of problems that may in turn reverberate in Galatians. The council at Jerusalem described in Acts concerns a controversy about how much, if any, of the Mosaic Law was to be enjoined upon Gentile converts to the new faith. Since for the Jews circumcision was a religious essential, could it be dispensed with? And if the answer was yes, did it follow that the entire Mosaic Law could likewise be set aside? Acts 15 in fact begins, "And certain men which came down from Judea taught the brethren, and said, Except ye be circumcised after the manner of Moses, ye cannot be saved." This appears flatly to contradict Galatians 5:2–4, which declares, "Behold, I Paul say unto you, that if ye be circumcised, Christ shall profit you nothing. For I testify again to every man that is circumcised, that he is a debtor to do the whole law. Christ is become of no effect unto you, whosoever of you are justified by the law; ye are fallen from grace." Peter speaks first at the council, declaring the universal embrace of Christian salvation, extending it to Gentiles as well as Jews. James speaks next, and seems to offer a kind of regulatory compromise: "Wherefore my sentence is, that we trouble not them, which from among the Gentiles are turned to God: But that we write unto them, that they abstain from pollutions of idols, and from fornication, and from things strangled, and from blood" (Acts 15:19–20). This looks very much like a selective list of items of the Law that must continue to be observed even by Gentile converts, and it brings up, awkwardly and pertinently, the whole complex and insoluble problem involved in any attempt, Jewish or Christian, to codify and make doctrinal the expression and experience of the love of God, the "minimal requirements" for salvation, and the grounds for orthodoxy and religious authority. The chapter of Acts ends on a very divisive and disturbing note. "And the contention was so sharp between them [Paul and Barnabas, who was to accompany Paul on his mission to the Gentiles], that they departed asunder one from the other" (16:39). There is a lot of speculation about what brought on this dissension, and one view is that Paul's position regarding the liberty from Mosaic Law that was conferred by the crucifixion of Jesus differed profoundly from Peter's attitude, and that Barnabas, caught in the middle, or else largely disposed to agree with Peter, was summarily dismissed by Paul. If this were the case, it would simply confirm the view of his irascible personality that his epistles evidence.

As contrasted with "the Twelve," who were "called" by Jesus in his lifetime, Paul, a Hellenized Jew, first became a fanatical Pharisee, during which time he energetically persecuted Christians, and then, after a strange and much-debated *vision* on the road to Damascus, became not only a convert to the Christian faith but one who came to regard himself as divinely appointed by Christ to be the apostle to the Gentiles. He is evidently touchy about the validation of his claim to apostleship, and vigorous in asserting it. That claim is based, of course, on his private and unverifiable *vision*, and this is entirely consistent with his insistence on the doctrine of justification (i.e., acquittal from sin) by faith alone. Joseph Klausner, whose views I generally share, writes thus of the man:

> Paul fought all his life against the idea of his "inferiority," if it is possible to speak thus, as an apostle. The disciples and brethren of Jesus who were intimate with the crucified Messiah during his lifetime and had received instructions, parables, and promises from his own lips, would reproach Paul in this effect: You are not a true apostle, and in vain do you on your own authority set aside the ceremonial laws; for you did not attend the Messiah, you were not intimate with him, and you cannot know his teaching firsthand. To this Paul would reply, that the important thing is not corporeal knowledge ("after the flesh") but spiritual knowledge—the revelation by vision whereby Jesus revealed himself to him. The *heavenly* Jesus is more significant than the *earthly* Jesus. For the earthly Jesus is important only because of his sufferings and death, which were propitiatory sufferings and a ransoming death. [Joseph Klausner, *From Jesus to Paul*, p. 314]

What Paul does, quite brilliantly, by this kind of rebuttal is at once to turn what appears to be his initial disadvantage in never having known Jesus of Nazareth during his lifetime to a distinction denied the other apostles, and at the same time to adopt the position most likely to appeal not only to those of his contemporaries who likewise had never met Jesus but, by implication, to all posterity as well—an immeasurable advantage in terms of plain numbers. In fact, he makes his own inward experience the equivalent of Peter's recognition (in Matthew 16:13–18) of Jesus' messiahship at the moment of the Transfiguration, thereby effectually silencing any opposition. He even has the temerity publicly to rebuke Peter (Galatians 2) for hypocrisy in his fear of offending those Jewish converts who believed that Gentiles must accept the Jewish Law, including circumcision, before achieving salvation through Christ. If the doctrine of justification by faith alone, so central to Galatians, gave solace and ammunition to Luther in his revolt from Catholic orthodoxy, the doctrine of predestination, based on God's election of Jacob over Esau, is strongly implied in Romans 9:6–13. So the grounds for doctrinal rebellion seem to have been sown by a man Klausner characterizes this way: "Saul-Paul was lacking in humility, and boastfully condescending. But he knew his shortcomings, fought against them, and sometimes conquered them." In view of Paul's arrogance, are we to notice any connection between 2:6 and 6:3 of Galatians, which appear to be another slur aimed at Peter, though without naming him?

So curious is the personality exhibited by Paul that it invites us to puzzle over even his most famous pronouncements. His vituperations are almost as celebrated as his benedictions: in Galatians 1:8–9 he offers curses against any deviation from his theology, and in 1 Corinthians 16:22 he declares, "If any man love not the Lord Jesus Christ, let him be Anathema Maranatha," the final term being equivalent to "perdition at the coming of Christ the Lord." It is a tone of voice I recognize from news accounts of the desecraters of graveyards, synagogues, and even of churches; it is the tone of the fanatic. Yet perhaps of all Paul's utterances none is more ringing that 1 Corinthians 13:1: "Though I speak with the tongues of men and of angels, and have not charity, I am become as sounding brass, or a tinkling cymbal." Many a heart has melted at this thought, and cherished Paul for that exaltation of loving kindness, which is what we have taken the verse to intend. But we must remember that Paul was a celebrated evangelist and preacher, and this verse sounds very much like ostentatious self-abasement, as if the golden-tongued hierophant were saying, "Not by my skills or merit am I made persuasive, but by the grace of God," and we are expected to be struck by this exemplary modesty. Doubtless we would be more struck by it if it were not so frequently in abeyance. Again, in Galatians 5:6, which puts observers of the Jewish Law and nonobserving Gentiles on an equal footing, Paul declares, "For in Jesus Christ neither circumcision availeth any thing, nor uncircumcision; but faith which worketh by love." And who could find fault with so admirable an impulse, save those for whom orthodoxy and authority were themselves matters of reverence? Is not *love*, after all, the generous solution in which all factions dissolve? Yet it doesn't need much reflection to see how easily love in its finer throes can become zeal, and zeal in its fiercest devotion can become fanaticism, and demand persecution.

It has been the troubling and virtually impossible task of many sects, Jewish and Christian, to furnish a codification of love, and a doctrine to define it. There is no more mistaken and self-serving Christian commonplace than the one that makes the New Testament the gospel of love and the Old Testament the book of law, a distinction almost universally maintained, in bland contradiction to Mark 12:28–31:

> And one of the scribes came, and having heard them reasoning together ["certain of the Pharisees and of the Herodians" had been attempting "to catch Jesus in his words"], and perceiving that he had answered them well, asked him, Which is the first commandment of all?
>
> And Jesus answered him, The first of all the commandments is, Hear, O Israel; The Lord our God is one Lord:
>
> And thou shalt love the Lord thy God with all thy heart, and with all thy soul, and with all thy mind, and with all thy strength: this is the first commandment.
>
> And the second is like, namely this, Thou shalt love thy neighbour as thyself. There is none other commandment greater than these.

In these verses Jesus is quoting Leviticus, though this point seems always to be forgotten or suppressed; but the arrogation to the New Testament of the primacy of love is a curious act of piracy.

A good deal of puzzling has gone into the question of just what it means to love one's neighbor. In *The Genesis of Secrecy* Frank Kermode has presented a set of illuminating and irreconcilable interpretations of the parable of the Good Samaritan, some of which are eschatological (Saint Augustine's, for example) and have nothing to do with the normal ethics of human behavior. Some have wondered long and thoughtfully about just who one's neighbor actually *is*, a problem complicated by translation: " 'Thou shalt love thy fellow as thyself' . . . is expressly stated to include the non-Israelite stranger," writes Rabbi Isidore Epstein, in commentary on Leviticus, and adds, "This is the precise meaning of the Hebrew term *rea*; the usual rendering 'neighbor' is misleading."

If "neighbor" has led to puzzles, "love" has led to disagreement, bewilderment, rancor, and violence. Most commonly it has been Christians who have set up the opposition between Law and Love, an opposition of the most unsound and perilous kind. It may in fact be that the Pharisees of the sixties were the hard-line hawks who maintained that since America was at war, even an undeclared war, and conscription was in effect, no citizen had the right to resist military service on the grounds of personal moral repugnance, because this was simply choosing which laws one cared to observe and which ones to flout. And the law is not to be subject to the caprices of personal taste. Any tendency to rely on one's instincts, on the dim standards of solipsism, on the evasions of the private psyche, the warp of individual feelings, leaves us hopelessly adrift, and not merely in secular matters. "Certainly, anyone who is wholly sincere and pure in heart may seek for guidance from the Holy Spirit," writes T. S. Eliot in *Thoughts After Lambeth*, "but who of us is always wholly sincere, especially where the most imperative of instincts may be strong enough to simulate to perfection the voice of the Holy Spirit?" Such thoughtful scruples seem not to have troubled Paul. Eliot was concerned here with the question of whether communicants of the Church of England should be required to consult ecclesiastical opinion and advice regarding birth control at all times or only when they are "perplexed." This may to some seem a minuscule or trifling consideration, but for sound reasons *de minimis non curat lex* does not apply to matters of reverence.

It is not always easy or possible, and arguably not desirable, to distinguish between laws that are purely ceremonial and others that are purely ethical. The love of God may be expressed, among other ways, ceremonially; and the love of one's fellow human being is shown, in what Jesus declares to be a part of the First Commandment, to be itself an expression of the love of God. "The meat of animals killed by strangling," writes G. G. C. MacGregor, "considered a delicacy in pagan society, would contain blood which, in accordance with the principle that 'the life is in the blood,' was strictly prohibited to the Jews (cf. Gen. 9:5; Lev. 3:17; Deut. 12:16, 23–25)." This is not merely a ceremonial consideration, since it reflects upon the sanctity of life itself. And Rabbi Epstein reminds that according to the Talmud "it is . . . sinful to give someone an address without being sure that it is the correct one. It is likewise sinful to go into a shop and ask the price of an article when there is no intention of buying it." These adumbrations of the Law might seem fussy in their detail and in the slenderness of their moral import; but in fact they are based upon the importance of respect for human feelings, and are therefore regarded by pious Jews as graver than a wrong caused to fellow men in respect to material values.

The retreat to private instincts of morality need not have any bearing upon either reverence for God or even a real respect for fellow human beings, and can end at best with the cloying sentimentality of comfortable Dickensian piety, which was able to find ample room for two varieties of anti-Semitism: it is a hard choice between the wicked passivity (and complicity) of Mr. Riah and the active villainy of Fagin. Dickens himself saw no implied slur to Jews in either portrait, which all by itself suggests that his is not a vision of love that could be sustained as doctrine; and some of his best-known commentators have seen no more in the matter than Dickens.

II

Paul begins his Epistle to the Galatians by reproving them for being in danger of backsliding and relapsing into Jewish orthodoxy and dependence on the Law; and the chief burden of the entire text is that the Law has been abrogated, and bondage under the Law has been ended by the emancipation of Christ's sacrifice. The metaphors that weave throughout the Epistle are drawn from the realms of law and of slavery, and the two themes are related and intertwined. To try to fulfill the Law is to be "in bondage under the elements of the world" (4:3), but Christ came "to redeem them that were under the law, that we might receive the adoption of sons . . . wherefore thou art no more a servant but a son; and if a son, then an heir of God through Christ" (4:5, 7). In place of the King James Version's "servant," other versions have "slave." This is perhaps why Raymond Stamm calls Galatians "the Magna Charta" of the Christian faith, though he may have had sectarian reasons as well. It may also be why commentators as different as Hyam Maccoby and Paul Johnson have been at one in calling Paul the *founder* of Christianity. In any case, Galatians tells us that Christ frees us from the bondage of the Law, and once freed we are no longer slaves or children but sons and heirs. The "slavery" metaphor must have meant a great deal to Paul, a sometime Pharisee well acquainted with the history of enslavement and emancipation that was annually and ceremonially recalled at the Passover.

By one of the painful and characteristic ironies of history, Paul's metaphor of slavery, applied to those who, by failing to adopt the Christian faith, were not freed from the bondage of the Law, was changed from metaphor to literal truth by the Dominican Pope Paul IV (1555–59), "acting in everything with a bitterness agreeable to the virulency of his nature," according to one of his contemporaries. He enclosed the Roman Jews within the walls of the Ghetto and commanded the men never to set foot outside it unless they wore distinguishing hats, which, according to Rodolpho Lanciani, the eminent archaeologist and historian, were conical caps "not unlike in shape to the one characteristic of our popular mask, Pulcinella"— i.e., a dunce cap. These hats had to be yellow; and women who came beyond the Ghetto walls had to wear yellow veils, because, as the papal bull *Cum nimis* declared, "It is most absurd and unsuitable that the Jews, whose own crime has plunged them into everlasting slavery, under the plea that Christian magnanimity allows them, should presume to dwell and mix with Christians, not bearing any mark of distinction, and should have Christian servants, yea, even buy houses." Under Gregory XIII (1572–85) the Jews were forced to hear a sermon every week in a church appointed specifically for them, and on every Sabbath police agents were sent to the Ghetto to drive men, women, and children into churches with scourges and to lash them if they appeared inattentive. To this barbarity had come the plea of Jesus "Suffer the little children to come unto me, and forbid them not." Robert Browning remembers this behavior in a poem called "Holy Cross Day." So Paul's metaphor had terrific consequences which he himself might not have foreseen, confident though he was of the illumination and eternal truth vouchsafed to him. It is that confidence of his that may in the end be most alarming, and may serve as a warning against my replacing his fixed convictions with fixed convictions of my own.

III

As a Jew living in a society essentially secular but nominally Christian, I have felt a need to learn the ways and something of the faith of the majority, for a Gentile is no longer, as in the Hebrew liturgy, "the stranger dwelling in our midst." It is impossible to be a Jew of my generation without being keenly aware of anti-Semitism, and sensitivity on this point alone has invited a study of Christian doctrine. My training in my own faith was of the most rudimentary and desultory kind, but over the years I not only grew to know it better but became increasingly acquainted with the convictions of my Christian neighbors. Many of these were good people whom I admired, and from whom I learned goodness itself, among other things. And there was much in Christian doctrine that seemed appealing as well. But few things struck me with more force than the profound and unappeasable hostility of Protestants and Catholics toward one another. The blood hatred of the Old World was brought over, with pike and Bible, to the New, undiluted but never so finely focused that there was none left over for the Jews. I heard an Easter Sunday sermon in a Catholic church on Lexington Avenue in New York in the middle 1950s (that is, before the Second Vatican Council) in which, on this day of unique Christian rejoicing and gratitude, the preacher devoted the whole of his discourse to proclaiming Jews the murderers of Christ, and all living Jews of our time as guilty of the crime by inheritance. The fierceness of such hatred is the more pronounced in direct ratio, it would seem, to the fervor of religious piety and conviction. Klaus Scholder's book *The Churches and the Third Reich:* Vol. 1, *1918–1934* plainly details the enthusiasm with which both Catholics and Protestants rose to embrace Nazism, including its most hideous racial policies. Karl Adam, a Roman Catholic theologian, declared that the "purity and freshness" of German blood was not only a "requirement of German self-expression" but "in line with God's revelation in the Old Testament." And, as Harvey Cox has reported in a review of Scholder's book, Emanuel Hirsch, in a five-volume history of Protestant thought, wrote in 1933, "If the Protestant Church . . . wishes really to proclaim the Gospel, then it must take as its natural standpoint the circle of destiny of the National Socialist movement."

Even as I write, the bishops of the Anglican church have irresolutely concluded their conference at Lambeth Palace. Most Americans who interested themselves in these deliberations were concerned with the question of the consecration of women as bishops. But a far more serious matter presented itself to the council and was, perhaps understandably, left unsettled. It has to do with the "justifiable use of force" to eliminate manifest and intolerable social wrongs. As I understand it, Archbishop Desmond Tutu was eloquent in arguing that the huge black majority in South Africa must not be categorically denied the last resort to such violent force. He seems to have been met with almost universal sympathy. But the bishops were understandably troubled by the fact that the same argument, based on the same principles, could be advanced in behalf of the IRA.

IV

I can remember being assigned in grade school to read *The Merchant of Venice.* It was mortifying, and in complicated ways. I was being asked to admire the work of the greatest master of the English language, and one universally revered, who was slandering all those of my race and religion. I was not even allowed to do this in private, but under the scrutiny and supervision of public instruction. And it took many class periods to get through the whole text. I can also remember the unseemly pleasure of my teacher in relishing all the slanders against the Jews in general and Shylock in particular. It was a wounding experience, and the beginning of a kind of education for which I received no grades. And it has continued for the rest of my life. Despite that early anguish I went on to find myself increasingly devoted to Shakespeare, and to literature in general, always tensely alerted to the possibility of being wounded, nearly always surprised by genuine kindness and understanding in matters that touched upon race and religion. And increasingly I found that it was nearly impossible to read the canon of English and American literature without becoming mired or entangled in questions of doctrine. There have been those who have tried to exempt Shakespeare from these controversies, by claiming that they were matters of indifference to him. In any case, my profession as teacher has required of me, in pursuance of an understanding of the works I teach, that I understand the parti pris that may color or define them, and these are often religious positions and doctrinal stances. It is impossible to read authors as different as Kafka and Hawthorne, Bunyan and Joyce, or any major poets, from Chaucer and Milton through Donne and Herbert to Hopkins and Lowell, without an acquaintance with their doctrinal and spiritual preoccupations. I have given some thought to these matters over the years and have read a good deal, though in a disorderly way. And it has occurred to me that the best and most telling answer to the solipsism and contemptuous repudiation of the Law of Moses by Paul is made by Jesus himself in words reported in Luke 16:19-31:

There was a certain rich man, which was clothed in purple and fine linen, and fared sumptuously every day:

And there was a certain beggar named Lazarus, which was laid at his gate, full of sores,

And desiring to be fed with the crumbs which fell from the rich man's table: moreover the dogs came and licked his sores.

And it came to pass, that the beggar died, and was carried by the angels into Abraham's bosom: the rich man also died, and was buried;

And in hell he lifted up his eyes, being in torments, and seeth Abraham afar off, and Lazarus in his bosom.

And he cried and said, Father Abraham, have mercy on me, and send Lazarus, that he may dip the tip of his finger in water, and cool my tongue; for I am tormented in this flame.

But Abraham said, Son, remember that thou in thy lifetime receivedst thy good things, and likewise Lazarus evil things: but now he is comforted, and thou art tormented.

And beside all this, between us and you there is a great gulf fixed: so that they which would pass from hence to you cannot; neither can they pass to us, that would come from thence.

Then he said, I pray thee therefore, father, that thou wouldest send him to my father's house:

For I have five brethren; that he may testify unto them, lest they also come into this place of torment.

Abraham saith unto him, They have Moses and the prophets; let them hear them.

And he said, Nay, father Abraham; but if one went unto them from the dead, they will repent.

And he said unto him, If they hear not Moses and the Prophets, neither will they be persuaded, though one rose from the dead.

THE EPISTLE OF
PAUL THE APOSTLE
TO THE EPHESIANS

—

Rita Dove

On the mysteries of vision, H.D. writes: "We begin with sympathy of thought." One of the last great modern mystics, H.D. scribbled her *Notes on Thoughts and Vision* in a notebook marked "July, Scilly Islands" in 1919, when she retreated to these islands off the coast of Cornwall in order to recuperate—from war, from illness and the breakup of her marriage, from the death of her brother and the hazardous birth of her daughter Perdita. Sea air and salt light to heal a wounded spirit: "The doctor prescribes rest."

I am reading H.D. on a grassy knoll overlooking the grounds of the Villa Serbelloni, the "Study and Conference Center" of the Rockefeller Foundation on Lake Como in northern Italy, trying to ignore a niggling restlessness I've had ever since my arrival. Do I feel displaced in the serenity of this splendid retreat, high above the tourist traffic of the village of Bellagio, here where terraced hills plunge into clear waters and cypresses slope into the mists at evening? Five weeks of hydrangeas and tiger lilies, white-coated butlers and silver candlesticks—what sumptuous reward for all the hours spent hunched in a sixty-watt circle of light, smudging my way through a wilderness of words! At last no meals to cook or phones to answer;

little mail, no children; a room of one's own, a study in the woods, and all around, beauty . . . but I'm not writing.

I've told myself it takes time to unwind, and I try to relax by reading afternoons when the *breva* sweeps the fog from the lake, freshening the shore. I read sprawled in a rattan chair set up outside, next to my study, hoping the sun will burn off the stress and fill the emptiness with magic.

While browsing in the villa library this morning I talked with a poet from Canada; he was convinced that the jewellike medieval painting of Saul on the way to Damascus that's mounted near the dictionaries is an unsigned Bono. Unsure who Bono was but unwilling to show my ignorance, I scrutinized the canvas for a signature—nothing in the tufted grass, the parched and rutted road, no scrawls in the surreal blue heaven or bright curls of the seraphim— and before I remembered to put on my museum demeanor I was captivated by the wistful sincerity of the scene before me. Saul looked utterly terrified, his horse rearing and his fellow travelers baffled by such strange behavior on an ordinary day. How devastating an experience for a man so certain of his convictions! No wonder he spent three days in darkness afterward, emptied of himself, until Ananias came to claim him in the name of Christianity. No wonder his name changed, the same sound but a different beginning.

H.D.'s *Notes* drop to the grass. A few yards away, three goldfish hidden under the lily pads send up their perky semaphores: I hear this infinitesimal percolation even as wild birds overhead belt out Italian chorales and a speedboat growls across the lake. So that's what's been bothering me: the germ of a poem dealing with religion. But, as if I were a Jewish dyer trading in royal purple, I struggle against the notion of Christianity acquiring a poem from me—just as I struggle against the ideologue who has haunted me since adolescence, whose stony gaze I still feel whenever I rail against the strictures of institutional belief.

———

Life before Paul was milk and honey, grapes and warm bread, cardboard-and-glitter crèches. In those early Sunday-school years we were fed on floods and famines, raining toads and babies in baskets.

Come twelve and the age of accountability, Christ appeared in the Temple and there followed a progression of sun-drenched miracles—Lazarus rising from his shroud, fish gleaming on proliferating hunks of bread. We loved the repetition of blessings, the palms fanning above the stolid head of a donkey, even the thirty pieces of silver. Blood and vinegar on the cross was swept over quickly, and Sunrise Services emphasized the rock rolled away, shining wings, astonishment, and His Glorious Resurrection. That was what a miracle was, after all: absence and light.

I was thirteen when the man who would introduce me to the apostle Paul walked into our senior Sunday-school class. He was tall, dark, and hellishly handsome, severely dressed in a matte-black narrow suit and black shirt from which rose a ring of shocking white, like a slipped halo. Never before had I seen a clerical collar (our minister wore standard suits with striped ties which peeked from his velvet-trimmed "preaching" robe); I thought the collar was his own invention, a kind of symbolic leash worn as a token of his service to God. He was the new assistant minister, straight out of theological school in the South (an exotic country to us in Akron, Ohio), and would take over the twelve-to-fifteen-year-olds, leaving our former teacher with the less unruly high schoolers.

Of course all the girls developed an immediate crush on him. We followed him breathlessly across the hall to a smaller, pale green classroom and without being asked formed a semicircle around the table he leaned against, like a male model from *Ebony* magazine, pin-striped trousers draping elegantly just above the buffed black wing-tips. On his left hand glinted, to our disappointment, a large wedding band.

"What do you know of mortal sin?" he asked.

We goggled at him and tittered nervously. "Mortal" sounded all right to us. He frowned, straightening the crease in his pant leg, then patiently unveiled to us the concepts of irretrievable error and purgatory. Since we were past the age of twelve, he explained, we were accountable for our sins against the Ten Commandments, which were inviolable. And our transgressions against any of those laws—whether actual or committed *in thought only*—were unforgivable except through Jesus Christ.

We barely heard the Jesus Christ part. We were doomed, for we had just coveted another woman's husband; we had also disobeyed our parents, stolen, lied, cursed—and if one counted thinking (how can you control your thoughts?) as well, then we committed these transgressions all the time. In an instant, flirting had changed from harmless entertainment to hellfire.

Our church was A.M.E. Zion. The acronym stands for African Methodist Episcopal, an appellation that contains all the contradictions and acclimatizations black Americans have gone through to accommodate both the African memory and the American dream. Basically Methodist, our church believed in a moderate liturgy (responsive readings) but did not tolerate kneeling or chanting; the "Episcopal" distinguished us from the Baptists not only in decorum— we baptized with a few drops of water on a baby's forehead—but in class. Determinedly of the bourgeoisie ("boojy" we called our parents, among them dentists, general practitioners, dry-cleaning moguls), we did not approve of hee-hawing sermons, though the minister was permitted to shout out the last sixth of his text.

"African" meant many things. Sometimes it was the license to wear proud colors and hats piled high, as extravagant as platters—unlike the drab skirt-and-blouse attire of the white Lutherans one street over. "African" also referred to our intimate relationship with God and Christ, the permission to wipe Christ's sweat from our brows and talk to him like a brother, to identify our lot with that of the Israelites under Pharaoh. Martin Luther King, Jr. was our Moses, charged with delivering his people across the Selma bridge. "African" bore the very cadences of nostalgia for our lost homeland, wherever it may have been—though in those turbulent years of Miriam Makeba and Malcolm X there was an edge to that nostalgia as well, a defiant hope from those who wished for mercy but just might choose, if pressed, to prevail by whatever means necessary.

But "African" always meant righteous singing. I particularly loved the "old hundred" hymns, standard oldies sung during the formal catechism of the service, before the sermon, as well as the choral outbursts from the white-clad women in the front pew.

Ah, the deaconesses! Mostly widows with massive bosoms, all ancient, these women put on their blinding white shirtwaists, their chalky nylons, and Shinola-white shoes every Sunday. Some wore tiny starched bonnets, very much like nurses or pilgrims, and others preferred the pure ornament of a scrubbed dark face lifted to the Lord. They were the self-appointed brides of Christ and the acknowledged mothers of the church, the arbiters of the Holy Spirit, and they disapproved of flash and frivolity and black militancy. (Though they never complained about Afros, since several of them had let their hair "go back" to furry halos.) The deaconesses were already seated when the rest of the congregation trickled in. Usually they were bent in prayer, humming vigorously to the mumbled supplications of a deacon, usually the oldest male, who by virtue of his sex and age was permitted to kneel on the first step leading to the altar.

The deaconesses were also intimate with what W. E. B. Du Bois called the Sorrow Songs—older hymns, prehistoric canons that resembled nothing familiar or comforting. They had very few words and were frightening in their near-inarticulate misery. For at least a half hour before the processional signaled the official start of the service, the old women hummed, rocked, wailed these chants as parishioners arrived and drifted into the pews. Unlike gospel, "big / with all the wrongs done done," these songs reeked with unappeasable loss and pain. They were the moans of slavery, the rhythms of an existence dulled by rote and brutality and hopelessness, an isolation so complete there could be no words.

The deaconesses led the congregation in that complex courtship between the Holy Spirit and mortal endeavor; the give and take, the surge and ebb between the minister's sermon and their shouted counterpoint was our clue to how well the minister was doing in bringing us closer to holiness, indeed, bringing us *in Christ*, in Paul's complex, mystical phrase, until heat and pinching waistbands dropped away and the message from the pulpit entered us directly, like an injection.

What is the mystery of grace? What does it mean to be *in* Christ? I watched the older women of the church "get happy"; I could see them gathering steam, pushing out the seams of their composure until it dropped down, the Holy Spirit, falling upon them like a hatchet from heaven. Instead of crumbling they rose up, incandescent, to perform amazing feats—they tightroped the backs of pews, skipped along the aisles, threw off ushers and a half-dozen ablebodied men with every shout. (Men rarely got happy; when they did, theirs was a decorous performance, hardly an experience at all.) A woman "full of the Spirit" was indomitable; one could almost see sunbeams glancing off the breastplate of righteousness, the white wings twinkling on the sandals of faith. And when it was over, they were not diminished but serene, as if they'd been given a tonic.

Why couldn't I be filled, transfused with glory? The most I'd experienced was a "quickening"—a mini-transformation characterized by shortened breath and an intense longing for the indefinite . . . what? I was tongue-tied, hopelessly guilt-ridden and self-conscious to boot. The most I could do was get teary-eyed. In the face of those bolder ecstasies, I'd fall back into my own ashes, quenched.

Witnessing these transformations usually made me churlish for the rest of the day. I decided God didn't like intelligence. And though we hadn't been meant to sample the Tree of Knowledge, surely we couldn't be blamed for the intelligence we'd been saddled with.

Sunday evenings after "60 Minutes" my father would push off his slippers and shrug into his overcoat, keys jangling. We knew the signal: another trip to Grandma's on the East Side. It was a long way through town, along the gorge and then the slow climb up Market Street, past the defunct oats silos and the Fir Hill Conservatory of Music, then down Arlington and into the purgatorial Furnace Street, where the smoke and brimstone miraculously began, spewing from Plant One of the Goodyear Rubber Company and the smaller infernos of Mohawk and General Tire. This was the part of the journey I waited for. The backlit plumes of smoke and murky variations of exhaust and light were exciting, a negative snapshot of power and hope; the mere sight of a belching smokestack at night made me think of evening gowns and diamond lavaliers.

All across town the accompaniment was radio—the staid ministerial admonitions of a local Presbyterian congregation on the way, and afterward the surging gospels of Shiloh Baptist, my grandmother's own church, whose evening service she attended faithfully via the airwaves, rocking in her armchair in the back bedroom. I was awed by so much fervor: that one could go to church on Sunday morning and still have ardor left over to attend an evening service seemed strange, yet weirdly desirable. How simple life would be if one could believe that much! Later, in bed, I'd tuck my transistor radio under the pillow and tune into the Catholic broadcast at ten—

after Shiloh Baptist's creaking ship of lamentations what a relief, a balm, *Hail Mary full of grace Blessed art thou among women and blessed is the fruit of thy womb Jesus* whispered over and over until I dozed off, safe for another night.

Into the intact world of childhood, Paul had introduced Doubt, and I resisted. As far as I was concerned, Saul/Paul was altogether too fervent—his persecution of the Christians too single-minded, his conversion too spectacular, his teachings too humorless. It wasn't the gaudiness of his martyr's life I distrusted (John's vision of the Apocalypse, in contrast, seemed absolute to me and vividly *correct*); rather, it was the contradiction between his life and his words. "Do as I say, not as I do"—we'd learned in Sunday school to nod, straight-faced, when reciting the commandments but to watch as scandals erupted in that orchestrated adult world: a senior usher ogling a pair of fine hips rolling under orange shantung, the occasional girl burgeoning under her choir robes. We waited for public recriminations, but all went on as before. We had a saying: Saints can backslide, but never trust a person who can't dance. Paul couldn't dance, but he shore could talk. Our assistant minister felt it his duty to initiate us into the world of words, the irretrievability of a vow.

I also distrusted the name change, from the Jew Saul to the astringent New Age Paul. Paul—a name without history. Somehow I suspected him of abandoning with his born name the Old Testament, where Sauls and Jeremiahs flourished, and his desert treks and prison tenure had no aura. He was a traveling salesman, his epistles little more than shtick.

And Paul had no music; neither did he make a joyful noise before the Lord. He despised pageantry and silver ornament. His was a ministry of noon—no shadows or respite from the all-reaching rays of righteousness. I could not think of Paul without imagining parched mesas and the emblazoned killing ground of a Colosseum. Even the olives he preferred must have been sharp with rosemary, chewy and bitter.

But the god I knew understood the value of a wink. He was nothing like this Paul with his blind stare, his frozen faith burning in his eyes. Leave such clenched fervor to human beings; gods and angels are casual. No wonder he saw life in terms of architecture, and the body become church, a sacred building you entered silently and where you'd better not spit. And farther up the wine-dark aisle, the path of blood transfixed, this sacrificial artery leading to the plateau where no body lived but Thought reigned, gold and wax and velvet, paltry adornment designed to render palpable to the congregation the ineffable integrity of the spirit. This, then, was Christ presiding over the church, and Man presiding over Wife.

The mystery of Paul's ideology is revealed through his metaphors: comparing the church to a marriage. To be saved, to establish a mystical and *ongoing* spiritual strength, one does not try to become Christ or to identify with Christ; instead, one develops a *relationship to* him. This is a "primitive" concept: the ancient Greeks mingled freely with their gods and goddesses, with sometimes disastrous (poor Leda), sometimes beneficent (Odysseus guided to Ithaca by Pallas Athene) results. African slaves in America transferred their attitudes toward divinities to the abstract figures of Christianity, telling Mary not to weep, exhorting Jonah not to despair, and rejoicing that Christ had personally reached down to lift them up. Black worshipers sat down to talk with God as with an old friend. When I was in my early teens, black disc jockeys favored a popular song that went: "I had a talk with my man last night; / He reassured me everything was all right." It was years before I heard the gospel song that had been its inspiration: "I had a talk with God last night." I was not as shocked by this discovery as perhaps I should have been; I was already on the way to secular humanism. After all, I had been talking to God for several years, bargaining and wheedling from the cave of my pillow, protesting my good intentions.

Human agency. I rolled the phrase around in my mouth as I perched on the curved lip of the pew, willing myself to remember the words through the sermon's climax and the preacher's ecstatic Call to Altar so that I might carry them home and find a use for them. *Human agency* was the key I'd been looking for in the rigid latticework the New Testament had raised around my daily living. Obedient though I was, I could not believe the thoughts that entered my daydreams so easily were forbidden. To hold the mind accountable—surely this wasn't what God had meant. Surely he did not want robots as children; surely a doll's house would be a bore for such a mighty spectator.

The world is protean. Every adolescent knows this, lives this . . .

and is astonished at adults' ability to fasten onto the order of things with smug attentions. How can they skim the surface of such stormy oceans? Mother snapping her facial compact shut with a satisfied click, Father Turtle-waxing the Ford on Saturday afternoon: where is the pleasure to be located in these routines when the ultimate pleasure (as every adolescent discovers) is sexual—the disintegrating joy of a French kiss, the utterly selfish desire of the body to *know more?* Of course, we didn't understand the concept of guilt, major guilt—the kind that can't be erased from heart and mind, that distresses even ten, fifteen years later, whenever buried incidents float unbidden to the surface. How could we? We hadn't lived very much.

Saul watched as Stephen was stoned to death; Paul was celibate in order to serve his Christ more ardently. Aren't these flip sides of the same coin? And if not, where did Saul go? Who, if anyone, was in the body that sat three days in darkness in Damascus, who spoke before the crowds, who crouched in that dark prison cell and built up the body of Christian thought into a white and pillared building? Did he remember Saul at all—or had he, as Paul, burned away his past self so completely that with it fled the childhood words for stone and bread? What initially fills the void when the old self is struck down and out—what rushes in before the light, what rides the arrow tip of redemption into the benighted soul?

In the rattan chair beside the lily pond, far above the unspeakably blue waters of Lake Como, the poem for Paul takes shape:

ON THE ROAD TO DAMASCUS

They say I was struck down by the voice of an angel:
flames poured through the radiant fabric of heaven
as I cried out and fell to my knees.

My first recollection was of Unbroken Blue,
but two of the guards have already sworn by
the tip of my tongue set ablaze. As an official,

I recognize the lure of a good story:
useless to suggest that my mount
had stumbled, that I was pitched into a clump

of wild chamomile, its familiar stink
  soothing even as my palms sprang blisters
under the nicked leaves. I heard shouts,

the horse pissing in terror—but my eyes
  had dropped to my knees, and I saw nothing.
I was a Roman and had my business

among the clouded towers of Damascus.
  I had not counted on earth rearing,
honey streaming down a parched sky,

a spear skewering me to the dust of the road
  on the way to the city I would never
enter now, her markets steaming with vendors

and compatriots in careless armor lifting a hand
  in greeting as they call out my name,
only to find no one home.

———

Paul's first visit to Ephesus lasted over two years, during which time he argued in the synagogue and converted "divers souls." Afterward he made for Jerusalem, sending back to Ephesus two disciples to keep the flame burning. In Paul's absence, the disciples met resistance from the silversmiths, who had a hefty business in shrines to the goddess Diana and naturally resented the loss in trade the new icon-less religion would occasion. Led by the silversmith Demetrius, the people rose up in defense of their goddess; when the disciples tried to speak, the crowd outshouted them, for two hours chanting "Great *is* Diana of the Ephesians." Forced to retreat, the disciples were recalled by Paul, who "embraced them" and set out himself for Ephesus, where he gave the heretics "much exhortation" (Acts 20:1–2).

Did Paul's harsh words succeed at Ephesus, or did Diana prevail? The Bible is curiously silent on this point. In fact, the authorship of the Epistle to the Ephesians is heavily disputed among theological scholars—and it was almost certainly not written for the Ephesians, though of course we have other testimonies of his ministry there. It hardly matters whether Paul wrote this epistle or not—the spirit of his thought is still intact. We know from Acts that Paul appeared at Ephesus with a bag of tricks, handkerchiefs emerging from his sleeves to heal the sick and raise the dead . . . and yet the artisans with their silver statuettes of Diana were still able to rouse the people: We want Diana, thousand-breasted deity, they told Paul's disciples, who were forced to retreat. Was the light in Paul's eyes too empty? Or was it simply that two mysticisms—the matriarchal vision of fertility and wholeness, the patriarchal vision of order and clarity—were insisting on their separate paths to glory?

———

When I was a teenager Paul seemed to be a hard man with an unrealistically severe code of sacrifice, a fanatic who devised silly laws of diet, dress codes, and impossible rules of behavior; an ideologue who equated belief with ethics and transformation with institutional rhetoric. This was the world view our assistant minister promulgated; Paul was his boogeyman.

I see now that Paul's proclamations were demanded of him. At that time Christianity was still a heresy within a larger tradition; Saul's persecution of Christians, his conversion, and his consequent wrangles with the priests of the Temple—these events were all in the family, so to speak. At the time when the Pauline Epistles were written, the biggest question for the new religion was whether or not to accept Gentiles; once that quandary was settled, more mundane issues (Can they remain uncircumcised? Must they obey the Judaic rules of diet?) were the order of the day. The disciples attempted to thread a path through the existing Old Testament laws; they sought an extension, and fulfillment, of Judaism. Paul's public needed concrete rules, so he gave them restrictions to hold on to: Wife, obey your husband; husband, love your wife—just as you obey Christ and He loves you. Children, obey your parents. Servants (this is the tricky one), obey your masters—followed by a telling conditional: "according to the flesh, with fear and trembling, in singleness of your heart, as unto Christ" (Ephesians 6:5–6). And because pictures are worth a thousand words, he gave them metaphors: the Church as a bride, Christ as bridegroom, and martial imagery sure to delight a city devoted to the huntress Diana. Gird the loins with truth, slip the feet into the Gospel of peace, take up the breastplate of righteousness and the shield of faith! Blatant theatrics, but it worked.

Yet Paul *was* a mystic. Only a mystic would address the newly converted with "And you *hath he quickened*, who were dead in trespasses and sins." Or: "the fulness of him that filleth all in all." Devising a system for connecting and reflection, a guide for conducting a life of energized joy—this is Paul's abiding light.

———

Whenever I move to a new place, the first thing I usually do is "cozy up" my study; I throw down rugs, mount marionettes on the walls, place a crystal or a hand-carved elephant on a shelf where my fidgety gaze might fall for a moment and rest. This time, though, it was different. After leaving the Rockefeller Study and Conference Center in Bellagio, I moved into what was easily the most nondescript room I have ever written poetry in—white brick, gray industrial-strength carpet—and yet, six months later I still could not bear to tack up so much as a single poster.

It was as if the photographs and paintings that used to provide companionship in my solitary hours of composition had ceased to serve as windows and begun to block the view. It seemed I required no distraction from the void. To put it less negatively: I no longer felt the need to focus in on an object in order to allow my thoughts free rein, unsupervised—a window had opened in me.

I was nearly finished writing "On the Road to Damascus" before I understood what about the gold-leaf-and-lapis universe in the painting the Canadian poet attributed to Bono had so moved me that morning in the Villa Serbelloni. Saul was terrified because the eyes that had studied the Law and looked calmly on at the slaying of another man had for the first time failed their owner. The Roman world, once as compact and manageable as the toylike apparition of the city of Damascus hovering on the horizon, had split apart, and he was falling into a mystery, bottomless and widening.

Paul's account of his conversion, on the other hand, is essentially the story of a seduction. He has been entered by Christ the Bridegroom and remade in the image of his Love. Then, as in any marriage, one must work at redemption; one must learn to forgive oneself.

H.D. writes: "We must be 'in love' before we can understand the mysteries of vision." This does not mean penetrating the mysterious, nor does it mean being taken by storm. Grace is a state of being, not an assault; and enlightenment, unlike epiphany, is neither brief nor particularly felicitous. The Saul in the painting knew better. Anyone who feels the need to connect the outside world with an interior presence must *absorb* the mysterious into the tangle of contradictions and longings that form each one of us. That's hard, on-going work, and it never ends.

THE EPISTLE OF
PAUL THE APOSTLE
TO THE PHILIPPIANS

—

Dana Gioia

A poet writing about the New Testament faces two kinds of intimidation. First comes the challenge of biblical scholarship. Probably no other area of human study has generated so much research, commentary, and criticism as the Bible. The New Testament alone has inspired two thousand years of continuous annotation and elucidation across every European language. The mass of writing on the subject is not merely unmanageable but unthinkably vast. (In comparison with the evangelists and apostles, Shakespeare is just a young playwright getting his first notices.) When a theologian can spend a lifetime of research without mastering the full heritage of Christian Scripture, what is the nonspecialist to do, especially when the learned commentators often cannot agree even on fundamental issues of authorship, chronology, historical fidelity, textual accuracy, and translation—not to mention the central problem of interpretation?

The second problem facing the writer is one of religious belief—not only his own but also those (for there will be many different ones) of his audience. In the West no texts are more charged with moral, spiritual, and even political significance than those of the New Testament. The author knows that each reader will bring a lifetime of preconceptions to whatever text he discusses. A cleric writing to fellow members of one particular sect (be it Roman Catholic or Southern Baptist) can assume a common set of beliefs. But someone trying to address a more general audience knows there will be disagreements about basic issues no matter what he chooses to say. For many readers every passage of the New Testament is the living word of God, infallibly speaking the literal truth to humankind. For others it is a magnificent account of tribal myths no different from the Hindu *Bhagavad-Gita* or the Egyptian Book of the Dead. And for still others—including most American intellectuals—it is a great moral document in which great truths are unfortunately tangled up with discredited supernatural legend.

Faced with these intellectual and spiritual obstacles, most contemporary writers have stopped discussing Scripture. Their reticence has largely left the subject to specialists. As a result, both American letters and religion have been the poorer. Moreover, as literary and religious writing have divided, so have their audiences. Today few literary readers know the Bible well. The little they have read—like the Book of Job—was usually last encountered in a college survey course. (Their knowledge of the Bible comes mainly from visual sources, most notably Renaissance painting.) The divorce between high culture and religion has now progressed so far in our secular society that even sophisticated readers now have difficulty understanding biblical texts. Buttressed neither by familiarity nor by faith, they lack both the intellectual and religious frames of reference to interpret them with even minimal accuracy. They may understand the words of any given scriptural passage but often miss the cultural context that gives it meaning.

The obstacles to understanding are particularly confusing in the epistles of Saint Paul. These central Christian documents promise the clarity and directness of personal letters, but to most modern readers their contexts often seem obscure, their purposes clouded, and their structures elusive. They lack the narrative accessibility of the Gospels and the Acts of the Apostles, where the story pulls the reader along. Nor do they have the poetic splendor and enticing obscurity of Revelation. Everyone loves a puzzle, especially one that promises to explain the end of the world. With Revelation, the reader expects to be mystified initially, and John of Patmos does not disappoint with his eschatological roman à clef. Among the books of the New Testament, only the Epistles fail to satisfy the generic expectations they raise.

Paul himself is also a difficult figure for modern readers. While he ranks as the most important personality in early Christianity (after, of course, Jesus, who even to nonbelievers occupies a special status), Paul remains very much a man of his distant time and place. Energetic, argumentative, intellectual, he lacks the simple human touch Jesus characteristically exhibits in the Gospels. While Jesus taught by parable and proverb, Paul most often instructed by abstraction and ratiocination. One cannot dispute that Paul's method was effective in his time. More than any other individual, he built the formal enterprise of Christianity by codifying Jesus' teaching into a systematic set of principles—a new covenant designed quite literally to replace the older, Hebrew one. But one must also recognize that the practical and ideological nature of Paul's first-century mission now makes his writing less accessible. While Jesus' sermons still seem fresh and immediate after two thousand years, Paul's homilies usually require explanation and amplification.

Amplification and explanation have, of course, been forthcoming. Commentary on Paul's epistles began at his death and has never stopped. Sometimes the commentaries even took the form of pious imitations. While the Epistle to the Philippians is genuine, half of the other New Testament epistles bearing his name were probably written by his followers. These pseudo-Pauline letters, in which early disciples probably took a few genuine scraps of his writing and elaborated them into complete fictive letters, were the earliest responses to Paul's work. Likewise, much subsequent Christian theology from Augustine to Schweitzer has taken the form of creative reinterpretation of his ideas. Since writers must often wrestle with their most powerful predecessors in order to win intellectual independence, for ambitious theologians it has most often been Paul the tent maker waiting for them in the ring.

If imaginative writers like me have anything to add to the understanding of Paul, it is probably mostly our innocence and humanity. We know the epistles, but not so well that we forget how foreign and confusing they seem to a new reader. We realize that the critic's job—like the artist's—is one of translation, in this case not simply from Greek into English but from an ancient mind to a modern one. Part of that translation comes from scholarship. We are of no use there. But the other part can come only from imagination—not in its everyday sense of making up fictions but in its higher sense of the intuitive discovery of reality. Perhaps the major difference between the artist and the scholar is in the role of the imagination. Scholars use imagination, but it is a secondary faculty, always in service to the known facts. For the poet or novelist, the imagination is primary. It employs facts as a point of departure, not into mere fantasy but toward relevant speculation. Likewise, the artist prizes the concrete and human detail and shies away from the theoretical and abstract. A poet may miss the theological implications in a phrase of Paul's but will immediately catch the psychological state or emotional tone. By virtue of training, a literary artist is alert to the human side of a text.

I will examine Paul's Epistle to the Philippians, therefore, in the only way I can—as a poet. I write knowing my impossible position as middleman between the erudite scholar and the uninformed general reader. But today any artist writing about a classic faces the same problem. How does one discuss a work about which everything has been said while no one outside the classroom was listening? The answer does not come from ignoring scholarship. Honest inquiry begins in knowledge. But the artist must resist letting academic scholarship dictate the issues to be addressed. One must try to engage the work itself and discuss only what frankly interests (or annoys) one about it.

For me, the most remarkable feature of the Epistle to the Philippians is its tangible humanity. Although ideas from the letter have been enormously influential, it constitutes no theological treatise. Paul's ideas develop less through any sustained argument than by emotional association. The design is therefore not so much intellectual as dramatic. To discover the underlying structure, one must understand Paul's personal situation at the time of its composition and his relationship with the church members he addresses. Tracing the implied narrative is the best way to approach this difficult epistle.

Let me begin, however, by acknowledging that it is not easy for the first-time reader to piece together the human story of Philippians. The letter is short (only 104 verses in all) but packed with information. The structure is subjective and digressive. There is no single line of thought or narrative. Even the circumstances that occasioned the letter are initially hard to unravel. Paul's thanks for the Philippians' assistance occurs so late in the epistle that it seems like an afterthought (a peculiarity that has led some scholars to suggest that the surviving text is actually a composite of several letters written by Paul at different times). Finally, the epistle deals with several issues, such as ritual circumcision, that make little sense to the contemporary reader untutored in early Christian ideological debate.

Despite its confusing organization, the first-time reader can immediately feel the emotional intensity of this extraordinary letter. Written while Paul, an old man worn out by years of travel and persecution, waited in Roman custody with the threat of execution over his head, the epistle achieves a spiritual clarity of the most intimate kind. Paul talks as much about his own struggle for salvation as he does the Philippians' situation. In a moment of uncharacteristic weakness, he even confesses that he would prefer to join Christ in death than to persevere in life against so many obstacles:

> For me to live is Christ, and to die is gain.
> But if I live in the flesh, this is the fruit of my labour: yet what I shall choose I wot not.
> For I am in a strait betwixt two, having a desire to depart, and to be with Christ: which is far better:
> Nevertheless to abide in the flesh is more needful for you.
> [1:21–24]

Reading Paul's intimate words, one naturally wonders who the people were whom he addressed and how they came to have such a candid and affectionate relationship with the stern and formidable apostle. In biblical studies such questions are usually impossible to answer. But in the case of Philippians, we are fortunate to have the personal background of Paul's relationship with the Macedonian church presented in some detail elsewhere in the New Testament. In his Acts of the Apostles, Luke gives an especially vivid account of Paul's first visit to Philippi because the evangelist apparently accompanied him on the journey. Not only is Luke's story interesting as an account of early Christian missionary work; it also helps explain the privileged position the church at Philippi occupied in Paul's heart.

Luke tells how, early in his missionary career, Paul had preached in Palestine and Asia Minor, but each time he turned to go eastward into Asia, the Holy Spirit had stopped him. Finally one night Paul, Timothy, Silas, and Luke were in Troas, at the tip of Asia Minor, pointing toward Greece. That night Paul had a vision in which a man appeared and said, "Come over into Macedonia and help us." They quickly sailed to Macedonia and went directly to Philippi, the major city of the region, which was located on the main road between Rome and the East. Their arrival in Philippi marked the inaugural Christian mission to the West, and the congregation they founded there became the first Christian church in Europe.

The Jewish community in Philippi was apparently too small to maintain a synagogue, so the faithful gathered on a riverbank outside the city walls. Paul preached there and made a convert (the first European Christian on record), a well-to-do fabric dyer named Lydia, who took the apostle and his company into her home. Paul then began preaching in the city until a curious event led him into legal trouble. A possessed slave girl, who had earned her masters considerable money with her gift of prophecy, started following Paul's company, crying, "These men are the servants of the most high God, which show unto us the way of salvation." (In the New Testament the demonically possessed always seem to recognize the sanctity of Christ and his apostles, even if the normal folk do not.) Paul finally took pity and exorcised her, to the annoyance of her masters, since she now had lost her profitable ability to tell fortunes. They brought criminal charges against Paul and Silas, who were then beaten, put into stocks, and thrown in prison.

Locked in an inner dungeon, Paul and Silas prayed and sang hymns until midnight, when, according to Luke, a miraculous earthquake opened all the prison doors and shook off their chains. The jailer, who thought all of his charges had escaped, was about to take his own life when Paul called out from the dark cell that none of the prisoners had left. The jailer was immediately converted and took the Christians into his own house. The next day the local magistrates, who were equally fearful of Paul's supernatural power and his Roman citizenship (which should have protected him from the peremptory beating they had inflicted), quickly set the missionaries free and begged them to leave the city. Once liberated, Paul and his companions briefly visited the house of Lydia and then departed Philippi.

Luke's account of Paul's mission to Philippi raises an inescapable issue for any modern reader—namely, the presence of miracles. In this brief episode one finds the following supernatural events: the intervention of the Holy Spirit, the prophetic apparition in Paul's dream, the possessed girl who can tell fortunes, the publicly acknowledged exorcism, and the wondrous earthquake. Paul and Luke take all of these events as matters of course, but since the Enlightenment, biblical scholars have fretted over the miraculous episodes in the New Testament. Many experts have tried to explain such supernatural events as literary symbols, unreliable hearsay uncritically accepted by New Testament authors, or even later textual additions. But in Acts Luke appears to offer an eyewitness account of the events at Philippi, and throughout the authentic Pauline Epistles Paul repeatedly alludes to similar wonders done in Christ's name. Even if one discounts the reports of such incidental miracles, a more extraordinary problem remains. Both Paul and Luke claim that Paul gained his knowledge of the Christian gospel not from the man Jesus—whom Paul never saw in the flesh—or even from the other apostles, but from a miraculous vision of the risen Christ on the road to Damascus. There can be no textual ambiguity here. As Paul himself makes clear in both First Corinthians and Galatians (1:11–12), he does not preach a gospel "given to him by man but directly by the revelation of Jesus Christ."

Contemporary scholars may lament Paul's dependence on supernatural evidence to assert the verity of the Christian faith. They may wish he practiced a more modern theology emphasizing the abstract ethical nature of Christ's gospel. But the facts are undebatable. Paul believed in Christ's divinity because he was given direct physical proof—not only outside Damascus but also repeatedly by divine guidance and miraculous intervention throughout his travels. What made Christ important for him was not merely Jesus' glorious moral vision but the fact that Jesus rose from the dead, ascended into heaven, and soon would come again in glory to judge all humanity.

Nor was his message even particularly farsighted. Paul believed that Christ would return within the lifetime of his newly converted church members. As he says in Philippians 4:5, "The Lord is at hand." There was nothing abstract or philosophical at the center of Paul's gospel. He was—in his own eyes—a passionate realist. Surely his accounts of miracles would have struck ancient readers as strongly as they do modern ones as the most extraordinary claims in his message. If Paul was inaccurate or extravagant in reporting these dramatic claims, how can one trust his veracity or rationality in any other matter? The reader has no choice but to view Paul as either a psychotic or a saint.

I have no desire to dictate the reader's choice between the alternative interpretations of Paul. I insist only that the issue cannot be avoided. Scholarship, however masterful, will resolve nothing. Enough authentic letters by Paul have survived to make his central claims of direct divine guidance unambiguous. The diagnosis one makes of Paul's reliability will affect one's reading of every book in the New Testament, and this verdict will depend ultimately on one's assumptions about Christ's divinity. According to human reason the Incarnation is impossible. A believing Christian must endorse it against both logic and common sense. The Christian faith, as Tertullian asserted, is based on an absurd proposition: *Certum est quia impossibile* ("It is certain because impossible"). And if one takes the leap of faith, it must be done, as Paul tells the Philippians, "in fear and trembling," for it changes every assumption about the purpose of human existence.

At the end of Flannery O'Connor's chilling story "A Good Man Is Hard to Find," there is a conversation between a murderer nicknamed The Misfit and an old woman. The Misfit's men have just murdered her family, and he is about to kill her. She mumbles "Jesus, Jesus" out of fear, and he unexpectedly begins to discuss Christianity with her in coldly rational terms that Paul would have understood:

"Jesus was the only One that ever raised the dead," The Misfit continued, "and He shouldn't have done it. He thown everything off balance. If He did what He said, then it's nothing for you to do but thow away everything and follow Him, and if He didn't, then it's nothing for you to do but enjoy the few minutes you got left the best way you can. . . ."

Paul said nearly the same thing, echoing Ecclesiastes, in 1 Corinthians 15:32: "What advantageth it me, if the dead rise not? Let us eat and drink, for to morrow we die."

Writing to the Philippians, Paul does not feel the need to argue forcefully about the reality of the central Christian message. He can take the Philippians' faith in these difficult matters for granted. Although he did not stay long in Philippi during his first visit, the church he founded stayed exceptionally strong and loyal. Not only did the church members remain sober and devout, they also supported Paul financially on his ministries in Thessalonica, Corinth, and Rome. The occasion for his Epistle to the Philippians comes directly out of their steady support. Paul wrote his epistle while in prison to thank the Philippians for sending him both money and a helper. He tells them that Epaphroditus, the assistant they sent to help his mission, has been seriously ill and now wants to return home. The epistle was presumably carried by Epaphroditus to Philippi, where it was read and preserved.

Although Philippians is a short epistle, its structure is digressive and conversational. Because it lacks one sustained argument unifying its various parts, some scholars have maintained that the text we have inherited is actually a composite of several separate letters Paul sent to the fledgling church. Yet this relaxed epistle seems no less unified than most long letters one might receive. Paul is full of news and advice. To concentrate on structural deficiencies in Philippians is to miss the quality that makes this gentle and candid letter unique among Paul's epistles.

A particular beauty of Paul's letter to the Philippians is the tangible affection and trust the apostle felt for the recipients. Philippians is not only Paul's warmest surviving epistle, it is also the most joyful. As many commentators have noted, the words for "joy" and "rejoice" appear twenty-two times in a relatively short letter. Paul's tone is friendly and intimate rather than defensive or excited. For once he relaxed his frequently argumentative and intellectual manner. Unlike the Galatians or Corinthians, the church members at Philippi gave him no cause for outburst and admonition. Of course, complete serenity is too much to expect from Paul. He does have one explosive bout in the epistle's third chapter, where he warns of the danger from the Judaizers, who demanded that Christian converts strictly follow Jewish Law concerning male circumcision. But even this brief harangue seems friendly by Pauline standards. One even suspects that the Philippians would have become worried about their old teacher's health had he not gotten his temper up at least once.

The opening verses of Philippians highlight its special qualities. Paul begins in his usual way by identifying himself and his companion Timothy as well as his recipients in Philippi. But then the letter takes an unusually personal and emotional turn as Paul admits his special affection for the members of this church. He confesses he cannot remember them without thanking God for the joy their exemplary fellowship in the Gospel brings him. He also confides how much he misses their company. Paul frequently wrote to advise and admonish local churches. He wrote to the Philippians, however, mainly to praise and thank. He does not ask the church members to change their behavior but to continue it.

The real heart of the epistle, however, is its second chapter, which outlines the goals of Christian life and sets Christ as the model for humility and obedience to God. The thirty verses of this chapter are one of the central texts of Christianity, and they have influenced spiritual thinkers from Augustine to Bonhoeffer. Paul begins the chapter with a series of conditional statements beginning with "if." As any student of Paul's rhetoric knows, when the apostle begins a statement with "if," then rhapsodic affirmation will usually follow:

> If there be therefore any consolation in Christ, if any comfort
> of love, if any fellowship of the Spirit, if any bowels and mercies,
> Fulfil ye my joy . . . being of one accord, of one mind.
> Let nothing be done through strife or vainglory; but in low-
> liness of mind let each esteem other better than themselves.
> [2:1–3]

At the center of this crucial chapter is a magnificent poem that constitutes the spiritual and literary focus of the epistle. Six particular verses (2:6–11) had long been recognized as the most eloquent and mysterious part of Paul's epistle. But it was not until 1928 that the German scholar Ernst Lohmeyer demonstrated that the oddly worded passage generally fell into a regular poetic rhythm in the original Greek. Though skillfully woven into the prose of Paul's letter, once separated, the lines form a hymn to Christ's incarnation and death. Paul introduces the hymn by reminding the Philippians to imitate Christ. Then he switches into poetry.

> *Being in the form of God,*
> *He considered it not a thing to be seized*
> *To be equal with God;*
>
> *But emptied Himself*
> *By taking the form of a slave,*
> *Coming in human likeness.*
>
> *And appearing on earth as Man,*
> *He humbled Himself,*
> *Becoming obedient unto death*
>
> *[Indeed, death on a cross]*
>
> *Wherefore God exalted Him*
> *And bestowed on Him the name*
> *That is above every name:*
>
> *That in the name of Jesus*
> *Every knee should bow*
> *In heaven, on earth, and under the earth,*
>
> *And every tongue confess:*
> *"Jesus Christ is Lord;"*
> *To the glory of God the Father.*
>
> *[Translated by Ralph A. Martin]*

There is much scholarly debate as to whether Paul himself wrote the hymn or simply quoted it from early Christian liturgy. Its originality hardly matters to the common reader. Who can doubt that the author of the thirteenth chapter of First Corinthians ("Though I speak with the tongues of men and of angels . . .") was capable of composing sublime poetry? If Paul did not author the Christological hymn, then there is no doubt that he quoted it with total approval. What matters is the spiritual vision of the hymn. It transforms the human qualities Paul celebrates earlier into the divine values embodied by Christ's incarnation.

The hymn at the center of Philippians articulates the radical change in values offered by Christianity. Jesus provided his followers with a new form of divinity, one based not on power and pride but on self-abasement and compassion. Paul glorified the virtues of humility, charity, and obedience—the essential Christian qualities, as difficult for his contemporaries to cultivate as for us today. Paul knew his commandment to esteem others more than one's own self went against the weaker side of human nature, but he believed the aspiring Christian would be aided by God. As he wrote in words that Søren Kierkegaard would later take to heart: "Work out your own salvation with fear and trembling. For it is God which worketh in you both to will and to do his good pleasure" (2:12–13). Paul also testifies not only that God does expect the faithful to show humility, charity, and obedience but that the Lord would reward those virtues on the coming Day of Judgment. In a particularly moving passage the apostle asks the Philippians to strive for spiritual perfection despite the evil around them, so that their example will prove before God that his own life has not been spent in vain:

> Do all things without murmurings and disputings:
> That ye may be blameless and harmless, the sons of God, without rebuke, in the midst of a crooked and perverse nation, among whom ye shine as lights in the world;
> Holding forth the word of life; that I may rejoice in the day of Christ, that I have not run in vain, neither laboured in vain.
> [2:14–16]

What makes Paul's hopes and fears about the impact of his mission especially moving is that he wrote the Philippians from prison. Once again there has been much scholarly debate about where Paul was incarcerated when he drafted the epistle. Most experts conclude that the letter to the Philippians was sent from Rome, where Paul was awaiting trial for disturbing the peace in Jerusalem. This theory places the composition of Philippians late in Paul's career. Consequently, some scholars maintain that it is Paul's last surviving letter.

Wherever he was imprisoned, Paul made the general circumstances of his situation clear to his friends at Philippi who had sent him assistance. He was waiting in custody for a judicial decision from the emperor which would either set him free or condemn him to death. Samuel Johnson once remarked that "when a man knows he is to be hanged in a fortnight, it concentrates his mind wonderfully." Johnson's flippant but accurate maxim applies even to the clear-sighted Paul. His letter focuses on eternal things and demonstrates remarkable serenity and capacity for joy in the face of possible martyrdom. There are no complaints, only resolution. If he lives, he knows, he will continue to preach the gospel. If he dies, he will join Christ. Either way, he claims, "Christ will be magnified in my body, whether it be by life or death." Paul may be in the custody of the state, but his mind refuses to be fettered by Caesar's laws.

Seen from this perspective, the Epistle to the Philippians plays a germinal role in the tradition of prison literature. Along with the dialogues Plato wrote depicting Socrates under the death sentence (the *Apology*, *Crito*, and *Phaedo*), the Pauline prison epistles (Philippians, Philemon, and Colossians) created the genre that would provide models for writers from Boethius through Dostoevsky, Gramsci, and Bonhoeffer. Philippians sets the visionary tone of this tradition. Paul's letter also reveals the spiritual paradoxes that later writers would adopt. If one is trapped in finite space, one will contemplate infinite things. If one must face mortality, one will meditate on eternity. If one is held in the worst place society offers, one will dream of the just city. Augustine's City of God began in Paul's cell. The word can free the spirit, if not the body. The quality of the vision, however, is only as good as the moral character that produces it. Prison has also occasioned the diseased writings of Sade and Hitler. But for some men the adversity of imprisonment set the ultimate spiritual challenge which provoked their greatest work.

If Paul's Epistle to the Philippians is indeed his final work, then this intensely personal testament suggests the continued spiritual growth of his last years. Facing death, he achieved a psychological independence from his physical circumstances and gradually transformed his own personality closer to his own Christian ideal. The toughness of his earlier public self softened into an unguarded gentleness and compassion. His often explosive temper relaxed into joy. Living his difficult principles, he attained the security he promised his friends at Philippi, "the peace of God which passeth all understanding."

According to Catholic tradition, Paul was eventually condemned to death by the authorities in Rome. He was taken to the place now called Tre Fontane and beheaded. His body was then buried where the Basilica of Saint Paul Outside-the-Walls now stands as a monument. But his greatest memorial remains the church he founded at the riverbank outside Philippi, which became European Christianity. If ever a monument proved more durable than bronze or loftier than the pyramids, that loyal congregation was it.

THE EPISTLE OF
PAUL THE APOSTLE
TO THE COLOSSIANS

—

Gjertrud Schnackenberg

Despite its proximity to the Gospels, its aura of inspired authority, its canonical weight and gravity, and the fame of its momentous Christological hymn-creed, the Letter to the Colossians is less a sacred text—a record of the word of God—than a pointed directive, written perhaps by an associate of the apostle Paul, to a wayward Christian congregation in western Asia Minor. The ancient Church's habit of hallowing the Pauline Letters, authentic and pseudonymous, as nearly equivalent in holiness and import to the matter of the Gospels, was well established by the time of the Apostolic Fathers (Ignatius, Polycarp, Clement) in the second century C.E.; by the mid-fourth century, Paul's Letters were collected, canonized in the New Testament, and thus fixed, in perpetuity, as vastly consequential documents, cherished sources for authoritative pronouncements. Certainly such a document as Colossians provides an extraordinary shaft of light to penetrate the crypt of the decades between the Resurrection and the writing of the Gospels, illuminating a distant, jumbled, narrow fragment of the early Christian movement called the Way. Still, it is notable that this letter, written perhaps only thirty years after the crucifixion of Jesus in Judea, does not refer to the

history of Jesus or mention any of his teachings. Colossians is inter-
pretative, theological, secondary, and ahistorical; and from a distance
of over nineteen hundred years we may see it as a formulation—
occasional, reflexive, highly particular—by a worried Christian
thinker, to answer a crisis in one of the "infant churches of Asia,"
in the minor city of Colossae, in the angel-worshiping kingdom of
Phrygia, where a small congregation of Greek-speaking, recently
evangelized Gentiles is in danger of losing its Christian faith.

In my edition of the Bible, Colossians stands only seventy-one
pages from the last Gospel (itself a far more encompassing Christological masterpiece). Within this fraction-inch of paper an abyss
opens up in the New Testament, interposing a discouraging distance
between the kingdom Jesus proclaims and the church his apostles
establish. Of course, a great gulf divides Jesus of Nazareth from the
apostle Paul—it would be impossible to recover the former from the
writings of the latter—but in Colossians we are presented with yet
a third region, rich in material entirely alien to Jesus and almost
impossible to reconcile with Paul. Entering into this book, we enter
into a realm where Jesus never set foot—the novel realm of deutero-
Pauline thought (works based on Paul's theology but not written by
him), here summoned as an authoritative challenge to the worrisome
and proliferating heresies of Asia Minor.

The four chapters of Colossians offer, in addition to the dramatic
hymn to Christ's cosmic preeminence (1:15–20), a collection of prayers of thanksgiving, baptismal allusions, admonishments against sub-
Christian superstitions and practices, and a conventional (perhaps
partly Stoic, partly halakhic) list of ethical duties (3:18–4:6) diamet-
rically opposed to the moral teachings of Jesus of Nazareth. The
structure of the letter is modeled upon the structure of Paul's authentic letters, but this work offers several novel theological drifts
not found in Paul's work, such as the amazing announcements that
the Christian initiate *already* is transferred to the Kingdom of God,
and that in the baptismal rite the Resurrection *already* is accomplished
within the life of the individual, who has, in effect, died and risen
with Christ—a radical soteriological elaboration which leads one right
back into the recognizably Pauline conundrum of wondering where
one is to locate the foundations of moral life. The style of the letter

is liturgical, prolix, melismatic, and copious; the tone is impersonal and highly tactful.

Perhaps owing to this great and uncharacteristic tact, the personality of Paul—usually an unmistakable entity—is blurred in Colossians. When we step backward from Paul's undisputed letters (such as First and Second Corinthians, and Galatians), as from a large mosaic, we see his personality emerge: we make out the features of his singular humanity (his humor, his vexations, his tender anxiety for his friends, his sarcasm with opponents, his ferocious loyalty, his deliberate unwisdom, his mystical gift, his impetuosity, his original genius, his incredible persistence, his fearlessness—a second-century writer records the tradition that Paul "breathed friendliness"), as well as the essential nature of and tension of his personality (controversial, oxymoronic, dialectical—as if one of John Donne's religious sonnets were turned into a human being). The crux of Paul's existence, and the solitary factor about it that he considers important, is, of course, his conversion, the central image of his spiritual drama. From the accounts of this event in Acts, we first see Paul, almost as a creature in a story problem about Flatland, angrily riding off in one direction, steaming with righteous hatred, the terror of the primitive church. We then see him flattened (and raised), shattered (and exalted), destroyed (and saved), blinded (and illuminated), humiliated (and chosen). A broken man, too weak to support himself, he needs his companions to help him through the city gates of Damascus. When he revives, he seems to be awakening in Backwardsland, himself his former "enemy," his hatred evaporated into love, having arrived at the place from which he meant to flee. Paul never ceases to repeat that this is a *divine* encounter; it is this experience, and nothing else, that gives him the authority to preach the Way. It is this experience that his authentic writings track, in manifold and ever-modulating confidences, in dialectical whirlwinds, in catalogues of travails, in mesmerizing theological prisms, in outbursts of groaning exasperation (as when he writes to his backsliding Galatian congregation, "SEE IN WHAT BIG LETTERS I AM WRITING"), in prayers of love, in soliloquies, in prescriptions and directives, in rabbinical disputations, in repetitions of baptismal epithets, in cascades and waterfalls of poetry, in anger, in floods of joy.

But in Colossians this personality is difficult to detect. This letter is a mosaic from which, no matter how far back we step, no sharp image emerges. Instead of encountering Paul himself (his "sharp-foolishness," his leaps and starts, the very human comedy of his brilliant but pigheaded mind having been traumatized and transformed by divine love), we encounter in Colossians an abstraction or imitation, featureless and pious. A comparison of two autobiographical passages may help light up the difference between the authentic Paul and the imitation. First, in a passage that can be and has been approached from innumerable angles, for innumerable reasons, Paul dashes off a self-portrait so filled with his personality that it seems we can feel his living breath near us as we read it. In its excitement, intensity, controversy, unwisdom, competitiveness, and faintly ridiculous self-portrayal, as well as in its indisputable heroism, this passage has Paul's fingerprints all over it:

> But whatever any one dares to boast of—I am speaking as a fool—I also dare to boast of that. Are they Hebrews? So am I. Are they Israelites? So am I. Are they descendants of Abraham? So am I. Are they servants of Christ? I am a better one—I am talking like a madman—with far greater labors, far more imprisonments, with countless beatings, and often near death. Five times I have received at the hands of the Jews the forty lashes less one. Three times I have been beaten with rods; once I was stoned. Three times I have been shipwrecked; a night and a day I have been adrift at sea; on frequent journeys, in danger from rivers, danger from robbers, danger from my own people, danger from Gentiles, danger in the city, danger in the wilderness, danger at sea, danger from false brethren; in toil and hardship, through many a sleepless night, in hunger and thirst, often without food, in cold and exposure. And, apart from other things, there is the daily pressure upon me of my anxiety for all the churches. Who is weak, and I am not weak? Who is made to fall, and I am not indignant? [2 Corinthians 11:21–30]

But an autobiographical passage from Colossians shows us fingerprints so smudged and blurred we can't identify them. For all the considerable theological beauty of this paragraph, particularly the apocalyptic reference to the revealing of a mystery hidden for ages, when we look for Paul here we don't find him, only an oddly impersonal version, somewhat woolly, pietistic rather than passionate, and—I can't avoid the anachronism—"saintly":

> Now I rejoice in my sufferings for your sake, and in my flesh I complete what is lacking in Christ's afflictions for the sake of the body, that is, the church, of which I became a minister according to the divine office which was given to me for you, to make the word of God fully known, the mystery hidden for ages and generations, but now made manifest to his saints. [Colossians 1:24–26]

Of course, this sort of reading proves nothing; and certainly the author of Colossians, if it is not Paul, is someone who knows Paul's work very well. But how many worlds away from the Passion in Jerusalem we are, a tremendous distance when we consider how close this letter is, chronologically if not geographically, to the events of Jesus' life. If this letter is correctly dated to the early 60s C.E. (the date is not firmly established, and probably it never can be), then we are peering into an era—I am agitated to think of it—when many hundreds of people would still be alive who would have known Jesus of Nazareth, who would have been healed and taught by him, who would have been witnesses to his resurrection—people including his brother James, with whom Paul spent fifteen days in sequestered conversation in Jerusalem. Paul, who never met Jesus, speaking with Jesus' own brother—this must be one of the most tantalizing and fascinating of all the alluded-to but unrecorded conversations in the history of the world.

The text of Colossians is sewn together with threads of baptismal imagery, and with reiterative, liturgical elaborations on the theme and meaning of this ritual immersion in (or anointment with) water which, in memorializing the baptism of Jesus, unites the Christian initiate with the risen Christ in a new life. John the Baptist, whom Jesus so especially esteemed, called the people of Israel to repentance—that is, to a change of heart—symbolized in the baptism he offered in the river Jordan. We know that John's baptism of Jesus precipitated a crucial, lightninglike encounter between Jesus and God; in that instant, the Spirit descended upon Jesus, and his mission to the house of Israel began. This moment is not only overwhelmingly sacred, but it is also, of course, terribly difficult to fathom, to put into words, to repeat, to grasp. What happened to Jesus at that moment is beyond the reach of all interpretation. Jesus asks baptism of his apostles; and it is understandable that his followers, wanting to entrust this event to others, and feeling compelled to memorialize its precious character, should attempt to repeat it, and then finally to institute a ritual yielded up by their efforts at interpretation. In Acts, they themselves become baptists, seeking to offer union in the risen Christ to others, through calling up Jesus' baptism.

In the Colossian interpretation of baptism, the Christian initiate undergoes the death and resurrection of Jesus, immersed (buried) and retrieved (resurrected), as the old and broken image of Adam is restored in the healed and purified image of Christ. The initiate is raised from this death "through faith in the working of God" (2:12) and, thus kept in the mystery of the Christ, is "transferred . . . to the kingdom of his beloved Son" (1:13), is "qualified" (1:12) and "reconciled" (1:21). This spiritual identification between the initiate and the risen Christ gives rise in Colossians to hortatory ethical passages (particularly the sermon of 3:5–17), although it isn't clear, exactly, how the ethical system that is being advocated is established within this Christ-initiate identification. (If one's resurrection already is accomplished, why does one require an ethical exhortation? If one is transferred to the Kingdom through faith, then why must one "put to death therefore what is earthly in you . . ."? Is the initiate to be saved more than once? Through ethical good works as well as through faith? Through both together?) Whatever we make of this problem in Pauline Christianity, still the most beautiful and exalted element of the baptismal formula is sounded in Colossians (as it is sounded in Galatians and in 1 Corinthians): the announcement of the non-preferential, limitless love God feels for His creatures:

There is neither Jew nor Greek, there is neither slave nor free, there is neither male nor female; for you are all one in Christ Jesus. [Galatians 3:28]

For by one Spirit we were all baptized into one body—Jews or
Greeks, slaves or free—and all were made to drink of one Spirit.
[1 Corinthians 11:13]

Here there cannot be Greek and Jew, circumcised and uncircumcised, barbarian, Scythian, slave, free man, but Christ is all,
and in all. [Colossians 3:11]

Here, in this overcoming of distinctions, reaching back through the
disguises of race, gender, class, and nation to the reality of the created
soul, in this vindication of the preciousness of the spirit over against
the multiple, conflicting claims of "identity," we indeed encounter
the seeds of universalism shining in Jesus' life and teachings.

Still, cultic ritual in and of itself—even so inclusive and profound
a rite as this—presents an intractable problem, in light of Jesus'
teachings, to the Christian conscience. We needn't rehearse the perversity of human limitations, so exhausted and crowded by history
as we are, to remember that in the general run of things our own
rituals are likely to seem profound, beautiful, moving, and wonderfully ancient, whereas the rituals of others are likely to seem superstitious, silly, uninspiring, and lacking in efficacious merit. Ritual,
hallowed to the inner group, is also exclusive and divisive. That is,
if the rite of baptism simply replaces one identity with another, then
that rite doesn't inevitably fully bear out the beautiful words of
Galatians 3:28. It would be an absurd suggestion that cultic ritual,
in itself, is alien to Jesus of Nazareth, for of course he is an observant,
ineffably religious Jew. The rite of baptism clearly devolves from the
mikveh, the ritual purification intended to separate the pure from the
defiled, the clean from the dirty, the saved from the rejected; and
this element of ritual purification echoes through the institution even
as baptism evolves away from symbolic ritual toward mystical union.
And yet, how many times, and in how many ways, does Jesus say
that he has come to the lost sheep of the house of Israel, to the
outcast, the ritually unclean, the rejected, the poor, the forgotten,
to all those who do not feel assured of salvation? That the pure, the
chosen, the clean, the assured are the ones most insensible to the
need to open their hearts? Once we enter, through this rite of baptism, into the inner group of the saved, haven't we stated our as-

surance? Are we any longer the people to whom Jesus came? As we draw a boundary line between the saved and the unsaved, aren't we drawing a map that will lead us, over and over, to the places of stoning and crucifixion?

Geography, lying somewhere between "the starry heavens above and the moral law within," may yield up its metaphysical dimensions less readily to a traveler than to a map reader—to someone who studies the earth from a supposedly aerial, atemporal point of view. Of course, traveling too is a way of reading maps; and certainly, in my own travels, when I seek out the ruins and visible fragments of the Roman Empire and Magna Graecia, I can't help seeing—in those vast apocalyptic images, fallen towers, stairways leading up to vanished second stories, the grassy geometries of ancient streets, foot-high walls that once loomed overhead—the backdrop of the first-century proclamation of the Resurrection, an empty theater for pressing yet again, to no one in particular, the question his fellow Jews so clamorously pressed on Jesus: "Master, when is the Kingdom of God?" The century of the apocalypse is far behind us, and yet sheep safely graze over what is left of the era when Paul journeyed thousands of miles to enter the synagogues and dwelling places, the arcades and basilicas of cities and villages throughout the empire, to announce, "He is risen." Was Jesus mistaken about the precipitous, cataclysmic end of the world? Or do the ages hang by a thread; are the mountain ranges of time—unutterable himalayas—merely a grain of sand before the Creator? Yet doesn't the light shine only upon the present moment? Doesn't nature lavish everything—everything—upon the present moment, plunging the past out of view and out of existence, and lighting up nothing of the future? And isn't the present moment the "time" of the morality Jesus reveals? Still, when one gazes down into the trenches of Roman excavations, it can seem that it is the dead who have been made real by death, whereas, before that massive, impenetrable finality, that monumental consequence, the living are changed into transitory ghosts.

And yet, in a library, seated before an atlas of classical antiquity, tracing with a fingertip the system of Roman roads in Asia Minor along which this Letter to the Colossians would have been carried (if the letter were sent from Ephesus, it traveled about 120 miles inland to the east, to Colossae, on the way to Syria and *Arabia Deserta*), touching the map, I am better able to see something that is hidden from me at an excavation site or when I am driving along what is left of a Roman road surface in a rented, hesitating Fiat. The sight of the Roman road system, sketched out in its totality on a map, is nearly as telling and as exciting to me as the sight of verses on a page. Like lines of poetry, the Roman roads are lines humming with communications, lines of awesome directness and force, lines that cut through confusion, connecting distant objects and events; like lines of poetry, the roads flow with multiple associations and images, they are open to all subjects, they break through borders and boundaries, they take the highest way, affording the largest views; like lines of poetry, the roads, in all the rhythms of their branchings, favor change, variation, mental evolution, and they culminate, finally, in a kind of self-portrait—for certainly, as I trace the empire's road map, I feel as much that I am tracing a portion of the empire's self-portrait as if I were touching the marble ear of a portrait bust of Augustus.

And, like lines of poetry, the Roman roads have a depth to their foundations that, finally, we cannot touch, foundations bound to crumble away or dissolve at our probing, backward into a time gulf. In Asia Minor the highway of the Roman senatorial province would overlay the road of the Greek colony, which would overlay the local Phrygian roads, which would overlay the thoroughfares of shepherds and sheep, then footpaths finally swallowed by the grasses of the open fields or lost in the rock cliffs of the local mountains.

And, like lines of poetry, the Roman roads were conduits of divinities, who, contrary to all myths and rumors, were not airborne, but traveled as pedestrians and ship passengers together with everyone else in the empire. The gods poured into Rome along whatever highways Rome could build (together with the *cursus publicus*, troops, food, curios, elephants, flamingos, merchants, traders, captives). The early Christian movement enters onto the highways in the midst of this traffic of gods and angels. Indeed, it is called the Way; indeed, it is on the road that Paul's encounter with the risen Christ shatters him. The road map presents us with a communication system through which the Christ-event in Judaea will be explored, interpreted, and expressed no less than in such lines of poetry as the hymn to the preexistent Christ in Colossians.

Colossae is an unexcavated archaeological site, in a country now called Turkey but once called the kingdom of Phrygia—a country so wealthy that Midas was its king; in Phrygia the Gordian knot was tied. A lavish and prodigal gesture overhangs Phrygia, for King Attalus III of Pergamum bequeathed it to Rome in 133 B.C.E. in the tribunate of Tiberius Gracchus (who accepted the windfall with what his advisers felt to be unseemly eagerness): Asia Minor became a Roman senatorial province overnight. Colossae and its neighboring cities were famous in antiquity for the manufacture of a luxury good, the naming of which provokes associations both Virgilian and Biblical: dyed purple wool. And Phyrgia exported to Rome something more important than dyed purple wool: the great goddess Cybele, who, upon her arrival and installation on the Palatine in 205–04 B.C.E. assumed the features of one of the most important deities the Romans could conceive, the Magna Mater, goddess of Nature (and, surely, a forerunner of the Italian Madonna).

A modern map will show us something else about Colossae: that it is located near the Turkish-Aegean tectonic plates, in the center of earthquake country, a part of the huge landscape of earthquakes that wrinkle the continent in a northward push toward the Caucasus mountains, repeatedly overthrowing or swallowing cities (as recently as 1988 producing the huge destruction of several Armenian cities). Colossae was destroyed by an earthquake, perhaps as late as the fourth century or as early as the 60s C.E., perhaps within only months or years of receiving this apostolic dispatch, perhaps even before Paul was beheaded by Nero's henchmen in Rome (c. 67 C.E.). And so the small congregation of Colossian Christians, who would have fervently awaited the apocalypse of Jewish charismatic prophecies, "fell asleep" (in the vocabulary of the early Christian movement) in the kingdom of Phrygia, to be disturbed and exposed sooner by the spoons and trowels of an archaeological team than resurrected by hosts of angels. To date, though, Colossae, with its turbulent "heresy," its Greek-speaking, angel-worshiping Gentile Christian congregation, is lost to history—or abandoned to eternity.

And the Colossian "heresy" is lost to modernity as well, long since exiled, like the angels of Asia, to the dim regions of sub-Christian practices and superstitions. The heresy apparently is a multicultural, multifaceted cultic aberration to which this letter provides numerous clues but no definitive description: we need to picture Colossae's location, on the heavily trafficked east–west imperial trade route, and its population of Phrygian natives, Greek colonists, Italian immigrants, and multitudinous Diaspora Jews—that is, we need to picture a population that includes (in order) angel-worshiping proto-Gnostics, cosmopolitan, skeptical, wisdom-loving philosophizers, pantheistic pagans, and exclusivistic, monotheistic, cultic ritualists. Especially there is a prominent Judaizing influence in this heresy, of course, for not only is Christianity in the 60s C.E. a Jewish sect, but the Diaspora Jews (with a population estimated between two and five million) were in the midst of a tremendous, highly successful missionary effort, seeking to convert the heathen nations to the worship of the one God. Pagan males who were drawn to Judaism but were unable to face the ordeal of adult circumcision, were allowed to attend the synagogue as marginal adherents—proselytes—tolerated by the Jews as "God fearers"; and surely many of the Gentile Christians in Asia Minor would have come to Christianity from this population of proselytes, given that Paul decided the circumcision obligation was not binding upon Gentiles (a decision that Israel could not, and would not, tolerate). From the Israelite point of view, Asia Minor was an infamously cosmopolitan, glamorous, curious, exuberant, experimental region, bewailed by the rabbis in the Babylonian Talmud as seductive of Jews, who, establishing roots there, would be exposed to all manner of extravagant perversities. A most marvelous description of the conversation between the Greeks and Jews is supplied in Acts 17, just before Paul makes his famous pitch to the Athenians:

> Now while Paul was waiting for them at Athens, his spirit was provoked within him as he saw that the city was full of idols. So he argued in the synagogue with the Jews and the devout persons, and in the market place every day with those who chanced to be there. Some also of the Epicurean and Stoic philosophers met him. And some said, "What would this babbler

say?" Others said, "He seems to be a preacher of foreign divinities"—because he preached Jesus and the resurrection. And they took hold of him and brought him up to the Areopagus, saying, "May we know what this new teaching is which you present? For you bring some strange things to our ears; we wish to know therefore what these things mean." Now all the Athenians and the foreigners living there spent their time in nothing except telling or hearing something new.

It is difficult not to be amused at the mutual assessments of vulgarity we see in this passage, as the "enemies of God" (the Jewish epithet for pagans) meet up with the "enemies of mankind" (the pagan epithet for Jews). But still, despite the wishful thinking of Jewish and Christian missionaries, these various cultures and religions did not exist in a discontinuous sequence, one replacing and extinguishing the next in chronological order; nor did they exist as contiguous but well-barricaded and isolated modes of life (although ancient cities had ethnic neighborhoods or regions just as modern cities do); rather, they lived all together in what must have been cacophonous and constant conversation (Greek), mutually giving and receiving influences and ideas—and changing one another.

And so, gazing into this mare's nest of conflicting claims, the author of Colossians warns the new Christian congregation:

See to it that no one makes a prey of you by philosophy and empty deceit, according to human tradition, according to the elemental spirits of the universe, and not according to Christ. For in him the whole fulness of deity dwells bodily, and you have come to fulness of life in him, who is the head of all rule and authority. In him also you were circumcised with a circumcision made without hands, by putting off the body of flesh in the circumcision of Christ; and you were buried with him in baptism, in which you were also raised with him through faith in the working of God, who raised him from the dead. And you, who were dead in trespasses and the uncircumcision of your flesh, God made alive together with him, having forgiven us all our trespasses, having canceled the bond which stood against us with its legal demands; this he set aside, nailing it to the cross.

He disarmed the principalities and powers, and made a public example of them, triumphing over them in him.

Therefore let no one pass judgment on you in questions of food and drink or with regard to a festival or a new moon or a sabbath. These are only a shadow of what is to come; but the substance belongs to Christ. Let no one disqualify you, insisting on self-abasement and worship of angels, taking his stand on vision, puffed up without reason by his sensuous mind, and not holding fast to the Head, from whom the whole body, nourished and knit together through its joints and ligaments, grows with a growth that is from God.

If with Christ you died to the elemental spirits of the universe, why do you live as if you still belonged to the world? Why do you submit to regulations, "Do not handle, Do not taste, Do not touch" (referring to things which all perish as they are used) according to human precepts and doctrines? [2:8–22]

This is the sum description of the Colossian heresy; it strikes one as a loud and speculative discussion. We hear the Phrygian proposal that Christ must be one of the angels, and the proto-Gnostic phrase "elemental spirits of the universe" (whoever they are); we hear the Greek proposal that Christ is the founder of a new school of wisdom, perhaps in the style of the Platonic, Stoic, or Epicurean schools (a proposal that would drive Paul to distraction, by the way, provoking his pronouncements about the foolishness of God); we hear the Judaizers insisting on circumcision, on cultic regulations, and obligations to observe festivals, new moons, and Sabbaths; and we see that these things are being mixed all together. But it is not only the Colossian congregation that is picking and choosing from among protean and intriguing possibilities and applying these to their new-found Christian worship; for the author of this letter—even as he attempts to assert the transcendent Christian way of life—himself employs phrases, advice, and metaphors from every part of the imperial map, including, for example, the phrase about the shadow and the substance, which is clearly Platonic; a phrase about "walking in the way of the Lord," which is clearly a phrase of the Jewish halakah; several phrases that have a distinctly Gnostic tinge (such as 1:9 and 1:12); and a shocking metaphor describing Christ as a triumphant

Roman military general, dragging behind him the "principalities and powers" (Gnostic spirits or Jewish angels, perhaps?) as if they were captives in a triumphal parade of imperial conquest.

Nor was heathendom the only quarter of the world inhabited by a potentially overbearing supernatural population, for the cosmology of the turbulent and anguished population of Israel (and not only the world picture of the Greek- and Latin-speaking Jews of the Diaspora but the Palestinian cosmology overhanging Jerusalem) was overrun with angels, archangels, principalities, powers, "forces" of good and evil, unknown intermediaries, Satan (or the Prince of Darkness), the Shekinah (the "numinous immanence of God" said to inhabit the First Temple but not the Second Temple), and the preexistent figure of Wisdom, who kept God company "before" the Creation; God did not dwell in the total, transcendent, abstract, solitary apartness that modernity mistakenly attributes back to him. He existed "together" with Torah; and he and Torah both could and would descend to earth in various forms, mixing into history. And underneath this complicated supernatural throng, all across the Judean countryside, widely various factions raged in discussions more heated, more demanding, and more immediately dangerous than the conversations along the Stoa or in the Forum or under any of the shaded arcades of urban heathendom.

So, into these swarming cosmologies and heavenly pavilions, Hellenistic, Judean, and proto-Gnostic, the Letter to the Colossians delivers, for the first time in the surviving records of the Way, a hymn to the preexistence and the preeminence of Christ—a poetic work that is all the more striking when we reflect that it may precede the astonishing opening sentence of the Gospel of John by as much as thirty years. (It is striking as well to think that both of these works may emanate from the city of Ephesus.) In the tradition of psalms, poems of thanksgiving, and mystical hymns of praise, the universe is portrayed as the luminous home for the enactments of God, the domain of Torah glimpsed in the starry night—as in Psalm 119, "For ever, O Lord, thy word is firmly fixed in the heavens"—and the hymn's singer seems to look backward and forward in time and space, and down through all the generations, with nothing less than the

universe as the background of the revelation. We hear this same
sound when David sings his love poems to the Law:

> *The heavens are telling the glory of God;*
> *and the firmament proclaims his handiwork.*
> *Day to day pours forth speech,*
> *and night to night declares knowledge.*
> *There is no speech, nor are there words;*
> *their voice is not heard;*
> *yet their voice goes out through all the earth,*
> *and their words to the end of the world.*

> [*Psalm 19*]

Such intimations are recorded in Greece as well, and we know that
Paul was acquainted with Cleanthes' great hymn to Zeus—or rather,
to Reason, or Law, or Logos—for Paul alludes to it during his speech
to the Athenians when he is "standing in the middle of the Areopagus," perhaps in an effort to reach his Greek audience through
their own poetry. When we turn to this hymn, we may hear the note
of the Psalmist's hymn to Torah, and we may see shadows of the
Colossian Christ-hymn as well:

> *Thou, O Zeus, art praised above all gods: many are thy names and*
> *thine is all power for ever.*
> *The beginning of the world was from thee: and with law thou rulest*
> *over all things.*
> *Unto thee may all flesh speak: for we are thy offspring.*
> *Therefore will I raise a hymn unto thee: and will ever sing of thy*
> *power.*
> *The whole order of the heavens obeyeth thy word: as it moveth around*
> *the earth:*
> *With little lights and great lights mixed together: how great thou*
> *art, King above all for ever!*
> *Nor is anything done upon earth apart from thee: nor in the fir-*
> *mament, nor in the seas:*
> *Save that which the wicked do: by their own folly.*

But thine is the skill to set even the crooked straight: what is without
fashion is fashioned and the alien akin before thee—
Thus hast thou fitted together all things in one: the good with the
evil:
That thy word should be one in all things: abiding for ever.
Let folly be dispersed from our souls: that we may repay thee the honor,
wherewith thou hast honored us:
Singing praise of thy works for ever: as becometh the sons of men.

In Colossians it is the Christ, rather than Reason (or Zeus) or
Logos or Torah, who holds all things together, whose precedence is
celebrated in exalted and emphatic cadences (although the hymn is
not metered); the text is noticeably creedlike in its clear and simple
declarations, intended, perhaps, to quell argument and to still the
mind. The hymn's opening line rings a change upon the most mysterious bell in the Hebrew Bible, in the first and ninth books of
Genesis, in which we hear the note struck three times, that man is
created in the divine image—a riddle so deep, an action on the part
of the Creator so fearful and sublime, that human discussion dwindles
and subsides before this utterance; the most that we can do is to
hold this strange statement in awe; our explanations falter before it.
Now, in Colossians, this story is touched once again: the broken and
defiled image of God—Adam, defaced in the catastrophe in the Garden—is, in Christ, restored and healed (again, this bears the mark
of the baptismal rite); and, as the defilement of Adam is felt, communicated, and inherited throughout all the generations—Adam's
defilement isn't simply his own, but everyone's—so too this restoration of the divine image is felt, communicated, and inherited
throughout all creation. Other Christological passages in the New
Testament will present or emphasize other aspects of Christ's flooding into the universe: John 1:1–2 will present the Christ as the Word
of God, identified with God; Philippians 2:7 will present the Suffering Servant prefigured in Isaiah; 1 Corinthians 1:23 will present the
stumbling block and folly of the crucified Messiah; Hebrews 1:1–4
will present the Christ who reflects, who inherits, who bears the
stamp of God's nature. But here in Colossians, because in this interpretation the Kingdom of God is effected already for the faithful,
we encounter the cosmic and glorified *imago Dei*. This is the Christ

we will come to know depicted in the enormous mosaic domes from the spheres of Byzantium: the Pantocrator, floating far overhead, between heaven and earth, in clouds of abstract gold "space," preexistent, omniscient, gigantic, grave, translated into the Kingdom and yet perpetually identified with all creatures and all Creation, holding together the universal church and all of history—and even presiding over the little congregation as it gathers to worship in Philemon's home in Colossae. The hymn's orientation toward origins rather than Parousia gives it a Hellenistic rather than a Hebrew stamp, for the Greeks did not share the Hebrew obsession with the outcome, the end of things, the moral, historical, personal longing for justice; and yet this Christ is the lord of history, and at its close the hymn plummets suddenly down to the shocking sight of Jesus' blood on the cross:

> *He is the image of the invisible God,*
> *the first-born of all creation;*
> *for in Him all things were created,*
> *in heaven and on earth,*
> *visible and invisible,*
> *whether thrones or dominions*
> *or principalities or authorities—*
> *all things were created through him and for him.*
> *He is before all things,*
> *and in him all things hold together.*
> *He is the head of the body, the church;*
> *He is the beginning,*
> *the first-born from the dead,*
> *that in everything He might be pre-eminent.*
> *For in Him all the fulness of God was pleased to dwell,*
> *and through Him to reconcile to Himself all things,*
> *whether on earth or in heaven,*
> *making peace by the blood of His cross.*

To anyone not acquainted with either the ancient Greek schools or the Judaism of the first century, it will seem a rare thing indeed that here Jesus of Nazareth—crucified as a criminal under the heel of the Roman Empire, in an obscure outpost of what the West calls the East—that Jesus here is proclaimed as having been present together with God "before" the Creation, in the unimaginable realm "outside" of time and space, "before" God chose life over not-life. But the sources for this perhaps bewildering proclamation are preserved all around us to this day, and not only in the famous syncretistic Logos of the Greek-speaking Jewish apologist Philo. In the Judaism of antiquity, Torah is the inspiration, the reason, the aim, the meaning of the universe; a midrash says: "God looked into the Torah and created the world." Torah preexists creation—unfathomably to human beings—in letters of black fire upon white fire; what is revealed to Moses in the stone tablets is a fraction only, a glimpse, of Torah's splendor and incommensurable beauty. God and Torah exist "together," transcendent and unutterable, yet they do not hold aloof from the Creation but descend to earth, enter into history. God's voice walks in the Garden of Eden. The "word of the Lord" appears to Abraham by the oaks of Mamre, a mysterious figure who brings Abraham out under the night sky to look up at the heavens and "number the stars." At Sinai, Torah is glimpsed; the divine presence (mediated by angels, perhaps) appears in the form of the burning bush. Spectacularly God manifests himself to all of Israel—"even to the handmaidens"—in the overwhelming communal revelation at Sinai, with thunder and lightning, smoke and fire, earthquake and trumpet blast. Repeatedly God speaks through the Prophets: repeatedly he sends angels and intermediaries. Now, in the Christian tradition, God comes nearer than angels or prophets can, turning toward us the face of Jesus: now the whole of the Law, in its mystical totality, is revealed: the love of the Creator, indiscriminate, unjust, nonpreferential, for his creatures, expressed in Jesus' hair-raising, divine, transcendent moral claims, and in his example and sacrifice, and in his Resurrection. What had been broken and lost—the *imago Dei*—is now restored; what had been partial and particular—the Sinaitic revelation—is now limitless and universal. The human being is invited to "see" with a vision lent by God rather than to "see" according to fallen human nature, and to participate in the love of God—that point at which the Kingdom, the *malkhut shamaim,* looms in the Creation. As Paul writes, using the sublime phrasing appropriate to this end-of-time: "From now on, therefore, we regard no one from a human point of view; even though we once regarded Christ from a human point of view, we regard him thus no longer." [2 Corinthians 5:16] That is: *It is finished*. But still the Parousia would not come.

To "the reader in the future" (in Mandelstam's phrase), something other than the Kingdom, or the Parousia, or even the catastrophic earthquakes of Phrygia, looms into the Letter to the Colossians: the specter of Byzantium, due north of Colossae about 220 miles as the crow flies, and about 260 years into the future. The Colossian Christ-hymn is not *only* an answer to the incipient heresies of Asia Minor; it is not *only* an attempt to fathom the unfathomable identity of Jesus; it is not *only* an attempt to organize the early Christian movement under the cosmic leadership of the Word of God; it is not *only* a historical example of the first stirrings of creed making; it is not *only* a heart's cry which testifies to the disappearance and absence of Jesus of Nazareth from the midst of his followers—although it is all of these things. Colossians is, as well, a foreshadowing—ingenuous, but nonetheless—of the Christendom of the third and fourth centuries, of the great councils and synods, and of the dust devils of feuds, denunciations, power struggles, and anathemas that tear through the highly politicized administrative bodies in Nicaea, Constantinople, Ephesus, and Chalcedon. In Colossians Christ is the head of the universe, the mystical monarch, the potentate; we can't help seeing something taking place in the shadow of this exalted declaration, something beyond the routine substitution of zeal (which Jesus despised) for devotion, piety for faith, ceremonial scruple for righteousness, power for love. We see the first century's evangelical mission attaining "success" and finally "supremacy," a bitterly, lamentably cruel paradox when we think of how Jesus of Nazareth rejected precisely this sort of "success" and "supremacy." We see the kingdom of God being interpreted as cosmography, cosmography mapped as geography, geography translated into empire, empire divided into real estate, real estate crumbling into treasuries. We see the emperor Constantine, wholly lacking in even the most primitive sense of contradiction, entering the hall of the Nicene Council dressed in purple and jewels, and taking his seat, among his ambitious bishops and the mutilated survivors of the persecutions, in "a modest gold chair." In the decade since his "conversion," he has continued to order execution by crucifixion; and one year into the future he will order his eldest son and wife steamed—or perhaps boiled—to death in the baths. We can't help recalling that the decapitated head of his rival Maxentius was sent to Africa as a trophy of Constantine's ascendancy only days after Constantine's vision or dream of the Chi-Rho. Time has taken a trophy of Constantine's head as well, in that overbearing, goggle-eyed, gigantified, severed marble head of the Constantinian colossus, captive and on view for a true Roman *aeternitas* in the courtyard of the Capitoline (an appropriate cage for it, considering that Michelangelo's enigmatic design for the Campidoglio does not incorporate a single Christian element or reference). This colossal head rolled from a colossal figure that his laborers had assembled, in haste and pillage, as a patchwork of plundered statuary parts affixed to an empty shell. Of course, the personal crimes of Constantine, to say nothing of the works of art produced in his reign, are not a concern of the church. History's perversity is, quite simply, history's perversity: still, the individual soul quails before the utterance of Constantine's third son, Constantius III, who inherited the East on his father's death and, wanting to secure the condemnation of Athanasius, told his church: "Let my will be deemed a canon among you."

We can rightly attribute limited knowledge of the future to the author of Colossians, not prophetic power. In the Pauline evangelical mission (as opposed to the Jerusalem Orthodox Jewish-Christian sect, headed by James, the brother of the Lord, and other of Jesus' family, until the destruction of the Temple in 70), the Way is polymorphous, universalistic, and, despite Paul's occasional muttering of anathema, not coercive; it arises as an invitation to all human souls as children of God. Furthermore, the Way in the 60s C.E. is a minority sect, soon enough to undergo wave upon wave of persecutions; as such, it is more seditious than conquistatorial, burning, from underneath and within, across the conventional barriers of gender, class, culture, race, religion, nation, from the desert into the city and out across the rural landscape. The Way is not a centralized institution authorizing itself to develop a core of elaborated dogmas and official theological sacraments (although the Christian congregations would have had some sort of circulating Gospel, some sort of liturgical body of "psalms and hymns and spiritual songs" [Colossians 3:16], perhaps a creed, perhaps some sort of delegation of authority under the sponsorship of the apostles). Furthermore, surely the author of Colossians, despite his shocking metaphor of Christ as a Roman military officer, and despite his assertion of Christ as the supreme ruler of the universe, would be stricken speechless at the (soon to be applied) implicit comparison of Christ, the Lord of the universe, and the emperor of Rome—and not in the least because overlording this decade is the Antichrist himself, Nero, crucifier of Christians and Jews, bestower of martyrdom on Peter and Paul.

Yet even at this early date—even with so fresh and raw a memory of how viscerally Jesus pitted his life against the sanctification of cultural habits, the idolization of human prescriptions and incremental, binding interpretations, the routinization of religion, and the death's head of rote institutional religious authority—even so, the Letter to the Colossians was written for one reason only: to answer, to stave off, to extinguish, a "heresy." Rather than looking back to the condemnation of Jesus of Nazareth as a blasphemer, Colossians looks forward to the reestablishment of norms by which blasphemers may be judged and condemned. Only thirty years after Jesus' death, we detect the assertion of orthodoxy, cultural tradition, conventional prescriptions, and boundary-creating dogmas which—to paraphrase that critically sad moment in Acts—will become the cloud that will take Jesus out of our sight. The role of Christology in this, if only partial, is indisputable, and perhaps inevitable, given that the world did not end, and given his inexplicable divinity; the mystery of Jesus' identity demanded to be solved.

Certainly we cannot hope that, by pressing backward through the history of the primitive church to the reality of Yeshua ben Ha-Notzri, we can, in Robert Frost's phrase, "Drink and be whole again beyond confusion"; for surely Jesus disquiets and distresses as much as comforts us, surprises as much as answers us. The divine love he teaches, welling up within each present particle of time, forever available among all of the complex claims of each particular moment, is destabilizing of present order, inexhaustibly creative, unsystematic, spontaneous, unformulaic. He speaks in the evocative, twinkling, perplexing idiom of moral poetry, in parables, paradoxes, mysterious figures, epigrams, and piercing summations which can dissolve history in an instant; he is able to superinduce poetry in even his most thickheaded conversants (perhaps poets may be comforted to find that poetry, apparently, is the idiom of the Kingdom). He teaches the morality of the Kingdom of God, not of human affairs; he teaches us about God, not about ourselves. And his counterclaim to earthly grandiosity and power, his opposition to the self-authorizing prestige of the religious institution's picture of itself as a divine bequest, is unwavering, absolute, and extreme. When a man rushes up to him and kneels before him, saying, "Good Teacher . . ." we hear Jesus' passionate, flashing retort: "Why do you call me good? No one is good but God alone."

The path to Golgotha, and its aftermath, is a path that presses beyond religion and identity, beyond the dissolution of identity that religion intends to confer; religious practice is displaced by this awesome, harrowing, inward feat. In Philippians Paul quotes a Christological hymn far starker, far less dazzling, and more profound than the Colossians hymn, saying that Jesus

> . . . *though he was in the form of God,*
> *did not count equality with God a thing to be grasped,*
> *but emptied himself,*
> *taking the form of a servant. . . .*

> [*Philippians* 2:6–7]

In the saying that Jesus "emptied himself," the followers of Jesus may feel themselves to be in the presence of a phrase that emanates from the silence surrounding the cross itself, where one may glimpse, in the "mystery hidden for ages and generations, but now made manifest" (Colossians 1:26) the dimensions of God's own suffering and pity—and of God's awe.

As for the efficacy of this letter, there are numerous indications that for centuries Phrygia could not, or would not, give up its angel worshiping, no matter how forceful the canonical blasts delivered against it. In 363 C.E. the Council of Laodicea (about ten miles from the site of Colossae) published, as its thirty-fifth canon, the following: "It is not right for Christians to abandon the Church of God and go away and invoke angels. . . . If therefore any one is found devoting himself to this secret idolatry, let him be anathema." In the fifth century, Theodoret records that the "disease" of angel worship long hung over the Phrygians, and that shrines and oratories to Michael dotted the Phrygian countryside.

From this we learn that Hermes, the chief pagan angel-messenger, had at least had the decency to adopt the Hebrew name and history of Michael. And, although it was enough to make a church father bury his face in his hands, in the still semipagan world view in rural Asia Minor, Michael did seem a reasonable and worthy rival of Christ's—for Michael, after all, is the greatest angel who ever existed, in Israel, Christendom, or Islam. In a *Dictionary of Angels* I find Michael's honorific titles and breathtaking accomplishments (such as overthrowing mountains) taking up column after column: this is the angel whose hand grabbed Abraham's wrist from the sacrifice of Isaac; this is the angel who may have appeared to Moses in the form of the burning bush; this angel is nothing less than the forerunner of the Shekinah; he is the Prince of Israel, the conqueror of Satan, the ruler of the fourth heaven.

But most of all, the *Midrash Rabba* (Exodus 18) suggests that Michael is the author of Psalm 85. I am arrested by this bit of information, picturing the chiefest of the archangels shut up in his own realm—the fourth heaven, one heaven higher than the heaven into which Paul was caught up—and enshrouded in the solitude and loneliness that surrounds the act of writing. Writing is a testament to absence, to otherness. Jesus does not ask us to write; the poetry poured from him; he wrote nothing down. Perhaps the moral-metaphysical Kingdom literally *at hand* was too urgently upon him. Perhaps he knew the Bible by heart—as poetry is meant to be known; perhaps he alone in Israel wholly grasped the ungraspable "letters of black fire on white fire," and therefore was repelled by the contrast of the Scribes' exaction. Perhaps he knew, in an instant's understanding, what the rest of us learn through all the great trudging length of history: that writing does not bring the Kingdom nearer. Or perhaps Jesus wrote nothing because, at least until his last moment on the cross, he had never known the absence of *Abba*.

THE FIRST AND
SECOND EPISTLES OF
PAUL THE APOSTLE
TO THE THESSALONIANS

—

THE LONG, LONG WAIT

Amy Clampitt

In the Sunday school of my childhood, chanting the names of the books of the Bible was a favored learning device; and up to a point, anyhow, it worked. I can still hear "Joshua, Judges, Ruth"; "Isaiah, Jeremiah, Ezekiel"; and likewise "Acts, Romans, First-and-Second-Corinthians." Beyond such clusters of three, I tended to stumble. What I did not learn, and what needs to be digested before one can begin to consider the Epistles of Paul to the Thessalonians, is that chronologically we had the New Testament all wrong. It's not only that of the four Gospels, Mark is earlier than Matthew, and John comes a long, long way after. It's also that Paul's First Epistle to the Thessalonians turns out to have been written before any of the four Gospels: chronologically, it is the earliest book in the entire New Testament.

The ramifications of this discovery are not to be perceived at a glance. They need tracing and pinning down. The date, first of all, is around 50 C.E.—that is, approximately twenty years after Jesus of Nazareth was arrested and put to death on a charge of sedition. Paul's earliest Epistle is also the earliest known document to mention Jesus by name. Not only was there no written account of his life and sayings; the word "Christian" had yet to be invented. That the religion it has come to designate would one day be the official cult of the Roman Empire, or an official cult of any kind, would hardly have occurred to anyone. Among dozens of religions, in a period rife with initiations and secret gatherings, a more likely candidate—or so historians tell us—would have been the worship of the Persian god Mithra.

At all events, the founding of an official religion was not what the apostle had in mind when he announced himself, along with two colleagues, in the earliest known Christian document: "Paul, and Silvanus, and Timothy, unto the church of the Thessalonians in God the Father and the Lord Jesus Christ." To know even dimly what he did have in mind, the words he used need to be looked at closely. In 50 C.E. the entire congeries of domes, steeples, gargoyles, stained glass, choir robes, candles—whatever is automatically summoned up by the English word "church"—was in the future; and equally so was the monolithic hierarchy that springs to mind when the word is written with a capital. The Greek word *ekklesia*, which Paul used, originally had no such associations, any more than the word *synagoge*, which is to be found elsewhere in the New Testament. The word *synagoge* meant originally a gathering, a bringing together; *ekklesia* referred, somewhat more specifically, to a civic assembly. The assembly of believers whom Paul addressed at Thessalonica met in one another's households, as any newly formed, essentially subversive group did then, or would do now.

As Paul uses it, however, the word *ekklesia* is qualified: he writes to the church of the Thessalonians *in*—or, as a more recent translation has it, the church "founded on"—God the Father and the Lord Jesus Christ. The etymological subtleties of this formulation, and more particularly of the phrase "in Christ," which Paul uses again and again, have been the subject of long and earnest debate, among those for whom the word *Christos* itself would call for none. For the rest of us, it needs likewise to be looked at. The literal meaning of *Christos* is "anointed one," from a verb meaning "to be rubbed" (most commonly with an oil or salve). It is the Greek equivalent of the Hebrew word "Messiah," similarly derived from a verb meaning "to anoint." Among the Jews up until the time of the Babylonian exile, the word "Messiah" referred to one of the kingly line of David, whose anointing by a priest or prophet was taken as a sign that he had been chosen by the Almighty to rule over the children of Israel. By the time of Paul, to pronounce the word "Messiah" was to set loose a flood of religious and political overtones: when Messiah came, it would be as a liberator of the Jews, bringing centuries of foreign domination to an end.

The Thessalonians to whom Paul was writing were not Jews, however. They were ethnic Greeks—sometime pagans who had turned, in the apostle's words, "from idols, to serve a living and true God." The Greek word *eidolon*, which Paul used, derives from a verb meaning simply "to see" and denotes a thing seen, an image. Among the Jews the worship of such images was of course proscribed. It had been regarded with particular horror since the reign of the Hellenistic Syrian tyrant Antiochus IV, who had desecrated the Temple at Jerusalem by setting up there an altar to the Olympian Zeus, whose image was enshrined in many a Greek holy place. The view of the world which the converts at Thessalonica had accepted, in turning away from all such worship, was essentially a Jewish one. As set forth by the Hebrew prophets, that view had a severity and an Asian excess such as the Greeks, in their concern for balance and clarity, would have put in its place by making it into an art form—a ritual drama or a graven image. The Hebrew prophets had no time for art forms. Their message was far too urgent: "Blow ye the trumpet in Zion, and sound an alarm in my holy mountain; let all the inhabitants of the land tremble; for the day of the Lord cometh, for it is nigh at hand." Thus the prophet Joel, calling on a backsliding Israel to repent and mend her ways.

The Hebrew Bible resounds with such summonings. Here is the prophet Jeremiah on the subject of those heathen art forms: "Behold the voice of the cry of the daughter of my country because of them that dwell in a far country: Is not the Lord in Zion? Is not her king in her? Why have they provoked me to anger with their graven images, and their strange vanities?" And here is Isaiah taking up the ageless prophetic denunciation: "Howl ye; for the day of the Lord is at hand; it shall come as a destruction from the Almighty. Therefore shall hands be faint, and every man's heart shall melt; And they shall be afraid; pangs and sorrows shall take hold of them; they shall be in pain as a woman that travaileth."

When the dour ascetic known as John the Baptist made his appearance—"the voice of one crying in the wilderness, Prepare ye the way of the Lord, make his paths straight," calling on all Judaea to repent and be cleansed in the waters of the Jordan—it was as one in the same fierce succession. During a time of political volatility within the Roman Empire, of threatened insurrection and growing factionalism among the Jews themselves, references to the day of the Lord were frequent. Since the desecration of the Temple, there had been a tendency to regard the enemies of Israel (rather than her own backsliding) as the real target of the wrath to come. For the strictly pious sect known as the Pharisees—among whom Paul had himself been prominent—the day of the Lord meant, in fact, the end of the world.

This kind of thinking was not altogether new. A tradition of apocalyptic writing went back at least two hundred years, to an anonymous Hebrew work that we know as the Book of Daniel. Along with predicting the end of time, it contains this declaration: "And many of those who sleep in the dust of the earth shall awake, some to everlasting life, and some to everlasting shame and contempt." The books of the Law and the Prophets had said little hitherto concerning the fate of the individual soul. But such apocalyptic forecasts would have been familiar to believing Jews and especially to the Pharisees, who looked for the coming of Messiah, the Chosen One, to usher in a new age and reign forever. In the writings of Saint Paul, the effect of such thinking is unmistakable. The First Epistle to the Thessalonians has an echo of Isaiah: "For you yourselves know well that the day of the Lord will come like a thief in the night. When people say, There is peace and security, then sudden destruction will come upon them as travail comes upon a woman with child; and there will be no escape." It has also an echo of the Book of Daniel:

For the Lord Himself will descend from Heaven with a cry of command, with the archangel's call, and with the sound of the trumpet of God. And the Dead in Christ shall rise first; then

we who are alive, who are left, shall be caught up together with
them in the cloud to meet the Lord in the air: and so we shall
always be with the Lord.*

This, for churchgoers of every sect and persuasion, is the central
message of Paul's First Epistle to the Thessalonians. I can't remember
now when I first heard it in so many biblical words; but I had been
acquainted with it by way of a hymn that was a regular part of the
opening exercises at Sunday school. Since I haven't heard it sung,
or so much as seen it in print, for more than half a century, it evokes
for me the damp of the church basement in which the youngest of
us were corralled while the adult Bible classes met upstairs. I hear
the pumping wheeze of the reed organ, with its rows of buttons for
adjusting the stops, as we sang the refrain:

When he *com*-eth, when He *com*-eth *to* make up His *jew*-els,
All the *pure* ones, all the *bright* ones, *His* loved *and* His own . . .

"Jew-ulls" was the way I still hear it, and "love *dan*dy zone." For
sheer inanity there can't have been anything to surpass it before the
advent of the sung commercial. Not a few of the hymns I remember
best provided a foretaste of the commercial's rollicking glibness:

> *Oh*, Beulah Land, *Sweet* Beulah Land,
> As *on* thy highest mount I stand,
> I look away across the sea
> Where mansions are prepared for me. . . .

Such rollicking is hard to resist, and I entered in as lustily as anyone
else. All the same, it sounded to me like a travesty of something I
didn't believe a word of. What I did believe, crassly and from an
early age, was that out in the real world, religion—i.e., having to go
to church—was already obsolete. And in fact (I am not trying to
excuse myself here) the little country church where I wriggled
through several hundred mornings of Sunday school, followed by

* *The Writings of St. Paul: Annotated Text and Criticism*, ed. Wayne A. Meeks (New
York, 1972).

preaching, praying, and the singing of hymns, was to a degree be-nighted. The community had been settled by members of the Society of Friends (or Quakers, as they didn't mind calling themselves), who in the welter of late-nineteenth-century evangelism had lost track of precisely who they were, or had been: they no longer sat in silence to await the promptings of the Inner Light but relied on a pastor, as well as a choir, to guide them. They omitted baptism and would have bridled still more at the idea of Communion, even when the wine was only grape juice; but in what mattered they differed hardly at all from any evangelical denomination.

What to the evangelical denominations mattered above all, and to the practical exclusion of very much else, was of course the Second Coming. Not that any such expression is to be found in the Epistles of Saint Paul. The one he did use, the one from which so enormous a freight of doctrine now depends, is the Greek word *parousia*. De-riving from the verb *pareinai*, "to be present," it has the pristine meaning of a presence, a being-there, and by extension came to denote an arrival, a visit, an appearance—or, as the King James Bible has it, a Coming. Unmodified, it is a word the apostle used over and over. "For what is our hope or joy or crown of boasting before our Lord Jesus Christ at his coming?" he wrote to the Thessalonians. And again, "that he may establish your hearts unblameable in holiness before our God and Father, at the coming of our Lord Jesus Christ"— and yet again, "we who are alive, who are left until the coming of the Lord. . . ." By the time of the Second Epistle to the Thessa-lonians—and concerning just when Paul wrote it, or indeed whether he or someone else is the author, scholars disagree—there had begun to be confusion and uncertainty, such as have not abated from that day to this: "Now concerning the coming of our Lord Jesus Christ and our assembling to meet him, we beg you, brethren, not to be quickly shaken in mind or excited, either by spirit or by word, or by letter purporting to be from us, to the effect that the day of the Lord has come."

Drawing repeatedly on the imagery of the Old Testament— "mighty angels in flaming fire, inflicting vengeance upon those who do not know God and upon those who do not obey the gospel of our Lord Jesus"—the letter proceeds to outline what had become, among the Jews, a familiar apocalyptic scenario:

Let no one deceive you in any way, for his day will not come unless the rebellion comes first, and the man of lawlessness is revealed, the son of perdition, who opposes and exalts himself against every so-called god or object of worship, so that he takes his seat in the temple of God, proclaiming himself to be God.

If the Thessalonians, those exemplary converts from paganism, could so easily be deluded into supposing that the advent of the Chosen One had, in some invisible and secret fashion, already occurred, what hope is there for any of the rest of us? Given *their* confusion, the casuistries, the contortions, the outright monstrosities that have been brought forth in the name and under the rubric of eschatology—the study of last things—are hardly a cause for wonder. For those who withstood the temptation to think, as the Gnostics were condemned for doing, in wholly incorporeal terms, there was nothing left to do but wait.

In the rural community where I grew up, the old silent waiting for the still small voice, for that which is of God in every man, as the old Quakers had put it, amounted perhaps to a homespun sort of Gnosticism. But it had been superseded. The waiting now was for something noisier, for the upheaval that would signal that the Second Coming was at hand. I remember hearing the son of perdition, the expected Antichrist, equated with Adolf Hitler. If so, the world had not long to wait. The jewels must be gathered up, the sinners called to repentance. There must be, in words I remember hearing from the pulpit, Sunday after Sunday, a revival.

Of that particular revival, if it can be said to have occurred, I was never a witness. The nearest I came to it was a mildly prurient report from the "hired girl" with whom I shared a room, of indignities she had witnessed at an evening's call for sinners to come forward. From somewhere or other I had snobbishly absorbed a belief that to be Saved in so public a manner was for those who Didn't Know Any Better, and thus of no consequence. Otherwise, the evangelical note was a long-winded nostalgic drone, or else a form of teasing:

"Tell me something. Are you a Bryl-Creem Christian? A little dab'll do ya? Are you an Alka-Seltzer Baptist? Put him in the water and he'll fizz for half a minute? Are you a C & E Christian—Christmas and Easter?"

And so on with On and Off, Hot and Cold, Lost and Found, Mini and Maxi, Before and After, Sweet and Low, Short and Sweet, Brown and Serve. The attendant bouquet of Gethsemane Christians smile and murmur their laughter at one another, and Kingsley finishes the series with an upbeat appreciation.

"With all your faults and blemishes, I contend that you are the best crowd. God's crowd is the in-crowd, the only crowd that will make it in heaven. . . ."*

Thus Rebecca Hill in *Blue Rise*, a novel set in rural Mississippi, but with so exact an ear that it transcends locality. The diction of evangelism in the second millennium of waiting is nothing if not strenuously up to date.

Just think of it . . . in the flash of a second every living believer on earth will be gone. Suddenly, without warning, only unbelievers will be populating planet earth. . . .

We will suddenly one day just blast off into space. Faster than the eye of the unbeliever can perceive, every living believer on earth will disappear. The world will probably hear a great sonic boom from all our transformed immortal bodies cracking the sound barrier. But the rest will be a mystery.

Thus *The Rapture*, by Hal Lindsey, an author of note (his first book, *The Late Great Planet Earth*, is reported to have sold eighteen million copies) as well as a pastor and broadcast evangelist. Nor is this quite all. As the apocalyptic scenario is fulfilled, he tells us,

the whole world will probably see this by satellite television. We now have the technical ability to fulfill what is predicted, "And those from the peoples and tribes and tongues and nations will look at their dead bodies for three days and a half, and

* Rebecca Hill, *Blue Rise* (New York, 1984).

will not permit their dead bodies to be laid in a tomb." [Revelation 11:9]*

As Susan Sontag has observed, reality bifurcates: there is the event and there is the image of the event.†

For Hal Lindsey himself, the strategy meanwhile has been to "gain a combat knowledge of the Bible in order to be able to face the perilous times that precede the Tribulation. It motivates me," he declares, "to win as many to Christ as possible before it's too late. I want to take as many with me as I can."

That is one extreme—an alarming one, surely, for anyone less confident than the Reverend Mr. Lindsey. It is to his credit that he evinces concern for the fate of the people of Israel. "Most believe," he says (evidently referring to other fundamentalist spokesmen) "that [a] place of protection for believing Israel will be the ancient fortress city of Petra," in southern Jordan—though given its history of sudden flooding, among other drawbacks, one wonders.

The opposite extreme, among those disposed to consider the matter at all, is less stark but more problematic. It entails an admission such as only the most dogmatic of literalists can fail to be troubled by:

With each passing generation, the person of Christ became more absent, more tenuous. To counteract the withdrawal of the historical Christ, believers had the words of Christ concerning the Spirit and the Second Coming: the present and the future promises. . . . The experience of the Spirit is necessarily mystical and enthusiastic by nature (in enthusiasm's original sense of being possessed by a god). . . . The Second Coming is equally problematic as a focus for belief. Its promise is dependent on Christ's words, which are in themselves dependent on the certainty or uncertainty of the written text, their inseparable matrix. . . .‡

* Hal Lindsey, *The Rapture: Truth or Consequences* (New York, 1983, 1985).
† Susan Sontag, "AIDS and Its Metaphors," *New York Review of Books*, October 27, 1988.
‡ Anthony Kemp, *The Estrangement of the Past* (New York, forthcoming).

Thus Anthony Kemp in *The Estrangement of the Past*, which as a work in progress has been of great help to my own thinking. The problem is elaborated in a book called *The First Coming*,* by Thomas Sheehan, a professor of philosophy at Loyola University in Chicago, who examines the early history of what he calls the "Jesus Movement":

> The problem was not that the disciples frequently met resistance from the religious establishment: That, in fact, was grist for their mill. . . . The serious problem, rather, was the lengthening of the supposedly brief interval between Jesus' hidden vindication at his death and his public reappearance in glory. Not only was the parousia being progressively delayed, but within thirty years of Jesus' death the founders of the eschatological movement within Judaism would begin dying off, with no return of Jesus yet in sight.

Once Professor Sheehan has stripped back the layers of dogmatic accretion from the slight and brittle fabric of historicity, there is not much that can be said with certitude. However, I believe that something can—otherwise this look at what Saint Paul wrote will have been an empty exercise.

As a matter of historicity, Paul was himself a latecomer. He had never met the man Jesus. He did not claim to have done so, only that "as to one untimely born, He appeared also to me." Here, again, is Professor Sheehan on that event:

> Paul hears a voice but *sees nothing*. In fact he is rendered temporarily blind by "a light from heaven, brighter than the sun" (Acts 26:13; cf. 9:3, 22:6). Even more important, when Paul himself described his experience some fifteen years after it happened, he called it not a vision but more neutrally an apocalyptic "revelation." [apokalypsis, Galatians 1:12]

* Thomas Sheehan, *The First Coming: How the Kingdom of God Became Christianity* (New York, 1986).

Though it happened to a saint of the church, an experience of this sort is not beyond the ken of ordinary humanity. Such experiences are perhaps not uncommon. They can be, and frequently are, reduced to clinical terms—which in no way, as William James was at pains to demonstrate, invalidates the effect, the forces that may have been set in motion. For Saint Paul himself, zealous opposition had prepared the way for the reversal, the conversion of energies that empowered him to become a founder, if not indeed sole inventor, of what we call Christianity. Many of us, in our own minor fashion, have experienced some such conversion of energies. In my own small instance, the way had been prepared by exposure to music and painting, as well as to the writings of the likes of Dante, Donne, Hopkins, and (I dare say) T. S. Eliot. Of the immediate particulars, I recall mainly that on a Sunday afternoon I had wandered into the museum familiarly known as the Cloisters, where in the midst of listening to a piped-in motet, for an unasked-for moment all habitual concerns gave way to a serenity so perfect that it amounted to a lapse of consciousness—or perhaps it is clinically more accurate to speak of a lapse so complete that it amounted to perfect serenity. The event was so totally unasked for, and the lapse so infinitesimal, that it passed almost unnoticed. It was only later, in astonished retrospect, that I found a word for what by then felt like an intervening flood. The word was "Grace." Though nothing from that day to this has caused me to gainsay it, the flood soon had me spinning out of control. I was about to be a famous poet, perhaps even the founder of a new religion. Elation became mania, which acquired by degrees the complexion of terror. The term I found for my condition now was "mortal sin." Outside of my private turmoil, it happened to be Holy Week. I found myself in church; there seemed literally nowhere else to go. And having gone in, I stayed in. With the enthusiasm of the typical convert, I was now a churchgoer.

While the enthusiasm was at its flood, I had no doctrinal worries. I believed whatever I was asked to believe. The flood stage passed; years passed, and I began to discover just how rigidly callous a preserve I had wandered into. The trouble, finally and above all, was its callousness toward the Jews. What goes on in an Anglo-Catholic house of worship may be in better taste than most others. The music at any rate can be gorgeous, and was one reason I gravitated there.

But when it comes to the people of Israel, the fundamentalist bodies are more respectful. Perhaps T. S. Eliot was never really an anti-Semite—the record is muddled, as records tend to be—but polite Anglicanism unmistakably harbors the chill of bigotry; and so, it would seem, does the entire institutional structure that is the Church.

The flaw is there, like the flaw in Henry James's allegorical golden bowl, before the sumptuous gift can be offered: the assurance, that is, that the Chosen One would come to make up his jewels—Saint Paul declaring, early in his First Epistle to the Thessalonians, "For you suffered the same things from your own countrymen as they did from the Jews, who killed both the Lord Jesus and the prophets." To whatever in the way of extenuation and qualification this statement, by a man who was himself a Jew, may lend itself, the effect in practice is by now incalculable.

From the Good Friday liturgy, in which for years I was an enthusiastic participant, Pontius Pilate emerges as rather a nice man, at least by comparison with the yelling mob who are the Jews personified. Not Pilate's fault, according to the liturgy. The historical record, as bluntly set forth by Thomas Sheehan, is otherwise:

Pontius Pilate . . . had arrived in Palestine in the Roman year 779 (26 C.E.). . . . Today he would probably, and correctly, be called an anti-Semite. His main jobs were to collect taxes and keep the public order as he put in his time in the provinces, awaiting a better assignment; but from the moment he arrived in the country he seemed never to miss a chance to offend pious Jews and in more than one instance to threaten and murder them. . . . In any case, whatever Pilate's reasons for deciding to have Jesus put to death, it is not true that the Jewish crowds shouted out that Jesus should be crucified (Mark 15:12ff.) or that they took his blood upon themselves and their children (Matthew 27:25). Nor did the high priest tell the prefect "We have no king but Caesar" (John 19:15). These sentences, which were later written into the accounts of Jesus' passion, are the products of a bitter polemic between early Christianity and Judaism and have helped to cause the horrors of two millennia of anti-Semitism.

There remains to note a terse report from the *Annals* of Tacitus, written around C.E. 114, that a man named Christ was put to death by Pontius Pilate during the reign of Tiberius.

This record notwithstanding, most churchgoers continue to believe what they absorbed at an early age: the Jews did it, or if the Romans did it, it was because the Jews wanted them to. Can so longstanding a calumny be extirpated? At this late date, there are theologians at work. Here is one, Lloyd Gaston, quoting the words of another:

> Rosemary Ruether has posed in all its sharpness what must surely be *the* theological question for Christians in our generation: "Possibly anti-Judaism is too deeply embedded in the foundations of Christianity to be rooted out entirely without destroying the whole structure." It may be that the church will survive if we fail to deal adequately with that question, but more serious is the question whether the church ought to survive.*

All this is somewhat grimmer than anything I quite expected when I set out to consider the earliest known document to mention the name of Jesus of Nazareth. Who was he? A Jew with no plans to found a new religion, who simply *was* what he proclaimed—that the Kingdom of Heaven is here and now. I think of modern Thessalonica, where the authentic residues of a Byzantine past amount to little more than a glimmer of mosaic, defaced, covered over and uncovered, further defacement being the price of salvaging anything at all.

Some such traces persist of a historical person, a blithe, severe, and luminous exemplar whom neither the accretions of time nor the effort to dislodge them can quite obliterate.

What, if anything, those traces may have to do with the kind of experience I have described—with those vivid energies rushing in from beyond one's own resources—I am not so foolhardy as to attempt even a guess. The conviction flowing from such an experience, that what is most real is the incorporeal, is borne out by what physicists tell us of the material universe. Yet such a conviction has inevitably to contend with an overbearing weight of evidence to the contrary. The accretions of history, of its folly and turpitude, stare

---

* Lloyd Gaston, *Paul and the Torah* (Vancouver, B.C., 1987).

us down. Any effort to return that stare, with all one's sympathies in place, would be next to intolerable. We inhabit a ruin of embattled certitudes, an incarceration of error fossilized, of an injustice so appalling that for any response at all there seems nowhere to turn but to the Hebrew prophets. With such a condition, humankind can deal only in very small doses: T. S. Eliot was right about that. One can concur, and at the same time be persuaded, with another Christian poet, that nevertheless "there lives the dearest freshness deep down things." For all its institutional horrors, the strength of Christianity remains that it is founded on a paradox: whatever we know of incorporeal reality is to date inseparable from the channels that received it. The long wait continues for the power of the incorporeal to manifest itself in one final dogmatic showdown. But in what is discernible of the life and teachings of Jesus himself, the incorporeal, in all its freshness, is here and now.

THE FIRST EPISTLE OF
PAUL THE APOSTLE
TO TIMOTHY

—

Marina Warner

My convent school was hard to find. There was one gate at the end of a private, unpaved road leading through the birch trees and azalea bushes of a dormitory suburb, and another entrance, turning abruptly off a side road, which opened onto the rhododendron-shrouded front drive. This approach was tarmacked and—at least in my memory—always reptilian shiny from the rain. The school only emerged into view at the end of the deep drive, and seemed very imposing, the many tall red-brick buildings attached to the Gothic chapel like spokes to a hub. Also, after the dripping shrubberies on the way, it always looked preternaturally tidy. The begonias, which were installed in rows in the front flowerbed display, would drop their heads in the English damp: the only disorder in the sweep up to the small front door.

I went back once, in secret, just up the drive and then—quick turn around—out again, no harm done, the flypaper didn't catch me, and I experienced again the loneliness I used to feel at the beginning of term, when the school received me back into its enclosed world.

Saint Paul, by contrast, was a traveler, a man with contacts, on the move and firing off letters as he went. We followed his different journeys in different-colored inks on maps of the Mediterranean; unlike the evangelists, who seemed separate from history, Paul could be grasped as a character in the past. Matthew and Mark were shadowy; Luke, the companion of Our Lady in old age and the painter of her portrait, had a bit of life in him, of a gentle, bedside-manner variety; John belonged in a vivid sequence of posed tableaux, ending in fierce old age sitting on his rock wrapped in visions. But there were adventure stories about Saint Paul that followed a familiar dramatic structure, of hubris and peripeteia, of shipwrecks and widows, riots and imprisonments, and, above all, the blinding moment on the road to Damascus.

Some years ago, in the church of Santa Maria del Popolo in Rome, I came upon Caravaggio's painting of that conversion: the fallen saint, the stepping, bewildered horse, the penetrating radiance impacted together as if the edge of the picture had been cut down in order to tighten the drama. Paul, for all his movements, never lost contact with the center of energy—or, rather, he carried it with him, like a magnet storing power. By contrast, enclosed at school, we were immobilized, and very far away from the heart of things. He enjoyed intimacy with the Lord, and all that meant in terms of power and love and light; we sat at our desks facing the blackboard in classrooms with high windows so that the view outside should not distract us, journeying with Paul on his many roads, by land and sea, along the lines of green and red ballpoint. In the fifth form (aged around fifteen) we could bicycle with permission to the local village beyond the shrubs and birch trees, but never farther afield. It was important to learn the love of Christ by sitting still and being good; Paul, dynamic, adventurous Paul to whom so much had happened, was the architect of this view of girls' proper conduct.

The result wasn't hatred of the saint, or even reproach. Saint Paul was beyond such familiarity. Besides, it was only much later that I ever heard of the idea that the New Testament might not be the revealed word of God but could be questioned, discussed, that individuals could take issue with it, that the Pastoral Letters, such as the First Epistle to Timothy, might not all originate from Paul but might have been composed pseudonymously by an interpreter who honored him and wished to propagate his teachings.* No, Paul's heroism inspired in us love of those who had been fortunate to enjoy the company of this traveling hero, to participate in his adventures—like Timothy, characterized as young in the epistles (though commentators now reckon his age to be thirty or more), who had been adopted as Paul's beloved son.

At a boarding school, with parents visiting only three times a term, young women create—or at least try to create—clusters of affection around them which will replace the missing mothers, fathers, brothers, and sisters. Sometimes their absence is experienced as straightforward loss, and the substitutes simply become temporary surrogates. But sometimes, the family back home inspire complicated emotions of anger and bitterness, for their disappearance can seem a kind of forsaking. In a convent, Christ's teaching that the true disciple leaves behind mother and father to follow him is fulfilled by the constant presence of nuns, who have renounced family even to the point of blotting out the name of their birth. Their choice complicates the issue of family love and loyalty, holding up the possibility that another family altogether could usurp the biological group of home and origin, that bonds could be forged willingly not by accident of birth but by election. Ah, the child who dreams, as Freud described, that she was switched in her cradle and given over mistakenly to these cruel and ordinary parents as their daughter, though she knows, if truth be told, that she is a princess, finds rich stimulus in the New Testament, where the constellations of relationships do not follow the usual social pattern, where Timothy can become the beloved son of Paul without the interference of a mother, shed all memory of earlier obligation or home, and fulfill his new father's orders like a hereditary prince.

Discipleship attracted us strongly, as a calling as well as a source of affection. We picked favorite nuns—and some among the community picked out favorite girls. When I was first sent to school, aged nine, Mother Barbara, the principal of the lower school, inspired deep attachments in many of the children. She was the lead voice in

* See J. N. D. Kelly's introduction to *A Commentary on the Pastoral Epistles: I Timothy, II Timothy, Titus* (London, 1972), pp. 1–36. He believes they are by Paul himself. See Elaine Pagels, *Adam, Eve, and the Serpent* (New York, 1988), pp. 23–27, for the opposite view.

the choir, singing antiphons and masses composed by our Reverend Mother Cecilia, named for the patron saint of music. Mother Barbara had Italian blood and an Italian soprano's voice, surprisingly muscular for its pitch, and rather loud for the lullabies she chose after lights-out in the dormitory, where we lay in separate cubicles with our clothes folded on stools at the foot of the bed, beyond the flowered curtain.

> *Sellellullellu bye bye*
> *If you want the stars to play with*
> *And the moon to run away with*
> *They'll come if you don't cry. . . .*

We were—almost all of us—sure we preferred Mother Barbara to our own mothers; though I used to feel this was disloyal, especially as I already had one Italian mother.

The nuns themselves understood, however, that their care for us might not suffice, and they allowed the children in the lower school to be visited at bedtime by an older girl of their choice—not every night, but sometimes. The moment would come, as we were sitting up in bed, with our hairbrushes in our hands, when the prefects would enter the dormitory and disperse down the aisles, looking past the curtains for the little girl who had requested their goodnight kiss. There was sometimes competition for the same older girl—stars of the tennis court and the hockey pitch were in great demand. My first allegiance went to the head girl, known as P.J., who seemed to me then the most beautiful being in the world. But other people thought so too, and I had P.J. to myself only once. I think she found me rather intense; I think she also would have made my happiness then if she had said to me, as Paul did to Timothy, "Go, my true and beloved child, take this message from me across the sea and defend it against all comers."

Mother Barbara placed us all *in loco filiarum*, but she wasn't exactly a mentor; P.J. was my "crack," as we called such passions, and I would have walked across a bridge of knives for her, as I say. I also longed to be tall and fair and cheerful and breezy like her, instead of stout and dark and anxious.

The relation of master-disciple, folded within the parent-child bond Paul and Timothy also claimed for themselves, did not really develop until later, when pupils reached the fifth and sixth forms, and then not among themselves but between teachers and girls, a certain nun and her student, though special friendships were terribly discouraged, of course. The imagined model tie was masculine, fraternal rather than filial, because the adventure of learning, the enterprise of traveling, even if only figuratively, was a male domain. When Sister Christina and I braved the lusts of pagan Rome in the company of Catullus, I saw myself as a wanderer in time, like Dante, or like Christian from *Pilgrim's Progress*. It was never me as I was then, in navy skirt and strap shoes and band holding my hair off my face, making the journey.

At the time I didn't know the Acts of Paul, for we were sheltered from the New Testament apocrypha. But when I came across the text later, and read there the story of Saint Thecla, I recognized something I had wanted to be. Thecla was forbidden to leave the house to hear Saint Paul preach, but she stood at the window of her parents' house in Iconium in Asia Minor to listen; accepting his message, she then rejected the rich marriage her parents had arranged for her, and proclaimed her new faith in virginity and Christ. Her rejected bridegroom had Paul driven out of town for leading young people astray. For her part, Thecla was condemned to death by burning alive. Miraculously, a rain cloud put out the bonfire, and she escaped. She then ran away to follow Paul. But Paul did not want her, because she was a girl. So Thecla cut her hair and put on boy's clothes and proved her devotion and courage until he at last agreed to allow her to preach as his disciple, like Timothy.*

When I lay in bed at night laying plans for my future, I saw myself intrepid, unstoppable, self-willed like Thecla—and in boy's clothes. When I read recently Karen Horney's critique of Freud's theories about femininity and the female castration complex, I was glad that someone within psychoanalysis had understood that young girls envy boys for social reasons, that Thecla did not cut her hair and put on the dress of a young man because she felt anguish at her lack of a

---

* See the Acts of Paul in *The Apocryphal New Testament*, trans. M. R. James (Oxford, 1969), pp. 274–77; Pagels, *Adam, Eve, and the Serpent*, pp. 18–20.

penis but because Paul would not let her speak her mind in the shape of a girl.*

My school copy of the New Testament shows many places scored in the margin of the First Epistle to Timothy, for it is a letter in which Paul has a great deal to say about both women's behavior and the correct Christian treatment of certain categories of women. He's above all concerned with women's tongues, as the author of the Acts of Paul was aware when he portrayed the apostle resisting Thecla's thirst to evangelize. It is in the First Epistle to Timothy that this verse appears: "Let the woman learn in silence with all subjection." (2:11).

The nuns who taught us Scripture and church history as well as all the other subjects in our curriculum did not keep silence. At times, in their secluded quarters at one end of the convent buildings, they did not speak, and at times we kept vigil with them, during three-day retreats or in memory of the dead on certain feasts. But on the whole, their calling as teachers contradicted in its essence the injunction of Saint Paul. And indeed, Mary Ward, the foundress of the order to which they belonged—the Institute of the Blessed Virgin Mary—had been persecuted in her lifetime for her independent and resolute desire to establish an order of nuns who would teach girls in the same way as the Jesuits taught boys. (The order was suppressed by the Pope and was not restored until 1877.)†

Mary Ward did not believe in silence for women or, perhaps, in their subjection. Her younger counterpart in New Spain, the poet and thinker Sor Juana de la Cruz (1648–95), also joined battle with the authorities when she listed many learned women of the past to whom she was beholden in her own studies and then continued with an attack on the male clergy's prerogatives: "The interpretation of holy scripture should be forbidden not only to women, considered

---

* Karen Horney, "On the Genesis of the Castration Complex in Women" and "The Flight from Womanhood," in *Feminine Psychology*, ed. Harold Kelman (New York, 1973), pp. 37–53, 54–70.

† Mary Ward (1586–1646) entered the Poor Clares in 1606, founded the Institute of the Blessed Virgin Mary three years later, and opened convent schools for girls in France, Belgium, Germany, and Italy until the suppression of the order. She returned to England in 1639 and continued her struggles to reestablish her ideas of an active female vocation.

so very inept, but to men, who merely by virtue of being men consider themselves sages. . . . There are many who study in order to become ignorant, especially those of an arrogant, restless and overbearing turn of mind."*

Saint Paul rather inclines to extravagant breast-beating, the attention-seeking gesture of a man who must always outstrip his peers, if only in abjection. In this First Epistle to Timothy, he writes of his turbulent past and calls himself, in the translation of Ronald Knox, which we used in the convent, "a man of violence, author of outrage" (1:13).† (In the King James Version he calls himself "injurious"; in the Jerusalem Bible, "a bully.") He reproaches himself for his sins: "I was the worst of all" (1:15). But he never grows to consciousness—nor did we then, reading him—that violence remained with him, that he continued to show an arrogant, restless, and overbearing turn of mind when it came to discussing the expectations and potential of women.

"Let the woman learn in silence with all subjection" continues with the ban at which Mary Ward and Sor Juana—and many others—chafed: "But I suffer not a woman to teach, nor to usurp authority over the man, but to be in silence" (2:12). He then gives his reasons, moving in a characteristically Pauline way to an allegorical exegesis of the Fall: that Adam was made first, to symbolize his precedence over woman, and that since Eve, the type of all women to come, sinned through speech, by tempting Adam to eat, speech must be denied her daughters.

In the Vulgate, Jerome used *seducta* for Eve's transgression: the serpent led her astray, and she then "seduced" Adam. The connotations of the verb are already sexual. Women's words are mixed up with women's wiles—beauty and expression go hand in hand, as Paul implies when he also lays down that women should dress modestly,

---

* From "Reply to Sor Philothea," in *A Sor Juana Anthology*, trans. Alan S. Trueblood (Boston, 1988), quoted by Michael Wood, "The Genius of San Jerónimo," *New York Review of Books*, October 13, 1988.
† Using the Ronald Knox translation, published in 1945, reflected the special pride of English Catholics in their heritage: Monsignor Knox was a scholar connected to the recusant families, the aristocracy of the faithful, about whom Evelyn Waugh wrote in *Brideshead Revisited*. I never liked his version as much as the King James or the Jerusalem Bible. I have used the King James in this article—its style still remains a standard for all writers of English.

without show of jewels or elaborate coiffures (2:9). Eve sinned by mouth: she bit into the apple of knowledge; she spoke to the serpent and to Adam; and she was in consequence cursed with desire, to kiss and be kissed ("Thy desire shall be to thy husband").

The seduction of women's talk reflected the seduction of their bodies; it was considered just as dangerous to Christian men, and condemned as improper. Paul, in the First Epistle to Timothy alone, proscribes at least five different kinds of speech which he attributes to women: the wives of deacons must not be "slanderers" (3:11); Timothy must not listen to "profane and old wives' fables" (4:7); younger widows are "not only idle, but tattlers also and busybodies, speaking things which they ought not" (5:13); he also fears gossip, and warns that young widows' behavior will give rise to talk unless they remarry. By contrast, he exhorts his disciple to be "an example of the believers, in word, in conversation" (4:12) and, at the end, to avoid "profane and vain babblings" (6:20). The translators of the King James Version had no difficulty finding English words for these different types of condemned speech. In this matter, Catholics and Protestants were in agreement: garrulousness was a woman's vice, and silence—which was not even considered an appropriate virtue in the male—one of the chief ornaments a good woman should cultivate. It's a commonplace that what counts as articulateness in a man becomes stridency in a woman, that a man's conviction is a woman's shrillness, a man's fluency a woman's drivel. The speaking woman also refuses subjection, and turns herself from a passive object of desire into a conspiring and conscious stimulation: the *mulier blandiens* or *mulier meretrix* of Ecclesiasticus 25:17–36 and Proverbs 6:24–6 comes in for much vituperation; the biblical text "A man's spite is preferable to a woman's kindness" (Ecclesiasticus 42:14) provoked much nodding of male heads.* Female curiosity had brought about the Fall and so must be quelled. The virtue of Prudence sometimes wears a padlock on her mouth, and sixteenth-century morality tales painted the portraits of the Wise Man and the Wise Woman, showing the latter with her lips firmly under lock and key:

---

* See Ian Maclean, *The Renaissance Notion of Woman: A Study in the Fortunes of Scholasticism and Medical Science in European Intellectual Life* (Cambridge, 1980), pp. 16–17.

1 Timothy

Everyone look at me because I am a wise woman . . .
A golden padlock I wear on my mouth at all times
so that no villainous words shall escape my mouth
but I say nothing without deliberation
*and a wise woman should always act thus.**

The tongues of women were associated with curses and spells, the central activity of witches. There even exist, from the seventeenth century, scold's bridles—contraptions like dog muzzles designed to gag women who had been charged and found guilty for something they had said; a law against cursing was passed in 1624.†

In cautionary children's literature of the late nineteenth century, a similar asymmetry between the value of men's and women's expressions governs the laws of good behavior. The wife of Monsieur Croquemitaine the bogeyman comes for little girls who show too much curiosity and shuts them up in a trunk.‡ Father Flog, Croquemitaine's American counterpart, brandishes a knife with which he cuts the tongues of liars—in this case "untruthful children" regardless of sex.§ The other day, in a tobacconist's shop in Jalisco province in Mexico, I found two postcards, drawn in lurid caricature. In one, a bent old harridan hauls her shopping while two lounging men look on approvingly: she has a huge padlock through her lips. In the other, a sharp-featured woman's eyes are popping in terror as a hairy fist pulls out her tongue and prepares to cut it off with scissors.

We weren't discouraged from talking at school; the nuns carried on teaching us Paul's view of womankind in their articulate and independent way without alerting us to the contradiction. But it was odd and painful to read, in such places as Paul's First Epistle to Timothy, that there was another standard of conduct to which we should conform if we were to be proper disciples. No one could miss the apostle's tone when it came to women: in our own sex we

---

* Woodcut by Anton Woensam (1525) in Carol Megan Armstrong, "The Moralising Prints of Cornelisz Anthonisz," unpublished doctoral dissertation, Princeton University, 1985, fig. 129, pp. 129–33.
† Antonia Fraser, *The Weaker Vessel* (London, 1984), facing p. 101, pp. 153–55.
‡ Seen in exhibition "L'Enfance et l'image au XIXe siècle," Musée d'Orsay, Paris, 1988.
§ "Father Flog," broadsheet, printed by the Humoristic Publishing Co., Kansas City, Mo., n.d.

were unworthy, in spite of being created equal and being saved equally and there being neither male nor female in Christ Jesus. And there was no means of redress, because the means—thought, learning, social reform—cut across the Scriptures' commands.

The First Epistle to Timothy tries to soften the blow against women by promising: "Notwithstanding she shall be saved in childbearing" (2:15). We had a central notice board at school, in which notices of old girls' engagements were posted, and news of the babies born to them. Often the names were foreign—Spanish families, Italian families (preferably princely) were much in favor with the daughters of Catholics in England. The nuns would glow with approval, looking in their voluminous habits as if they were actually inflating gently. If the harsh self-immolation of Thecla eluded us, we could be saved by having a Catholic baby with a Spanish prince; it was a comfort. We believed it. I believed it, and in some ways still do, because I have found with age that although I see clearly the fallaciousness and the unkindness of fundamental principles I was taught, I bear the stamp of them ineluctably, and feel myself to be a renegade, a kind of voluntary outcast. For I sometimes feel a pinch of regret that I was not married in Saint James', Spanish Place, wearing lilies and white lace, to the scion of an ancient Catholic line to whom I would bear an heir. For this was the secondary romance, after the high mission of Timothy and Thecla—though I was at odds with it, too, as well as called by it: I had read Shelley and became a votary of free love, scorning the designs for foaming lace wedding dresses which my classmates doodled in lessons.

Biblical scholars now argue that the mitigation of the apostle's usual stringent asceticism in the First and Second Epistles to Timothy and the Epistle to Titus points to a follower and imitator of Saint Paul who sought to "domesticate" Pauline doctrine and adapt it to a traditional Jewish idea of the worth of marriage, the importance of hierarchy within the family, and tribal obligations to widows.* This explains, very satisfyingly, the contradiction on which we were impaled at school between a heroic, otherworldly vocation on the one hand and the silent mission of motherhood and wifely obedience on the other.

* See Pagels, *Adam, Eve, and the Serpent*, pp. 22–31.

Since leaving school, I have written about the Virgin Mary, and about Joan of Arc, and about many other Catholic heroines, imaginary and historical, who first captured my imagination when I was at the convent in the rhododendrons and I was taught to aspire higher and ever higher. I was not schooled to silence; but I learned that a woman's silence is especially golden. Reading Saint Paul confirmed those longings I already felt to be other than what I was: I became a house divided against itself.

But I hope that the wind that blows in the cracks has a speaking voice.

THE SECOND EPISTLE OF
PAUL THE APOSTLE
TO TIMOTHY

—

Guy Davenport

> For wee wrestle not against flesh and blood, but
> against principalities, against powers, against the
> rulers of the darknes of this world, against spir-
> ituall wickednes in high places.
>
> Ephesians 6:12 (1611)

This sentence, in which we can see oiled athletes grappling in the dust of a gymnasium at Tarsos, was first written down, from Paul's dictation, by his secretary Tykhikos, around the year 60, when Nero was still sane and Plutarch, over in snowy Boiotia, was an adolescent about to set out for Athens to study mathematics and philosophy with Ammonius, who, like Paul and Jesus, was a peripatetic teacher. What interested me in this strong sentence when I came across it out of context, having previously paid more attention to the sentences before and after—about putting on the whole armor of God, or as Samuel Butler's mother said, girding one's loins with the breast-plate of righteousness—was Paul's seeming to have a good word to say about the flesh. The context was Blake's *The Four Zoas*, where it serves as epigraph and is in Greek. Blake was a congenial Christian and, like Kierkegaard and Bunyan, had that gift of analogy and integrating vision which makes a prophet a prophet.

"For our fight is not against human foes," the New English Bible translates, "but against cosmic powers, against the authorities and potentates of this dark world, against the superhuman forces of evil in the heavens." No good word about the flesh here. The imagery of Paul's *haima kai sarka* (where "blood" had the sense of courage, liveliness, strength, life itself, and "flesh" meant the whole body, not a portion of it) is missing. When Jerome made his Latin translation in the fourth century (in Bethlehem, with his lion), he reversed the order: *carnem et sanguinem*, the "flesh and blood" of kinship, of being human.

The air around Jesus and Paul was full of devils. It is easy to see these for what they were: we call them viruses, bacteria, epilepsy, depression, phobias, obsessions, blindness, lameness, scleroses. And something subtler: meanness, cruelty, selfishness. We see Jesus healing both disease and the ungenerous heart, scarcely making a distinction between them, as if the wounded body and the wounded mind were the same kind of hurt crying out to heaven to be healed.

What I at first found liberating in Paul's sentence is that he was saying that the flesh is not in itself evil. Evil is in the mind, in the will. Evil is in the power one person has over another, in governments, and especially in official views of virtue which conceal ill will, jealousy, and a great fear of the flesh and the world.

My upbringing was Baptist. Aside from the holiday warmth of Christmas and Easter, what the church had to teach was the opposite of good news; it was bad news, dreary and dull, all the way. With adolescence came a questioning of it all. To identify bigotry and narrow-mindedness in a Southern Baptist congregation is no great feat. Our church was for white people only; members of it belonged also to the Ku Klux Klan. I have no musical gift and thus hated all the hymns; and Miss Lottie Estes told us in Sunday school that Jesus' nudity on the cross was far more painful to him than the nails in his hands and feet. And I was already having trouble with the absurdity of the Christian proposition: namely, that belief in a set of incredible events would get me to heaven post mortem.

Meanwhile, I was actually being raised by my parents to believe that a moral life, polished manners, and an ambition to be moderately well off were the essence of acceptable behavior. Both my parents tacitly agreed with Trollope that a strong interest in religion was a prelude to insanity. The good is the enemy of the better. The ancient code of middle-class propriety has stuck with me. Religion has yet to put down even a tentative root in my soul.

The Bible, however, I've read over and over across the years, not only because a literary scholar must know it well but because I find in it a spiritual resourcefulness, an imaginative engagement, an excitement of curiosity and wonder. I find Amos to be a wholly good man. Ruth and Naomi move me to tears. The only integral survival of the deep past is in the Bible, in Homer, in the archaic Greek poets. I see a Jesus in the Gospels who is not quite like anybody else's (except perhaps Bulgakov's) and is decidedly different from the one of the Baptist sermons I have endured.

Paul I see as a figure in Plutarch's world, an intellectual with both a Jewish and a Greek education. He belongs to a renaissance of that moment in the fifth century when one could hear Aristarchus or Diogenes or Socrates in an Athenian gymnasium. He echoes them, sometimes literally. Diogenes said that the love of money is the marketplace for all evil; Paul changed "marketplace" to "root." Paul, like his Greek predecessors, was a man of cities. Jesus preferred villages, hillsides, lakeshores. In my imagination I see Jesus as a man so attractive (eyes, gestures, a man whose genius was compassion) that people might easily drop what they were doing and follow him. Paul, however, I see as a bald and seriously bearded official, born to administrate.

He was something like an Eichmann when we first see him. He seems to have been present at the stoning of Stephen. He was a zealot, an authoritarian, a pedant in the law.

His conversion is a swerving of world history. Two renaissances suddenly flow together, like the Missouri flowing into the Mississippi. John the Baptist had awakened the old tradition of the prophet—a new Elijah, Jonah, Amos—and Jesus had joined his revival. The turbulence they introduced can be measured by John's and Jesus' executions, only a few years apart. Their converts took stock within a few years of the crucifixion. They kept the spirit of Jesus' teaching alive. Scholars posit collections of his sayings which would find their way into the Gospels. The oral tradition must have been extensive; how else can we account for such folklorish elements as walking on water and feeding thousands with a few fish and loaves?

An epic amplification had made Jesus' life a myth before a single

Gospel was written. Paul saw none of the Gospels. What would he have thought of them? Did he have a hand in the first, the one written by Marcus in Rome? He mentions a Marcus in 2 Timothy, and deems him "a useful assistant." Why didn't Paul himself write a biography of Jesus?

I can remember, years ago, when it occurred to me that the very essence of the Gospels is the fact that they are incredible, that these crucial accounts are, like everything else man has made, stained with human error and uncertainty. We see this as much in the canonical Gospels as in the very moving Gospel of Thomas and in the near-idiotic Gnostic gibberish from Nag Hammadi. Jesus spoke—in Aramaic? in common-market Greek?—and what he said was written down for us years afterward. Paul wrote: and we aren't all that certain about his texts.

The Tykhikos who took down Paul's letters to the Colossians and the Ephesians turns up in Beckett's *Waiting for Godot* to dramatize the Christian predicament. He has a rope around his neck and carries "a heavy bag" (Bunyanesque, this), "a folding stool" (Jesus when he comes will want a throne, the archaic English meaning of "stool"), "a picnic basket" (for the loaves and fishes, in case Jesus wants to do that again), "and a greatcoat." He is haltered like a beast of burden and subject to the whip of one Pozzo. His name is Lucky, the Greek for which is Tykhikos. We see him go stark raving mad. Jesus, like Monsieur Godot, promised to return "soon." We Christians have been waiting, as of this writing, for 1,955 years. Soon! And what if he came, some years back, and was shut up in an insane asylum, or lynched all over again, or, as Dostoyevsky imagined, dragged before the Inquisition? Ruskin remarked that if an angel appeared in the English sky, a sportsman would bring it down.

Waiting for Godot is but one of Beckett's statements about Christianity; *Endgame* is another, where the word "nail" in three languages gives us the names of the characters other than Ham, whose name provides the hammer. Christianity in Beckett's comedy (his designation "tragicomedy in two acts" is part of the joke) is an agony of waiting, a proposition vitiated by taunting uncertainty, a galling frustration. Joyce, Beckett's master, had seen Christianity as a myth that had displaced human nature itself. But the history of Christianity is not Christianity. It is a religion that can constantly return to its sources and renew itself, as with Milton and Blake, Kierkegaard and Luther. There are perhaps only Christianities.

I have a sharp feeling that Paul's Christianity is at great variance with Jesus'. Paul, under house arrest in Rome, a city of moral philosophers all under the eye of Nero's police (C. Musonius Rufus, Apollonius of Tyana, Epictetus' school, all suspected of sedition and fleas), was a religious philosopher who had assumed the role of a prophet, much as Muhammad was to do in Islam. His task was to explain, convert, spread the good word. Jesus had, in a paradoxical sense, removed the scaffolding of the law to show that the structure would stand by itself—by faith. The tribe was to be replaced by a new kind of community. Goodwill was to replace legality.

What Jesus had done was to cancel the classical idea of fate, silencing the oracles, unifying the human spirit under one dominion, which all of us are to find in our hearts. The law and life itself would then be identical. Others were to be another self, treated as such. The bond would be love, respect, loyalty, a kinship for which the metaphor would be that we are all children of one father. So redeemed, Cain would embrace Abel rather than kill him.

The awesome simplicity of this vision was what Paul had to implement. The authority Jesus constantly invoked—the origin of man in a natural unity that was not at war with itself, whose tribal deities and demons were all myths—Paul placed in Jesus himself, whom he understood to be the creator of all that is. Jesus strove to reconcile man with himself: to make a unity of the divided self, and to make a unity of the brotherhood of man. Paul, striving to bring man and God together in a philosophical unity that he called *faith, redemption, salvation, worship*, inadvertently divided us all over again. Christ's return was the diffusion of his spirit through all mankind: the descent of the dove. Paul relocated this return in historical time, and made Christianity a preparation for fullest life, rather than the fullest life itself. In the very act of spreading the good news of man's liberty under a new dispensation he imprisoned us in a corrosive anxiety, in mandates to persecute, to bind the good news in an obfuscation of fear and superstition.

We cannot blame Paul; we can only say that with the best will in the world he unwittingly returned our spiritual life to the bonds from which Jesus freed us.

Thus the strong sentence in Ephesians about the spirit of evil in things heavenly has become an irony central to those who try to be followers of the loving and gracious rabbi with the dusty feet, the agile mind, the loving heart, who healed and told vivid parables.

When, some fifteen years ago, I began to write stories, I found that I was assuming that my subject was precisely this dialogue between Jesus and Paul, and that the student teaching what he had learned was a process that engaged my imagination and my moral sense. In my first book of stories, *Tatlin!*, I wrote about a Soviet artist and engineer, Vladimir Tatlin (1885–1953), whose creative genius had to be expressed under the eyes of Lenin and Stalin; and did I first become aware of this confrontation of power and liberty in a Baptist Sunday school, when the antagonists were Jesus standing manacled before Pontius Pilatus, and Paul in Rome?

The other stories in this book also explore themes essentially religious: Herakleitos' understanding of the unity of mankind and of the world; Kafka's encounter with a new machine, the airplane; the discovery of the prehistoric caves at Lascaux; Poe's spiritual discovery that he was an Orpheus in the nineteenth century; and the meditations of a Dutch philosopher in our time on a complex of observations derived from Samuel Butler and Charles Fourier, masters of happiness.

These early stories are all written out of the perception that the modern world is a renaissance generated by our new knowledge of civilization's archaic beginnings. Fourier took Jesus' "Render unto Caesar, the things that are Caesar's; unto God, the things that are God's" as a mandate for us to redesign Caesar's things, that is, our political structures, to be in harmony (his great word) with the things that are God's. His new design is so eccentric, so radically a revision, that I imagined my Dutch philosopher seeing it in terms of Butler's Erewhonians, who, while satirizing Victorian hypocrisies (or, as Paul would say, the spirit of evil in things heavenly), are also Butler's sly imagining of a secret utopia. (Modern writing has many secret Christians like Butler: Wittgenstein, Joyce, Beckett, Kafka).

In "The Dawn in Erewhon" (the story about the Dutch philosopher) I quote Ephesians 6:12, along with a veritable subtext from the New Testament. Eventually these concerns would appear more openly in my stories. In *Eclogues* I bind the double tradition of Greek and Roman pastoral to the pastoral metaphor in the Gospels. I make a story out of Acts 14:6–20, where Ovid's account of Baukis and Philemon coincides with Paul and Barnabas in Lystra, an event of which Paul reminds Timothy in his second letter to him. (And Timothy was a native of Lystra.) Paul's relationship with Timothy is the pattern for most of the relationships in *Eclogues*: teacher and fond pupil, mature and young shepherd. I felt, also, that there should be a story that translates this relationship into modern terms; hence "The Death of Picasso," which is not so much about the redemption of a young man as about the finding of his spirit inside squandered and misdirected energies.

In *Apples and Pears* I take up and expand my Dutch philosopher's fascination with Fourier in a novella which occupies most of the book. The other three stories, placed before the novella, are about Henri Gaudier-Brzeska, a spiritual forager of great genius crushed by the things that are Caesar's; Bashō, another spiritual forager; and Kafka, yet another.

The Jules Verne Steam Balloon (1987), nine stories, is my most open meditation on religion. In three interlocked stories, "The Bicycle Rider," "The Jules Verne Steam Balloon," and "The Ringdove Sign," a young Danish theologian who is writing a doctoral thesis on certain Gnostic colorings in the Gospels (finding traces in figures dressed in white linen—the Lazarus of Secret Mark [quoted by Clement], the naked young man in the garden at Gethsemane, the angel at the tomb—of a daimon who instructed Jesus). This theologian is thoroughly Danish and modern; his father is a Lutheran pastor of much charm and broadmindedness. The fate of the thesis I leave to your imagination. Ephesians 6:12 occurs in Danish in this text, for its flavor, and because translations always act as symbols of the incarnation in a linguistic world. *Et Deus erat verbum.*

I have written a story about Jonah, who was a favorite of Jesus'. I find a significance in the prophet who had a hard go of it, who spoke as if through thick plate glass to his audience. So there are stories about Robert Walser, about Leonardo, about Pyrrhon of Elis, about T. E. Hulme, about C. Musonius Rufus, about Victor Hugo (at a moment when no one would listen to him), about Paul.

Paul's letters, even when not addressed to congregations, are meant for public reading (or were they later made to be so?). The Second

Letter to Timothy, scholars say, is probably not Paul's work at all. Its vocabulary and style differ from letters that are certainly Paul's. But this cannot be wholly true: it is too much like a real letter. There is a grouch against one Alexander, a coppersmith, warning Timothy away from him. "Bring the coat I left with Karpos at Troas, and the books, especially my notebook."

The great Pauline note is struck in his sports image about having run a good race, the whole course (is he thinking of the marathon?), and expects the Olympic crown of wild olive. Timothy's father was a Greek, his mother and grandmother Jews converted to Christianity. Timothy could not be very old. Images of wrestling, running, fighting in armor come so readily to Paul's stylus that we suspect he comes from a culture in which Jewish, Roman, and Greek elements harmonized. His name Saul is from the Old Testament (and was pronounced Shaul); Paulus is a Roman name, and he would probably have had a Gaius or Julius added on, to go with his being a Roman citizen.

Timotheos is "his son." He, like Titus and others, is to carry on Paul's teaching. So the letter is a short treatise on being a teacher, with much good advice.

It is also wonderfully prophetic. Paul sees things getting worse before they can get better: "Men will come to love nothing but money and self." (Spengler, who treats Paul as the real founder of Christianity, ends *The Decline of the West* on the same note, saying that all spiritual value was draining from moral splendor, breeding, and culture into money.) "They will be arrogant, boastful, and abusive; with no respect for parents, no gratitude, no piety, no natural affection; they will be implacable in their hatreds, scandal-mongers, intemperate and fierce, strangers to all goodness, traitors, adventurers, swollen with self-importance." (The New English Bible, this.) Diogenes in full spate!

And, he continues to Timothy, there will be "men who preserve the outward form of religion, but are a standing denial of its reality." This was a theme of Jesus'. In his First Letter to Timothy, Paul had described ideal bishops, elders, and deacons. We who live in an age of popes bent under the weight of diamonds and wrought gold, of evangelists as wealthy as gangsters, and of Christians far richer than Nero at his greediest, can legitimately ask if Christianity exists in any form even resembling that of Paul, much less that of Jesus. Early Christianity was against a ground of Judaism of strictest moral rectitude and ritual piety. On classical ground it was in the midst of a thousand altars to generous gods a belief in whom was thoroughly rational. The Eleusinian mysteries, the cult of Mithras, the temples of Aesculepius, local deities in their groves (Castor and Pollux, Pan, Artemis)—both Romans and Greeks had made a lovely syncretic harmony of these (pious Romans *collected* religions). What perversity in Christianity balked at tolerating them until they, as indeed happened, could be absorbed into their *mythos?*

If my writing, involved as it is with allegiances and sensualities, with its animosity toward meanness and smallness, has any redeeming value, it will be in its small vision (and smaller talent) that Christianity is still a force of great strength, imagination, and moral beauty if you can find it for the churches and dogma. I remember, years ago, walking with Thomas Merton in the woods back of Gethsemani on a frosty autumn day. I forget what occasioned his remark. "Oh, there's salvation all right," he said, grinning broadly, "but not in the Church." *The* church. (My capital may be gratuitous.) It amused him to say that I was the only real pagan he'd ever known, and he made no attempt to convert me: a hopeless case, I suppose. "All bishops are mad," he said on another occasion (we were talking about Bishop Pike). And: "Martin Heidegger had no notion what Being is." And it was Tom who came up with the translation of Herakleitos of the fragment variously translated as "Religion is a falling disease" or something equally nonsensical: "Bigotry is the disease of religion."

I include these obiter dicta of the great Trappist because I think I saw in him a real Christian, as I see in Edward Schillebeeckx another; and have seen others in Christopher Smart and Blake and Wittgenstein; in Kierkegaard and the elder Grundtvig, in Elizabeth Gaskell and Mother Ann Lee; Thoreau and Martin Luther King, Jr. I will make my peace someday with Jesus' terrifying death on the cross (every breath costing him unimaginable pain in lifting himself by his nailed hands). Meanwhile, the Jesus who moves me is the one whose feet were washed at Simon the Pharisee's house. (Paul was once a Pharisee.) Simon was scandalized to see Jesus allowing a woman ("which was a sinner" says the King James Version) to wash his feet. And Jesus had "somewhat to say to Simon." He said: "I entred into thine house, thou gavest me no water for my feete: but shee hath washed my feete with teares, and wiped them with the haires of her head. Thou gavest me no kisse: but this woman, since the time I came in, hath not ceased to kisse my feet. Mine head with oile thou didst not anoint: but this woman hath anointed my feet with oyntment." Jesus forgave the woman her sins, and the Pharisee grumbled about that, too.

THE EPISTLE OF
PAUL
TO TITUS

—

LIARS AND EVIL BEASTS

Josephine Humphreys

I have a form of spiritual hypochondria, that is, a suspicion that my soul is unsound. It's a vain, pleasure-loving soul, guilty of a million sins—but no worse in that respect, maybe, than most. It's within, I think, the sin norms. What worries me more is this soul's deviant nature in matters of faith. It is not exactly heretic, though various heresies have appealed to me. The main symptom of unsoundness is a general difficulty in professing any doctrine at all. I have trouble saying the Apostles' Creed, that brief list of things I am supposed to believe. But any good hypochondriac harbors a secret faith in health. I think belief is possible. I try, in church, to say the creed, even though I usually have to stop after two words.

Yet I can say those two. I believe. After that, the list gets too particular. I need more information, and I have a lot of questions. I can't stand and swear to the details, have had trouble with them since I was twelve. Nevertheless, *credo*. That much won't satisfy a church, but it's a start. I can say it without a shred of doubt.

And I look for a completion of the predicate. That's one good thing about incomplete belief: it keeps me awake and on the lookout. If I did not believe, I wouldn't be expectant, as I am at every moment, of encountering the object of that verb. The avenues are open; I may turn a corner and happen on truth tomorrow, or today, or now. Even daily life, the small domestic world I inhabit, is charged with anticipation. I feel not like the stout explorer coming suddenly upon the Pacific, but like one who isn't there yet. Something is over the rise, something clear and immense, and I think I can get to it.

Its sure but so far unseen presence accounts for my love of the natural world and my love of the written word. Nature and language both seem likely haunts for truth. So I look there, and I look also in the lives of men, and when possible I look into myself.

But sometimes when I'm looking, even in the sacred texts where others have traditionally found their creeds, I can get discouraged. The Letter to Titus is one book of the Bible that discouraged me. When I first read it, I felt pretty far from discovery.

Paul (or one of his followers; I'll call him Paul) writes to his emissary Titus in Crete, with instructions for fortifying the fledgling church. There is trouble in Crete; the church is threatened by disorder within and attack from without. I turned to this letter because it seemed promising. A personal letter, written in a situation of immediate danger, seemed apt to embody the essence of the apostle's message. Titus was dear to Paul, had been his companion on the journey to Jerusalem and his messenger to Corinth, a Greek who probably had been converted by Paul himself. Along with the two Letters to Timothy, the Letter to Titus is one of the "Pastoral Epistles," rather different from Paul's other letters in their focus upon the duties of pastors and the obligations of the flock. It's a short letter, urgent as a telegram. I thought, Here's a chance to discover the crucial thing. Telegrams get right to the point.

But I was disappointed. Paul's bare-bones directive is threefold: appoint elders who are above reproach; rein in the congregation and make everyone behave; and rout the heretics, who are asking troublesome questions and disturbing the faith of the believers. The emphasis of the letter is on upright behavior. Slaves and women are told to be submissive. Questions and doctrinal disputes are forbidden; Paul recommends kicking out anybody who is fractious more than twice. People must behave properly so that outsiders can find no cause for criticism.

I have nothing against upright behavior; I can understand the need for it. But is it really the heart of Christ's message? The Letter to Titus discourages me because it sounds like the voice of fear, not the voice of love. I'm intimate enough with my credo to know that its object will never be found in fear. I don't believe in evil as a force in the world; but what we call evil is fear on the offense, taking the forms of greed, racism, cruelty. I have had enough of fear. For a long time it paralyzed me and kept me from work, kept me from risking myself. But Paul, writing to Titus in Crete, is afraid.

He is afraid of corruption, one of the worst fears, leading always to fortification and withdrawal.

"This is why I left you in Crete," he writes, "that you might amend what was defective" (1:5). Behind his exhortation is the understandable need to make and protect an exemplary community and keep the church intact. The church needed protection, in those wild times and that wild island. There were sinners galore, and heretics nibbling away at the not-yet-solid doctrine. The church needed walls, and in the Letter to Titus we see them going up.

But the question of sinners is troublesome. Christ loved them, after all. I've always been drawn to them myself. Even as a child, I found the lists of sinners intriguing. Heretics, revilers, idolaters, fornicators, blasphemers, sodomites, whoremongers—what variety, what mystery! Their names were strange; I was never quite sure what some of them did, technically. And yet they were all to be saved. That was part of the central truth, surely. The church can't protect itself from sinners; the church *is* sinners.

The great variety of sin makes it possible for all human beings to be sinners. Upright behavior cannot remove us from the sinning crowd; we are in it, and thus within the scope of grace and salvation. That's how I reason it, anyway. In spite of the soul's faults, something in it was worth rescue at great cost to the rescuer. This is a mystery, not a list of rules. It is hard to spell out.

But by the time of the Letter to Titus, the church seems to be moving away from single mystery and toward multiple rules, in an effort to organize and solidify. The letter talks mainly about respectability, the appearance of goodness. Respectability certainly doesn't negate goodness; but I can't think that it constitutes goodness. A man may be, as Paul desires, sober, not violent, serious, having an honorable occupation and one wife, and still not be good.

If I could take this letter merely in its own context, it would not bother me so much. I could say, that was then; a certain amount of Polonial advice was necessary and useful to the early church. Unfortunately, the Letter to Titus represents to me an operative aspect of the modern church. The notion of a Christian elite, of a church walled against those who do not in one way or another qualify for full membership (women, for example, or homosexuals, or those who have not been "saved") is a discouraging one. It's different from an elect, a people chosen by God to receive his message. I don't mind the idea of God electing a certain bunch, initially; he had to start somewhere. In the course of time, and in contrast with the universality of the message delivered, the election hardly seems to matter much. But an elite chooses itself, and perpetuates itself through time, and loses the sense of gift and grace.

What is the Letter to Titus really about? I ask this question whenever I read a book or story: what was on this writer's mind? Paul was writing about behavior, but he was thinking about truth and lies, and how to hold on to the one under attack from the other. Right away, he says his purpose is to further the "knowledge of the truth which accords with godliness" (1:1). Knowledge of the truth is possible, because a message has come from "God, who never lies" (1:2).

That phrase is overpowering, convincing, mysterious. *God, who never lies*, has told his truth to man. What better beginning could be possible? But that truth is endangered. The writer is scared of the human mind, of language itself, for the damage it can do to God's truth. God's message must be passed on by men, in words, first by the apostle, "through the preaching with which I have been entrusted by command of God our savior" (1:3), and thence through bishops like Titus and his appointees in the outlying churches. Titus is Paul's "true child" in the church (1:4), but he has to name other ministers of the truth, each of whom "must hold firm to the sure word as taught, so that he might be able to give instructions in sound doctrine and also to confute those who contradict it" (1:9). The ministers must be careful to "avoid stupid controversies, genealogies, dissensions and quarrels over the law" (3:9).

If, as seems probable, the letter writer was not actually Paul himself but a later follower writing on his own or expanding a fragment of one of the apostle's letters, it makes sense that he should fear losing the truth. He sees years passing. The Kingdom that was imminent may be a longer time coming than anyone expected. Mystery is hard to hold on to, and hard to pass down to future generations, becoming more and more dependent on human words. The original mystery was somehow beyond language, did not need it, had a force that was evident without explanation; it could be told indirectly, in parables. But now truth is no longer manifest and omnipotent, the word of an always honest God. It must be transmitted by men. It can be corrupted.

"For there are many insubordinate men, empty talkers and deceivers, especially the circumcision party; they must be silenced" (1:10–11). And Cretans, he says, are especially famous for damaging the truth; they are known to be "always liars," by testimony of one of their own (1:12). "Therefore rebuke them sharply," Titus is told, "that they may be sound in the faith, instead of giving heed to Jewish myths or to commands of men who reject the truth" (1:13–14). Twice in the course of the letter Paul feels called upon to interject reassurances of the truth: "This testimony is true" (1:13) and "The saying is sure" (3:8).

Now, there aren't a lot of jokes in the Bible. But here's one, an old brainteaser: the poet who said Cretans are always liars was a Cretan himself—therefore he lies, therefore Cretans cannot be always liars, etc. But look: Paul doesn't get the joke. "This testimony is true," he says. Intent on shoring up *the* truth, protecting it from language and disputation, he misses a fallacy in his own language.

Last year I was driving across northern Alabama and was for a short while within an area in which the only radio stations were "Christian." I had never heard the full argument for Christian home education before, but I heard it in detail in Alabama, and the rationale was similar to that of the Letter to Titus. Schools were not to be trusted; they might expose children to the speculations of philosophers and scientists. Human reason was presented as not only flawed but sinful, heretic. The word of God could be corrupted by schools, and Christians ought therefore to keep their children at home, educating them from Scripture alone. Too much thinking and too much talking is dangerous.

And yet, if God never lies, won't his truth be strong enough to withstand anything our poor minds can do to it? I think a God who never lies must be one who never fears for the safety of truth. Surely language and thought, gifts from him, can only strengthen our grasp of truth and improve our understanding, even of a truth that lies outside the effable realm. I trust words, though I'm aware of their limitations; I believe they lead us generally toward discovery, not into confusion. Only by trusting language can we recognize the blind alleys down which it occasionally leads.

I have been in Crete, where Titus was—went there with my mother, who had been waiting all her life to see the ruins at Knossos. In college she had studied Minoan and Mycenaean art. I think she also hoped that the trip would help me. My life at the time was in some disarray.

I had spent it being respectable. She had done the same with her life. We were two good women, Titus might have said, having accomplished all that Paul required of women in his letter. "Bid the older women likewise to be reverent in behavior, not to be slanderers or slaves to drink; they are to teach what is good, and so train the young women to love their husbands and children, to be sensible, chaste, domestic, kind, and submissive to their husbands, that the word of God may not be discredited" (2:3–5). My mother had married directly out of college, postponing Knossos; had gotten a job, raised three children, joined the Junior League, led the March of Dimes, taught Sunday school. I had done the same, with three more years of schooling and one less child.

But something had gone wrong with me. I didn't know exactly what. I'd begun having chest pains and nightmares. A doctor said nothing had gone wrong with me physically. Maybe I was working too hard, he said. When he left the room, I read his notes upside down. He had written "anxiety reaction." That was not *nothing*, I thought; but still the diagnosis didn't help me much. I wanted to talk to my mother about what was happening to me, but I didn't know where to begin. How could I say that all this goodness was not enough? That I needed something else?

Not that I meant to jettison my whole good life. I wanted to keep my family. But none of the rest. I was losing my hold on it anyway— the job, the volunteer work, the community life, the household duties. I was more and more drawn to writing fiction, something I had started young and then quit, out of fear. Writing was risky. It was difficult, presumptuous, disturbing, unprofitable, maybe even sinful (writers being the original liars). It was certainly not "sensible" or "domestic," qualities admired by Paul. Not an "honorable occupation." And it had no easily explicable purpose.

So I hadn't done it. I had been good instead; in other words, had protected myself—withdrawn and fortified. My fears came partly from me, from the kind of person I was (aloof-timid) and partly from my place and upbringing (Southern-Episcopalian-conservative). My mother had the same fears. She was happy with her life, but she was also not happy. I think I know why she took me to Crete: she knew what was there and wanted me to see it. She was not the kind of woman who would overtly encourage a daughter to throw off respectability. But she took me to Crete.

We roamed the ruins. It was a strange day, quiet and empty, halfway round the world from our real lives, and made even stranger by the anticipated visit, in this remote spot, of Teddy Kennedy. That was why we were the only people there; tour groups were not allowed in today, the guard said, and when Kennedy came, we would have to leave—go across the road to the taverna, he suggested, have a retsina. I was miffed. I wanted Knossos and my mother to myself. When we spotted a string of black limousines approaching from Heraklion, we reluctantly made ready to vacate the ruins. But the motorcade didn't stop. We watched it pass and snake into the hills beyond. I've always been grateful to Kennedy for bypassing us that day. I was superstitious then, as people can be when their lives are falling apart. I thought fortune kept him away, and left us there for a whole day alone in a place my mother considered holy.

The ruins are not extensive. We might have seen everything within two hours. But we took the day. We were not through until sunset.

Maybe in Paul's time the people of Crete were liars and evil beasts and lazy gluttons, but I could not believe it of the earlier Cretans, the builders of Knossos. Those seemed something far different to me, judging from their traces. The ruins suggested not a palace at all but an airy structure of human proportions: small rooms lit by shafts of sunlight, the whole complex crisscrossed by stairways and open passages, completely without defense. The place was neither fort nor temple. On the walls, dolphins played. The throne room was more like a sun parlor; the throne, a small stone chair. I could tell that the builders were at home in the world, crazy about the sea and sun and animals and plants. Of their religion, not much evidence remained—a few votive figures, some pots depicting a festival ritual.

"What did they believe?" I asked my mother. We were sitting on the roof, looking toward the hills where Kennedy had disappeared. Crete seemed brown and dry; it was November.

"I don't know," she said. "Whatever was in the dolphins."

She was right. Those dolphins, those bulls and flying men, those girls . . . I imagined a Crete in which truth was visible in every earthly thing, and artists showed it. The dolphins were lies, of course; a painter had made them into birds, drawn them into an untrue world. But they were lies that, far from damaging truth, seemed to be getting at it. A writer could do what the painter did. Homer had.

In South Carolina I was a good housewife. In Crete I was a communicant. I thought I could love the world as thoroughly as the Cretans had, love *through* it, to what was on the other side. I thought some lofty thoughts at Knossos, but lofty thoughts are possible and not always unreliable in an ancient place. One such experience in a lifetime is not excessive. As I stood in the Queen's Megaron, writing did not seem so dangerous to me. It seemed like the only thing to do. When I got home, I started.

Starting was hard enough. Working long hours for years was harder. And eventually my Minoan vision of nature and art proved inadequate. I had always thought that I had novels in my head, simply waiting to be transcribed. That was a delusion. What was in my head was only puffs of fiction, mutable and quick to evaporate. Words didn't come to me; I had to beat them up out of nothing. My characters seemed sunk in torpor; they hardly moved. When I asked my own question—what's this story really about?—I had no answer. But gradually an idea took hold, began to make sense. I found a way to encourage (give heart to) the characters. Though I didn't know it at the time, what I came to depend on was akin to something Paul had said.

In the Letter to Titus, the really curious thing is that, for all its concern with the need for protecting the truth, and all its stress on conduct "befitting" Christianity, there is little space given to the truth itself. But it's in there. Hidden, but present.

And when it comes, it calls into question everything else that the letter says. Maybe I overlooked it before because the words are so familiar, having become the rote of doctrine. But there at the heart of the letter, nearly the exact middle, are the words *"For the grace of God has appeared for the salvation of all men"* (2:11).

I don't think the Minoan scheme provides for such a thing. But I believe it. I believe that the grace of God has appeared for the salvation of all men. "All," Paul says, instantly embracing even those against whom he has been railing, all the empty talkers, all the deceivers, the liars, evil beasts, lazy gluttons, those corrupted in mind and conscience. The "all" is not modified; it must include Cretan, Jew, man, woman, slave, master, sinner, heretic, me.

And as sinners are included among the saved, the saved are included among the sinners. "For we ourselves were once foolish, disobedient, led astray, slaves to various passions and pleasures, passing our days in malice and envy, hated by men and hating one another; but when the goodness and loving kindness of God our Savior appeared, he saved us, not because of deeds done in righteousness, but in virtue of his own mercy" (3:3–5).

I believe in the salvageability of humanity, and that's what I try to write about. My understanding of salvageability is probably not orthodox. I don't mean that people can be saved by churches, or by belief, or by writers; I only mean that they are worth saving. They are valuable. If that were not true, fiction would have no reason to be.

It may always be difficult for me to profess a Christian faith. The other day I read in the Episcopalian newsletter a description and condemnation of pantheism, an old heresy. Like a hypochondriac reading up on the symptoms of disease, I recognized the telltale signs; I had it, without question. I've got others as well, heresies whose names I don't even know, and my personal spiritual life may well be forever plagued with them. I don't think a church will ever want me.

But fiction doesn't require the writer to profess. In it I am free to work from the most inchoate of creeds, following what leads turn up, secure in the knowledge that most exploration leads somewhere. When I begin a book, I don't know what's in store; I trust in discovery. It usually comes. Fiction speaks indirectly, does not lay down laws. Sometimes I think of Crete when I'm writing, because I do try to love the material world so thoroughly that I may not escape a spiritual vision. But I think also of the parables, Christ's fiction, in which nothing is spelled out. I think of God who does not lie. He imagined us as like himself, and so I think of even fictional characters as having a soul, even the villains—especially the villains. I don't try to present a correct Christian vision of the world; I'm still not sure what that would be. What I love is the great miscellany of souls, their mystery and their value, the thing in them that may be sacred, their truth.

Paul, I think, knew that truth and lies cannot be opposites, because they are not equals. We speak of "the truth" but have no precise antonym for it. Truth is big and singular and not of our making. Lies are little human darts, *words*, in the long run no match for truth, nor even its enemy.

THE EPISTLE OF

PAUL

TO PHILEMON

—

A PRISONER OF CHRIST

Jonathan Galassi

The letter to Philemon is the shortest of Paul's epistles, and, except for 2 John, the shortest book in the Bible. It concerns the fate of a wayward slave, Onesimus (the name means "profitable" or "useful" in Greek, and Paul characteristically puns on it), who had earlier escaped from the household of Paul's friend and fellow Christian Philemon, and who may also have robbed him. Paul, who is writing to Philemon from prison, has met and converted Onesimus and has come to love him—he calls him "a part of my own self." He is sending him back to his master with the request that Philemon receive him "not as a slave any more, but something much better than a slave, a dear brother."*

A runaway slave, if caught, could have faced crucifixion, but Paul is clearly expecting no such response from Philemon. He offers to repay anything owed him by Onesimus, at the same time reminding Philemon of his own debt to Paul, "which is yourself"—presumably a reference to Paul's conversion of him. Some commentators have suggested that Paul is hinting that Onesimus be returned to him to

* All biblical quotations are drawn from the Jerusalem Bible.

help him in his work. Whether or not this is the case, Paul appeals to Philemon's good nature and to Paul's own high standing in Philemon's eyes, rather than to his authority over Philemon, in asking him to receive and forgive his slave:

> Now, although in Christ I can have no diffidence about telling you to do what is your duty, I am appealing to your love instead, reminding you that this is Paul writing, an old man now and, what is more, still a prisoner of Christ Jesus. I am appealing to you for a child of mine, whose father I became while wearing these chains.

The circumstances of the writing of the letter are cloudy. It is generally considered to have been sent from Rome sometime during Paul's first period of imprisonment there in the early 60s, for the metropolis was a haven for runaway slaves. At least one commentator, however, Eduard Lohse, argues that Colossae was too far from Rome for a runaway slave to have reached, and that from Rome Paul could not have contemplated visiting Philemon shortly, as he mentions in verse 22.* Lohse believes the letter was written from Ephesus in the mid 50s, which would make it one of the earliest of the epistles, along with Thessalonians and Corinthians. Though it is known that Philemon was a Colossian, there is no evidence that he was living there at the time Paul wrote him; as Paul never visited Colossae, he must have converted him elsewhere.

Philemon has been canonical since the second century, but it was largely ignored by the ancient church because it dealt with "questions about life in this world and 'the gospel is not concerned with trivia,' " as Lohse observed. Jerome had to defend it against his contemporaries who believed its theme to be "beneath the dignity of an apostle," in the words of G. B. Caird.† Yet Caird points out that for modern commentators the practical nature of Philemon's theme can be seen as an argument in favor of its authenticity, "since to our way of thinking the letter would surely not have been preserved at all

---

* Eduard Lohse, *Colossians and Philemon: A Commentary on the Epistles to the Colossians and to Philemon*, tr. William R. Poehlmann and Robert J. Karvis, ed. Helmut Koester (Philadelphia, 1971), p. 188.
† *Paul's Letters from Prison* (Oxford, 1976), p. 213.

without a strong tradition that it came from the hand of Paul." Even so, the manner in which the letter is written, its affectionate, cajoling tone, its imagery, rhetoric, and intellectual temper, seem to identify it as Paul's. It is a brief note to a brother-in-arms about a not quite everyday matter, yet it is imbued with Paul's frame of mind, and in its own microcosmic way it is revelatory of his fundamental concerns.

The rhetoric of Philemon is consistently familial, the terms "brother" and "sister" being used no less than seven times in a text of less than five hundred words. Paul refers to Philemon and all his fellow Christians as his brothers, and indeed the essence of the letter is that the fraternity has now expanded to include Onesimus as well. The slave has also, paradoxically, become Paul's "son," since as his converter Paul is his Christian father—as he is Philemon's. But the overriding relationship is the "brotherhood" of faith—a term borrowed from the existing vocabulary of family relations, to describe a relationship that supersedes the familial. "Brother," according to Caird, "is almost a synonym for Christian"* in the early church, and this initiate's use of the term can be traced back to Jesus' revolutionary words in Matthew 12:46–50:

> He was still speaking to the crowds when his mother and his brothers appeared; they were standing outside and were anxious to have a word with him. But to the man who told him this Jesus replied, "Who is my mother? Who are my brothers?" And stretching out his hand towards his disciples he said, "Here are my mother and my brothers. Anyone who does the will of my Father in heaven, he is my brother and sister and mother."

Jesus' words are revolutionary because they reject the established order, the family hierarchy, in favor of a new relationship. (See also Matthew 10:35: "For I have come to set a man against his father, a daughter against her mother, a daughter-in-law against her mother-in-law. A man's enemies will be those of his own household.") Within the new family of God the Father, all who have faith are brothers— that is, they share equally in the benefits of his love. Onesimus, through his conversion, has become the "brother," the spiritual if

---

* Ibid.

not the temporal equal, of Paul and Philemon and all other Christians.

The notion of equality before God is the central tenet of Paul's interpretation of Jesus' teaching, not only the basis for his insistence of the primacy of love over duty, as here in his appeal to Philemon on Onesimus's behalf, but the underlying justification of his mission to the Gentiles, which would eventually transform Christianity from a sect of Judaism into a world religion. Though Paul himself demonstrates ample pride in his Jewish ancestry and education, he came to regard the Jewish Law (which he elsewhere calls "the yoke of slavery" [Galatians 5:1]), with its emphasis on obligation and observance and its highly restricted notions of kinship, as irrelevant—and thus an obstacle—to the fundamental import of Christ's teaching. For Paul "the whole of the Law" is summarized in a single command: *Love your neighbour as yourself* (Galatians 5:14). It is through one's approach to others, through the earthly metaphor of interpersonal relations, that man's relationship with God is to be apprehended. This is the basis of every other commandment:

> Avoid getting into debt, except the debt of mutual love. If you love your fellow men you have carried out your obligations [literally, "fulfilled the Law"]. All the commandments: *You shall not commit adultery, you shall not kill, you shall not steal, you shall not covet*, and so on, are summed up in this single command: *You must love your neighbour as yourself.** Love is the one thing that cannot hurt your neighbour; that is why it is the answer to every one of the commandments. [Romans 13:8–10]

This subversion of the Judaic dispensation can be seen as the crucial moment in the development of Christianity, and for his insistence on it Paul more than deserves his title of second founder of the religion. It is a deeply radical shift in perspective, which envisions an entirely new and more intimate relationship with God and, because of this, with other men. Not only the spiritual and psychological but the racial, ethnic, and political categories of Paul's previous world are implicitly dissolved:

* A note in the Jerusalem Bible points out that while "in Leviticus, 'neighbour' was a fellow countryman, here it is any member of the human family which is made one in Christ."

You have stripped off your old behaviour with your old self, and you have put on a new self which will progress towards true knowledge the more it is renewed in the image of its creator; and in that image there is no room for distinction between Greek and Jew, between the circumcised or the uncircumcised, or between barbarian and Scythian, slave and free man. There is only Christ: he is everything and he is in everything. [Colossians 3:9–11]

Such assertions have highly inflammatory political implications, and one can well understand both the Jews' and the Romans' eagerness to suppress their promulgator. But Paul is careful throughout his writings not to attack the political status quo directly; the worldly is always only a way of speaking, *faute de mieux*, about the divine order. Paul's stated concern is always spiritual status, and in the specific matter of slavery he makes clear that the slave must obey his master. Colossians, which if it is not by Paul himself is certainly a faithful expansion of his ideas, has this to say about the issue:

Slaves, be obedient to the men who are called your masters in this world; not only when you are under their eye, as if you had only to please men, but wholeheartedly, out of respect for the Master. Whatever your work is, put your heart into it as if it were for the Lord and not for men, knowing that the Lord will repay you by making you his heirs. It is Christ the Lord that you are serving; anyone who does wrong will be repaid in kind and he does not favour one person more than another. Masters, make sure that your slaves are given what is just and fair, knowing that you too have a Master in heaven. [Colossians 3:22–4:1]

The author of Colossians, whether he is Paul or not, makes use of Paul's technique of appropriating a specific vocabulary for the uses of his argument. Here, the master-slave nexus becomes a metaphor for God's relationship to man, and the transformation by inference casts a new light back upon the original subject. For Paul and his coreligionists, everything in the world is re-created, metaphorized, by faith, which means that every worldly condition has a spiritual counterpart which it symbolizes. One consequence of this is that slavery loses some of its force as an actual predicament. The true "slavery" is not a physical condition; for the early Christians, as Robin Lane Fox has noted, "the greatest slavery was man's slavery to his passions."*

Paul does not draw out the metaphoric connection between Onesimus's literal condition as a slave and man's spiritual "slavery"; yet the link is there, hovering in Paul's description of himself as "a prisoner of Christ." He uses the phrase three times in this brief note, and it is the unspoken equation of himself and Onesimus that is the true basis of his appeal to Philemon. The text makes clear that Paul was a literal prisoner at the time he wrote Philemon, whether in Rome or in Ephesus, yet characteristically the phrase has a more than literal significance. "Paul," Caird writes, "was fond of vigorous metaphor";† indeed, as we have seen, metaphor was essential to his rhetorical method. Six of the epistles refer to him and others as "slaves" or "servants" of Christ;‡ here, similarly, he is a "prisoner of Christ": literally a prisoner because of his promulgation of Christ's teaching, and figuratively a captive of the overwhelming Christian vision of existence. The term as Paul uses it is a mark of honor; he may even be guilty of self-congratulation. As Caird puts it, "For Paul to be Christ's prisoner is high rank, not cause for pity."§ In a sense, Paul is experiencing the most total form of Christianity possible: utter submission to the higher will apprehended through Christ's teaching. In such a condition, worldly status can only be irrelevant:

A slave, when he is called in the Lord, becomes the Lord's freedman, and a freedman called in the Lord becomes Christ's slave. You have all been bought and paid for; do not be slaves of other men. Each one of you, my brothers, should stay as he was before God at the time of his call. [1 Corinthians 7:21–24]

Paul never addresses the contradiction in the last two sentences of this passage. He does not ask Philemon to free Onesimus, only

---

* *Pagans and Christians* (New York, 1987), p. 296.
† *Paul's Letters from Prison*, p. 1.
‡ See Romans 1:1; 1 Corinthians 7:22; Galatians 1:10; Ephesians 6:6; Philippians 1:1; and Colossians 4:12.
§ *Paul's Letters from Prison*, p. 218.

to forgive him his transgression and to accept him as a brother on the higher plane of faith. He does so by implying how close his own situation is to Onesimus's. Each is inescapably encumbered in the world—Paul in chains, Onesimus in the shackles of slavery. But they are also united in belief; and because Philemon is their brother in belief, Paul is asking—not ordering—him to show mercy and forgiveness, to love Onesimus: that is, to submit.

Martin Luther, in his preface to Philemon, emphasizes how irrelevant "rights" are for Paul, and how coercive is the nature of his appeal through love:

> This epistle gives us a masterful and tender illustration of Christian love. For here we see how St. Paul takes the part of poor Onesimus and, to the best of his ability, advocates his cause with his master. He acts exactly as if he were himself Onesimus, who had done wrong. Yet he does this not with force or compulsion, as lay within his rights; but he empties himself of his rights in order to compel Philemon also to waive his rights. What Christ has done for us with God the Father, that St. Paul does also for Onesimus with Philemon. For Christ emptied himself of his rights (Phil. 2:7) and overcame the Father with love and humility, so that the Father had to put away his wrath and rights, and receive us into favor for the sake of Christ, who so earnestly advocates our cause and so heartily takes our part. For we are all his Onesimus's if we believe.*

If we believe . . . For Luther, too, what is fundamental is submission to Christ, "emptying oneself" of "rights" in order to be open to receive the influx of divine love made available through Christ's intercession. In this battle of wills, God's one commandment is bound to prevail over any sublunary, legalistic notion of justice. Yet it is precisely in Paul's notion of universal equality before God that the modern notion of "rights" is born. Though the idea of the equality of persons in the sphere of politics would lie largely dormant for centuries, it is here in Paul: the foundation "for what are usually

---

* "Preface to the Epistle of Saint Paul to Philemon, 1546 (1522)," in *Luther's Works*, American Edition, vol. 35, ed. E. Theodore Bachmann (Philadelphia, 1960), p. 390. Quoted in Lohse, *Colossians and Philemon*, p. 188.

described as liberal values in the West—for the commitment to equality and reciprocity, as well as the postulate of individual freedom," as L. A. Seidentop has written.* The slogans of the American and French revolutions are imbued with Paul's rhetoric, except that the metaphors have been literalized and the language reactivated in the arena of the world. The notion of otherworldliness and of submission to a higher will was essential to the survival and development of Paul's Christianity; but the seductions of the temporal eventually proved too great for his church and its adherents. In spite of his strictures, it was the literal dimension of Paul's idea that was to prevail, eventually supplanting faith itself as the cornerstone of Western beliefs; it is the notion of secular equality—of "rights" justified by "love"—that keeps reappearing as a corrective force to channel the energies of history in the direction of an ever broader democracy. One has only to think of the American civil rights movement of the 1960s or of the current Western concern for "human rights" to realize how deeply and continually influential this "reductive" reading of the imagery and ideas of Philemon continues to be.

Even more than his ideas, though, it is the extraordinary unitary nature of Paul's vision that strikes us most deeply in reading him today: the force of intellect that permitted the formulation and elaboration of his Christianity; the rugged poetry of his language; the steely spiritual and physical courage that stood by him as he endured the consequences of his bearing witness. Paul's letters show him to be one of the most vivid personalities of the ancient world: brilliant, proud, quixotic, quick to anger, deeply loving, deeply humble, and profoundly confident of his mission. All of this is present in Philemon—his humanity, his courage, his stubbornness, and, above all, his capacity to see every event within the framework of his overriding vision. If few who have followed in his footsteps have matched his certainty of the efficacy of faith, hope, and love, the residual power of his voice is such that it still attracts and compels today. He was prodigious; his conviction animated every action he took, every word he wrote. And this singleness of purpose is the most inimitable and unforgettable thing about him.

* "Liberalism: The Christian Connection," *Times Literary Supplement*, March 24–30, 1989, p. 308.

THE EPISTLE OF
PAUL THE APOSTLE
TO THE HEBREWS

—

Robert B. Shaw

I

A friend, on hearing that I was writing this essay,* recalled an apt sentence from one of the novels of E. F. Benson. Two ladies are exploring an English village where their presence is recognized as unusual: "They wandered down the main street, exciting as much commentary as the Epistle to the Hebrews." Biblical criticism, as I should have remembered from the year I spent in divinity school, has frequently the atmosphere of a village: ingrown, voluble, disputatious, daunting to outsiders; unable to agree on questions of who, where, and when. What little Greek I once knew is long gone, and it is only as an outsider that I can approach this topic. What I have to offer is not scholarly commentary but some personal meditation on this strange book which has intrigued me since I first read it. If part of what I write seems autobiography, I can only plead that this witnesses to one effect of the Bible on me, as on many of its readers. It is a great spur to self-examination.

Without getting caught in scholarly quicksand I should mention

* The King James Version of the Bible is quoted throughout this essay.

briefly some of the issues that have detained others at length. (1) The Epistle to the Hebrews, once ascribed to Paul, is not by Paul. The author's style and theological preoccupations determine this much, but who he was remains a mystery. Early in the third century Origen concluded famously, "But who wrote the epistle, in truth, God knows," and scholarship has so far not got beyond his statement of the case. (2) The work is most likely not an epistle. It carries no salutation, and the first twelve chapters are homiletic rather than epistolary in form. The final, thirteenth, chapter has more the air of a letter, but it is generally regarded as a later addition, possibly with the intent of having the work accepted as Pauline. (3) No one is sure where the Jewish Christians to whom the work is addressed were located. While one commentator argues strongly for connecting the author and his audience with Rome, another will argue for Palestine with equal fervor. (4) There is just as much uncertainty surrounding the date of composition. If one takes its description of Jewish worship as referring to the Temple in Jerusalem, then the work would have to precede the destruction of the Temple in C.E. 70. This date ceases to be a benchmark, however, if the author, as some would argue, is describing not the worship practices of the Temple but the earlier ones of the tabernacle, gleaned not from personal experience but from his reading of Exodus. Hebrews is quoted in the letter known as 1 Clement, which was written very near the end of the first century and so must predate that. But the date, even within decades, remains debatable, like so much else.

Of course, when I first read Hebrews such difficulties were not mine to grapple with. I read it not particularly out of piety but because in those days I read anything I could get my hands on. This was in adolescence, and to me the text presented obscurities enough without worrying over matters of provenance. I was moved to continue pondering the work, despite its opacities, because of the power the language of certain passages exerted over me. Some of these passages still carry much the same effect. I am not in general given to what the eighteenth century would term enthusiasm when reading literature. Some readers are more susceptible. A. E. Housman notoriously testified that he tried not to think of poetry while shaving, "because, if a line of poetry strays into my memory, my skin bristles so that the razor ceases to act." He adds, "This particular symptom is accompanied by a shiver down the spine. . . ." Emily Dickinson was yet more extreme: "If I read a book and it makes my whole body so cold no fire can warm me, I know that is poetry. If I feel physically as if the top of my head were taken off, I know that is poetry. These are the only ways I know it. Is there any other way?" Well, yes, there is. I read much of the poetry I prize most with the greatest delight, but without such dramatic physical sensations. The exceptions to this are chiefly Shakespeare (especially *King Lear*) and the Bible (King James). Many passages in Scripture do literally make my hair stand on end, and some of those horripilating lines are in Hebrews.

Probably when I first read the book the verses that made my neck bristle were admonitory ones. Like other writers who are convinced that the end is near, the author couples warnings to exhortations. A good example comes toward the end: "Wherefore we receiving a kingdom which cannot be moved, let us have grace, whereby we may serve God acceptably with reverence and godly fear: For our God is a consuming fire" (12:28–29). The last words thrilled me like a glimpse into a volcano soon to erupt. I am less moved by them now, having seen over the last several years so many abuses of evangelism. We may, by looking honestly at ourselves, be frightened into religion (and that may be a good thing), but I take a skeptical view of preachers who attempt to do the frightening for us.

A verse that comes much earlier is daunting in a subtler way and continues to affect me now as much as it ever did: "For the word of God is quick, and powerful, and sharper than any two-edged sword, piercing even to the dividing asunder of soul and spirit, and of the joints and marrow, and is a discerner of the thoughts and intents of the heart" (4:12). Of course "the word of God" here means more than the text of the Scriptures. It means the fearsomely acute discernment by which God searches and knows us. But for most of us such unexpected piercing is sustained in hearing the dangerous Book read to us or in reading it ourselves. Here, then, the word of God holds up a mirror to itself, celebrating its power to cut through pretense and bring unacknowledged inward realities to light. It is uncomfortable, and it is sublime.

The way to sublimity is often through the mundane. The dangerousness of God's word became clearly apparent to me when I read the Bible myself, but I was aware of it as something set apart from ordinary language even before I could read. My mother's father was a Presbyterian minister, and until I was four my parents, my brother, and I lived with my grandparents next to the church. We spent a lot of time there, perforce. My first impressions of Christian worship were vividly sensory in ways that my age would explain. Parents attempting to make small boys look proper for Sunday dressed them in suits with short pants then, and I remember how the cushions of the pews, stuffed with horsehair, prickled my legs as they dangled above the floor. Sitting next to my mother or grandmother, I would look at the stained glass (the windows were in the style of Tiffany and so caught a child's eye) or at the people around us, most of whom seemed very old. The white-haired ladies, always wearing hats, all knew my name, although I could never tell them apart. They carried large pocketbooks (never, then, called handbags) which were black in the winter and white in the summer, and out of which came lavender-scented handkerchiefs, change purses, spectacles, peppermints, and much else. My grandmother had her own supply of peppermints which she doled out to me if I seemed restive.

My grandfather was at the center of things, which is to say, in the pulpit. He was liberal in theology, kindly and humorous in manner; indeed, the only harshly Calvinistic thing in that church was the horsehair cushion I sat on. But although he was unfailingly gentle with both children and adults, my grandfather was possessed of immense natural dignity. Standing at more than six feet in his black Geneva gown, with his snowy hair smoothed faultlessly down and his wire-rimmed eyeglasses glinting, the impression he gave was august. His appearance no doubt furnished my earliest image of God the Father. His elderly flock cherished him. When he was made a Doctor of Divinity one lady congratulated him. "I'm so glad," she said, "that yours is an honorary degree, not one of those *earned* degrees." (Anyone who has gone to the trouble of earning a few must sometimes suspect that she was right.) Had I been older, I imagine, he would have riveted my attention. As it was, I was often prey to distractions, being diverted when an old tremulous usher spilled a whole tray of communion glasses on someone's dress, or simply when the sun falling through some paler panes irradiated the motes dancing in the air around me. Once on a dark winter's day at just the moment when my grandfather was preaching about the Valley of the Shadow all the lights went out, and there was a startled hush as one of the ushers stumbled to the fuse box. Afterward the adults of the family laughed about this, but I was left somewhat in awe by it.

I mention these trivial details in order to emphasize what follows. Interleaved with such mundane distractions, and with the stretches of tedium they interrupted, were moments of a different character. In memory I have no visual image of these; there is only the sound of my grandfather's voice reading or expounding some inspired words. Something new came into his voice when he quoted Scripture, and as I listened something came into me which had little to do with intellectual understanding. There was nothing put on or actorish about his voice at such times, but it had a ritual deliberateness which stemmed, I would suppose, from due reverence. And for me the sound of the words momentarily effaced the familiar Sunday scene, even subduing the aggravation of the horsehair. There was a sense in all this which I could not have articulated then, of an order of being different from mine: an invisible world which interpenetrated the one I saw (or at these moments, did not see). I use the word "moments," but the intimations I had hung free of time: it was in eternity that the Word was uttered, startlingly enough underpinning this quotidian world of small children struggling with boredom and old people long since resigned to it. If these were moments, they were moments out of time, spells of disembodiment. Was this not perhaps the word of God fulfilling its office as described in Hebrews, "the dividing asunder of soul and spirit"? I realize now that when I read such verses what I hear in my head is my grandfather's voice.

II

Hair-raising eloquence is achieved in brief phrases in Hebrews, but such phrases are concentrated summations of a powerfully conceived and elaborated argument. All commentators, agreeing that the author has the most stylistic polish among New Testament writers, take note as well of his skill in extending an argument over twelve chapters, thus offering the longest sustained discussion in Christian Scripture. I will set down the gist of that discussion now.

The author is principally concerned to show his audience how Christ's perfect atonement for their sins must alter their practice of worship and the assumptions underlying it, as they pass from the old Covenant to the new. Christ is an effective mediator of the new Covenant by virtue of both his divine and his human nature. His divinity is stressed at the outset, when the author, drawing heavily on Scripture, demonstrates the superiority of the Son of God to the angels. Angels are mere "ministering spirits" (1:14), whom the Father sends to minister to us, but the Son is "the brightness of his glory, and the express image of his person . . . [who] upholding all things by the word of his power, when he had by himself purged our sins, sat down on the right hand of the Majesty on high" (1:3). Quoting Psalm 110, our author asks, "But to which of the angels said he at any time, Sit on my right hand, until I make thine enemies thy footstool?" (1:13) Passing on from these comparisons, however, we find equal stress placed on the Son's humanity. This exalted being united himself to humankind so that we might regain our lost kinship with divinity: "For both he that sanctifieth and they who are sanctified are all of one: for which cause he is not ashamed to call them brethren" (2:11). Of his free will he came to "taste death for every man" (2:9), and it was fully *as* man that he tasted it, as the author's vivid evocation of the Passion emphasizes: Christ "in the days of his flesh, when he had offered up prayers and supplications with strong crying and tears unto him that was able to save him from death, and was heard in that he feared; though he were a Son, yet learned he obedience by the things which he suffered" (5:7–8).

Such cognizance of the two natures of Christ may be found elsewhere in the New Testament; it adumbrates the creedal statement that Christ is "true God and true man." What is unique in Hebrews is the use the author makes of this perception, speaking chiefly not of Christ's person but of his office: the office being that of high priest, of one presiding at the new rite established by his sacrifice. The center of the argument is an intricate contrast of the worship of the old Covenant, led by the Levitical priesthood, and that of the new, instituted by Jesus, who was "made like unto his brethren, that he might be a merciful and faithful high priest in things pertaining to God, to make reconciliation for the sins of the people" (2:17).

In the course of explaining the priestly role of Christ the author says a great deal about the priests who stood before God for Israel in earlier times. With what seems a fascination with liturgical detail, he sketches the outer sanctuary of the tabernacle (and, as some would argue, of Jerusalem's Temple as well) with its candlestick, table, and showbread; and he dwells even more on the inner shrine "after the second veil," the Holy of Holies, where the Ark of the Covenant was housed. In the outer sanctuary the priests officiated at services every day, but the Holy of Holies was entered once a year on the Day of Atonement, and by the high priest alone, "not without blood, which he offered for himself, and for the errors of the people" (9:7).

In the author's view the necessity of repeating such sacrifices year by year proves they failed to "make the comers thereunto perfect" (10:1). Conscience of sins persisted which the blood of animals could not purge. In contrast he offers what we would be tempted to call a daring analogy except that for him it is not an analogy at all but a decisive fact. Once and for all, at his ascension into heaven, Christ as high priest entered the true Holy of Holies with the one fully efficacious sacrifice:

> But Christ being come a high priest of good things to come, by a greater and more perfect tabernacle, not made with hands, that is to say, not of this building;
> Neither by the blood of goats and calves, but by his own blood he entered in once into the holy place, having obtained eternal redemption for us. [9:11–12]

We are invited to follow him into that sacred precinct now laid open to us, to have, as the author puts it, "boldness to enter the holiest by the blood of Jesus, by a new and living way, which he hath consecrated for us, through the veil, that is to say, his flesh" (10:19–20). One reading this will be reminded of the Gospel account of what occurred when the sacrifice on the cross was accomplished: "The veil of the temple was rent in twain from the top to the bottom" (Matthew 27:51).

This remarkable argument proceeds from a world view which some have called Platonic. Certainly the author perceives two levels of reality within which his contrasted modes of worship operate. There is the earthly tabernacle or Temple in which the Levitical priesthood offer the sacrifices as the Law prescribes. And there is the "greater and more perfect" one in which the Son offers himself in our behalf to his Father. The earthly tabernacle and its rites are, in this author's persistent vocabulary, "shadows" or "figures" of those in heaven. He declares that "Christ is not entered into the holy places made with hands, which are the figures of the true; but into heaven itself, now to appear in the presence of God for us" (9:24), and speaks of "the law having a shadow of good things to come, and not the very image of the things" (10:1). Yet "Platonic" does not seem quite the term to apply to this author's metaphysics. The notion of an eternal form or archetype may seem to be there in what he says of the heavenly tabernacle, but he does not seem to go as far as Plato in disdaining the material world. Plato's unruffled Socrates, taking the hemlock in calm certainty that he is escaping the prison of physical nature, is a figure very different from the Christ of Hebrews, offering in his Passion "prayers and supplications with strong crying and tears." As with the divine and human natures of Christ, the heavenly and earthly spheres have each a substantial reality and coexist, albeit at times with a certain tension. In speaking of the worship of the Levitical priesthood as a "shadow" of Christ's sacrifice the author is questioning not its reality but its efficacy for atonement.

"Shadow" in fact seems often a more understandable concept if we transpose it from the category of space to that of time: to this author the worship of Israel was a *foreshadowing* of what Christ has now accomplished; his sacrifice achieves what all previous sacrifices aimed at, and thus is a culmination of all the spiritual aspirations of Israel since the giving of the law. Christ as high priest gives humanity access to "the true tabernacle, which the Lord pitched, and not man" (8:2). Belief in that unseen reality, and a conviction that Christ has made worship a way of taking part in that transcendence, underlies the entire argument.

Taking part in transcendence, becoming aware of a supersensual order of being, seems to me to be the height of human experience in worship. I would place my childhood intuitions under this head, and I have had later experiences (not many, but some) that I would place there as well. For much of my adult life I have been intrigued by ritual, as I suppose the author of Hebrews to have been. The delicate relation of aesthetically striking forms in liturgy to the sometimes obstreperous religious message they convey first held my interest when I was in college, and it still engages me. It had a lot to do with bringing me into the Episcopal Church, where liturgy was in more plentiful supply than in Presbyterianism. I attended divinity school for a year and then and for some while afterward considered the possibility of ordination. During that time, and even after I had made a different vocational choice, I grew more intimately involved in the liturgy than I might have simply as a member of the congregation, for I served frequently as an acolyte and more occasionally as a subdeacon at solemn mass. I used to intone the Epistle, and sometimes it was a passage from Hebrews that I chanted. (Singing in public does not abash me so long as it is all on one note.) Girded, draped, and festooned in cassock, amice, alb, cincture, chasuble, and maniple, I felt as sacerdotal as a layman likely could. The decor was of course more elaborate than in my grandfather's church, a more florid Gothic and more distinctly sacramental. The altar, not the pulpit, was the focal point, and behind it rose not a bare cross but a reredos of Caen stone presenting the crucified Savior with a panoply of some fourteen angels and saints. The atmosphere was literally headier, clouded with each Sunday's incense.

After I ceased to be nervous about which altar step to stand on I found I was experiencing liturgy in a new way, not simply as language but as motion and gesture. The word "choreography" naturally comes to mind, and more than one devout thinker has spoken of the Eucharist as a kind of dance before God's altar. And ideally one cannot tell the dancer from the dance, for personality is subsumed in the impersonality of ritual and in the corporate nature of worship. As I had as a child, I felt fleetingly the impinging presence of an invisible world and a suspension of consciousness of time. Some, I know, would classify such responses as aesthetic. To this I can only answer that I have had aesthetic experiences, and the apprehensions I speak of here were of a different nature. I think that both priest and communicant can become aware of their actions as a showing forth of the cosmic drama of redemption, and know that what is done at the altar is not their own doing. In any sacrament the true celebrant is Christ, and the bedizened ministers plying their hieratic gestures catch their rhythm from him and follow in his steps.

I would not care to assert that the author of Hebrews would feel at home in an Anglo-Catholic parish. In its elaboration of vestments, furnishings, and ritual actions, would the mass seem to him uncomfortably close to the Levitical ceremonies he labeled "shadows"? Would he prefer a Presbyterian service or, for that matter, a Quaker meeting? Unanswerable questions. I myself read this author not as hostile to ritual but as concerned that it fulfill its purpose, that of bringing worshipers into "the true tabernacle." And I feel that he would approve of any ritual in which such an aspiration is realized. It is worth emphasizing that even as our rites share with the ancient ones of Israel the aim of entering the divine presence, they allude to them in some aspects of form. The vestments of the Church today recall the robes of Aaron, and the container where the consecrated host is kept is called the tabernacle. Although the author of Hebrews may seem to stress in his argument the differences between the old Covenant and the new, the modern reader, considering his language of sacrifice, is likely to be struck rather by how much this author's spiritual imagination draws from the faith into which Christ was born. And one is left finally in awe of the great collective spiritual striving that is liturgy, continuing and ramifying throughout history.

III

I have been dealing chiefly with the theological ideas of Hebrews. Now I want to say something about the literary artistry of its author and the scope of his thought. I move to more comfortable ground here, for as my thoughts of becoming a priest receded, my efforts as a student of literature became more intense, and have since continued. Lacking Greek, I can still discern some aspects of this author's literary skill, particularly in his use of quotation and typology. I sat in Harold Bloom's class when he was formulating the theory expounded in *The Anxiety of Influence* and later books. I could make little, then or later, of Bloom's "revisionary ratios," but his radical insistence that books are made out of other books, and that a writer's passionate struggle with his precursors is often at the center of his art are conceptions I still find useful. Listening to Bloom read poetry did not at the time remind me of listening to my grandfather read the Bible. Perhaps it should have: Bloom, too, was a kind man deeply involved in his text, and his intonations were at times oracular. I suppose that he would describe the author of Hebrews as a "strong revisionist" in the use he makes of the Prophets and the Psalms. All of his quotations (drawn not from the Hebrew Scriptures but from the Septuagint's Greek version) are deployed to buttress his concepts of Christ's divine nature and priestly office. His explications of such passages may seem strained, and his casting aside of contexts cavalier, but such practices fall within the tradition of midrash, or biblical exegesis, which the author inherited. Some of his midrashic flights seem as bold as any of the secular ones I used to have proffered me by Harold Bloom, a modern master of the method.

A prime example of his boldness is his quotation in Chapter 10 of some verses of Psalm 40. In the King James version of the psalm these verses read:

> Sacrifice and offering thou didst not desire; mine ears hast thou opened: burnt offering and sin offering hast thou not required.
> Then said I, Lo, I come: in the volume of the book it is written of me,
> I delight to do thy will, O my God: yea, thy law is within my heart. [Psalm 40:6–8]

In Hebrews a variant text of the Septuagint is followed; we find the word "body" substituted for "ears" in verse 6, and the whole speech is ascribed to the preexistent Christ, announcing his purpose in coming into the world:

> Wherefore when he cometh into the world, he saith, Sacrifice and offering thou wouldest not, but a body hast thou prepared me:
> In burnt offerings and sacrifices for sin thou hast had no pleasure.
> Then said I, Lo, I come (in the volume of the book it is written of me) to do thy will, O God. [Hebrews 10:5–7]

So the "body" is that offered on the cross, and the one who offers it here makes plain his intention. This is but one of many examples of scriptural quotation and gloss that remind us of the indissoluble links, literary as well as spiritual, between the two Testaments.

Even more intriguing in its forging of such links is this author's use of typology. Arcane to us but easily familiar to the first audience of Hebrews was the interpretation of persons, places, objects, or events in the Old Testament as foreshadowings of Christ and the events recounted in the Gospels. Typology is used most ingeniously and elaborately in Hebrews to set forth the nature of Christ's priesthood. Israel's priesthood was hereditary, and was exclusively assigned to the tribe of Levi. The author wishes to explain in what sense Jesus of the tribe of Judah could be a priest, and with this purpose he describes him as one "made a high priest for ever after the order of Melchisedec" (6:20). Who was Melchisedec?

We find him by turning back the pages in the Book almost to the beginning. In the fourteenth chapter of Genesis, Abraham, returning victorious from battle, meets Melchizedek (the Old Testament spelling), who is described as "king of Salem" and as "priest of the most high God." Bringing forth bread and wine, he blesses Abraham's triumph and Abraham pays him tithes of the spoils. Three verses suffice for this tale (18–20), and Melchizedek disappears from the record forthwith. In his exposition in chapter 7 the author of Hebrews turns the paucity of information, as well as what few details are known, to positive advantage. Part of his interpretation is etymological. The name Melchizedek means "king of righteousness," and his title, king of Salem, means "king of peace." With much more interpretive liberty he concludes that since Scripture says nothing of Melchizedek's genealogy, of his birth or his death, he may be seen as resembling the Son of God; like Christ, he "abideth a priest continually" (7:3). And he is a priest of a superior order to that of the tribe of Levi. Abraham paid him tithes; hence, the ingenious argument goes, Levi also paid him tithes, "for he was yet in the loins" of his ancestor Abraham "when Melchisedec met him" (7:10). (The author seems to realize how far he is stretching here; he introduces this thought with "And as I may so say" [RSV: "One might even say"], acknowledging the metaphoric nature of his language.) All these features allow him to recognize Melchizedek as a type of Christ, who became our new high priest "not after the law of a carnal commandment, but after the power of an endless life" (7:16). The messianic Psalm 110, which he has quoted before, furnishes the one other mention of Melchizedek in Scripture, and presents this author now with a conclusive citation: "The Lord sware and will not repent, thou art a priest for ever after the order of Melchisedec" (Hebrews 7:21, referring to Psalm 110:4). Earlier he had quoted from the first verse of the psalm: "The Lord said unto my Lord, Sit thou at my right hand, until I make thine enemies thy footstool." Now he shows that the conquering prince is also a priest; the words of the psalm are those of the Father ordaining his Son to his atoning mission.

Typological interpretations of this sort impress us with their intricacy, but to most of us they seem somewhat musty as well—mental exercises alien to modern habits of thought. And yet, from biblical times through the Renaissance this method of superimposing one scriptural text upon another proved an immensely potent resource, not only for theology but for literature. Dante's *Divine Comedy*, Spenser's *Faerie Queene*, the religious lyrics of Donne and Herbert, and the major works of Milton are suffused with it. No one can doubt that when more rationalistic modes of biblical study became the fashion, scholarship made great strides, but one may feel that by the same token art was in some respects hobbled. If we think of the author of Hebrews as practicing biblical criticism, his procedures are bound to seem strained and quaint. But if we view him as exercising poetic intuition through typology, we can appreciate the imaginative power of his parallels. We see this not only in the Melchizedek-Christ collocation but in numerous others as well, such as the comparison near the end of the work, of Sinai, the fearful mount of the old Covenant, with Mount Sion in "the city of the living God, the heavenly Jerusalem" (12:22). Sometimes the analogy is greatly condensed, as in the reference to "Jesus the mediator of the new covenant, and . . . the blood of sprinkling, that speaketh better things than that of Abel" (12:24). Abel's innocent blood cried out for vengeance from the ground, whereas the blood of Jesus pleads forgiveness for those for whom he died. Typology is a poetically potent endeavor particularly because it brings into bold relief not only the similarities but the differences in the things being compared.

Something was lost for literature, and maybe for life at large, when the Western mind gave up such ease of allusiveness. Of course typology assumes an audience thoroughly steeped in Scripture, and this is so far from being true today that an author would be utterly quixotic to depend on it. Conservatives often lament the fact that most children in our society grow up without exposure to the Bible, and they seem to assume that what they see as an increase in immorality may be assigned to such ignorance. I am skeptical of this, tending to believe that the level of human depravity remains fairly constant through history, although it does lately seem to me that shamelessness is on the rise. What saddens me about the biblical illiteracy of the students I teach is realizing how much resonance they miss in the older literature they are attempting to read. And for writers, too, the eclipse of the Bible as common intellectual currency has meant a certain impoverishment. The metaphors of modern poetry, striking as many of them are, can seem a bit thin when compared with typological figures, for they are drawn from individual perceptions which others may not share rather than from a communal hoard of images. Most readers, of course, aren't aware of this. Like people raised on skimmed milk, they don't know what they're missing by forgoing the real thing.

Something similar can be said with regard to historical consciousness. As long as the typological outlook persisted, the Bible could be viewed as a single record of God's acts rather than two Testaments awkwardly sutured together. The old view stressed the providential design of history, in which the promises to Israel were fulfilled in Christ's coming, and were thus the common heritage of believers. To an extent we find hard to imagine, the author of Hebrews was at home in history: it was a continuum, with a point and plan which knowledge of the Scriptures could make plain. The historical breadth of his vision is especially apparent in chapter 11, when he seeks to strengthen the faith of his audience by listing in a rapt catalogue the examples of great believers in times past. It is a roll call of heroes, of those who risked everything by putting their faith in "things not seen" (11:1). He extols Abel, Enoch, and Noah, and especially Abraham:

> By faith he sojourned in the land of promise, as in a strange country, dwelling in tabernacles with Isaac and Jacob, the heirs with him of the same promise:

For he looked for a city which hath foundations, whose builder and maker is God. [11:9–10]

Sarah, Isaac, and Jacob, Joseph, Moses, and even the harlot Rahab are held up for admiration, until at last the author is driven to even more condensed summary:

And what shall I more say? for the time would fail me to tell of Gideon, and of Barak, and of Samson, and of Jephthah; of David also, and Samuel, and of the prophets:

Who through faith subdued kingdoms, wrought righteousness, obtained promises, stopped the mouths of lions,

Quenched the violence of fire, escaped the edge of the sword, out of weakness were made strong, waxed valiant in fight, turned to flight the armies of the aliens. [11:32–34]

It is, as it is meant to be, an inspiring account, and all the more for concluding with a reference to those "of whom the world was not worthy" (11:38), who suffered persecution or martyrdom. The author, however, does not wish his audience to be passively edified, but actively engaged. All these champions remained faithful *without* seeing the promise fulfilled; therefore are not Christians, who have seen its fulfillment, bound all the more to follow their example? This thought lies behind the famous exhortation which opens Chapter 12:

Wherefore, seeing we also are compassed about with so great a cloud of witnesses, let us lay aside every weight, and the sin which doth so easily beset us, and let us run with confidence the race that is set before us,

Looking unto Jesus the author and finisher of our faith; who for the joy that was set before him endured the cross, despising the shame, and is set down at the right hand of the throne of God. [12:1–2]

In this author's view of history the past remains vitally present for the fulfillment of divine purpose. We are not simply to pay homage to the heroes gone before us; we are to augment their record with our own belief and deeds. Indeed, as the author earlier says, God's design for history provides "that they without us should not be made perfect" (11:40). The idea expressed so magnificently in the image of "a cloud of witnesses" is a sobering one. It imagines our spiritual progress proceeding under the urgent scrutiny of countless holy souls of patriarchs, prophets, and martyrs, not to mention God himself. We all know how uncomfortable it is to be watched, and there may be a more daunting note here for some of us than the author intended. But the notion that faith is an ongoing enterprise, bringing together the living and the dead across the gulf of time, even as it persuades us of many things which for now remain unseen—this seems to me a heartening message in a time when the patterns of history have grown obscure, and believers may once again think themselves "strangers and pilgrims on the earth" (11:13). Those who read Hebrews with not a scholarly but a spiritual purpose will no doubt mentally populate the "cloud of witnesses" according to their own histories as well as the sacred history this author draws upon. When I read the phrase I think of some saints carved on a reredos, of my grandfather and others of that generation of my family, of those old ladies with their pocketbooks, whose names I will never know, and of many more.

THE GENERAL EPISTLE OF
JAMES

—

PASSION AND PATIENCE

Michael Malone

> But let patience have her perfect work, that ye
> may be perfect and entire, wanting nothing.
>
> James 1:4

> Be patient therefore, brethren, unto the coming
> of the Lord. Behold the husbandman waiteth for
> the precious fruit of the earth, and hath long
> patience for it, until he receive the early and latter
> rain. Be ye also patient.
>
> James 5:7–8

Called to write about *the* Book, the book that calls us to a mystery and a ministry, I abruptly developed writer's block. For months, I shied away every time I started the first sentence to this essay on my faith, this essay on the Epistle of James, this essay about . . . well, what?

Ye know not what shall be on the morrow. . . . For that ye ought to say, "If the Lord will, we shall live, and do this, or that."

But I haven't even been able to decide on the kind of "this or that" I should be doing. I've been sheering off, quick as a school of turquoise fish taking a blue turn, because of something sensed in the sea ahead. But what? Fear of failure? Fear of an immodesty in proclaiming faith? After all, in a world that preaches secular success, failure and faith are the final taboos. Christians in the arts today are likely to find acquaintances sniggering and pals blushing at their confessions of belief. They are likely to see their secular friends incredulous, embarrassed—as if from watching otherwise sophisticated people getting shamelessly gulled by a carnival scam.

One isn't often asked to talk about faith, or is asked with challenging suspicions. In such cases, it sometimes helps (joked my godfather—younger than I, a professor at Yale Divinity School), to toss in a few frank sexual revelations. It makes one's Christianity more palatable these days. In novels, we can talk of faith unasked—unasked, and often unanswered by critics who simply don't know what to make of modern "religious" fiction. At the final curtain today, a feast is just a feast, a dance is just a dance. Shakespeare, or even Dickens, might safely take for granted an audience of shared faith—at least an audience with some knowledge of the *language* of faith. But writers here at the end of this century dare not assume that readers will even catch their references, much less be sympathetic to, much less share, their beliefs. Misreading is particularly likely for comedy, as the foolish interpretations inflicted on Flannery O'Connor's stories attest; religion is apparently more obvious if gloomy or tortured. Perhaps I should take as a promising sign the report that a Princeton bookstore had shelved my novel *Handling Sin* as nonfiction among the self-help books. Perhaps it's cause for comfort that in these secular days a bookstore owner could conceive of a customer coming in to say, "Hi there, I'm having a little trouble handling sin. Could you suggest something helpful?"

As a Christian novelist, my occupation (my work) and my vocation (my calling) come, at their best, together. My work is sitting quietly in a room, translating differences, listening to voices, hearing the stories of human hearts, and writing them down. My labor is the slow, still act of writing down words. Writers write. Sadly, writers need to be also authors, roaming Manhattan to ensure the worldly success of their imaginary characters. So writers become authors. Writing is a job, but authoring's a profession. Authoring is contracts, contacts, the page position of a review, the number of figures in an advance; it's working the room, protecting the back list, doing the performance art of the world. James warned us about this: "*Whosoever therefore will be a friend of the world is the enemy of God.*"

Out of this private act, writing, comes a public, a *published*, claim to talent, wealth, fame, immortality. Comes self-promotion. Comes self-justification. "My book was better than his" . . . "I've written more books than she has" . . . "I've worked longer, harder, better than her [or him]." We know how high the price of such self-justification. James warned us about this: "*For where envying and strife is, there is confusion and every evil work.*"

Authors easily take the stance of a mistreated and miserable Job who cries out for a judge, eager "to order my cause before him, and fill my mouth with arguments"; who longs to record the injustices done him by the world.

> *Oh that my words were written!*
> *Oh that they were inscribed in a book!*
> *Oh that with an iron pen and lead*
> *they were graven in the rock forever!*

Oh that my novels were given the notice they deserve, oh that Manhattan knew their worth, oh that my books stayed in print forever. Writers sit and write, but authors sit and fret. They fret, impatiently, in the long still stretches before, during, and after publication. They fret when work is rejected, and when it's accepted: for work unpublished is lost, and work published may be publicly abused and abandoned. Authors talk of reviews as if their lives as well as their livelihoods depended upon them. They talk of criticism as merciless, brutal, devastating, they tell horror stories of how they and their fellows have been skewered, savaged, destroyed. Poor Keats, claimed Shelley, slain by a bad review. Poor Charles Lamb standing in the theater box booing and hissing his own play, rather than let the audience suspect him of authorship. Authors fretfully talk about writing. "God, how little I've accomplished! If I were Keats, I would have been dead for a quarter of a century now. Dickens, my God! A novel a year, *two* novels a year!" Authors talk. Writers listen.

Let every man be swift to hear, slow to speak, slow to wrath.

Just that virtue praised by James—swiftness to hear—is the gift given fiction makers: "He's a good listener, she has a great ear." But listening seems on the surface so inactive, so unadult, so even un-American! Because writing is done passively and privately while books appear noisily in public, some writers need to pump the act as full of macho anguish and agon as possible. So Byron swims the Hellespont and dies fighting for Greek freedom. So Hemingway is reduced to challenging Dashiell Hammett to a "spoon-bending con-test" in a nightclub. In lieu of physical bravado, wars of alcoholism, drug addiction, suicidal impulses become the Khyber Pass, the Al-amo, the Iwo Jima of artistic struggle. Scott Fitzgerald and Dorothy Parker share with us the suffering of their Crack-ups. Movies about writers try to make *typing* look macho. Writers staring at typewriters are said to be "sweating blood."

But writing is not bullfighting or lumberjacking. When one is writing, one needs to sit still and listen. As Milton listened to his "Celestial Patroness, who deigns / Her nightly visitation unim-plored, / And dictates to me slumb'ring." As Blake, a secretary, took notes from God. It's what Emerson meant when he described poetry as a kind of ice skating that takes us we don't know where. You have to go there passionately, you have to go there passively. The paradox is in the word itself, the way paradoxes always are. "Passion" and "passive" and "patience" are rooted in the same Greek word, *pathos*. In fact, "passion" once meant "being passive," "being affected from without." To be passionate, to be patient, to be passive, is to feel suffering.* The Passion of Jesus Christ is the story of his suffering. The active faith of his passive, patient hanging on the cross, with his arms nailed open to receive our pain. His *act* is his quietly awaiting the time, his allowing, his enduring, his redeeming the Passion.

Writers trade in passion. We fill pages with the moods, fits, ado-rations of our characters, their emotions and appetites, their out-bursts, passionate lusts, impassioned pleas, pathetic tears. To write passionately, we have to passively suffer passions to happen in the imagination. But then we must *make* something of them.

---

* Latin deponent verb *patior, pati, passus sum*: to suffer, undergo, experience, allow. And the participle *patiens*: capable of enduring.

But be ye doers of the word and not hearers only.

In making art of actions, we become doers of the word, and not hearers only. It may be that our doing takes place as we're sitting monotonously at a desk. It isn't dramatic to write dramas. But just sitting still, in active faith—as Gandhi knew—can stop a train. The passive resistance of protest can change a nation. The passive act of writing can change a heart. They also serve who only sit and sing. They are doers of the word.

When I think of choosing to spend my life as such a doer of the word, I think of the active faith of certain women who led me to that calling. In *Handling Sin*, Raleigh Hayes, my North Carolinean middle-class, middle-aged Job of a hero, is guided—nudged, yanked, prodded—on his road trip to salvation by three psychopomps. They're all women. As Lewis and Clark knew, women make the best guides; they have a very good sense of direction. It was women who found their way, after all, to Christ's tomb. In the comic quest of *Handling Sin*, Raleigh's guides are his wife, Aura; his elderly aunt Victoria, retired seller of missionary supplies to the Far East; and his grandmother's ancient black maid, Flonnie Rogers, a woman with the "Power" to cure warts, with a burning contempt for "God's first mess-up, this old world of trash," and a faith as absolute and angry as Jeremiah's. Raleigh has this memory when he visits her in a wretched convalescent home.

Raleigh saw forty years back, the woman with her hoe, angrily stabbing weeds and flinging them over her shoulder out of her careful garden. That woman, her thin strong arms bright in the summer heat, was saying, "You think God Almighty cares how much you respect Him, a skinny little boy like you? He don't care what the President thinks."

"Well, I don't care about Him either. I think He's stupid," said the small boy behind her, the wicker basket so laden with soft red tomatoes he had to loop both elbows under the handle.

The woman spun around, clinched his chin in her dark hand, and jerked his head straight up at the hot, unclouded sky. "You make you one of *those*," she snapped, pointing at the blue horizon. "You fixing to try it, you so smart? Or one of *these*." She yanked a long crooked carrot sliding out of the earth. "See this little finger? Look here! You see this little nail on it?" She clicked the tiny finger. "That's just a little ugly thing. It ain't nuthin'. Well, little boy, you make me one, and bring it on here to me, and then maybe I listen to you telling me how you just as smart as the Almighty Lord."

Like Raleigh, I've been nudged, yanked, prodded on my road trip by women too. I have these memories of three who first led me, in the mid-1950s, to choose to be a writer. (To say so may be a little like W. C. Fields's saying, "A woman led me to drink, and I never even thanked her for it.") One was a majorette. Two were seventh-grade teachers. Mrs. Aberdeen, the art teacher, was a Yankee and a divorcée (related facts to many in my Piedmont pocket of the Bible-Belted South). Angular, with the long confident stride of a bohemian Hepburn, Mrs. Aberdeen wore a cape, and large misshapen clay beads, and leather sandals of a sort none of us had worn since our early childhoods. "Release! Let go!" she cried in her flat quick unfamiliar accent, as she threw buckets of paint at a wall of newsprint. "Read Lawrence Durrell!" she told me. "Write from your gut!" She had possibly the first so-called "apartment" in town, to which we came in enamored groups to sit inextricably caught in canvas butterfly chairs, listening to Tom Lehrer or to songs of twanging lament that had sounded redneck when my grandmother used to sing them, but full of "folk art" when played in an apartment on scratchy records. We imagined Mrs. Aberdeen in love with the new French teacher, Monsieur Lyons, also an exotic immigrant to the Piedmont, and an immense improvement over our former instructor, the basketball coach, who pronounced *bonjour*, "bone jar." Monsieur Lyons taught us French words for body parts by pointing them out on the poster of Brigitte Bardot (in *And God Created Woman*) that covered the blackboard behind our sidewalk café—where at the start of every class we sat at card tables pulling wax from candles stuck in Chianti bottles and warbling "La Vie en rose" along with Edith Piaf. His fingertips yellow, his breath rank from Gauloises—these were days when for all we knew, marijuana was a Mexican folk dance, and so a foreign cigarette looked wonderfully like iniquity—Monsieur

Lyons directed a production of Oscar Wilde's *Salome*, which was set by Mrs. Aberdeen in Nazi Germany. Soon after, the two of them left our junior high, whether by choice or together, I never knew.

Miss Taybee, my seventh-grade English teacher, never left. Though quite mad, in the extravagant southern manner, she was never fired either, being a native of the town and of good family. The South doesn't mind insanity, as long as it's local; when a Confederate general fell under the delusion that he was a bird, his fellow officers responded by serving him seed on a tin plate. That Miss Taybee floated through the cafeteria reciting Poe to no one in particular was not cause for counseling, much less dismissal. She was wispy and small boned, given to frail blue chiffon and opalescent scarves. Her "twin" sister, a stout-legged geometry teacher, told us she had a steel plate on her skull that occasionally interfered with her concentration. It was life that interfered with my Miss Taybee, a dreamer with a passion for passion on the page. She had always lived, as she said, for books; for beautiful stories, for poetry, for tragic love and suicide. Led by her, barbaric and innocent twelve-year-olds wandered all year in puzzling annals of romantic adultery. *Idylls of the King, Ethan Frome*, the death scene from *Anna Karenina*. We read *The Scarlet Letter* without knowing what the "A" stood for.

Miss Taybee, who was rumored to smoke five packs of Salems a day (though never in public), would rush to the coat closet during lightning storms, from which—perhaps smoking—she would wave out her long shimmery scarf, as if in mute surrender to brute nature, and call to us to go on reciting the sad tale of "the beautiful Annabel Lee / In her sepulchre there by the sea. / In her tomb by the sounding sea." Or "Remember me when I am gone away, / Gone far away into the silent land." On sunnier days, she would stalk the aisles, overlooking spitballs and notes folded into stamp-sized packets, stopping suddenly to touch a head with a fluttering hand. "A rock, a leaf, an unturned door," she would sigh. "I am looking for the next Thomas Wolfe. Is it you?" Years later, while I fretted over some balking revision, I would imagine a Muse lying on my couch, smoking, reading a huge novel by her old flame Thomas Wolfe, a beau who knew how to keep her on her feet, waltzing from morn to night. Swept over by remorse at how little I'd accomplished in the day, I would dream of Thomas Wolfe. I would follow the specter of this gigantic man, like Marley's ghost clanking chains of paper clips and typewriter ribbons, his size-fifteen feet thudding in time to the chant with which he roamed Manhattan streets: "I wrote ten thousand words today. I wrote ten thousand words today." (He not only managed to write them, he counted them, standing at his refrigerator, crumpling sheets of legal pad in his huge paws, tossing them to the floor.) In my dreams, the Muse resembled the young Miss Taybee I'd never met. "Is it you?"

And so in junior high I became ostentatiously a poet. While listening to Rachmaninoff, I wrote sonnets with purple ink on parchment. I was in love with a majorette. While at first she preferred Roy Orbison's lyrics to mine, and preferred Big Moochie Saddlefield to me, I kept writing. Big Mooch (known at home as Little Senior) was ostentatiously a hood. Of the sort to pick his teeth with a switchblade, to drag his lead motorcycle boots on the concrete as he drove, so that sparks flew out. To display not just tails but what looked like whole dead squirrels on his handlebars. To hiss at me, "I'd love to kill you." But I kept writing, wrestling with rhyme for love's sake. And I came to see more beauty everywhere, I came to want more and more to make what beauty I could. Wisely said Saint Augustine, "Show me a man in love; I'll show you a man on the way to God."

My mother was also a schoolteacher, a lover of books, a lover of poets. "It's imagination," she explained to my first-grade principal. I'd claimed she'd been unable to sign my first-grade report card (I'd done it for her in block print: MRS. MALONE) because she was suffering from "Blue Bonnet" plague. "Poets," she explained to the principal, quoting Emerson, "are liars who always tell the truth." To me, when I came to her chafed with boredom, she said, "Read. Write a story. Then you can live all times, get to know all kinds of people. But you know, the same will be true if you just look around you, even here in this horrible hick town. If you just listen. Be still and listen. The whole world's here. Look there out the window. See that drab little wren up there on the crab apple, singing for the love of creation."

"Oh, Mama, for God's sake!"

Yes. For God's sake, indeed.

In Asheville's cemetery, next to Thomas Wolfe's grave lies his brother, Fred. On Fred's tombstone is carved "Luke of *Look Home-ward, Angel*." What a extraordinary testament to the power of faith in fiction! I heard Eudora Welty, another guide to me, quote Willa Cather once: "Let your fiction grow out of land beneath your feet." I've learned to do that. In fiction I come quietly back to, of all the everywheres, that red clay Carolina I'd once been so eager to leave. "Remember me," Miss Taybee sang. "When I am gone away, gone far away into the silent land." And so I do. I'm a novelist. You can go home again. You can't help it. You need only keep faith, sit still, and listen. You need only have ears to hear.

———

"Yes," a friend said, "the General Epistle of James. Isn't it a wonderful choice for a novelist to talk about?" Wonderful? Would a novelist ever have *chosen* it? Short and disjointed, theoretical, impersonal, stuck way in the back of the book, after the Gospels and after Paul, one of the "Catholic," the General, Epistles, a moral sermon, a hortatory treatise hidden behind the weighty proportions of Hebrews, James has never been a star in the crown of the New Testament, never been anyone's favorite; was never even, for centuries, entirely safe from being dropped out of the canon, or at least demoted to second-rate standing. Erasmus said it lacked the gravity and majesty that mark the apostolic style. Martin Luther, with scant authority—beyond the fiat of an absolute certainty that often required him to do *nichts anders*—moved James (along with Hebrews, Jude, and Revelations) to the end of his 1522 New Testament, and chose not to number it in the table of contents. "A right strawy Epistle," he concluded, certainly not to be compared with Paul and John.* James? The epistle synopsized as early as Origen as the one about faith being

---

* Yet even Luther, while he found James of doubtful apostolic authority and of less value doctrinally, didn't dismiss it entirely, nor—Protestant that he was—did he demand that others do so: "I will not have it in my Bible in the number of the proper chief books, but do not intend thereby to forbid anyone to place and exalt it as he pleases, for there is many a good saying in it." Tyndale too thought James deserved a place in Holy Scriptures, despite its flaws—among them its failure to preach Christ's death, Resurrection, and the gift of salvation made us by the Covenant of His blood—for "[James] calls upon men to keep the law of God, and makes love which is without partiality the fulfilling of the law, as Christ and all the apostles did. . . ."

dead without works, the epistle Luther fought as a denial of Paul's justification by faith? "Yes," my friend said, "it's perfect for a novelist. Faith and works."

Ah, but the work of a fiction maker is to imagine local habitations, to give names to nothing. That's what I wanted for "my" epistle, a name and place, a James as real as Paul. In college, although I had little natural bent for theoretical abstraction, I stubbornly and foolishly insisted on majoring in philosophy, where I foundered finally among the stricter equations of logical positivism. To me philosophy was very concretely Plato's Ideal Chair, Ockham's razor, Hume's probable cue balls; when I thought of Husserl's phenomenological brackets, I imagined enormous spaghetti prongs.

"We are not so much interested," explained the chairman of my honors examination, "in what Descartes thought in Stockholm about tutoring Queen Christina. We are more interested in what Descartes thought in *The Discourse of Method*." These shrewd philosophers then joined those who'd advised me to consider fiction as a career as well as a habit of mind. "We are abstract. You are concrete," baldly summarized one of the examiners. How right he was. Thirty years later, I'm scribbling calls for the concrete on the margins of students' short stories: "*Look* at your characters. *Listen* to the scene. Find the detail. Where *are* we?"

On first reading, the Epistle of James, however wise and true a diatribe, adds nothing concrete, not a scene, not a character, not a detail, to the greatest story ever told. It has no indisputable author, no particularity of life, no local habitation. As an epistle, it's a chain letter. Addressed collectively to "the twelve tribes which are scattered abroad" and ending abruptly without a word of valediction, this encyclical guidebook of dos and don'ts is little more "letterly" than a mail-out headed "Dear Chrysler Customer."

Yes, on first reading, James is a disappointment. There is nothing as incarnate as this typical P.S. of Paul's: "Greet Priscilla and Aquila, my helpers in Christ Jesus: who have for my life laid down their own necks." Or this news from Hebrews: "Know ye that our brother Timothy is set at liberty; with whom, if he come shortly, I will see you." As a storyteller, James is no Paul. Through Paul's acts and in his letters we see a man whole; his brilliance, his extraordinary capacity for faith, the spasms of envy, self-pity, and boasting through which he keeps struggling for peace. We share his arrests, quarrels, shipwrecks. How he fled Damascus in a basket lowered by friends over the city walls. How hurt he was when Mark deserted him in Pamphylia. He tells us, "After three years I went up to Jerusalem to see Peter, and abode with him fifteen days." He tells us he challenged Peter and "opposed him to his face." We read the novel of a life, from a fall off a donkey on the road to Damascus to preparations in a Roman prison for death. "I have fought the good fight, I have finished my course."

The identity of "James, a servant of God and of the Lord Jesus Christ," who sends that terse "greeting" to the twelve tribes, is not indisputably known. There may not even be such an author. As early as Eusebius of Alexandria, commentators have felt compelled to point out that the epistle may be spurious. Later scholars have solved the problem of authorship by supposing a contemporary "pseud-epigraphic" compositor, or a "Hellenized redactor" putting together homiletic "sense units" as late as the second century, or, conversely, an earlier "pseudonymous Jewish source" with a subsequent "Christian overlay." One theory suggests a pre-Christian allegory addressed by *Jacob* to his twelve sons, the patriarchal tribes. Arguments abound.

There were many men called James in Christ's life. If one of them is in fact the author of the epistle, he is not (on this scholars agree) the best-known James—the apostle James, James the Greater, the tempestuous son of Zebedee, the Galilean fisherman who threw down his nets when Christ beckoned "Follow me," who with his brother John was named Boanerges, Sons of Thunder. Some say this James the Greater was also Christ's cousin—that his mother was Salome, Mary's sister. He was certainly, along with Peter, one of Christ's best friends, and it would be handy if he had written the epistle. But he didn't; Herod Agrippa had him executed too soon. (James the Greater was the first of the twelve apostles to be martyred.) There's a James the Lesser too, another apostle, James of Alphaeus, but no one much thinks he could have written the epistle. And there's possibly a third apostle with the same name, James of Clopas, but he's not really a contender, either.

Who, then? The most likely candidate, favored by traditional and modern scholars, is the man known as James the Just, the Righteous One. He was the presiding elder of the church in Jerusalem and is often mentioned in the New Testament, where he is called the "brother of the Lord." James, then, Jesus' brother.* But not one of the twelve original apostles. A Christian who had not been one of Christ's disciples, who was not among the twelve guests at the Last Supper, whose conversion did not happen until after Christ's death— perhaps at the sight of the resurrected Lord. (According to Paul, such a vision was in fact granted James, but belatedly, only after Christ had appeared first to the original apostles.)

I began to imagine the story of this younger brother James. He would have been raised in an artisan's home in Galilee, would have been known to his neighbors through his family, as Jesus was known back home: "Is not this the carpenter, the son of Mary, the brother of James, and Joses, and of Juda and Simon? and are not his sisters here with us?" Home in Galilee, after all, neighbors were skeptical. "Jesus said unto them, 'A prophet is not without honor, but in his own country, and among his own kin, and in his own house.' And he could there do no mighty work, save that he laid his hands upon a few sick folk, and healed them. And he marvelled because of their unbelief." (Mark 6:3–6)

I imagined a younger brother who heard the teaching but didn't see the glory. A brother to whom Jesus might be an object of admiration, envy, and embarrassment. When those close to Christ "laid hold of him" in the press of the mobbed house where he was casting out devils, they sent for his family. Fearing "he is beside himself," the followers yelled for help, and then let Jesus know: " 'Behold, your mother and your brethren without seek for thee.' And he answered them, saying, 'Who is my mother and my brethren? . . . Whosoever shall do the will of God, the same is my brother, and my sister, and my mother.' " I imagined that younger brother James standing right then with Mary, in the street with the crowd, calling to Christ to come out of the house, being told he was missing the point.

Afterward, at the end, did James follow Christ into Jerusalem? I

---

* Certain theologians (among them Catholics) are constrained by faith in the Virgin Birth to take "brother" either to mean the generalized, metaphoric "brother," as in fellowman, or to refer to a different familial relationship than the one the Greek term usually denotes: thus, they theorize that James might be Christ's half-brother by an earlier marriage of Joseph's.

think he must have, for following Christ's crucifixion, he became prominent in that city quite quickly: as soon as Peter miraculously breaks out of jail, he tells friends to go tell *James* the news. James himself is already news: Paul notes that when he arrived in Jerusalem, he saw none of the apostles save James, brother of Christ, "among all the apostles." A church official in the home church, James becomes the chief spokesman at the council at Jerusalem, possibly the author of a circular letter embodying its decrees. Could a Galilean artisan Jew have written the Greek of such a letter (or of the epistle)? Apparently, yes; bilingual skills were not at all uncommon at the time, particularly not for a man like James, engaged for thirty years as a religious debater and public speaker in a large city.*

The Jerusalem Council set forth the argument on the first doctrinal crisis for the faith—the issue of circumcision (which, with dietary laws, ritualized a Judaism some Christians rejected). In this debate James seems to have taken a leading role. It was his strategy, and inclination, to reconcile Christian Jews with that faction of Christians (both Jewish and Gentile) who were pushing to break free of the old Law. It was James who called for a sympathetic understanding of Jewish sensibilities; who persuaded Peter, temporarily, to stop eating with Gentile Christians—so as to avoid provocative contacts where the food taboos of Jewish Christians might be offended. It was James who talked Paul into paying his respects to Christian Jews in Palestine.

At this time of heightened Jewish nationalism, "zealots of the law," most of them poor, some of them slaves, were coming into conflict with Roman despotism. Christians had to make a political decision: should they align themselves with Judaism, or with Greeks and Romans against Judaism? By Roman law, they were protected against prosecution if they defined Christianity as a Jewish religion; all they had to do was pay a token fine and claim atheism. On the other hand, Jews were persecuting Christians. On the other hand, Jews were being persecuted by Rome, and so association with Jewish activists was dangerous. Dangerous times. A time for patience.

In early church legend, James, the Lord's brother, gained the rep-

---

* One theory has it that the epistle is a short Aramaic letter of homilies composed by James, then translated and expanded, perhaps by an amanuensis with good literary Greek.

utation of a deeply pro-Jewish, even pro-zealot leader. Hegesippus, a traveling story collector around A.D. 160, said that James prayed *in* the Temple for the salvation of the state of Israel until his knees grew as hard as camel knees, that he wore the robe of an orthodox Jewish priest, that he practiced the asceticism of a Nazarite. But the notion of James's zeal is likely to be exaggerated; like Paul and Peter, the Epistle of James calls for an avoidance of political strife and revolutionary activism. And this younger brother of Jesus seems, by nature, a peacemaker, a compromiser, a smoother-over of differences, a patcher-up of quarrels. A strong thrust of his epistle is, in fact, opposition to the materialized eschatology, the pie-in-the-sky now, of agitators among the faithful. His epistle sends a warning to those who believed the church should work to improve the status of lives in the world, believed that victory could be temporal, bliss could come here and now.

Although James attacks the rich passionately, he offers no assault on the state itself. Instead, he teaches an attitude to the world that calls for long-suffering patience and good citizenship, calls for no intrigues in response to dissatisfactions, no social aggression. If such acceptance seems appeasement, we need only remember that in the turbulent decades following Christ's death, the faithful anticipated an early and absolute solution to their temporal problems: the imminent coming of God's reign. The apocalypse would arrive and rebalance the scales. Low would be high, the poor would be rich in salvation.* James says, Lie low and wait. But within the boundaries of that quietism, his defense of Jewish traditions was clearly fervent. His position, and the probable esteem in which Jewish nationalists held him as a result, make his own martyrdom, therefore, the more ironic.† For in A.D. 62 he was executed apparently not by Rome but by Sadducees and Pharisees, who took advantage of an interregnum

* These themes were influenced by Qumran, an apocalyptic-pietistic cult of Jews, for whom the Book of Daniel was key; *de contemptu mundi* currents in the Hellenistic world (among Stoics and Cynics as well as Christian Gnostics) also had a recognizable impact on the Epistle of James.

† The Jewish emphasis in the epistle (the only place in the New Testament in which the word "synagogue" is used to define a Christian church) substantiates for some scholars the authorship of James. Other scholars reject James the Just as the author of the epistle because they doubt that so profoundly Jewish a Christian would have been so antizealotic: In the epistle, fellowship is explicitly founded on the basis of shared *faith*, not shared *nation*. The worldly focus is clearly not Jerusalem but the

between the colonial procurators, Festus and Albinus. One theory even has it that the high priest of the Sadducees, Ananus II, out of envy, ordered James, the brother of the Lord, stoned. It seems the right end to the story of the James I've been imagining.

———

Assuming this is the James who wrote the epistle, what of his letter to the world? It has nothing much to say about Jesus. Indeed, some scholars deny James authorhood on the grounds that the Lord's brother would never have written anything with so few specifically *Christian* references. There is no word about Christ as the Messiah, or about the cross, or about Christ's resurrection.* The epistle stresses the moral truths, the teachings, of Christ, but not his godhood. The focus moves not back to the past of Jesus' Passion but forward to political and social crises at hand. There is little talk of Christ's grace or of Christ's Passion; there is much talk of a Christian community, a restoration of a community of people within the church tribes, for whom Abraham is their father, Christianity their faith, and the Roman Empire their governor. Complex and dangerous allegiances to negotiate.

But throughout, the *language* of the epistle is deeply resonant of the language of Christ as recorded in the Gospels—especially in the Sermon on the Mount and in the Q material (Matthew and Luke). This work is familiar with, at home with, Christ's words. To me, the fact that the letter ignores Christ's divinity makes it *more*, not less, likely that James, "the brother of the Lord," might have a hand in its composition. To me it makes human sense that James would not need to remind himself, maybe would not want to remind himself,

———

Roman Empire. These scholars also fail to find in the epistle's moral dicta the strict legalisms that might be expected from James.

Some who deny authorship to James date the epistle A.D. 81–96 (under the rule of Domitian), or even as late as the third century. Some point out that had there been an epistle by an eminent church leader like James, it would have been more prominent in the early canon. Others offer in rebuttal that orthodox Gentile Christians would naturally silence in those early years so venerated a Jewish Christian as James.

* Calvin saw no reason to dismiss the epistle on those grounds: "It is not surely required of all to handle the same arguments." He went on to praise the variety of subjects on which James offers instructions.

maybe would not think to glorify as miracle, a life with which he had been intimate from birth.

What James does glorify is Christ's Word, taken out into the world in *active faith* and embodied in uncloistered virtue. Sent out, you might say, among readers. The core of James's message is that faith is not a theory but a life. Generations of exegetes have argued over this message, some praising a profound and organic spiritual essay, others faulting a fragmented succession of moral saws. I went through many readings myself, agreeing with the latter view, until I stopped picking at James and started listening. His message is whole, and can be summed up this way: a life of faith without patience turns evil; a life of faith without deeds turns dead. Here is what James can teach us and, yes, why he is good for a writer to listen to.

Have patience, even in troubles. In fact, rejoice in sufferings, for they try and they prove our faith. They teach us patience. Steadfastness is active, not passive; in it, we are making ourselves "perfect works," making ourselves whole, as opposed to unstable, "doubleminded" sorts who change with the world's circumstances.

Whosoever therefore will be a friend of the world is the enemy of God.

The world stirs up unquiet souls, made restless by doubt.

For he that wavereth is like a wave of the sea driven with the wind and tossed.

But God, "with whom is no variableness, neither shadow of turning," is constant light. God is never double-minded. He is all there, perfectly whole, perfectly steadfast and patient. His gift of Himself is wholly generous, without strings, without limits. It is a gift of salvation to be given eternally to the lowly and poor, while the transitory gifts of the rich and powerful, hustling to serve God and Mammon both, will fade.

As the flower of the grass he shall pass away.

For the crown of life, unlike the crown of a king (or, for that matter, the laurel wreath of a poet) is the gift of God, a gift given, not won, after trials have taught endurance, and temptations have strengthened patience. Every gift of God is good, every present is perfect. It is for us to *be there* to accept the gift. It is for us to cast off our unworthiness like a filthy garment and receive with meekness the implanted word.

But be ye doers of the word and not hearers only. Christianity is a life to be lived, not a theological debate. When the implanted Word (the Logos and the Torah, the Word and the Law together) takes root, it grows into conduct, it bears the fruits of our deeds. The Word saves our soul. First, then, we must hear it, and to hear it we have to be quiet.

Let every man be swift to hear, slow to speak, slow to wrath.

To listen, we have to bridle our tongues; passion (wrath) cannot be dispassionate, and so leads to sin, and so leads to death. And we have to *keep on* listening, keep on seeing—not, as it were, occasionally glancing in a mirror without really looking at it. What we see if we gaze patiently in the mirror of the Word is the "perfect law of liberty." Liberty because there is only one rule. Love God and love thy neighbor. That fulfills all law, motivates all reward, all judgment.

Pure religion and undefiled before God and the Father is, to visit the fatherless and widows in their affliction, and to keep himself unspotted from the world.

According to James, what "the faith of our Lord Jesus Christ" asks of us is not only to keep the self pure (undistracted by the world) but to exercise charity out in the world (go *visit* the orphans and widows) *while* keeping the self pure. We have to be *in* the world without being *of* the world. Our dealings there can have no "respect of persons." We must show no partiality between rich and poor, between the successful and the failures, between who's in, who's out. Don't, says James, be toadies to the rich; it's they who oppress you, anyhow. Don't strive to succeed over others; don't envy the successful. Don't curry favors with the powerful.

For if there come unto your assembly a man with a gold ring, in goodly apparel, and there come in also a poor man in vile raiment; and ye have respect to him that weareth the gay clothing, and say unto him, Sit thou here in a good place: and say to the poor, Stand thou here, or sit here under my footstool: Are ye not then partial in yourselves, and are become judges of evil thoughts?*

How do we *act?* That's what James is asking us. *"What doth it profit, my brethren, though a man say he hath faith, and have not works? Can faith save him?"* And here, of course, is the crux of the epistle *as* a theological debate. Luther profoundly objected to what he took to be James's challenge of Paul on the question of justification by faith. For Paul, faith (a response to hearing the Word) is the gift of God, fully offered, ours to accept. Yet clearly for Paul, faith involves a dedication of the whole self, actively engaged in relation to the world. We are justified by a faith acting, in Paul's words, through deeds of love, not deeds of law. It has seemed to most contemporary scholars that James, while his emphasis is different, in no real way contradicts Paul. Nor, if James is the author and the epistle was therefore written about 60 C.E. (when Paul was in prison in Rome), is it even probable that James is challenging Paul himself, by setting against Christian faith a Jewish view of salvation by works? No. James is more likely to be answering current perversions of Paul's position, challenging those who might think it sufficient to profess the faith without altering the sins or selfishness or sloth of their lives. James is saying that faith is barren, if theoretical. Knowledge is not enough. With this Calvin, for one, agreed: "Knowledge of God can no more connect a man with God than the sight of the sun can carry him to heaven."

James is not opposing faith and works, but opposing living faith and dead faith; he is saying not that genuine faith alone is insufficient, but that faith without works is not genuine.

For as the body without the spirit is dead, so faith without works is dead also.

---

* James 2:2–4. It has been suggested that this may be a critical reference to well-to-do Gentiles (especially Romans—the gold rings, the "goodly apparel" of togas) receiving preferential treatment over other converts to Christianity.

The passage does not read "though a man hath faith, and hath not works" but, rather, "though a man *say* he hath faith, and have not works." James is claiming that without works, protestations of faith are just that, protestations. Christ had warned the same: "Not everyone that saith unto me, Lord, Lord, shall enter into the kingdom of heaven; but he that doeth the will of my Father." We must show mercy in order to receive it. We must *act out* the law of liberty. And the law is indivisible, not a list of separate rules but a command to be obeyed wholly: Wrath is a kind of murder. A lustful heart is a kind of adultery.

I will show you my faith by my works. In Hebrews, we hear a long roll call of Old Testament believers who had faith in the "substance of things hoped for, the evidence of things not seen." Noah who built an ark, Abraham who went out, not knowing whither he went. Sarah who in her old age received strength to conceive seed. By faith Abraham offered up Isaac, his only begotten son; by faith Moses forsook Egypt and passed through the Red Sea. When the walls of Jericho tumbled, by faith the harlot Rahab "perished not with them that believed not." By faith David, Daniel, Samson—all the great "cloud of witnesses"—*acted* in the world, stopped the mouths of lions, subdued kingdoms.

James takes two of these witnesses—Abraham, the most revered of Hebrew patriarchs, and Rahab, a Gentile, a woman, a harlot—two extremes, as if to say again there can no respect of persons—to show how faith is completed by works. Abraham prepares to sacrifice Isaac. Rahab sneaks the spies into Jericho. They take action, they take risks.

When James wrote, tests and trials of faith had an immediacy they lack in our lives. Governors could have Christians put to death for treason by enforcing the law that all must burn incense before the image of the emperor. By 64 C.E., Nero would be throwing Christians to the lions. Within that context, we can hear the special urgency in James's warnings against the dangers of passing judgment, the dangers of laymen, political agitators, and demagogues usurping the role of teachers—exciting themselves and others into imprudent, provocative self-assertion. We can feel the political tension in his stressing that there must be a greater burden on teachers to teach well and to practice what they teach. All must guard their tongues, avoiding rancor, malice, wrath, strife, and slander. An uncontrolled tongue is like a fire, unruly, out of control: if you can control your tongue, you can control your whole body. False teachers will be known by their bitter envying and a selfish ambition which throws their minds into "confusion and every evil work." True teachers will be known by their quiet "meekness of wisdom." This higher wisdom, Christ's wisdom, is, says James,

> *first pure, then peaceable, gentle, and easy to be entreated, full of mercy and good fruits, without partiality, and without hypocrisy.*

True wisdom is shown by deeds. A teacher's deed is his or her "good conversation." In James, *words are works*. And patience is an act.

> *Be patient therefore, brethren, unto the coming of the Lord. Behold the husbandman waiteth for the precious fruit of the earth, and hath long patience for it, until he receive the early and latter rain. Be ye also patient.*

James calls on the whole community of Christians to see themselves as a tribe that stretches patiently forward to the New Jerusalem and proudly back to Job and Elias and the Old Testament martyrs. "Behold, we count them happy which endure." He calls upon his listeners to see themselves as a community in the present, steadfastly living out their faith. "Is any among you afflicted? Let him pray. Is any merry? Let him sing psalms."

> *Pray for one another, that ye may be healed. . . . Brethren, if any of you do err from the truth, and one convert him; let him know, that he which converteth the sinner from the error of his way shall save a soul from death, and shall hide a multitude of sins.*

In his last words, James, the brother of the Lord, calls upon the community of Christians to be a family.

———

I gather my characters at a communion rail to share in a mystery. The core of fiction is always to get at mystery. Together we are all reading the mystery of God's plot. We are reading for clues to our connectedness—to God, to the world; most of all, to each other. "What happened to you? to her? to him?" we ask each other. Because we are kin, we gossip. Because we are human, we tell each other our histories. We could define humans as the animals who listen to stories. Call television the modern equivalent of the monthly installment of Dickens, of the medieval bard chanting his epic tale in a mead hall, the primitive shaman telling his story to a tribe of pygmies. "What happened next?" everyone is asking. And to judge by the incredible number of hours spent in front of our television sets, we will apparently, if allowed the leisure, listen to "what happened next" day and night. In my local drugstore, I recently overheard two women in a passionate conversation: "She's going to leave him for Jack." "Jack? But Jack's in prison. My God, he murdered his own brother." "Was it his *brother?* Maybe she's making a mistake." They were talking about the people on a soap opera. People's stories. Who shot J.R.? What's this about Elizabeth Taylor's six weeks of dieting hell? Is Scarlett really going to lose Rhett? Can Dimmesdale find salvation? Is Prince André going to die?

There is a chapter toward the end of a novel of mine that moves late on Whitsunday eve through the entire town of characters, all of whom are reading stories.

At night when the gusty flotsam of life had settled, and the ghosts of the day sprang up grinning in the windows unseen, the readers of Dingley Falls read on. They read not merely to keep their eyes lowered so that they wouldn't see the goblins, not even if they thought of themselves as refugees from their own lives, or thought of their books as evacuation routes. . . . No, Dingleyans were reading because, unlike God and unlike the periscopes made by Dingley Optical Instruments, they could not see around corners; because from any one perspective life is so much less full than fiction and so much more painful. Safe in fiction, they were testing their hearts.

We are each of us a part of all we've read. Fiction lets us share familially in a communion of our humanness. As a writer, as a Christian novelist, my calling is to gather characters at the communion rail of our shared mystery, let characters tell their stories, let readers test their hearts.

I'm sometimes asked to what school of writers I belong. Since I'm American, a voice in me wants to say with Elvis, asked to define *his* school, "Man, Ah don't sing like nobody else." But of course I do. I'm one singer in the choir of the rose, and I've listened to other voices, ages old. I'm of a generation that grew up reading, maybe the last to do so. The generation that came of age in the 1960s— not, then, just a child of Dickens, but of Rosa Parks as well, and so a believer that in our patience, we must never lose our passion to feel wrongs, to write wrongs, to say no to wrongs. Those who wear Christ's armor should be willing to do battle against the world. To be doers of the Word. We can at least witness the courage, and the cost, to the prophets who war for us. In the ending of *Uncivil Seasons*, my hero, now in love and so on his way to God, says no to the cynical power of the world personified by an old industrialist. But he cannot yet say yes to that radical love of the cross which the world finds mad (as Havelock Ellis said, if Christ were alive today, he'd be locked in a lunatic asylum), and he rejects the challenge thrust at him by an elderly black woman, Sister Resurrection.

Outside, the afternoon sun glowed red on all the buildings. I stood with the old industrialist at the top of the broad stone steps that were guarded by empty antique cannon, fired last in 1865 for a lost dream and a cause undefendable. Beside me a long sigh rumbled from Cadmean before he spoke. "I'll tell you this, Justin. Sometimes I think when I think about my Baby looking up at those tired old stars of hers, what if it was my privilege to be up there, looking down? What do you think I'd see? Hunh?" His sulfurous, low-lidded eyes gazed down over Hillston. "Well, I'd see a little tiny ball of slime, wouldn't I? And nations of bugs crawling crazy all over it. And I bet up there I'd be able to hear something I've always suspected. God laughing his damn head off like a scorching wind. Am I right? Take care of yourself, son."

I stood there, watching him carefully descend the gray stone steps one by one, watching him stiffly pull himself into the backseat of the waiting limousine and with a wince of pain tug shut the door.

All he couldn't do was make his child want to spend a night under his roof. All he couldn't will, with the powers of influence, was love. Just as Joanna couldn't will it, not even with sorcery, or revenge its loss with death.

I stood there until from behind the stone balustrade, I heard the voice of Sister Resurrection, as always, faithful at her station by the house of law. She began to speak suddenly, as if she'd been listening to the old man whose bones, like hers, were brittle, and whose eyes were as ancient and as hard. I heard her before I saw her, so her sharp impatient chant came up to me in the warm sun like the keen of a ghost too haunted to wait for the dark.

"The time is come. How long, O Lord? God fixing to melt the mountains. Make a path. God fixing to overthrow Pharaoh. Joseph's neck in a collar of iron. Cut it loose. The blind shall see the mountains tremble. Make a path for the anger of the Lord. Praise Him!"

Around the corner of the cannon the small figure of rags came marching, her hair snow wool and matted with bits of earth. The filthy sweaters hung fluttering to her knees, and she had again her wood handmade cross in both small black hands. Leaning on my cane, I made my way down the steps to where she stood, still speaking. "God Almighty's sick and tired. He gonna loose the Devil's chains."

I touched her arm, and she spun to face me. I said, "Mrs. Webster, God knows I don't have any right to ask you this, but don't you believe there's any chance for love at all?"

The clouded black eyes blazed out at me like a sudden flame. *"I carrying it!"* She spit the three words up at my face, and then thrust forward her crossed sticks of wood. "You want it? Take it!"

Startled, I stepped back and said, "No, ma'am."

Clouds passed over the eyes like smoke and she turned away and began again to prophesy.

———

That's how my writing is about faith, and works, and the Word in the world, and why I suppose people are puzzled when I say I write "religious novels." Nor do I wave the banner of any political program, but my fiction is civic, communal, and political. My novels are of towns and cities, businesses, schools, military bases, courtrooms, churches. They are "long old-fashioned" novels. Comic epics in prose. Divine comedies.

I believe laughter, like music, can be a prayer. Laughter can be a celebration of God's creation, in which we humans are surely the most sublime and ridiculous inventions. I am talking here about laughter in response to *comedy*, not jokes, not humor, not wit. Comedy is profoundly serious, and dangerous. I'm talking about the comedy that is no respecter of persons, that says yes, without partiality. The comedy that says "Join in" to the outsider. The divine comedy that chooses life over death, chooses life after death. Christianity is a divine comedy, the crucifixion has a happy ending. I believe in that resurrection of laughter when, for love of Sophie, Tom Jones is cut down from the hangman's noose, when, for love of life, Falstaff stands and runs off the battlefield after his own funeral eulogy.

"I will show thee my faith by my works." My works witness the Word and say yes. The Word asks us all to a feast, invites us all to join in the dance of creation, when the morning stars sang together and all the sons and daughters of God shouted for joy. The Word asks us to let our quarrel with the world be a lover's quarrel. We are called by faith, you and I, to meet with all the other pilgrims on the road—James, Paul, a widow, an orphan, a man with a gold ring, Abraham, Rahab, Miss Taybee, Big Moochie Saddlefield, Luke of *Look Homeward, Angel*—singing, praying, and listening to one another's stories.

THE FIRST AND
SECOND EPISTLES
GENERAL OF
PETER

—

Marilynne Robinson

The beauty of the First Epistle of Saint Peter is a sufficient argument against attempts to cast doubt on its unity—such doubts are always raised about ancient texts—and a proof of its seriousness of purpose. Unfortunately, seriousness is an undeclared issue in the interpretation of First Peter, a deeply visionary work whose compression looks like brevity. Reading the commentaries this text has inspired, I am struck by the persistency with which it has been found either to rephrase non-Christian ethical teachings or to bless social relations whose character and history are at odds with the example of Christ, a standard the epistle invokes explicitly and powerfully. The effect of Peter's encyclical has been to discredit his church and, worse, to render it discreditable. The letter does not support the reading traditionally made of it, that it is a vindication of social hierarchy and that it gives authority to the idea that women are inferior to men. The letter seems to me to have been, in the phrase Peter borrowed from Isaiah, a stone of stumbling, an occasion for people predisposed to doing the wrong thing to act on their inclination. The Second Epistle of Peter, apparently written by someone wishing to recall the spirit of Peter's teaching, records and laments the vulnerability of

Christianity to abuse and corruption. The writer discovers a sad atavism behind the disfiguring of practice and belief; but this has seldom cautioned interpreters of 1 Peter from assuming that the apostle is putting his specific blessing on attitudes they would have espoused as readily if Jesus had never lived, and more comfortably, because these attitudes are not easily reconciled with the life Jesus led, a significant part of it in the company of Peter.

Peter is thought to have had the help of Silvanus, a man more learned than he, in composing his letter. The Greek in which it was written is said to be very polished. The elegance of its conception I attribute to Peter himself. Jesus valued him for the insight that made him first to recognize in Jesus the fulfillment of Scripture, a problem of interpretation requiring an understanding of the language and spirit of the prophetic tradition. In other words, there is every reason to assume that Peter was fully immersed in the poetics of Scripture. The letter is the work of an imagination stimulated and illuminated by a very great compassion and by the sense that the teachings contained in it are a precious gift to a specific community, and that the burden of all that is taught, first and last, is the love of God for the people to whom the letter comes, the value to God of the people to whom the gift is made. It is the object of the letter to create in its readers and hearers a reverence for themselves and one another which is to be the basis of their understanding of God.

In very few words Peter gives these converts a summary of doctrine, which assimilates Christianity to the teachings of the Old Testament. While it is always important to attempt to understand any work of literature in the terms it creates for itself, this is particularly true of the literature of the Bible. The Bible is composed of centuries of progressive interpretation and elaboration of its own texts, by writers to whom these were of consuming interest and inestimable value. Their own works became additions to canon by consensus among priests and others to whom the integrity of the whole body of writings was of equally passionate concern. Language has never been put to more ambitious use. The aptness of allusions and metaphors has never been considered with more care, and their implications, in themselves and as modes of thought, have never been mined more profitably. Biblical writers typically isolate moments of history as emblematic narratives in which God addresses his people, as if experience taught them in parables. These moments, like visions and waking dreams, are always immediate and urgent, and their meanings are at once inexhaustible and susceptible to misunderstanding or misrepresentation. The life of Christ, in both its mythic and its exemplary aspects, extends this tradition.

The effect of this pulling forward of certain moments, fixing them in narrative rather as they might be stabilized in ritual or iconography, is to make history, that is, experience, seem prodigious and numinous. The wrenching of time out of undifferentiated sequence is among the most brilliant accomplishments of the creators of biblical literature. For clearly there is a given-ness in things. Events do not occur in shapely forms as if they were the abstract of all possibility, or as if occasions were logical or Platonic structures that felt the pressure of chance and the tension of probability uniformly over their surfaces. It seems to me that actuality is a rupture in probability, and that energy flows toward event the way lightning pours through a fault in the atmosphere. It is precisely Scripture's eye for the prodigious, its catalogues of marvels, that should recommend it to the realist. We know now that gawdy phantasms swim the universe trailing tendrils and plumes, and that behemoths that swallow up light and make space curl in their wake are as native to being as oysters. Archaic cosmologies are sound in essential points. Rationalism is a rude child among the ideas it has set about to embarrass or explode.

With the freedom that the intellectual and aesthetic traditions of Scripture have won for him, which render the creative freedom of God, Peter gives an account of the destiny of his hearers, beginning before time began. He follows Scripture in undercutting ordinary notions of time and causality, while attaching the highest order of importance to the simplest business of life. The greatness of God by no means diminishes the significance of any human life, or of any action or thought. Peter, in an extraordinary elaboration of the teaching of Christ that believers are reborn, describes his hearers, each of them, as an adored child suckled with "pure spiritual milk," who has "tasted the kindness of the Lord." It is entirely germane to the method and meaning of his letter that Peter, having invoked the grandest conception of sacred history, makes of history an embrace, an intimate and tender act. It should be noted, too, that implicitly God is represented as a nurturing mother. The passage is wonderful as poetry, because it invests grandeur with tenderness and tenderness with grandeur, and because it puts before our eyes, for our reverent attention, an image of grace drawn from simple and ordinary life. Peter is eager to persuade his hearers of their own holiness. Therefore his images of God and Christ always give these converts a vision of themselves under the aspect of the sacred. He holds up to them the figure of Christ as servant. Every role he blesses is amenable to being described as obedience, or as solicitous attention which is servantlike in that it enacts a deep acknowledgment of the dignity and value of the person who is its object.

The investment of the humble and ordinary with the full burden of holiness is rendered in a radical distortion of narrative perspective. Peter describes God as having ordained, and also as suffering for, the rescue of these converts, yet his advice to them is as urgent as if the issue of Creation hung in the balance. This sort of sprung time throws their lives into the foreground the way figures in a medieval painting are set against landscapes that recede uncannily into an unplaceable remoteness. If Peter had made a painted image, a visual moment in which prophecy is vindicated, foreknowledge is confirmed, and the suffering of Christ is made good in the holiness of his people, we would see figures performing modest and beautiful kindnesses, like Jesus' washing his disciples' feet, or cooking fish for them on the shore when he had only just put off his graveclothes. It would be full of a sense of delighted recognition, as between Elizabeth and Mary when their infants leapt in their wombs, as between Jesus and John the Baptist at the Jordan River, as between the disciples who walked to Emmaus and the stranger who walked beside them. If these Christians are to understand what it means to be "sanctified," Peter must make them respond with recognition to the figure he holds up to them.

That the one letter confidently attributed to Peter, the friend of Jesus, should represent Jesus in terms of his humility and patience in suffering, surely ought not to be attributed to Peter's eagerness to endorse a pagan ethic of subordination, as is sometimes argued; rather, it describes the qualities of his teacher that most moved him, compelled his own belief, and seemed most central to the faith it was his particular responsibility to propagate. As a disciple he experienced the patience of Jesus in the face of betrayal. Perhaps it is the memory of the moment in which he himself injured Jesus that gives such power to his description of the quiet with which he accepted the abuse he suffered. In any case, it is surely reasonable to assume that Peter addresses servants and women because Jesus addressed servants and women. They are present in the new churches because in his teaching and life they and other humble folk are the particular objects of his attention and love, almost to the exclusion of other society. It is astonishing how these people have been harmed by Peter's making them the objects of his particular concern, no doubt in imitation of Christ.

Where Scripture is granted peculiar authority, it enjoys an implied existence behind textual difficulties and apart from the historical communities that derive from it and whose practices and traditions are assumed to interpret it. The penumbra of fallibilities that surrounds Scripture is by definition no part of it. This shedding of specific manifestations is no embarrassment because the disruption of error, contamination, or neglect is the characteristic occasion for the expansion of vision and understanding within the literature itself from the time of Moses forward.

I grant the Bible such authority for a number of reasons. Its sophistication is always impressive—for example, the preserving of creation narratives in Genesis, one beside another, with their differences unreconciled, a tactful recognition of the value of the accounts themselves apart from any factual content that might be claimed for them. These stories, which might have been new when fire was a novelty, and which might have been refined through a thousand preliterate generations, are attempts to articulate the character of the being of humankind in the world. This is a most amazing problem, since every term in which it is expressed eludes definition. These ancient narratives characterize evil as both prevalent and anomalous, and humanity as both holy and flawed. That they allow these contradictory ideas to be conceived of simultaneously is as important to the tradition that grows out of them as the perception that human time exists among other scales of time, in which it is comprehended and made, again, anomalous, or the perception that the darker side of human potentiality implicates the whole of earthly creation in the prospect of death. That these things should be true is so extraordinary that even now, when their truth looms over our existence, they elude our understanding.

I imagine primordial crones, husking and stemming the weedy staples of a tenuous life and telling old stories until they became strange and perfect. This to my mind is not at all incompatible with divine inspiration. It is no demystification to say that from the first the Bible feels steeped in human experience. So early the people of the Bible were ready to concede to one another innocence and dignity, not compromised by evil, only obscured by it. Their stories are a brilliant rescue of humanity's ingratiating essence from its brutal ways. The spirit of the stories is a revelation in itself.

Now, at what must be very nearly the end of history, reading these old documents, I fall to thinking how little seems to have happened. It is as true of Christendom as of humankind that its fall came so briskly on the heels of its creation as to make the two events seem like one. If a hint of divine origins has always been discoverable, the fact is owed to the continuous sense of failure, of falling short, that makes meaning float beyond the reach of language, that makes beauty slide away from every form we try to give it, that makes giant loneliness the measure of small love. The shape of what we ought to be, which we cannot fill, remains our nimbus, the best claim we have to our own loyalty.

Humankind is an extraordinarily isolated creature, whose history must appear from any distance a harrowing dream of frustration and fear and self-contempt, itself villain, itself victim. We have no other enemy, yet we are endlessly assaulted and besieged. This state of affairs is neither recent nor local, nor does it show signs of melioration. Everywhere harm is done on ingenious pretexts, even now when every risk is insupportable. With Utopia precluded fully and finally, truce would be accomplishment enough. But that has no hold on the imagination, perhaps because it cannot be made a pretext for violence.

The writer of the second epistle attributed to Peter explains why the Last Judgment has not come as quickly as the early church expected. To God a thousand years is like a day, and God is patient, wishing for the salvation of us all. Now we live in the knowledge that war, famine, and plague on an apocalyptic scale could befall us tomorrow, that the heavens may well "pass away with a great noise" and that the elements may well "melt with a fervent heat." If this were to happen, it could all be described without reference to any supernatural agency. It seems we have passed judgment on ourselves.

I have never understood the mythos of Fall and Judgment. Yet I am struck by its usefulness in describing humanity's passage through the world, which clearly will be continuously troubled, and very brief by the standards of life on this planet. Against the duration of the sun, for example, it will be quite literally no time at all. If time is an illusion, then Creation, Fall, and Judgment were one event, and all that has seemed to intervene has been the opening out of the implications of the offending act, or even its completion. Perhaps Eden was lost in the first instance in the sense that its ultimate loss was assured, and we have wandered in Eden all these years, with expulsion at our back and nature deteriorating around us. First Peter assures us that Jesus was ordained as Saviour from before the beginning of the world. This implies that the Fall had all its consequences in train a very long time before it occurred. I put aside questions of guilt and responsibility, which are clearly unanswerable in the terms that are given to us. Increasingly I am impressed that biblical narrative warps and strains human notions of cause and consequence. Clearly the events in which we are caught up exceed our powers of understanding. This is no less true if our circumstances are thought of in rigorously secular terms. It must now be acknowledged that the most important aspects of our collective life are the crimes we have done and the greater crimes we have prepared, oddly as this fact sorts with the relative harmlessness of the generality of people.

For whatever reason, Peter and his followers assumed what we must struggle to accept, that the world will pass away. The great recurring theme of biblical narrative is always rescue, whether of Noah and his family, the people of Israel, or Christ's redeemed. The idea that there is a remnant too precious to be lost, in whom humanity will in some sense survive, has always been a generous hope, and a pious hope. For Peter this remnant is the ragtag community spreading into Rome and throughout its empire, the new Christians. Therefore in characterizing them to themselves he is describing those aspects of humanity dearest to God.

The rhetorical method employed in the body of the epistle is a catalogue of parallel injunctions, the urging of one model of behavior, the humility of Christ, through a range of relations. The Sermon on the Mount is a more straightforward example of the same method. The strategy of the letter is to establish a unifying vision of mutual obligation, based on the figure of Christ as servant, while leaving intact relations which were, as the writer is clearly aware, burdensome enough in many cases to recall the suffering of Christ. By referring them always to one emblematic figure the letter resolves things that seem in their nature various or opposed, above all the exalted status of believers in the eyes of God and the intractable difficulty of their lives in the world.

First, Peter addresses the faithful as "sanctified by the Spirit for obedience to Jesus Christ." He tells them that in the great tradition of prophecy, from which the many Gentiles among them had always been excluded, the prophets "were serving not themselves but you." In "obedience to the truth" believers are to love one another. Having established the idea of obedience in these very lofty contexts, Peter then urges his hearers to "be subject for the Lord's sake to every human institution." To this point obedience reciprocates kindness and service and sacrifice, and requires only love. To obey the emperor and his governors is another matter, though Peter represents these authorities in charitable terms, strikingly willing to concede their merits even though the community had begun to suffer persecutions.

Then Peter brings the matter of obedience nearer home, instructing servants to "be submissive to your masters with all respect." He offers no instruction to masters, as he does to husbands to honor their wives, or elders to care for their followers. This may indicate the modest circumstances of the clutch of faithful to whom this elegant and tender letter is addressed. But it should be noted that Peter's invoking the suffering of Jesus in this context puts the unjust master in the unenviable place of Jesus' tormentors.

One wonders what alternatives servants could have had to obeying their masters. Peter describes them as enduring punishments even when they have done nothing to offend. Clearly they were extremely vulnerable people, whose resistance to their circumstances, if they were to offer any, would surely recoil upon them. Peter dignifies their submission by making it a religious duty, and he salves the humiliation of the injustices they suffer by reminding them that they are reenacting precisely the experience of Christ and, furthermore, that just as the prophets served them, Jesus suffered for them. Since Jesus made no secret of his bias in favor of the humble, Peter's teaching is by no means contrived to suit a particular audience or occasion. It is an aspect of the freedom of God that he values what the world despises. Yet, strange as it seems, this passage has been used to justify hierarchy, as if oppressing those with whom God in his humanity identified himself were consistent with the will of God.

When Peter urges wives to submit to their husbands, his argument in favor of obedience changes once again. He asks wives to adopt "reverent and chaste behavior" in order to convert their husbands by their example or perhaps to reinforce their conversion. Peter makes a very generous estimation of the motives of wives. He assumes that their husbands' good is their primary concern. Therefore submission in their case suggests nothing of the martyrdom explicitly invoked by Peter in urging the submission of servant to master. There is no reason to assume the writer considers oppression less onerous to women than to men. Women were servants as well as wives. Peter clearly assumes that their obedience to their husbands will be an expression of love, like all obedience within the community of the faithful. He also assumes that the wife will be in advance of her husband in matters of faith, and worthy and able to win him to obedience to the Word—the image recurs again—by her example. In other words, spiritual insight and the whole burden of prophecy can be mediated to men through their wives' understanding of it, embodied in gracious conduct. To be blunt, Peter is telling wives to be submissive to their husbands in order to lead them.

He seems almost playfully aware that his words will arouse invidious notions of female manipulativeness. He makes the image of woman as seductress explicit in order to dispel it. Wives should not adorn themselves outwardly, he says, but with "the imperishable jewel of a gentle and quiet spirit, which in God's sight is very precious." His language alludes to his own description of Jesus as "in God's sight chosen and precious." In other words, once again the idea of submission is associated with the figure of Christ. Women are not singled out or set apart. Indeed Peter creates for them the distinction of being the children of Sarah, clearly an equivalent for the ancient boast of descent from Abraham. In doing so he provides their obedience with a dignified precedent, while giving Sarah a prominence tradition had never allowed her. This is all entirely consistent with early Christian belief that human beings were not in their essence male or female.

Peter tells husbands to "live considerately with your wives, bestowing honor on the woman as the weaker sex." There is no suggestion that the weakness is other than physical. Frequent childbearing by itself would account for this gender difference, and to "honor" women seems more consistent with showing them consideration on such grounds than with making allowance for deficiencies of character or intellect. Elsewhere Peter tells his hearers to "honor all men" and to "honor the emperor." Neither in the context nor in the Latin or English translations is there any hint of condescension in his choice of words. When he describes women as "co-heirs" or "joint heirs" in grace he establishes them as full participants in the cosmic scheme. Even his metaphor would have seemed startling, when women were not customarily allowed to inherit. It is significant that women's submitting to their husbands should arise as an issue, since in ancient cultures generally and in Judaism the subordination of women would be assumed. No tradition anticipated the honor Jesus showed to women, and institutions and societies supposedly based on his teaching have seldom granted his example a moment's respectful attention.

The First Epistle of Saint Peter does not justify slavery or servitude or the subordination of the poor, or the devaluing of women, all characteristic of pre-Christian society. The Second Epistle, circulated under Peter's name to invoke the spirit of his teaching, laments the corruption of the church together with the decline of belief in the imminent return of the Lord. Peter did not foresee the naturalization of the church to the world, let alone prescribe the terms upon which relations in a notionally Christian society were to be established. He is clearly intent upon calming the expectation that Christian values would be expressed in social institutions. Instead he Christianizes the present circumstances of his hearers by interpreting existing authority in terms of the life of Christ. Peter promises these converts nothing but heaven. There is no suggestion that the world itself holds any release, reward, or vindication for them, or that any could be of interest, in light of the littleness of time, set against an eternity that all but overwhelms it. He tells a new, maligned, and persecuted sect how to live in the world it finds, while the world lasts.

Peter says, "Clothe yourselves, all of you, with humility toward one another, for 'God opposes the proud, but gives grace to the humble.' " God is indifferent to human order, as to human time, except in the degree that he expresses his otherness by subverting it; or to put the matter another way, the degree to which the world ignores things precious in the eyes of God is the degree of its difference from him. Peter's teaching that God values humility has been used to justify presumption. It is our strange privilege to err. Clearly we follow the bent of an injured nature. For if we had persuaded ourselves in the terms of reason or belief to extend to one another the reverence Peter's letter has urged on all the generations who have read it, we would have had another history, and we would enjoy other prospects than those that now present themselves.

It is all mystery. And the traditions of Scripture are observant of the workings of mystery. In fact they have made it their ornament, their dark pleasure. So late in the day I do not know what has been at issue in this little whorl of universe. I think the ancients bear consulting.

THE FIRST, SECOND,
AND THIRD EPISTLES
GENERAL OF
JOHN

—

Robert Hass

In my grade-school classroom in northern California, there were pictures pinned to the bulletin boards representing the Last Supper—not an item of spectacular interest, but something to think about through long stretches of afternoon. Each of the apostles wore a robe in a different shade of bright pastel. They looked like flavors of ice cream. Judas, off to one side, was, of course, chocolate—detestable Judas, the class treasurer, who betrayed the Lord and hanged himself later in his loneliness and remorse. Only Peter with his iron-gray beard and his impetuous brow and sky-blue robe did not suggest a flavor. There was no flavor then the color of the sky. It is one of the special pleasures of the story that the rock upon which the church was to be built was a somewhat comic figure: Peter, who rushed forward to chop off the centurion's ear, so that the Lord had to pick it up and put it back on; who swore that he would be faithful to the last and then, hours later, while Jesus was being grilled by the Sanhedrin, was spotted in the courtyard warming himself at a fire by one of the servant girls of the high priest. "You were with Jesus, the man from Nazareth," she said. And Peter: "I don't know what you're talking about." And, as in a fairy tale, the cock crowed.

The pretty young man who rested his head on the breast of Jesus wore a robe of goldish yellow, a sherbet color, something fragrant and a little exotic, perhaps pineapple. I knew, from the stories the nuns told us, that he was John, the Beloved Disciple. It was a role I understood very well: younger brother and best loved. I also knew that this boy grew up to write the most profound and mysterious of the Gospels, and that as a very old man, almost a hundred, years and years past the triumphal procession into Jerusalem when the crowd waved palm leaves, and the vigil in the upstairs room, and the arrest by torchlight in the garden, and the cry of despair from the cross, and the sunny morning and the rolled-back stone, he wrote an account of a vision he had been given on the island of Patmos of the coming of the end of the world.

The Epistles of John did not figure in this legend, and I am pretty sure I did not read them, since Catholics were tellers of stories and enumerators of lists—the four cardinal virtues, the seven fruits of the Holy Ghost, the ten Sorrowful Mysteries of the Rosary—and arguers of fine points of moral theology, rather than readers of Scripture. I must have heard fragments at mass on Sundays when brief excerpts from the Gospels and epistles were read from the pulpit in English. In the course of a summer when I have been reading the epistles and thinking about them, I've twice heard passages from the first epistle read at Christian services, once at a wedding and once at a funeral. It is why we need sacred texts, I suppose—to read them at occasions in human life. The second and third epistles are not much more than business letters; I doubt that they are much used in the liturgy. But the first epistle is written in a spirit of some urgency, and it rises to moments of sudden, aphoristic brilliance, when the language seems as alive as the current of a river or the touch of a living body. Still, it seems an odd thing that this letter, written no one is sure where, in a language that the learned are not sure they understand entirely, to a community of people it is hard for us to imagine, has become the text of festivity and bereavement on another continent after centuries and centuries. At the wedding I noticed that I was aware, because I had also been reading scholarly commentaries, that the lines read on the bright, hot morning, with an air of floral triumph, came from a particularly obscure passage in the Greek of the first epistle which may very well have meant exactly the opposite of what the English translation seemed to say.

———

It was in the course of these studies that I learned the word "Johannine." It means something like "relating to or characteristic of the apostle John or the books of the New Testament ascribed to him," though there are problems with this definition, since it's possible that the books ascribed to him have nothing to do with the apostle John.

The OED cites use of the word beginning in the 1870s and 1880s, which is a clue to its actual significance. It stands for the solution to a problem created when Europeans began to apply the methods of secular textual and historical scholarship to their own sacred books. When they did, it became apparent that the traditional attribution of the fourth Gospel, the three epistles, and the Book of Revelation to a single common author could not be sustained by their standards of evidence. But the texts that tradition had passed down together did seem to have common elements of thought and expression which distinguished them from the Synoptic Gospels and the epistles of Paul. If they were not written by John, they belonged together nevertheless. And if the Gospel was at least in a tradition of teaching connected to the apostle, then the epistles were, like the Gospel, Johnish.

Hence, Johannine. To know the term is to see that one stands on the other side of a rather painfully constructed bridge in the history of—what? I was about to write "Western Christian thought"—of one's culture's relation to the sacred, as it is more or less unconsciously absorbed.

———

The epistles were written, most scholars seem to think, between 90 and 110. By this time all the great events are over. The ministry of Jesus in Palestine has ended with his execution at Passover sometime between 30 and 33. The word of his miraculous resurrection from the dead has been carried by his disciples to almost all the cities of the Roman world. The ministry of Paul, begun with the conversion vision on the road to Damascus seven years after the death of Jesus, has ended with his martyrdom in Rome, where Simon Peter is also said to have died. Tacitus remarks that Nero "inflicted most exquisite tortures on a class hated for their abominations, called Christians by the populace." Paul is supposed to have been beheaded on the Ostian Way. Peter was crucified (upside down, according to tradition) in the Circus of Nero just south of Vatican Hill. At about the same time, the Jews of Judaea rose against Roman rule and were crushed. The great Temple at Jerusalem, only recently completed and one of the wonders of the world, was razed to the ground. Masada fell in 73. Sometime later, perhaps twenty years, perhaps thirty, the epistles appear. We have them in texts edited from old manuscripts and papyri, copies of copies of copies in Greek, Coptic, Latin, Syrian: two brief letters and a homily, or sermon.

———

To the compilers of the New Testament, they must have seemed precious fragments of what remained of the original vision. They were, like the letters of Peter, James, and Jude, the last words of the last witnesses.

Though the process of establishing a canon went on until the middle of the fourth century, one list of canonical books was made at Rome by a bishop and theologian named Hippolytus around 200. Discussing the doctrines of the fourth Gospel, Hippolytus comments on the epistles. It is one of the earliest references to their existence, and one gets a sense of the force they had for him as testimony: "What wonder, then, that John so emphatically brings out the several points in his epistles, saying in his own person, 'What we saw with our own eyes and heard with our own ears, and our hands handled, these things we have written you.'"

———

To modern scholars, the interest of the epistles has been the glimpse they give of a Christian church coming into being. The context of the first epistle, one realizes as one reads it, is heresy and secession. For scholars the striking fact is not that its author is claiming the authority of direct witness but that he is appealing to it to settle a controversy. Though he does not know it—he writes, for example, with a vivid sense of the coming apocalypse—he comes not at the end but at the beginning. The age of the miraculous had passed. What had begun was the puzzle of its meaning, heirs quarreling over the estate, a church.

The scholarly reconstruction of that church starts with the fact that no one can say with any certainty who wrote the books attributed to John. The last verse of the last chapter of the Gospel identifies the author as John, son of Zebedee. "This is the disciple who is bearing witness to these things and is writing these things." But most scholars think that the last chapter is a later addition. The author of the Book of Revelation also announces himself; he has had a vision, he writes, that God gave to Jesus and that Jesus sent by an angel "to his servant John, and John has written down everything he saw and swears it is the word of God." But once again the consensus, based mainly on considerations of style, genre, theology, is that the Gospel and the apocalyptic book were written by different people. The epistles were attributed to John in the first references made to them by the church fathers, some hundred years after they were probably composed, but there is no internal evidence to support this attribution. Though it was customary for an epistle to carry an introductory phrase identifying its author, the first epistle carries none. The author of the second and third calls himself "the elder" (*presbyter*) only. Nor is there any sure evidence that the author of the first epistle wrote the other two.

Scholars solved this problem by assuming the existence of a first-century community for which the main teachings about Jesus and his life derived from the apostle John. In effect, they accepted the tradition in general but not in particular. The point for them is that the Gospel, the epistles, and perhaps Revelation came out of teachings, oral and written, passed down in the sixty years between the death of Jesus and a particular moment in the life of the community that the epistles imply. They have added to this assumption the perception that the Greek of the Gospel and the epistles has an Aramaic cast, as if they were written by people who were thinking in Aramaic or who spoke a Greek idiom that had Aramaic coloring. And many of them have accepted the tradition that John's apostolate was centered on Asia Minor. This comes from Revelation, which, as we have seen, may or may not be related to the other writings. There is also a second-century anecdote that places John at Ephesus, a Roman merchant city on the Aegean coast of what is now Turkey, where he is said to have departed a bathhouse abruptly because a Gnostic teacher had come in. From this slim evidence a picture emerges of a group of Jewish Christian communities in the Roman cities of Asia Minor, which developed a Christian teaching somewhat different from that founded by Paul and based on his epistles and the Synoptic Gospels.

A Johannine tradition. Out of which came those startling formulations—"*In the beginning was the Word, and the Word was with God, and the Word was God*," "*God is light, there is no darkness in him at all*," "*Anyone who fails to love can never have known God, because God is Love*"—that seemed to connect Christianity with Greek metaphysics, with the symbolic dualisms from which Gnostic thought emerged, and with the sensibility of the mystical and purifying sects that were becoming increasingly common throughout the empire. It is a cast of mind that has influenced all European theological thinking. What the epistles, especially the first, give us, in Greek "more remarkable for energy than lucidity," as a French scholar has observed, is a brief look at that tradition in the process of formation.

In his *History of Christianity* Paul Johnson cites a telling fact. During the life of Jesus, he estimates, there were a million and a half Jews in Palestine, and four and a half million scattered around the cities of the Mediterranean. These overseas Jewish communities were prosperous, well integrated into the civic life of the empire, connected to one another by Roman roads and by the relatively swift channels of trade and commerce. They contributed substantially to the building of the Temple at Jerusalem. News of events in the Jewish world circulated through them rapidly, and it was through their synagogues that news of the Jesus sect spread. The church at Ephesus— or wherever the Johannine tradition was taking root—most likely emerged from such a synagogue.

There has also developed a scholarly tradition, since the discovery of the Dead Sea Scrolls, that John the Baptist, and perhaps Jesus, had connections to the Essenes, a Jewish sect that had withdrawn into the desert at Qumran, where the scrolls were found, in order to practice a purified Judaism. The Essenes developed a dualistic theology, an imagery based on light and darkness, an insistence on brotherly love, on doctrinal and ritual purity. Since the fourth Gospel seems to be at greater pains than the synoptic accounts to establish the relationship between John the Baptist and Jesus, and since there are similarities between the language of the Dead Sea Scrolls and the language of the Gospel, there has been a further guess that the synagogue or synagogues from which the John tradition emerged were colored by Essene thinking. It seems likely that by the time of the epistles the community included Gentiles as well as Jews. So the moment of the epistles may have been a secession by Christians of Gnostic leaning from a community of Greek-speaking, urban, probably middle-class Jews and Gentiles who were themselves a Christian secession from a synagogue of Essene tendency somewhere in Asia Minor.

This reconstruction is speculative and no doubt too refined. There are others, perhaps equally plausible.* All of them are an effort to set the stage for the controversy implicit in the epistle. It is hard to tell exactly what the opponents of the author, the secessionists, think; and as much scholarly ingenuity has been spent attempting to reconstruct it as has been spent on establishing the outlines of the Johannine church, with possibly even less certain results. But the heart of the controversy is clear. It is about the understanding of the relation between spirit and matter, a problem that troubled the roots of Christian thought from the beginning.

---

* I found the most helpful summaries of the scholarship in Raymond Brown, *The Epistles of John* (New York, 1982); Rudolf Bultmann, *The Johannine Epistles*, tr. O'Hara et al. (Philadelphia, 1973); C. H. Dodd, *The Johannine Epistles* (New York, 1946); and Kenneth Grayston, *The Johannine Epistles* (London, 1984). Raymond Brown's *The Community of the Beloved Disciple* (New York, 1979) is a detailed treatment.

Actually the issue is more astonishing than that. It is the understanding of the relation between matter and spirit as it bears on the question of eternal life. What the author of the first epistle says, in the Jerusalem Bible translation, is this: *"The Word who is Life, this is our subject. That life was made visible: we saw it and we are giving our testimony, telling you of eternal life which was with the Father and has been made visible to us."* Eternal life. Years of Catholic education had, when I began to read the epistles, dulled for me the extraordinary proposition of those words. I have come to tell you, the Christians said, about living forever. The phrase in Greek is *zoe aionios*.

Raymond Brown in the Anchor Bible edition of the epistles glosses it as follows: "Eternal life is qualitatively different from natural life (*psyche*), for it is the life that death cannot destroy. Duration (everlasting, or even without beginning) is not the primary issue; it is life from another eon (*aion*, whence *aionios*) or sphere." This must be, of course, an educated guess. We can't know what coloring exactly the phrase had for speakers of Hellenic Greek in Beirut or Alexandria or Smyrna in the year 100: *zoe aionios*.

———

The Gospel of Mark tells a story about John. He and his brother James—they were sons of a Galilean fisherman named Zebedee—asked Jesus for a favor. "Allow us to sit one on your left and one on your right in glory." In the version the nuns told us, Jesus answered them indulgently and diplomatically. "As for the seats to my right and left hand, they are not mine to grant; they belong to those to whom they have been allotted." The tone of the telling suggested to us that these boys in their charming and literal-minded way could only conceive of an afterlife in which there were chairs and lefts and rights, and that we, of course, knew better. I suppose that we tried to compose facial expressions to indicate that we did.

Thinking about these childhood stories, I realize that they inhabit the two eternities I know: childhood and stories. When I was describing Peter warming himself at the fire, beginning to inhabit whatever place in my imagination those stories dwell in, I started to write that he was warming himself against "the raw cold of early spring," and noticed the absurdity of the pretension. Then, sudden impulse,

I called a friend and asked him what the weather was like in Jerusalem at Passover. Mild during the day, he said, but cold at night. You'd want to wear a sweater. I thanked him and returned to my desk with the feeling that I had just crossed from one sphere to another and back again. *Aionios*.

It reminded me of going to see a pair of paintings by Caravaggio in the church of Santa Maria del Popolo in Rome on a sultry, overcast morning in early summer. The paintings, one of the conversion of Paul, another of the crucifixion of Peter, once you have left the light of the square and entered the dark of the church, come swimming right at you out of the gloom. Sinew and light is what they seem to be about, musculature and torque and chiaroscuro. One of the centurions is so tensed with the effort of torturing Peter to death that his nose is wrinkled, his upper lip drawn like a rabbit's.

Afterward I had a beer and a sandwich in the heat of the day at a café in the Piazza del Popolo. First crucifixion, then *crostini*. I was a tourist. I thought about what a long time these stories have compelled the European imagination, about the way Caravaggio had used them to speak about the body, to provoke wonder at the sheer force of bodily life. The rediscovery of that force, of the beauty of that force, had, I knew, invented the tourism I was embarked on. For speakers of English, it began with John Ruskin, who had used Italian art and the vivacity of Italian life as a weapon against the Christian and evangelical culture of Victorian England. Sitting in the piazza, watching the pigeons, watching the little surf of beer foam play against and then cling to the surface of my glass, I knew I was enacting a piety, not one that had much to do with Peter. It wasn't to an idea of spirit and the eternal that I was making this visit, but to an idea of art and mortal life.

————

I don't remember exactly when, in what stages, I shed my Catholicism. I see now that it was a completely predictable development. It is, after all, the existence of Christian artists that needs to be explained in the second half of the twentieth century, not infidels and aesthetes and Buddhists and spiritual drifters. "You must not love this passing world," the author of the first epistle wrote. *Kosmos* is the word in Greek. It probably meant the worldly world, or just the known social surround; it still has that meaning in some dialects of modern Greek, in which, according to one commentator, a gossip is someone who tells your business to the whole *kosmos*. At eighteen or nineteen the passing *kosmos* and its mortal glory were exactly what I thought I loved. I was also in love with writing. I read the books of my time and entered their way of looking at and thinking about things.

There was, of course, Joyce. Not just the figure of Stephen Dedalus, who assimilated Catholic thought so brilliantly to some idea— right out of Ruskin—of the artist as priest. "Joyce," said one of my professors, an Irishman, "wanted to have his Eucharist and eat cake, too." We all saw that Joyce had, in fact, undercut Stephen's pretensions with the figures of Bloom and Molly, those paracletes of the ordinary. I wasn't reading the New Testament (if I ever had) at the time of my poring over *Ulysses*. But if I had read Paul in Galatians, who wrote, "Those who belong to Christ Jesus have crucified the flesh," or the twelfth chapter of John, in which Jesus says, "Anyone who loves his life [*psyche*] loses it; anyone who hates his life in this world will keep it for eternal life," it might have been with the figures of Bloom and Molly that I would have tried to reply.

Or perhaps with these lines from Wallace Stevens's "Sunday Morning":

> "The tomb in Palestine
> *Is not the porch of spirits lingering.*
> *It is the grave of Jesus, where he lay."*
> *We live in an old chaos of the sun,*
> *Or old dependency of day and night,*
> *Or island solitude, unsponsored, free,*
> *Of that wide water, inescapable.*
> *Deer walk upon our mountains, and the quail*
> *Whistle about us their spontaneous cries;*
> *Sweet berries ripen in the wilderness;*
> *And, in the isolation of the sky,*
> *At evening, casual flocks of pigeons make*
> *Ambiguous undulations as they sink,*
> *Downward to darkness, on extended wings.*

For there is not much question that there is a seed of world-and-flesh hatred at the root of Christianity. It is also true that the tradition is full of life and that the founding doctrines are contradictory. The same Gospel of John that urges us to hate our lives in this world says that God loved the world so much, he gave his Son to save it. Still, it would be meaningless to think of the historical emergence of Christianity as a manifestation of respect for and celebration of the processes of physical life. It began in the idea of triumph over them, or perhaps in the hunger for triumph over them.

And of course there is every reason for that hunger, not just in the desire to evade death or to protest the cruelty of life and the horror of existence. It seems to emerge quite naturally from the conditions of consciousness. Wallace Stevens, having diagnosed the illness of Christianity in its desire to escape death in "Sunday Morning," came to think about the difference between the mental quail and sweet berries in his poem and actual quails and berries in the world, and afterward wrote a poetry reflecting on the relation between world and imagination which is full of palpable spiritual loneliness, haunted not by nature but by some other elusive or illusive object of thought. "The palm at the end of the mind," he would write, in nearly his last poem, "rises in the bronzed distance."

And this same argument between the word and the world—it has become an argument between nature and art—rages in the poems of William Butler Yeats. It comes to its most dramatic and lucid form in the prayer at the center of "Sailing to Byzantium":

> *Consume my heart away; sick with desire*
> *And fastened to a dying animal*
> *It knows not what it is*

and issues in this vow:

> *Once out of nature I shall never take*
> *My bodily form from any natural thing,*
> *But such a form as Grecian goldsmiths make*
> *Of hammered gold and gold enamelling*
> *To keep a drowsy emperor awake;*
> *Or set upon a golden bough to sing*

To lords and ladies of Byzantium
Of what is past, or passing, or to come.

I think when I first read this passage it seemed merely eccentric. To want to be a mechanical bird: I wrote it off to Yeats's aestheticism. It seems to me now near the heart of the human wish for eternal life, one in which we are not touched by pain, and are beautiful, and get to gossip forever about the *kosmos*. But, then, I was much more interested in the assertion that Crazy Jane made to the Bishop:

> *A woman can be proud and stiff*
> *When on love intent;*
> *But Love has pitched his mansion in*
> *The place of excrement.*

That seemed to make the right insistence on the relation between body and spirit. I did not know then what I know now, that the passage in the Gospel of John that enunciates the doctrine of the Incarnation, in honor of which I had been taught as a boy to kneel whenever it was uttered—"And the Word was made flesh, and dwelt among us"—uses a Greek verb, *skenoun*, for "dwell" that means, literally, "to pitch a tent." Yeats is echoing this locution in "Crazy Jane Talks to the Bishop." Spirit and flesh: it is the same quarrel as in the Johannine Epistles, and the same mystery.

———

The first epistle, it has to be said, rambles. It is rambling as high art. It rambles so well that generations of its students—Augustine, Luther, Calvin, even Isaac Newton—have not been able to adduce a secret order in its rambling. But for all the circling and repetition and contradiction—the first contradiction is that it preaches brotherly love while bitterly denouncing its enemies as the Antichrist; the second is that it urges our capacity for sin (rather than our sinfulness) throughout and then, in 3:9, says that no one who has been begotten by God sins—for all this, it is quite clear what the letter is about. That it concerns secession is evident from 2:19: "Those rivals of Christ came out of our own number, but they had never really belonged to us; if they had belonged, they would have stayed with us; but they left us to prove that not one of them ever belonged to us."

What the secessionists believed is not so clear. The author of the epistle, however, keeps insisting on two points: first, that Jesus is the Christ, the Anointed One and promised Redeemer, and second, that he came in the flesh. "The man who denies that Jesus is the Christ, he is a liar"; "Every spirit which acknowledges that Jesus the Christ came in the flesh is from God: but any spirit which will not say this of Jesus is not from God, but is the spirit of antiChrist." This makes it seem likely that the secessionists have denied, in one way or another, either the humanity of Jesus or his divinity. They did not believe that the Word pitched a tent in the physical world.

The writer of the epistle seems anxious to refute another idea as well. Exactly what that idea is has also been a matter of scholarly debate. "If we say we have no sin in us," he writes, "we are deceiving ourselves." "Anyone who says 'I know him' and does not keep his commandments is a liar." And again, "To say that we have never sinned is to call God a liar." At my first reading of these passages, I groaned. I thought it was simply denunciation of human sinfulness in the grand manner. But the argument is more nuanced than that. Its point seems not to be that we are sinners but that we are *capable* of sin. This suggests that the secessionists believed either that they were incapable of sinning or perhaps that what one did in this world didn't matter very much. "Flesh begets flesh," the Gospel of John says, "spirit begets spirit." As he argued against the idea of the un-alloyed spiritual nature of Christ by insisting on the mystery of an incarnate spirit, he argues against this ethical idea by insisting on the gospel of love. "This is the message as you heard it from the beginning: that we are to love one another." "His commandments are these: that we believe in the name of his son Jesus Christ and that we love one another."

The whole upsurge of antiworldliness and asceticism in the ancient world from which Christianity sprung led—even two hundred years or more after the epistle, at the time of Augustine—away from the world, from the empire and its cities, and into the desert, which was both an actual wilderness and a metaphor for some place in the self that did not belong to the world. The secessionists were Gnostics, or—there is a debate about when gnostic thought may be said to have emerged—crypto-Gnostics. They did not believe that the divine Word trafficked with the human body. They were inclined to discount the importance of bodily action. And in this they seem a natural development of Johannine Christianity. The Synoptic Gospels, after all, belong to the eternity of story, as Yeats's golden bird does. They are full of legends of the marvels of this world: the curing of lepers, the multiplication of loaves and fishes, the man who walked on water and died and rose from the dead. Though these same stories appear in John, it contains what the others do not—that astonishing leap to what is not figurable in human art, not tellable: the Word that was in the beginning and was with God and was God. This is not Jewish eschatology with its chairs in Paradise. It is something else that pulls away from the earth, wants to leave it behind. And clearly it speaks to a very deep place in the human imagination.

Writers know a version of it, because all art drives toward either representation or abstraction, or tries to negotiate the tension between them; it wants to render the thing and to be its pure essence, and never quite succeeds at either, fails to render human experience entirely, fails to soar free of its materials. *Logos and kosmos*. The first epistle is fascinating because it is the place, among the canonical Christian texts, where this issue reaches a kind of resolution. The Word that preexisted the world and will outlast it came, nevertheless, into this world, the teaching says, was born not of water only but also of blood. It not only saved souls; it made the physical world sacred by its presence. It planted eternity here in the moments of human existence. That this argument emerges so flickeringly in a somewhat wandering and repetitious letter with an air more of valediction than of apocalypse gives it an odd sweetness: "My children, we live in the last days."

Some scholars think that the Gospel of John was an essentially Gnostic document, and that its inclusion in the New Testament was made possible only by the inclusion of the epistles, which were, in effect, a non-Gnostic revision of the Gospel. Elaine Pagels, in *The Gnostic Gospels*, has suggested that the motive for this compromise, in the fourth and fifth centuries, was political.* A doctrine

* *The Gnostic Gospels* (New York, 1978). See also her earlier book, *The Johannine Gospel in Gnostic Exegesis*.

that embraced the world opened the church's way to earthly power.

This is probably what made possible a church with universal appeal. In this sense, the Gnostic Christians were—to draw an analogy with Buddhism—the "small boat," a Hinayana tradition, which went underground only to keep emerging in the history of the West, in Manicheanism, Catharism, in the poetry of William Blake. And Roman Christianity was the "big boat," a Mahayana tradition, which somehow managed, with its Johannine dualism and its Pauline fear of sexuality, to include large measures of Mediterranean earth religion in its worship of the mother of God, its seasonal rituals, and its pantheon of saints. This church preserved its core of asceticism, its insistence that man must not be reconciled to his own nature, and to this it grafted, through the doctrine of Incarnation, a liturgy rich in stories and human iconography. It also tied the promise of eternal life to a political institution deeply patriarchal in structure and deeply suspicious of the unruliness and ingenuity of human sexuality, which it has always treated as, in some sense, a rival repository of the mystery of body and soul—with results that, even if one loves the passing world, need to be loved selectively.

THE GENERAL
EPISTLE OF
JUDE

—

JUDE, NOT OBSCURE

Grace Schulman

I remember reading the General Epistle of Jude for the first time at Bard College, in a Great Books course that began with the Greeks, paused after the *Commedia*, then resumed with Marlowe after the semester break. It was an intense year. The teacher, Theodore Weiss, and his students were propelled forward by the winds that swept Ulysses and his crew, then disembarked at Ithaca only to sail again. We navigated the Hebrew Bible and the Gospels with no diminishment of energy.

In those early weeks, we grew years older as we perceived just how various were the cultures that supported Western literature. Essentially we were concerned with the Greek tradition, Judaism and Christianity, but we looked at Syrian, Ethiopian, Canaanite, Babylonian, and Hindu sources as well. The patterns of theophanic birth and sacrifice, the ways in which metaphors were employed, the rhythms of each language, the revelation of character, and the sacred ideas were the light of our books and thought. A member of an observant Jewish family, I had been familiar with even the minor characters of the Hebrew Bible and acquainted with Greek figures, but relatively ignorant of the Christian Bible.

At the same time, I felt the impact of diverse cultures every day of my life. My bookshelves held Louis Ginzberg's *Legends of the Jews*, Saint Augustine's *Confessions*, and a study of Sumerian marriage rituals. On the wall nearby was a poster of El Greco's *Saint James the Less*, a painting I had seen in a museum near Bard. Often I gazed at his hand that emerged from the ample blue-robes, the wrist flexed as though to instruct and to implore, to clarify his doctrine and to extend a blessing. The fingers, splayed, resembled at once a branch of white pine and the wings of a mourning dove I had seen outside my window. Light fell on the hand, on one of the shoulders, and on the face. The eyes glowed, and the face shone with passion and suffering. I was drawn to that saint, who appears only infrequently in the Bible. Among the few things that are known about him is that he is *not* the author of the General Epistle of James. For me the great painting also was an emblem of the uncertain authorship of the General Epistles and, in fact, of much of the Bible. In many cases, the writer's name can be discovered only by rationalization, and never with certainty. With reservations, a few scholars consider that James the Righteous may have composed the Epistle of James, and they are even more equivocal when speculating about the authorship of Jude. Still and all, a powerful writer compels us to characterize him through his language. Even when we are not seeking an identity, we intuit qualities from a voice, an attitude, a mannerism. So it is with the writer of Jude.

Jude is one of the seven General or "Catholic" Epistles, which include also James, First and Second Peter, and First, Second, and Third John. They are so called because they are not addressed to any single church, unlike, for example, the Epistles of Paul to the Corinthians, which are directed to the church at Corinth. The writer of the Epistle of Jude is probably not the same as Saint Jude the apostle, the patron saint of hopeless causes, intercessor for those in desperate situations, not the recipient of appeals and thanksgivings that are found to this day in the personal columns of *The Village Voice*.

Long ago I mistakenly identified the biblical author with the statue of Saint Jude the apostle a friend had given my father when he was ill. It was a white plastic figure carrying a walking stick. My mother kept it on the piano among her ivory Buddhas, a resolute, chalk-white idol in a tunic among yellowing gods with bare arms and legs. My father remarked that the saint's searching eyes set him on edge, but he gazed at the replica all the while he judged it. In fact, he recovered soon after.

Although it was not the only icon in my Jewish household—there was a bronze Saint Theresa and a wooden Saint Sebastian—that machine-molded Saint Jude was our only object whose significance was devotional, rather than an aesthetic expression of the cultures that informed our lives.

That Jude, Saint Jude the apostle, is named with the Twelve as "Judas the son of James" (Luke 6:16; Acts 1:13) and is called "not Iscariot" to distinguish him from the traitor (John 14:22). Saint Jude the apostle is designated also as "Thaddeus," or "Lebbaeus called Thaddeus," when Jesus gives the apostles authority to cast out sickness. Of the six others named Jude (Judas, Judah) in the Christian Bible, one that is thought to be a possibility for the epistler is Jude the brother of Jesus (Matthew 12:33; Mark 6:3). Both are unlikely, though, because the writer was of a later period. He tells us this when he reminds his listeners of the apostles' prophecies: "But, beloved, remember ye the words which were spoken before of the apostles of our Lord Jesus Christ . . ." (17).*

Apparently the author is a Christian convert who knows Hellenic poetry, the Hebrew Bible and apocryphal sources, such as Enoch. Perhaps he is not a Jude at all but a writer speaking in the persona of Jude, as may be the case with the Book of Daniel and the Song of Solomon. Possibly the writer follows the common literary practice of identifying with another for aesthetic purposes, as in Tennyson's "Ulysses," Lowell's "Mother Marie Thérèse," and Bishop's "Crusoe in England."

In that abundant Great Books course, I wrote on the General Epistles, surprised at their relative neglect, attracted by their structural logic, and moved by passages containing clear, precise metaphors. There was, for example, this passage from Jude, when the poet chides dissidents who make their way into the church as false teachers:

* Quotations are taken from the King James, or Authorized, Version.

These are spots in your feasts of charity, when they feast with you, feeding themselves without fear: clouds they are without water, carried about of winds; trees whose fruit withereth, without fruit, twice dead, plucked up by the roots;

Raging waves of the sea, foaming out their own shame; wandering stars, to whom is reserved the blackness of darkness forever. [12, 13]

Devoted as I am to the King James Version, I find the epistle striking the same chords years later in Richmond Lattimore's translation from the Greek. Indeed, his words reinforce my feeling for the work:

It is these who are blemishes on your love feasts when they join you in them, shamelessly looking after themselves: rainless clouds driven by on the gales, autumn trees without fruit uprooted and dying twice, wild sea waves foaming their own shame, wandering stars with the dark of hell in store for them.*

Again I marvel at those "wild sea waves foaming their own shame." The metaphor is exact but distorted, an image of human evil revealed in the natural scene. The writer's process of discovery recalls that of the Greek poets, who envision personal misery in objects or phenomena, rendered with exactitude. Lines come to mind from the *Orestes* of Euripides:

For, like a fast ship, whose sail was shaken by a god, you are thrown into a sea of terrible suffering in wild destructive waves.

and also from the Hebrew of Isaiah:

But the wicked are like the troubled sea, when it cannot rest, whose waters cast up mire and dirt. [57:20]

as well as from the Epistle of James:

* Richmond Lattimore, trans., *Acts and Letters of the Apostles* (New York, 1982), p. 277.

For he that wavereth is like a wave of the sea driven with the wind and tossed. [1:3]

From the time I first read Jude, the poetry outweighed my own indifference to the scoundrels he berates, corrupt teachers who "defile the flesh." It was of less consequence that I could not adhere to the concept of eternal punishment. *He* could, and I listened. The writer presented images in a chain transformed by time, curiously in relation to other works. He depicted things so vividly as to foster belief in the consciousness of his persona, using words that did not decay. Visualizing those waves, clouds, and trees, I trusted the character who despised an evil that I contemplated with detachment.

Jude has affinities to the Second Epistle General of Peter in its language, and to James in its awareness of Judaism's ethical principles along with the espousal of Christian doctrine. Unlike a letter, the Epistle of Jude is a formal document that enables the writer to speak to congregations he cannot address in person. It includes, in this case, a general salutation, a reason for the exhortation, the warning, a wish for steadfastness, and concluding words of praise.

This epistle, so brief that its thirty-five verses cover no more than a page in the King James Bible, implores the Christian community of its time to hold fast despite subversive influences. The writer chides the evil teachers for their unholy ways, deriding the "ungodly men, turning the grace of our God into lasciviousness" (4).

Scholars date the text in the postapostolic period, near the end of the first century C.E. Bo Reicke reasons that the epistle was composed around 90 C.E., when senators and aristocrats fought the emperor Domitian's tyranny, and before the monarch began persecuting the Christians, in 95 C.E. He argues that the epistle urges the faithful to obey the Roman government, as well as God, and to dismiss the anarchists who oppose the despot's reign.* Many scholars disagree with this reading, believing that Jude reproves only malcontents who fail to respect God.

Jude's language hardly resolves the question, but it does point up

---

* B. Reicke develops this argument in *The Epistle of James, Peter, and Jude*, the Anchor Bible (Garden City, N.Y., 1962), pp. xvi–xxxviii. Although his thesis has been questioned, his dating is well within the range of scholars' estimates, which extend from 70 to 120 C.E.

the complexity of the author. Primarily, he deplores the heresy of his adversaries. Sharpening his disparagement, he refers to traditional sources, especially the Hebrew Bible and other Jewish writings. He cites Genesis, Numbers, the First Book of Enoch, and a haggadic midrash called *The Assumption of Moses*, an odd document that the early church officials affirmed as material for the epistle. He recalls sinners such as Cain; the unbelievers in Israel's wilderness generation (Numbers 14:26–27); and the inhabitants of Sodom and Gomorrah (Genesis 19:1–29).

He alludes to biblical sins, which, however, are also classical examples of lawlessness. Having admonished the faithful to beware of those people who "despise dominion" (8), he invokes the revolutionaries led by Core (Corah, Korah), who rose up against Moses and Aaron (Numbers 16:1–35). From the First Book of Enoch he borrows an elaboration of the wayward angels in Genesis (6:14) who begat earthly beings. From *The Assumption of Moses*, the writer draws the legend of the archangel Michael's dispute with the devil over the leader's body. He contrasts the wicked teachers with the dutiful angel. The teachers "speak evil of those things which they know not: but what they know naturally, as brute beasts, in those things they corrupt themselves" (10). Unlike them, the good angel "durst not bring against him a railing accusation, but said, The Lord rebuke thee." (9).

The epistler's character is striking for its containment of opposite qualities. On the one hand, he reveres the law. His overriding care is for the Gospel law, but I suspect he is devoted to the state as well. He has a sensibility that respects obedience, whether to God or to society. His gratitude is muted but vigorous, a quiet version of David's praise for the Ark, which the king celebrated on harps and psalteries (2 Samuel 6:5). The Jude writer's regard for law resembles that of Moses, to whom he refers twice, once in connection with the Core rebellion and once with regard to the lawgiver's body. Those two allusions in this brief epistle imply his concern with legality.

On the other hand, he is too vehement, too quick to anger, to be slavish to human authority. Besides, he is a nonconformist in his imagination. For example, there is irony in his illustrating patient obedience by citing *The Assumption of Moses*, a nonscriptural legend of what happens to Moses after his biblical death. Then, too, he braces his own anger against rebelliousness by quoting from the Book of Enoch ("And Enoch also, the seventh from Adam, prophesied of them, saying, Behold the Lord cometh with ten thousands of his saints" [14]). There is further irony here, in that he defends Christianity against its detractors by quoting inaccurately from a source that is in the first place apocryphal. In his references, the ideas are preserved but the wording is inexact. It is as though he is quoting from memory, and the effect is inconsistent with the writer's usual precision.

The Epistle of Jude is remarkable for combining a number of cultural influences, sometimes in a single verse. Hellenic, Jewish, and Christian images accrue, enriching consecutive assertions. In another instance of using a noncanonical source to uphold Christian doctrine, he refers to the Book of Enoch's account of the angels in Genesis that took earthly wives before the flood. He tells of their punishment: "And the angels which kept not their first estate, but left their own habitation, he hath reserved in everlasting chains under darkness unto the judgment of the great day" (6).

The tale resembles Hesiod's *Theogony*, in the Greek poet's story of how Zeus destroys the Titans. There, Zeus's fighters, covering the Titans with missiles, "threw them under the wide earth and bound them in painful chains, conquering them despite their great courage, as far below the earth as heaven is above it."

Scholars differ as to just who Jude's adversaries are, whether antinomian Gnostics who scorned moral behavior, converts who lapsed into apostasy, or the divisive early Christians who are chastised in the First Epistle of Paul to the Corinthians. There is a range of opinion, even apart from the theory that they are Roman anarchists. Because the writer presents the offenders in such scant detail, the text shimmers with omens that point to a composite notion of fathomless evil. We know only what Jude considers essential about the unrighteous: they are treacherous people who have inserted themselves among the Christians, and who twist the grace of God into a rationale for sexual licentiousness. In their carnal desires, they are compared to those wayward angels of Genesis who married women. They are likened also to the residents of Sodom and Gomorrah who lusted for angels, "giving themselves over to fornication, and going after strange flesh" (7). The intruders dream, and "these filthy dreamers defile the flesh" (8). Apart from its sexual connotations, the image of "dreamers" shows the sinners boasting of visions while degrading others whose knowledge they lack. It calls back Isaiah 56:10–12: "His watchmen are blind: they are all ignorant, they are all dumb dogs, they cannot bark; sleeping, lying down, loving to slumber." The fraudulent prophecies of the heretics, heightened by wine and apparently given for money ("because of advantage" [16]), are perversions of wisdom.

The writer's technique is to buttress his argument by compounding the heretics' evil ways. In the manner of Enoch, he rails against them: "These are murmurers, complainers, walking after their own lusts; and their mouth speaketh great swelling words" (16). They are "spots in your feasts of charity" (the *agapais*, or Christian fellowship meals), distorting the ideal of amity by indulging in their own lechery. The image is of heathen revelry at a Christian celebration. He defames the evil ones utterly, calling them "they who separate themselves, sensual, having not the spirit" (19, "sensual" here rendered from *psychikoi*, or animal soul, as distinguished from *pneuma*, or spirit).

I am amazed by this writer's skill. However vehement his wrath, however unremitting his hatred of the dishonorable infiltrators, he sets forth his anger logically. At times his rage shakes the structure of the epistle, but always it is contained within the form, a scheme of contrasts between the faithful Christians and the faithless rebels, and between the faithless rebels past and present. Beyond that scheme, the writer uses a rhetorical pattern of assertions and illustrations, with occasional outcries, such as "Woe unto them! for they have gone in the way of Cain" (11).

Never does the language disrupt the pattern, nor does it break down. It must not, for it supports the epistle's theme of propriety.

To illustrate the process, Jude begins with an unspecific greeting:

Jude, the servant of Jesus Christ, and brother of James, to them that are sanctified by God the Father, and preserved in Jesus Christ, and called.
Mercy unto you, and peace, and love, be multiplied. [1, 2]

Directly after it, the writer reveals that his purpose has changed from a letter concerning their "common salvation" to an entreaty "that ye should earnestly contend for the faith which was once delivered unto the saints" (3). The comment refers to the apostolic tradition, or the transmission of the Gospels from Jesus to the apostles, and from them to the church. After depicting the "ungodly men," and likening them to the villains of Numbers and Genesis, the writer inspires terror by intimating that the biblical culprits are suffering "eternal fire" (7).

With gathering force, the scribe gives reasons for his wrath, his voice rising as he discloses their offenses. Always, though, his vigor is held in check by rigid attention to the patterns of comparison and contrast and of assertion and illustration. His fury resounds until the final verses. There he consoles the faithful, urges them to be firm, and counsels them to trust in him "that is able to keep you from falling, and to present you faultless before the presence of his glory with exceeding joy" (24).

Considering its literary power, I wonder why our major writers and critics have overlooked the Epistle of Jude. I would have expected the name of this figure to resonate in our literature and to inform our art, music, and thought. Ironically, the Jude that has cut the widest path into English and American letters is the traitor. None of the other Judes have been so widely cited. A few writers have remembered the apostle, including Rumer Godden in *A Candle for St. Jude* and, of course, the Beatles, in "Hey Jude." Hardy's *Jude the Obscure* is a less direct reference, the obscurity of his Jude epitomizing the obscurity of the epistle writer, whether or not Hardy intended it. Hardy's lack of specificity, though, is in keeping with his use of Christian consolations in general ways as ironic reminders of their irrelevance to his characters' dilemmas. In one sense, Hardy's Jude Fawley resembles the biblical writer: like him, Jude exhorts the populace, but does so in a travesty of the hortatory manner. Late in the book, when Jude Fawley returns to the city, he begs the crowd to consider his failure a result of his poverty, and his speech is called "well preached" by one Tinker Taylor. However, Jude Fawley has no particular biblical counterpart. And as for Hardy's own attitude toward this text, he whispered to his notebooks that he enjoyed the First Epistle of Clement to the Corinthians. He acknowledged that he preferred that work to either the Second Epistle of Peter or to Jude.

Although the Epistle of Jude is included in the canon of sacred Scriptures, it was from the first viewed with suspicion and still suffers some disfavor in the church. In the third century, Jerome questioned its canonicity because of the inclusion of apocryphal writings. In the sixteenth century, Martin Luther impugned its authorship. Those objections still cast shadows on the epistle. Pointedly, the Jude writer quotes Enoch as though that Genesis patriarch were the author of the Book of Enoch ("And Enoch also . . . prophesied" [14]). That reference to Enoch as author seems now a sad comment on the history of Jude. It suggests, too, his innocence of the stance taken by later biblical scholars: that textual authenticity resides in naming the author.

In the case of Jude, the writer's name is of less relevance to the epistle's strength than it is of interest historically. What matters more is the sense given of a writer who offers Christian followers a glimpse of an ideal world founded on the concept of a loving God.

I am moved by that vision, despite myself. I have always regarded literary religious systems as metaphorical. I can be stirred by the aesthetic function of, for example, Sophocles' notion of the cosmic order, or of Milton's reimagining of the Genesis story. However, reading Jude as mere fancy would be to slight its importance to the writer as a proclamation made in accordance with God's will.

It is the writer's personality that draws me to his exhortation. As a being, he is less appealing than he is intricate. He is given to self-denial and has an unsmiling distaste for physical intimacy. At the same time, his compassion for men and women is emphasized by repetitions of "beloved" and "love." He seems humorless in his amassment of rebels such as Cain and Core without regard for the vast differences in tone between those biblical accounts. On the other hand, his list of bad acts, making up a composite notion of evil, suggests a lively wit reminiscent of Juvenal or Swift.

Passion and restraint are the polarities that direct his thought, vary his tone, and rattle the beams of Jude's rhetorical scaffolding. Those opposites enliven his mind and his art. While he advocates containment of emotion, his images have that accuracy that strong feeling pressures into being. His "autumn trees without fruit uprooted and dying twice" resembles Hopkins's "See, banks and brakes / Now, leavèd how thick! Lacèd they are again / With fretty chervil, look and fresh wind shakes / Them. . . ."* Although they differ in tone, both passages have an actuality born of creating equivalents in terms of earthly things. In both, the imagery is so exact as to seem induced by some rage or grief.

The Jude writer is consistent in possessing the purity of heart essential to his vision of ideal love. Other than that, he fascinates for his contradictions. His language is heightened by paradox (the sinners insult what they do not understand and are destroyed by what they do [10]); contrasting acts (the Lord saved, the Lord destroyed [5]); and antithetical attributes ("sensual" persons who lack spirit [19]). True to his nature, he recommends obedience but is no passive servant of manmade law. I imagine him to have been an ambivalent follower of the reign, contemptuous of the anarchists who opposed the Roman emperor, and critical of senators who sided with the rebels. He was not, I think, devious, as one who speculates on the advantages to the church of honoring the monarch. Instead, he was loyal to the prevailing order as an extension of his loyalty to God, or perhaps he had in mind "Render unto Caesar that which is Caesar's."

He is impressive, too, for his range of tone. In the concise epistle, he roars with anger against the unrighteous, bristles with logic, and utters a benediction. To listen to his voice, bold and original, is to know that he is a person of conviction whose commitment to the right deeds can move others to be ethical. He is a poet who has made art out of a difficult subject: a warning to be virtuous and scorn the tempter.

———

My attraction to the General Epistles was not ephemeral. In fact, the whole of the Christian Bible was to be essential to my life and work, for it informed the Giottos and the Pieros I most admired, besides being the source of Leonardo's *The Adoration of the Magi* and Correggio's *The Ascension of Christ*. In great books, the Christian Bible's motifs may be manifest, as in the *Commedia*, or they may be inferred,

* *Poems and Prose of Gerard Manley Hopkins*, ed. W. H. Gardner (New York, 1985), p. 67.

as in the ambiguous "you" of a love poem, or allusions to the Incarnation, or the Grail legends, or an apostle's name.

In Christian legend, I turned to Saint Veronica, who, on the way to Calvary, used a handkerchief to wipe the blood and sweat from Christ's face and received an imprint of his features on it. The cloth designated as Saint Veronica's is preserved as a relic at Saint Peter's in Rome. I marveled that a miraculous image could be accurate and natural as well: the fabric was stained in accordance with his contours, as in a silk-screen print. In the Middle Ages, the word "vernicle" was used frequently to signify a copy of the veil that was venerated as a devotional object. Such a replica is worn by Chaucer's dishonorable Pardoner in the Prologue to *The Canterbury Tales*: "Swiche glarynge eyen hadde he as an hare, / a vernycle hadde he sowed upon his cappe."

Drawn to the contrast between the actual napkin and the replica, I dwelled on the term *vere icon*, or "true image," which, though not the root of the name Veronica, bears its sound as well as the meaning of her story. I called my first collection *Burn Down the Icons*, realizing that all of my early poems turned on the paradox of trying to fix things in images, rather than to accept the world's incessant mutability, and yet acknowledging that light changes to fire, water to vapor, rock to sand. I held the metamorphic condition to be inescapable, except in the case of the hero: my Aunt Helen, a Holocaust victim, climbed to the roof of a municipal building in the Warsaw Ghetto, tore the Polish flag to shreds, and was shot to her death. In "Letter to Helen," I wrote of her:

> *That is what icons are, indelible*
> *prints on the mind. Your image is a fresco*
> *that will not come down*
> *in dust. Because you lived your life I shine*
> *in flames, burning but not consumed,*
> *changing to be myself, as though if water burned*
> *it would be water all the more . . .*

Veronica's image persisted and prevailed. In a poem called "Birds on a Blighted Tree," I saw sparrows surrounding and appearing to move the stiff branch of a maple in winter:

Iconoclasts impress indelible
Veronicas on living things,
Leaving a branch leafless.
Free things breed freedom;
That dead arm beating.

I am a Jew whose mentors were devoted Christians who wrote in English. I remember visiting a synagogue when I was a child and hearing in Hebrew song an alternating sorrow and joy I wanted to capture in my native language. I remembered that convergence of opposite emotions when I first read Hopkins ("Mine, O thou Lord of life, send my roots rain" and "He fathers forth whose beauty is past change: praise him") and Herbert, who transforms a long sorrow into sudden joy ("It cannot be / That I am he / On whom thy tempests fell all night.")

I perceived then that praise born of sorrow was the dark, fierce joy that forces up the poet's song. I thought of Caedmon, the first English poet, in Bede's seventh-century story. An elderly illiterate farmhand who lived near Whitby Abbey, Caedmon was too shy to sing at a feast where scops celebrated battles of the kings they served. Instead, he ran to a barn and sang the Creation. Although he had never before shown evidence of ability, he had heard Latin prayer in masses at the abbey. Ingeniously, he combined the matter of the monks' songs with the Old English language of the scops' tributes: "Now we will praise heaven's keeper." His doxology was Christian, his word "keeper" an epithet for the Anglo-Saxon king.

In the early rondel I wrote of Caedmon, I identified with the somewhat obtuse Hild, abbess of Whitby from 657 to 680. Apparently she knew Caedmon and was aware of his illiteracy. When she overheard him singing in the barn, she reported that an angel had commanded him to raise his voice. It was only after Caedmon demonstrated that God had made him a poet that Hild invited him to the abbey to teach the monks to sing.

The Abbess of Whitby

There must have been an angel at his ear
When Caedmon gathered up his praise and sang,
Trembling in a barn, of the beginning,
Startled at words he never knew were there.

I heard a voice strike thunder in the air:
Of many kings, only one god is king!
There must have been an angel at his ear
When Caedmon gathered up his praise and sang.

When Caedmon turned in fear from songs of war,
Gleemen who sang the glories of the king
And holy men wondered that so great a power
Could whirl in darkness and force up his song;
There must have been an angel at his ear
When Caedmon gathered up his praise and sang.

That bleak gratitude follows me still. Recently I wrote a villanelle, "Julian of Norwich," named for a fourteenth-century woman who was the first writer of English mystical prose. Julian (also called Juliana) was an anchorite who lived in a cell attached to an East Anglian parish church. From one of her windows she could see the Eucharist; from another, people seeking spiritual counsel. I imagined those men and women to be plague-sored, hungry, crippled and scarred, for England was enduring the Black Death, the Hundred Years' War with France, the deposition of Richard II, who died in prison. In 1370 Julian experienced a series of revelations, or "shewings," of the crucified Christ, and constructed her art upon it. Through her country's suffering and confusion, she wrote that the extraordinary love of God is to be found in the ordinary. "Sin is necessary," she said, but added: "All will be well, and all manner of things shall be well."

I used her words as one of the repetends in my villanelle:

JULIAN OF NORWICH

Warped in the window-diamonds of my cell,
distorted, outsize primroses unfold:
I see all manner of things that shall be well.

Eyeless men with plague-sores come to chapel,
hungry, with blood-soaked poultices, and cold.
Warped in the window-diamonds of my cell,

they lurch and fall, inert. Another dead bell.
Their king gone, my King blesses (dressed in gold,
I see), all manner of things that shall be well.

Hermits recoil. If I were to foretell
doom, monks would believe. Instead, I'm called
warped. In the window-diamonds of my cell

are men who know Black Death and wars, and tell
of starless night, and will until I'm old,
I see. All manner of things that shall be well

deceive: dense glass in quarrel panes can spell
disaster, lunacy. Faces are bold,
warped in the window-diamonds of my cell.
I see all manner of things that shall be well.

For me, the benediction that grows out of torment is the essence
of art. It lies in Julian's awareness and in Caedmon's hymn. It resounds in Rilke's poems, notably in "Ich rühme," in which the poet
is given a list of the world's evils and praises them, one by one. In
Jude, the writer's fury is transformed, in the closing lines, into words
of celebration. It is the tension between bitterness and joy that I
first perceived in Hebrew melodies and later learned from Christian
writers to try to capture in English. It is the mainstay of my life and
work.

THE REVELATION OF
SAINT JOHN
THE DIVINE

—

John Hersey

Although there was much Bible of both Testaments drummed into me in my childhood, I grew up totally unacquainted with the last book of all, the Revelation of Saint John the Divine. I knew only its mystifying title. In Sunday school, as a reward for learning to recite the names of all the books of the Testaments, including that one, in the right order, I won a Bible bound in thin wooden boards, which were said to have been hewn from a tree on the Mount of Olives—an outrageous lie, I'm sure, but deliciously exciting for a gullible small boy. In my youth, I heard about the Four Horsemen of the Apocalypse; they were Stuhldreher, Miller, Crowley, and Layden, the backfield of the 1924 Notre Dame football team. Now, many years later, having been alienated for most of my adult life from the forms of religion, I sense in my reading of the apocalypse in this book some kind of blurred warning that may be thought appropriate for our troubled times, but I still feel very far distanced from Revelation—from its harsh crankiness and from what seems to me, insofar as I understand it, its wrongheaded message.

I was a "mishkid"—a son of missionaries. My father went to China in 1905 as a secretary of the Young Men's Christian Association; my mother went alone halfway around the world to join him the following year. The Boxer Uprising of 1900, in which a number of missionaries had been brutally slaughtered, had marked a turning point in the Protestant evangelical movement in foreign fields. The nineteenth-century missionaries had been bent on gathering sheaves for the Lord: converting the heathen, saving souls from damnation. A new wave of young men and women went out just after the turn of the century—it was for a few years distinctly The Thing to Do among campus leaders at Ivy League and eastern and midwestern denominational colleges—and this new generation came to call themselves Social-Gospel missionaries. They felt they had a somewhat different task from that of their predecessors.

My parents and their peers were as much concerned for the people of China, with the conditions of their life on this earth, as with the fate of their souls in heaven. The new wave of missionaries founded schools and colleges, set up hospitals, gave lectures on science and engineering, taught modern agronomy and forestry and flood control, and converted to Christianity, when they did so, as much by example as by exhortation. Among my father's duties was famine-relief work. Today, the Communist government of China, having long calumniated missionaries as "running dogs of imperialism," has begun to acknowledge their extraordinary contribution, for anyone can see that the thriving universities and hospitals of present-day China, almost without exception, were founded by them.

The crux of the Social-Gospel calling was its *active* nature. Its premise was that something like heaven on earth was a possibility, or at least that life on earth could be less hellish than it so often seemed—than it clearly was for most Chinese in those days—and that if such ameliorations were indeed possible, only human effort could bring them into being. This premise was firmly footed on the teachings of Jesus in the Gospels. One of the several reasons why the Book of Revelation did not figure in my life or, I assume, in my parents' lives is that there is simply no room in it for the Social-Gospel idea. Or for the Gospels themselves, for that matter.

To get at these exclusions, let us first consider Revelation as a piece of writing.

A reading writer listens with the ear of his eye for an author's voice. Reading Revelation, I hear at least three distinct voices. This is puzzling in a work which is entitled, in the King James Version, The Revelation of Saint John the Divine, as if it were definitely the work of one man. So we are confronted at once with a riddle of authorship. From early days of church history, it was assumed that this was entirely the work of the apostle John. Modern scholars, however, have doubted that he was the author and have attributed the book to John Mark, John the Elder, or some other unknown John. The Anchor Bible, a huge work of exegesis and clarification undertaken by an international consortium of Protestant, Catholic, and Jewish scholars, who since the 1960s have been devoting a volume to each of the books, suggests in its commentary on Revelation that there were probably three, or perhaps four, authors of the book.

The book does fall into at least three distinct parts, sounding those three quite different authorial voices. The first section, chapters 1–3, in which the "John" politely yet sternly addresses the seven churches of the Middle East, one by one, charging them to shape up, was probably written later than the rest of the book by a follower of Jesus, the Anchor Bible suggests. The next section, chapters 4–11, with its violent, hallucinatory images, was probably a revelation given to John the Baptist (which is mentioned in the Gospel According to Saint John, 1:15–34), and it reflects John the Baptist's expectation of a Messiah, "He that cometh," before he knew about the ministry of Jesus. This section certainly is in a more strident voice, more fiery and pessimistic, than that of John of the Gospel. The rest of the book, chapters 12–22, in a comparatively poetic though still often fearsome voice, seems to have been added later by a disciple of John the Baptist—one who knew a bit about Jesus—and its apocalypse predicts the fall of Jerusalem under the Romans in A.D. 70, a calamity that will come because of the moral collapse of the apocalyptist's fellow worshipers. There seem, finally, to be some interpolations in the last chapter by a Jewish Christian, perhaps in the late 60s, who is evidently better acquainted with the preachings of Jesus Christ.

This multiple authorship would help to account for the episodic form of the book, which is by no means linear but goes around and around. The end of the world is first seen in chapter 6. One can find a vague pattern of successive passages in clusters of sevens: seven churches to be chided, seven seals on the book of things to be revealed, seven trumpets announcing plagues, seven vials from which another cycle of harassments is to be poured. There remains a sense that the work, after it is introduced by the letter to the churches, has been broken into halves by two strong voices, and that parts within the two sections have been sewn together, sometimes with crude stitching.

The prose varies from a straightforward epistolary style to horrendously turgid to ravishingly beautiful. I gather that the grammar of the Greek version is very queer, and small wonder. Some of the imagery seems to be the product of one suffering a bad trip on a hallucinogen, or of a scriptwriter for a teenagers' horror movie. The whore of Babylon sits in the wilderness "upon a scarlet colored beast, full of names of blasphemy, having seven heads and ten horns"—which horns "shall hate the whore, and shall make her desolate and naked and shall eat her flesh." Each of the four beasts around the heavenly throne is "full of eyes before and behind." Even the Lamb of God, who opens the seals of the book, has seven horns and seven eyes. Locusts, emerging from smoke pouring out of a bottomless pit, are shaped like horses prepared for war, wear gold crowns, have men's faces and women's hair and lions' teeth, bristle with iron breastplates, fly on wings that sound like "chariots of many horses running to battle," and brandish scorpion tails with stings with the power to "hurt men five months." How far we are from the comfort and promise of the Gospels! "Blessed are the poor in spirit, for theirs is the kingdom of heaven. . . . Blessed are the meek, for they shall inherit the earth."

There is a spooky power in the prose. In crucial scenes, one feels drenched with a strange radiance, with glints of jasper, of chalcedony, and of "a sea of glass like unto crystal." One smells "odors, which are the prayers of saints." A star called Wormwood falls to earth, and one third of the rivers of the world taste bitter. Babylon is "a cage of every unclean and hateful bird." There is the haunting beauty, as the third voice takes over in chapter 12, of "a woman clothed in the sun, and the moon under her feet," who is "given two wings of a great eagle, that she might fly into the wilderness, into her place, where she is nourished for a time, and times, and half a time."

It is not surprising that this power and beauty of language—so different from the power and beauty of the Psalms, and of the Song of Solomon, and of the Gospels—has always beguiled writers and artists, not necessarily Christian ones. In 1511 Dürer, then twenty-seven years old, filled a book with grim, eloquent engravings: *The Apocalypse Illustrated*. Blake's visions are shot through with hints of Revelation; "The Four Zoas," for example, seems to have been suggested by the four beasts around the heavenly throne of chapter 4. Yeats's "A Vision" is an apocalypse that shows inevitable traces of Revelation—as well, more intimately, of other seers: Ezekiel, Blake, Shelley. Revelation provided the overarching metaphor for the carnage of the First World War in Vicente Blasco Ibáñez's 1918 novel, *The Four Horsemen of the Apocalypse*—a worldwide best-seller that was made into a somewhat less than apocalyptic film for Rudolph Valentino. The informing central image of Robertson Davies's magisterial *Deptford Trilogy* is the woman clothed in the sun, with the moon under her feet.

I sense one clue to the bizarre yet dazzling multiple grammars of Revelation in Northrop Frye's interpretation of Blake's title "All Religions Are One." The phrase, Frye suggests, means "that the material world provides a universal language of images, and that each man speaks that language with his own accent. Religions are grammars of this language." This brings us back to the question why Revelation would have been unlikely to figure in my parents' mission. For the question really is: If John the Baptist and a follower of his, both writing earlier than the Gospels, were the principal authors of Revelation, are the book's grammars truly Christian? That is, do they parse with the grammar of Jesus Christ? There are reasons to doubt it.

Jesus is not the central figure of Revelation, as he is of all other apocalypses in the New Testament—and in apocryphal Christian ones as well. The name Jesus or Jesus Christ appears just five times in the introductory letter of Revelation, in chapters 1–3, presumed to have had a Christian as its author. There is not a single appearance of the name in the section attributed to John the Baptist. It crops up only eight times in all the rest of the text, apparently written by a disciple of John the Baptist who has heard something of Jesus. The phrase "the Christ" appears twice and "his Christ" twice, but probably these should have been translated "the Messiah" or "the Anointed" in the pre-Christian sense, because each time the phrase occurs in connection with "kingdom," "power," "reigning," all of which Jesus foreswore.

The very idea of a surreal and monstrous apocalypse such as the one transacted in Revelation is foreign to the sane and gentle Jesus I was indoctrinated with as a child. In the Gospels, he is not seen as an apocalyptist or even as much of a visionary. His only clear, extensive apocalyptic utterance is in Mark 13 (and its parallels in Matthew and Luke), where he predicts wars, famines, earthquakes, and meteorological disturbances before the Son of Man goes to heaven, but his prediction has in it no hideously mutated beasts, no fumes of nightmare.

In its content, the Anchor Bible suggests, Revelation is much closer to Jewish apocalyptic literature than to Christian. The throne scenes, the sealing of scrolls, the calling of the roll of tribes, the two resurrections, and the apparent references to a Messiah—all these have Judaic sources. Most of the apocalyptic writings from before and during the first century were Jewish. Those that were adapted to Christianity had clear Christian references woven into the texts; these are missing in Revelation, which instead has a wad of Christian substance (chapters 1–3) patched onto the beginning, and four Christian verses (22:16–17, 20–21) stitched into the ending.

In apocalyptic writings, animals often serve as metaphors for human traits and even persons, and in Revelation, the Lamb of God, worshiped by the elders around the divine throne, opens the seals of the book of life, stands on Mount Zion, conquers the wicked, and gives light to the new city; and those who are saved wash their robes, till they are white, in his blood. The significant clue here is that the image of the Lamb of God, as it refers to Jesus, is found in the Gospels only in passages having to do with John the Baptist.

In my Oxford annotated edition of the Bible, the section of Revelation attributed to that John has more than four hundred allusions to the Old Testament, compared with relatively few to the New Testament. The beasts, the Temple, the tent of witness, the Ark of the Covenant, Jerusalem the harlot, the rider on the white horse named Word of God—all these and many other images and wordings have their origins in pre-Christian texts. Many of the images in the book reach back to pagan sources. Whereas Christian apocalypses draw on Greek mythology, Revelation has Babylonian, Zoroastrian, Egyptian, and Persian roots, in such images as the seven spirits at the throne, the woman clothed with the sun, the great red dragon. There are old, old astrological sources, too; that same dragon is defined by a constellation, and its tail sweeps through galaxies; Michael's war has its battlefield in the stars; and diviners have thought they could see with the naked eye the geometry of the New Jerusalem, ready to descend to earth, in the night sky overhead.

Particularly noticeable in this book is its numerology, something rarely seen in Christian writing. An earlier fascination with numbers apparently stemmed from a yearning for the Messiah and a wish to be able to count the years till his coming. In Revelation we see seven lampstands, seven seals, four horsemen, four beasts, twenty-four elders, four winds, seven trumpets, one hundred and forty-four thousand children of Israel with God's name written on their foreheads, two olive trees, seven plagues, ten thousand times ten thousand angels, a thousand two hundred and threescore days, and many other tallied things. There is, above all, the famous, ominous number of the beast: six six six. There seems to be some terrible contest in the book between the numbers six and seven and their multiples. To the Babylonians the number seven—the number of the perceptible astral powers, the sun, the moon, and the five visible planets—symbolized some kind of Gestalt, a completeness, a finality. Is the number six somehow uncomfortable with that rounding out, that sigh of stasis? Some scholars, who seem to have had mysterious reasons for disliking the idea of the book's being organized in clusters of sevens, have found it to be subdivided into bunches of sixes, and have been able to outline it that way fairly convincingly. As a writer I am especially repelled by this aspect of Revelation because of my sense that in our era numbers are growing more and more powerful, words weaker and weaker. Time was when we were invigorated by words: "nothing to fear but fear itself," "blood, sweat, tears, and toil." Now we are bombarded and moved to action (or inaction) by political polls, unemployment figures, the Dow Jones averages, the rate of inflation, the trillions of national debt.

———

So it has seemed to me that Revelation was not a book that would have guided my parents, and that it may not belong in the New Testament at all. (I am very much aware that the Christian church fathers put it there, for reasons they must have thought good, and that Christianity has clung to it ever since as an essential text of self-definition. There was some debate a few decades ago about whether it should remain in the canon, but it firmly does.) This issue aside, can Revelation serve, if even only in a literary sense, as an apocalypse for our time?

In our popular culture, the word "apocalypse" has come to have a false meaning. It has come to stand for any violent upheaval. A few years ago, a collection of journalistic pieces about the turbulent 1960s was entitled *Smiling Through the Apocalypse*. A film on the Vietnam war was called *Apocalypse Now*. But a true apocalypse—in its derivation the word really means just what this book calls itself, a revelation—has a double dualism. First, it opposes two cosmic powers of good and evil; we may call them God and Satan, or they may have other names. Second, it proposes two distinct times, a present that is hopelessly and irretrievably evil, with Satan or his equivalent in charge, and a future when God or his equivalent will defeat Satan and bring a perfect eternity—perfect, at least, for those who are seen as righteous in the god's eyes. An apocalypse is eschatological; that is, it foresees the end of the world as we know it.

Obviously, neither the 1960s nor Vietnam provided or justified such a foresight. Hiroshima didn't either, for that matter. Revelation does. Its very first verse says it will show "things which must shortly come to pass," and the book pictures a present age in which human beings will suffer, perhaps repeatedly, sevenfold horrors so grim that they will beg for death; and then a future time when there will be Armageddon, judgment, and paradise.

The text is enigmatic; it seems to be ciphered in a code of some sort. One way of cracking the code may be with historical keys—seeing the book as a message to the Jews (including Christian Jews) of the 60s A.D., when the writing of the book was apparently completed, and when warfare was heating up in Palestine between Romans and Jews, telling the latter that if they mended their behavior, God would take a hand in delivering their homeland from the oppression of the former. In this case the number of the beast would, in the counting of Hebrew letters, stand for Nero: *Neron Caesar*. The ten horns of the scarlet-colored beast bearing the whore of Babylon (meaning Jerusalem) would be ten emperors of Rome. The woman clothed with the sun who is given refuge in the desert would be the faithful band who fled from the Romans into the Judaean desert. The seven hills pictured at one point would be those of Rome. And so on.

If this interpretation works, what is wrong with applying the metaphor of its promise to our times? Revelation is intensely pessimistic, and we have reason to be. The book suggests that things will get much worse before they get better, and we can think so, too. Hasn't this century poured its vials of plague on us? Sores: AIDS. Seas of blood: slaughter of whales and seals and dolphins. Rivers and fountains of blood: the "conventional bombings" of World War II, Vietnam, wars of the Middle East. Fire: Hiroshima. Darkness: smog. Drought: drought, the greenhouse effect. Unclean spirits: you name them. And we can list other plagues not even dreamed of in the first century: overpopulation, mass starvation, mountains of garbage, epidemics of drugs, a glut of violent crimes. As we approach a new millennium, things do seem bound to get worse before they get better.

But Revelation offers what seems to me an obviously false hope: that after the worst of the coming misfortunes (Armageddon), God will intervene to bring to the chosen—and who is so modest as to exclude himself definitely from the band of the elect?—first a millennial, then an everlasting, paradise. We tend to picture Armageddon nowadays—"a great hail out of heaven"—as a nuclear holocaust. If that were to come about, would paradise ensue? Are we expected to accept the inevitability of this Armageddon? Even to welcome it, as the prerequisite to eternal peace?

Revelation puts mankind in an accepting, passive mode. This would not do for my Social-Gospel parents, and it won't do for their agnostic son. The book allows—almost commands—doing nothing about social ills and dangers; God will take care of those things. We must suffer plagues in order to reach heaven. In *Blessed Assurance: At Home with the Bomb in Amarillo, Texas* (the home of the final assembly plant for all American nuclear weapons), A. G. Motjabai quotes

Reverend Charles G. Jones, pastor of the Second Baptist Church there, as saying, "The Lord does not *need* nuclear war to help Him do what He chooses to do. If He chooses to use nuclear war, then who am I to argue with that?"

For literal-minded believers with temperaments too active merely to sit and wait for Armageddon and paradise, there is a grave temptation: to appoint themselves on God's side, as soldiers of his agency. The dualism of Revelation has its political attractions. We are the good guys; they are the bad. This makes it easy to speak of an Evil Empire, which is bound to be defeated, which we have a foreordained duty to fight and defeat. "I have read the book of Revelation," Caspar Weinberger, then secretary of defense, was quoted in the *New York Times* of August 23, 1982, as having said. "And yes, I believe the world is going to end—by an Act of God, I hope—but every day I think that time is running out." The speaker's phrase "I hope" implies the possibility of fateful Acts of Man, presumably to help God along.

The violent pessimism of Revelation has given it, over the centuries, a special appeal to the disaffected. In recent years a spate of racist and anti-Semitic hate groups have sprung up in the United States, known generically as "survivalists," who justify their armed communes and their terrorist tactics by their misreading of the dark prophecies of Revelation. These include organizations with names like Posse Comitatus; the Silent Brotherhood; the Christian-Patriots Defense League; and the Covenant, the Sword, and the Arm of the Lord. Here, one can think, are the beasts of Revelation in human form.

And so this strange book has brought us, finally, to a total negation of the hopeful words of the Gospels, "the good tidings." Revelation dismays me—as a son of missionaries who did what little they could to avert plagues, and as a writer who has felt obliged to write about some of those that we have already seen.

ABOUT THE CONTRIBUTORS

——

John Updike was born in Shillington, Pennsylvania, and attended the Shillington public schools, Harvard College, and, on a year's scholarship, the Ruskin School of Drawing and Fine Art, in Oxford, England. From 1955 to 1957 he worked on *The New Yorker*'s Talk of the Town department, and since 1957 he has lived as a freelance writer in Massachusetts. He has written more than thirty books of fiction, poetry, and essays; his most recent is a collection of art criticism, *Just Looking*. Baptized and confirmed as a Lutheran, he was for many years a Congregationalist, and is at present an Episcopalian.

Mary Gordon was born on Long Island, grew up in Queens, and was educated at Barnard College, where she now teaches. Author of the novels *The Other Side*, *Final Payments*, *The Company of Women*, and *Men and Angels*, the story collection *Temporary Shelter*, as well as countless essays and articles, she lives with her husband and two children in New Paltz, New York.

Annie Dillard is the author of eight books, including *Pilgrim at Tinker Creek*, which won a Pulitzer Prize in 1975, *Holy the Firm*, *An American Childhood*, and, most recently, *The Writing Life*, a memoir.

Reynolds Price is a novelist, poet, playwright, autobiographer, essayist, and translator. He is also James B. Duke Professor of English at Duke University. He has previously studied both the Old and the New Testaments in his book *A Palpable God: Thirty Stories Translated from the Bible with an Essay on the Origins and Life of Narrative*.

Larry Woiwode's fiction has appeared in *The Atlantic*, *Esquire*, *The New Yorker*, *The Paris Review*, and many other publications and has been translated into a dozen languages. His first novel received the William Faulkner

Foundation Award and his second, *Beyond the Bedroom Wall*, was nominated for both the National Book Award and the National Book Critics Circle Award. In 1980 he received an Award in Literature from the American Academy of Arts and Letters. He lives in North Dakota with his wife and children.

David Plante was born in Providence, Rhode Island. He received his early education from French nuns and Christian brothers in parish schools and later attended Boston College, where he studied French and philosophy. He has traveled widely in Belgium, Greece, and Italy, has lived in Rome and, since 1966, in London. He taught creative writing for four years at the University of Tulsa and was Writer-in-Residence at King's College, Cambridge, in 1985. He is a regular contributor to *The New Yorker*, and his work has also appeared in *The Paris Review*, *The New York Times Book Review*, and elsewhere. He is the author of the acclaimed Francoeur Family trilogy: *The Family* (1979), which was nominated for a National Book Award, *The Country* (1981), and *The Woods* (1982). His other novels include *The Ghost of Henry James* (1971), *Relatives* (1975), *The Foreigner* (1984), *The Catholic* (1986), and, most recently, *The Native* (1988). He has also published one work of nonfiction, *Difficult Women*. He has received a Guggenheim Fellowship and an Award in Literature from the American Academy and Institute of Arts and Letters.

Frederick Buechner was born in New York City. He was educated at the Lawrenceville School, Princeton University, and Union Theological Seminary. In 1958 he was ordained to the Presbyterian ministry. He has written ten novels, including *The Book of Bebb*, a tetralogy, and *Godric*, which was nominated for a Pulitzer Prize, together with a number of works of nonfiction, including *The Alphabet of Grace* (delivered as the Noble Lectures at Harvard), *Wishful Thinking, a Theological ABC*, *Telling the Truth: The Gospel as Tragedy, Comedy and Fairy Tale* (delivered as the Beecher Lectures at Yale), and *Whistling in the Dark*, illustrated by Katherine Buechner, the oldest of his three daughters. There have also been two autobiographical volumes, entitled *The Sacred Journey* and *Now and Then*, with a third, *Family Secrets*, soon to follow. He and his wife live in southern Vermont.

Alfred Corn is the author of five books of poetry, the most recent of which is *The West Door*. He has written a book of essays on literature, entitled *Metamorphoses of Metaphor*, and a novel, *Part of His Story*. Among the prizes awarded to him for his work are the Guggenheim, the NEA, and a fellowship from the Academy of American Poets. He lives in New York City.

Anthony Hecht used to sing in his college choir, for which he received a small emolument. He has published several collections of poetry, as well as one of critical essays, and has been awarded the Pulitzer Prize and the Bollingen Award. He served as Consultant in Poetry to the Library of Congress from 1982 to 1984.

Rita Dove's books of poetry include *The Yellow House on the Corner, Museum, Thomas and Beulah* (for which she received the 1987 Pulitzer Prize), and, most recently, *Grace Notes. Fifth Sunday* (short stories) appeared in 1985, and a novel is forthcoming. Ms. Dove has received Fulbright and Guggenheim Fellowships, two NEA grants, the Academy of American Poets' Lavan Award, and the GE Foundation Award. She teaches creative writing at the University of Virginia.

Dana Gioia is a businessman in New York. His poems and essays have appeared in *The New Yorker, The Hudson Review, Poetry*, and other journals. His collection of poems, *Daily Horoscope*, was published in 1986. His most recent book is *Mottetti*, a translation of poetry by the Italian Nobel Prize–winning poet Eugenio Montale.

Gjertrud Schnackenberg was born in Tacoma, Washington, and graduated from Mount Holyoke College. She has published two collections of poetry, *Portraits and Elegies* and *The Lamplit Answer.*

Amy Clampitt was born and brought up in rural Iowa, graduated from Grinnell College, and has since lived mainly in New York City. Her poems began appearing in magazines and literary journals in 1978. She is the author of *The Kingfisher* (1983), *What the Light Was Like* (1985), *Archaic Figure* (1987), and *Westward* (1990). She received a Guggenheim Fellowship in 1982 and the fellowship award of the Academy of American Poets in 1984, and in 1987 was elected to the National Institute of Arts and Letters. She has been Writer-in-Residence at the College of William and Mary, Visiting Writer at Amherst College, and Visiting Hurst Professor at Washington University.

Marina Warner is a novelist, historian, and critic. Her books include a study of the cult of the Virgin Mary, *Alone of All Her Sex*, and of the public uses of female allegory, *Monuments and Maidens*. In 1987–88 she was a Getty Scholar at the Getty Center for the History of Art and the Humanities. *The Lost Father*, her most recent work of fiction, won the PEN Silver Pen Award and the Commonwealth Writers' Prize (Eurasia), and has been translated into many languages. She is currently working on a study of fairytales as female literature and is writing a novel.

Guy Davenport, a professor of English at the University of Kentucky, is a critic and writer of fiction. His most recent books are *Every Force Evolves a Form*, *The Jules Verne Steam Balloon*, and *A Balthus Notebook*.

Josephine Humphreys is the author of two novels, *Dreams of Sleep* and *Rich in Love*. She was the recipient of the 1985 Ernest Hemingway Foundation Prize, a Guggenheim Foundation Fellowship, a Lyndhurst Foundation Fellowship, and a Danforth Foundation Fellowship. She lives in Charleston, South Carolina.

Jonathan Galassi is the author of *Morning Run*, a book of poems (1988). He has also published two volumes of translations of the work of the Italian poet Eugenio Montale, *The Second Life of Art: Selected Essays* (1982) and *Otherwise: Last and First Poems* (1984); his edition of the *Collected Writings* of John Cornford was reissued in paperback in 1986. He is currently preparing a translation of Montale's collected poetry from 1925 to 1956. He lives in New York City with his family, where he works as editor in chief of Farrar, Straus & Giroux.

Robert B. Shaw is the author of two books of poems, *Comforting the Willows* and *The Wonder of Seeing Double*. He has also published a critical study, *The Call of God: The Theme of Vocation in the Poetry of Donne and Herbert*. An associate professor of English at Mount Holyoke College, he previously taught at Harvard and Yale. In 1987 he held a Creative Writing Fellowship from the National Endowment for the Arts.

Michael Malone was born in North Carolina and was educated at the University of North Carolina and at Harvard. His novels include *Dingley Falls*, *Uncivil Seasons*, *Handling Sin*, and *Time's Witness*. He has also written books of nonfiction, as well as plays and screenplays; his essays, stories, and reviews appear regularly in national magazines and newspapers. As Visiting Writer-in-Residence, he has taught at a number of institutions, including Yale, the University of Pennsylvania, Swarthmore, and Yale Divinity School.

Marilynne Robinson is the author of *Housekeeping*, *Mother Country*, and numerous essays. She lives in Northampton, Massachusetts.

Robert Hass is the author of *Human Wishes* and two earlier collections of poems, *Field Guide* and *Praise*, along with a book of essays, *Twentieth Century Pleasures*. He has also collaborated with Czeslaw Milosz on the translations of his poems, most recently *The Collected Poems*. His many honors include a John D. and Catherine T. MacArthur Fellowship and the

1984 National Book Critics Circle Award in criticism. He has taught for many years at St. Mary's College of California and is currently a professor of English at the University of California, Berkeley.

Grace Schulman's books of poetry include *Burn Down the Icons* and *Hemispheres*. She is the author of a critical study, *Marianne Moore: The Poetry of Engagement*; co-translator of *Songs of Cifar and the Sweet Sea*, by Pablo Antonio Cuadra; and winner of a Present Tense Award for her translation of Hebrew poetry. She is poetry editor of *The Nation*, a professor of English at Baruch College of the City University of New York, and a former director of the Poetry Center of the 92nd Street YM-YWHA. Her poems have appeared in such publications as *Grand Street*, *The New Yorker*, *Poetry*, *The New Republic*, and *The Hudson Review*. Her essays have appeared in *Congregation: Contemporary Writers Read the Jewish Bible* and *Testimony: Contemporary Writers Make the Holocaust Personal*, among other anthologies. She lives in New York City with her husband.

John Hersey was born in Tientsin, China, and lived there until 1925, when his family returned to the United States. He studied at Yale and Cambridge, served for a time as Sinclair Lewis's secretary, and then worked several years as a journalist. He is the author of fifteen books of fiction and seven of reportage and essays. He has won a Pulitzer Prize, taught for two decades at Yale, and is a past president of the Author's League of America and past chancellor of the American Academy of Arts and Letters. He is married and has five children and four grandchildren.

FOR THE BEST IN PAPERBACKS, LOOK FOR THE

In every corner of the world, on every subject under the sun, Penguin represents quality and variety—the very best in publishing today.

For complete information about books available from Penguin—including Pelicans, Puffins, Peregrines, and Penguin Classics—and how to order them, write to us at the appropriate address below. Please note that for copyright reasons the selection of books varies from country to country.

In the United Kingdom: For a complete list of books available from Penguin in the U.K., please write to *Dept E.P., Penguin Books Ltd, Harmondsworth, Middlesex, UB7 0DA*.

In the United States: For a complete list of books available from Penguin in the U.S., please write to *Dept BA, Penguin, Box 120, Bergenfield, New Jersey 07621-0120*.

In Canada: For a complete list of books available from Penguin in Canada, please write to *Penguin Books Ltd, 2801 John Street, Markham, Ontario L3R 1B4*.

In Australia: For a complete list of books available from Penguin in Australia, please write to the *Marketing Department, Penguin Books Ltd, P.O. Box 257, Ringwood, Victoria 3134*.

In New Zealand: For a complete list of books available from Penguin in New Zealand, please write to the *Marketing Department, Penguin Books (NZ) Ltd, Private Bag, Takapuna, Auckland 9*.

In India: For a complete list of books available from Penguin, please write to *Penguin Overseas Ltd, 706 Eros Apartments, 56 Nehru Place, New Delhi, 110019*.

In Holland: For a complete list of books available from Penguin in Holland, please write to *Penguin Books Nederland B.V., Postbus 195, NL-1380AD Weesp, Netherlands*.

In Germany: For a complete list of books available from Penguin, please write to *Penguin Books Ltd, Friedrichstrasse 10-12, D-6000 Frankfurt Main I, Federal Republic of Germany*.

In Spain: For a complete list of books available from Penguin in Spain, please write to *Longman, Penguin España, Calle San Nicolas 15, E-28013 Madrid, Spain*.

In Japan: For a complete list of books available from Penguin in Japan, please write to *Longman Penguin Japan Co Ltd, Yamaguchi Building, 2-12-9 Kanda Jimbocho, Chiyoda-Ku, Tokyo 101, Japan*.

FOR THE BEST IN PAPERBACKS, LOOK FOR THE

☐ **FAITH, SEX, MYSTERY**
A Memoir
Richard Gilman

Gilman's memoir tells of the making and unmaking of a Catholic—as a young Jewish atheist undergoes a conversion, enjoys eight years of believing, and then gradually loses faith.   *254 pages*   *ISBN: 0-14-010587-5*   **$7.95**

☐ **THE EARLY CHURCH**
Henry Chadwick

The first volume of the *The Pelican History of the Church* follows the emergence of Christianity from the apostolic age to the foundation and explosive expansion of the Church of Rome.

304 pages   *ISBN: 0-14-020502-0*   **$5.95**

☐ **WESTERN SOCIETY AND THE CHURCH IN THE MIDDLE AGES**
R. W. Southern

Volume 2 of *The Pelican History of the Church* is the story of the birth and decay of a great Western ideal—that of an ordered society, religious and secular, as an expression of a divinely ordered universe.

376 pages   *ISBN: 0-14-020503-9*   **$5.95**

☐ **THE CHURCH IN AN AGE OF REVOLUTION**
1789 to the Present Day
Alec R. Vidler

The fifth volume in *The Pelican History of the Church* is a masterful assessment of a doubt-ridden and turbulent period in Christian history; it offers an incisive appraisal of the Church's endurance in the Age of Revolution.

302 pages   *ISBN: 0-14-020506-3*   **$6.95**

☐ **A HISTORY OF CHRISTIAN MISSIONS**
Stephen Neill

The sixth and final volume of *The Pelican History of the Church* traces the expansion of Christianity via missionary activity, from the Crusades to Colonialism to the present day.   *528 pages*   *ISBN: 0-14-022736-9*   **$6.95**